MY KID DUMPED FOOD ON ME.
UM...
MY PANTS ARE STAINED, BUT THE HALL IS DARK, SO NO ONE CAN TELL...
WHO CARES ?!
村田雄介

Yusuke Murata

We had a launch party for the anime. In the car on the way over, I thought over the speech I would make, but in the end it turned out like this.

Please, don't ever make me talk in front of people... There were a lot of people there (about 80), and I realized all over again how fortunate it was that so many people gave their support to the anime. Thank you very much to all of the staff who worked on it and to all of you viewers out there!

SNAP
SNAP
稲垣理一郎

Riichiro Inagaki

I've always tended to press too hard when I write. When I do the rough sketches (layouts prior to the final manga), I break off incredible amounts of lead. Snap! Snap! One after the next! I wonder where all those bits of lead go? When I clean the top of my desk, I never see any... Perhaps they've disappeared into another dimension...

Eyeshield 21 is the most exciting football manga to hit the scene. A collaborative effort between writer Riichiro Inagaki and artist Yusuke Murata, ***Eyeshield 21*** was originally serialized in Japan's ***Weekly Shonen Jump***. An OAV created for Shueisha's Anime Tour is available in Japan, and the ***Eyeshield 21*** hit animated TV series debuted in spring 2005!

EYESHIELD 21
Vol. 29: Second Quarterback
SHONEN JUMP ADVANCED Manga Edition

STORY BY RIICHIRO INAGAKI
ART BY YUSUKE MURATA

English Adaptation & Translation/John Werry, HC Language Solutions, Inc.
Touch-up Art & Lettering/James Gaubatz
Cover and Graphic Design/Sean Lee
Editor/Kit Fox

VP, Production/Alvin Lu
VP, Publishing Licensing/Rika Inouye
VP, Sales & Product Marketing/Gonzalo Ferreyra
VP, Creative/Linda Espinosa
Publisher/Hyoe Narita

Printed in Canada

Published by VIZ Media, LLC
P.O. Box 77010
San Francisco, CA 94107

10 9 8 7 6 5 4 3 2 1
First printing, December 2009

EYESHIELD 21

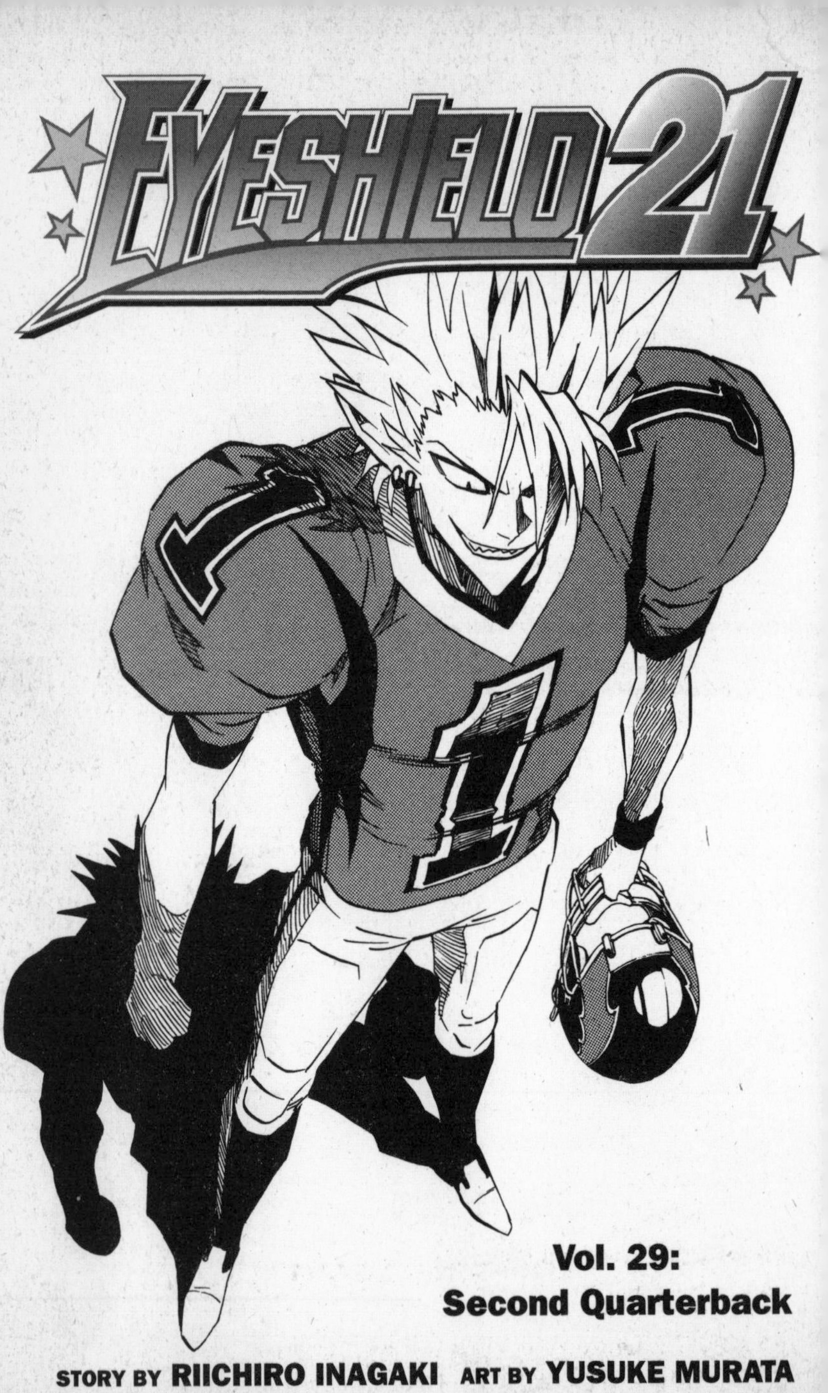

Vol. 29: Second Quarterback

STORY BY RIICHIRO INAGAKI ART BY YUSUKE MURATA

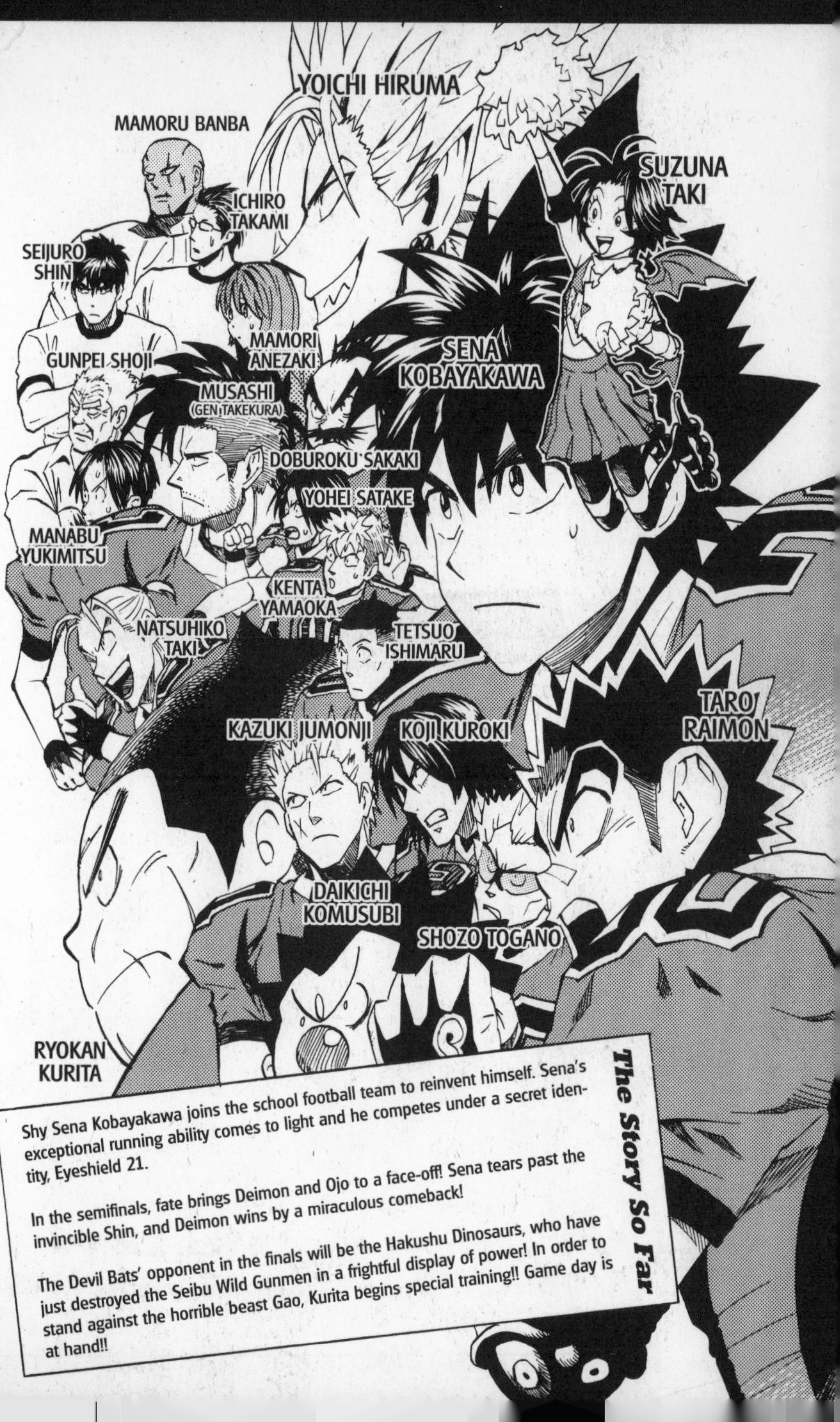
YOICHI HIRUMA
MAMORU BANBA
SUZUNA TAKI
ICHIRO TAKAMI
SEIJURO SHIN
MAMORI ANEZAKI
SENA KOBAYAKAWA
GUNPEI SHOJI
MUSASHI (GEN TAKEKURA)
DOBUROKU SAKAKI
YOHEI SATAKE
MANABU YUKIMITSU
KENTA YAMAOKA
NATSUHIKO TAKI
TETSUO ISHIMARU
TARO RAIMON
KAZUKI JUMONJI
KOJI KUROKI
DAIKICHI KOMUSUBI
SHOZO TOGANO
RYOKAN KURITA

The Story So Far

Shy Sena Kobayakawa joins the school football team to reinvent himself. Sena's exceptional running ability comes to light and he competes under a secret identity, Eyeshield 21.

In the semifinals, fate brings Deimon and Ojo to a face-off! Sena tears past the invincible Shin, and Deimon wins by a miraculous comeback!

The Devil Bats' opponent in the finals will be the Hakushu Dinosaurs, who have just destroyed the Seibu Wild Gunmen in a frightful display of power! In order to stand against the horrible beast Gao, Kurita begins special training!! Game day is at hand!!

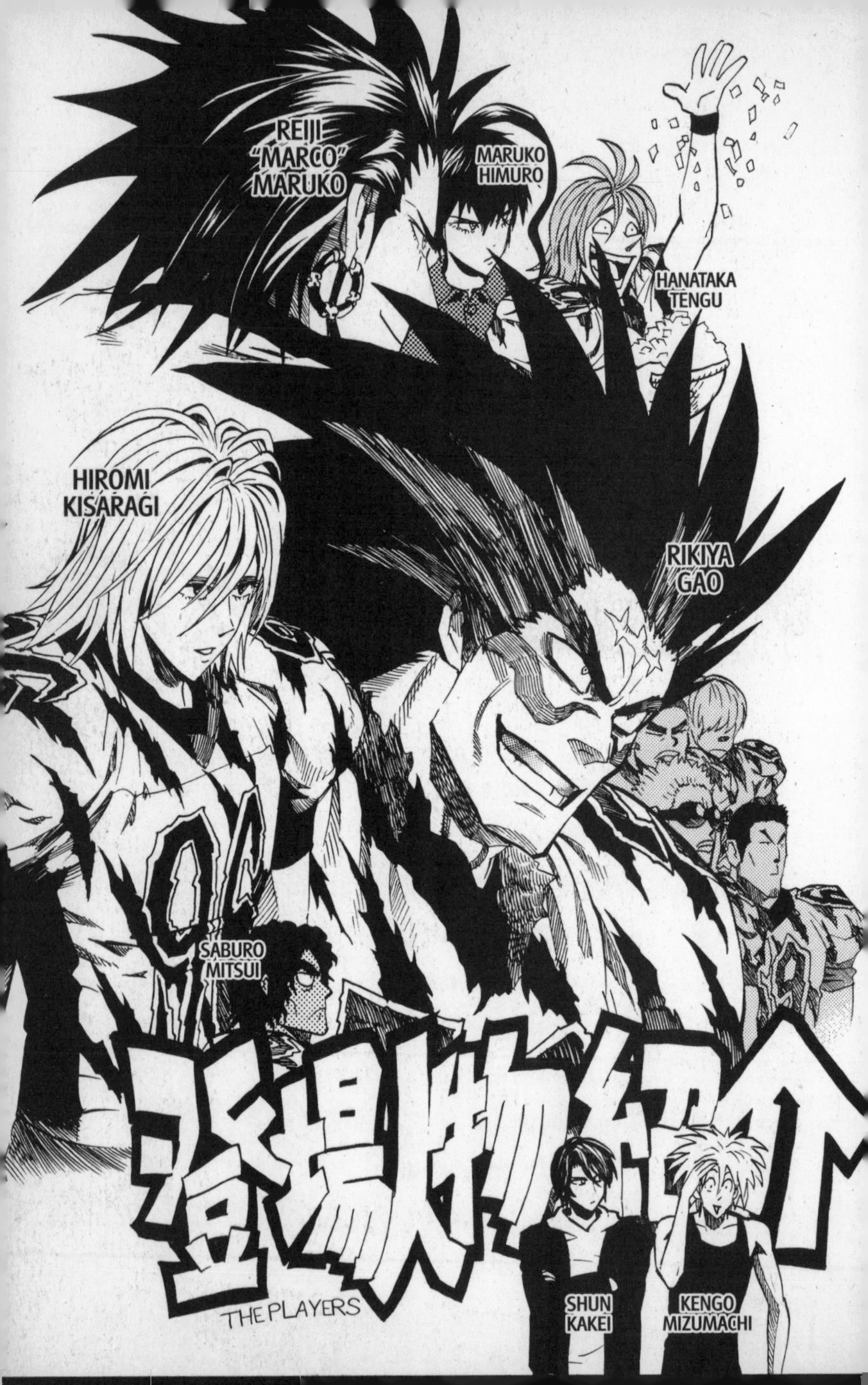
MARUKO HIMURO
REIJI "MARCO" MARUKO
HANATAKA TENGU
HIROMI KISARAGI
RIKIYA GAO
SABURO MITSUI
登場人物紹介
KENGO MIZUMACHI
SHUN KAKEI
THE PLAYERS

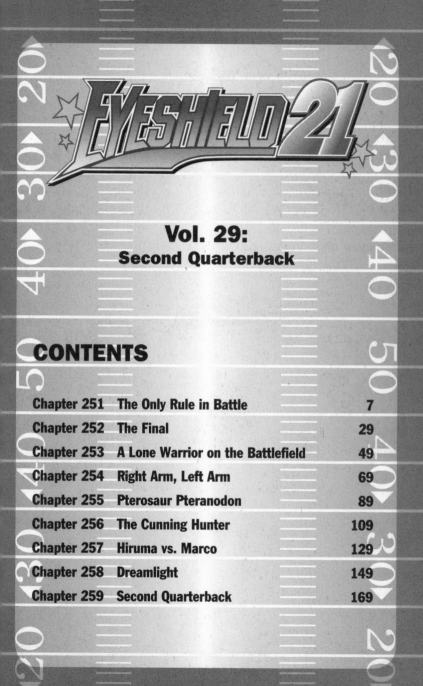

EYESHIELD 21

Vol. 29:
Second Quarterback

CONTENTS

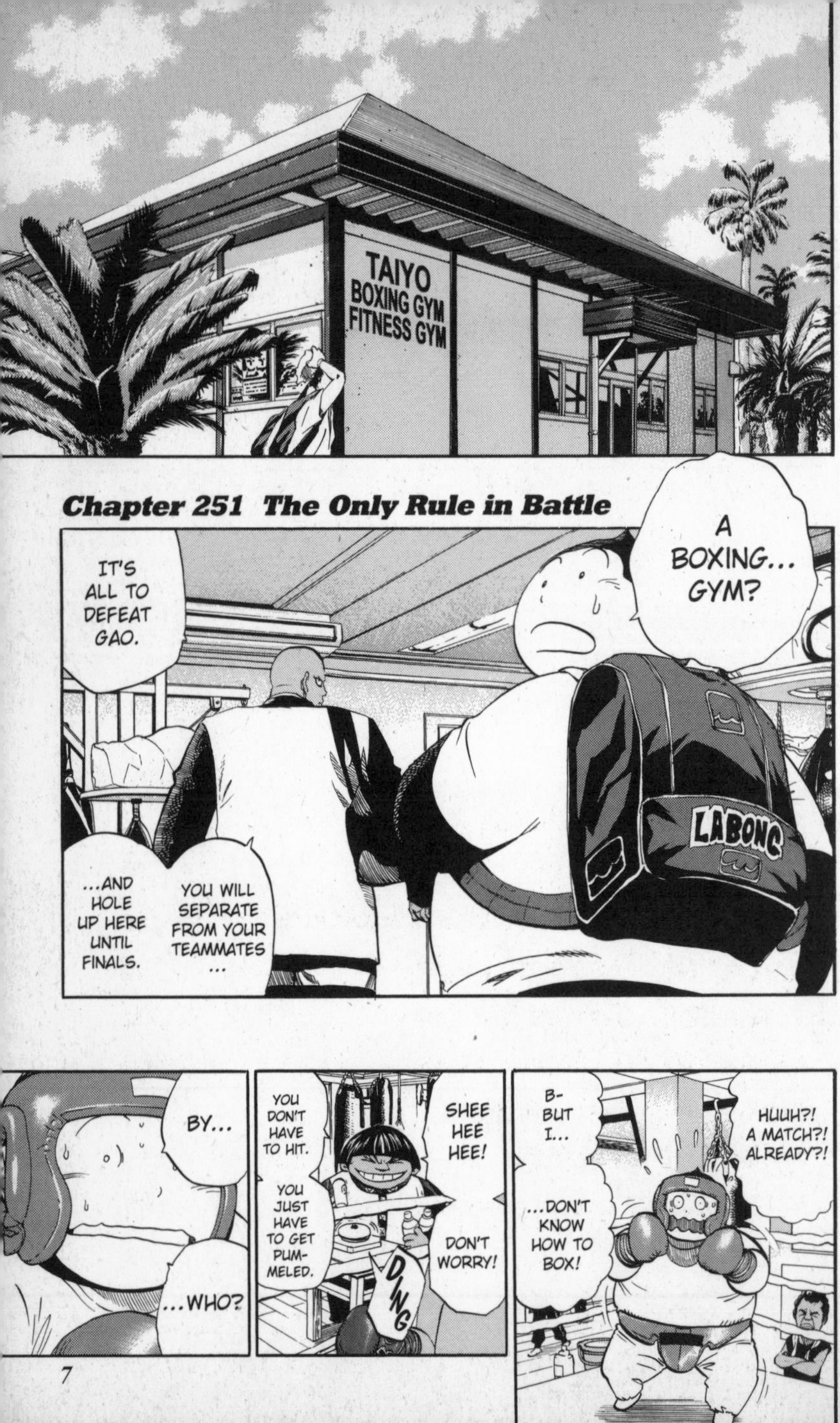
TAIYO BOXING GYM FITNESS GYM
Chapter 251 The Only Rule in Battle
A BOXING... GYM?
IT'S ALL TO DEFEAT GAO.
LABONC
YOU WILL SEPARATE FROM YOUR TEAMMATES ...
...AND HOLE UP HERE UNTIL FINALS.
HUUH?! A MATCH?! ALREADY?!
B- BUT I...
...DON'T KNOW HOW TO BOX!
SHEE HEE HEE!
YOU DON'T HAVE TO HIT.
DON'T WORRY!
YOU JUST HAVE TO GET PUM-MELED.
DING
BY...
...WHO?

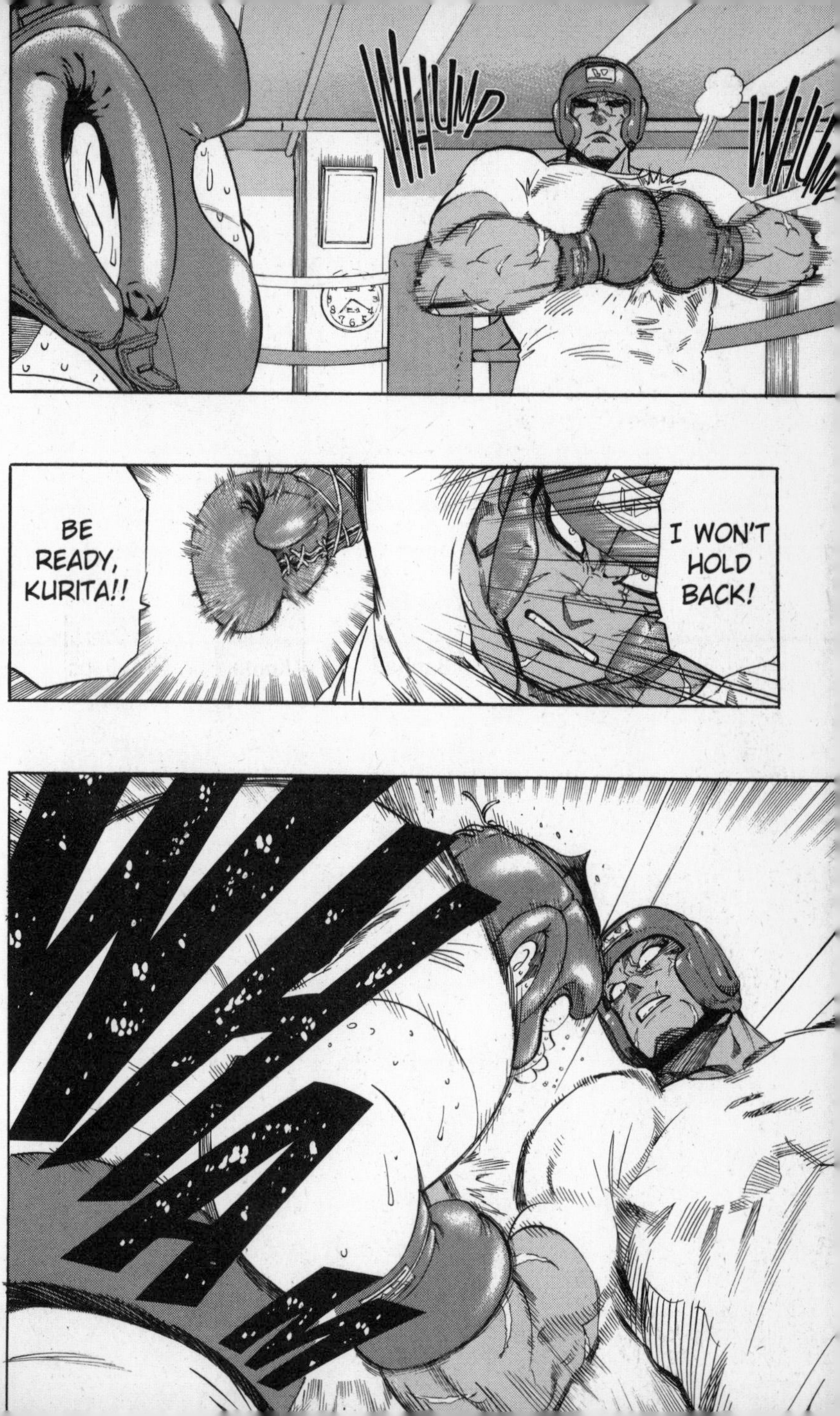
WHUMP
WHUMP
WHUMP
I WON'T HOLD BACK!
BE READY, KURITA!!
WHAM

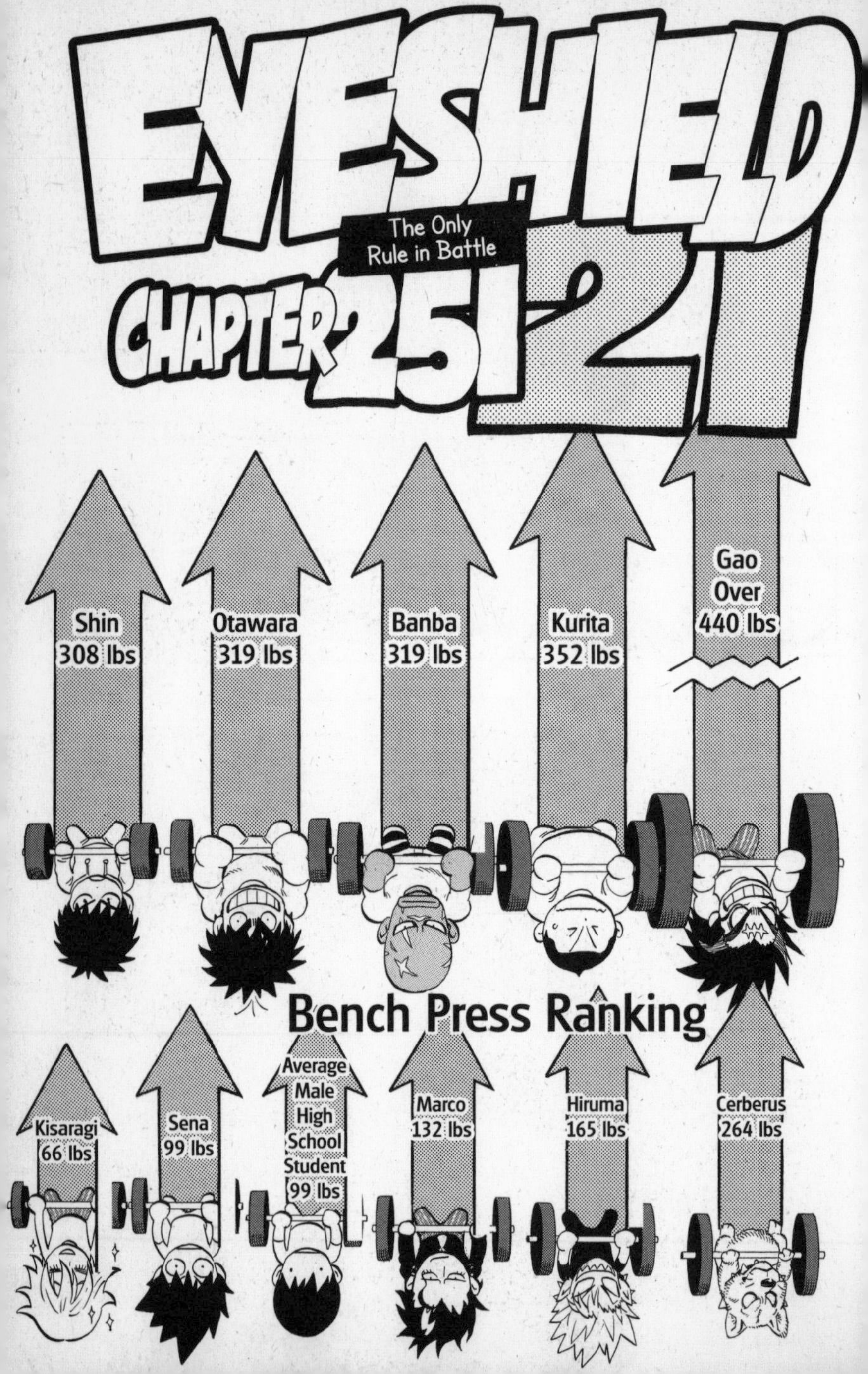
EYESHIELD 21
The Only Rule in Battle
CHAPTER 251
Gao Over 440 lbs
Kurita 352 lbs
Banba 319 lbs
Otawara 319 lbs
Shin 308 lbs
Bench Press Ranking
Cerberus 264 lbs
Hiruma 165 lbs
Marco 132 lbs
Average Male High School Student 99 lbs
Sena 99 lbs
Kisaragi 66 lbs

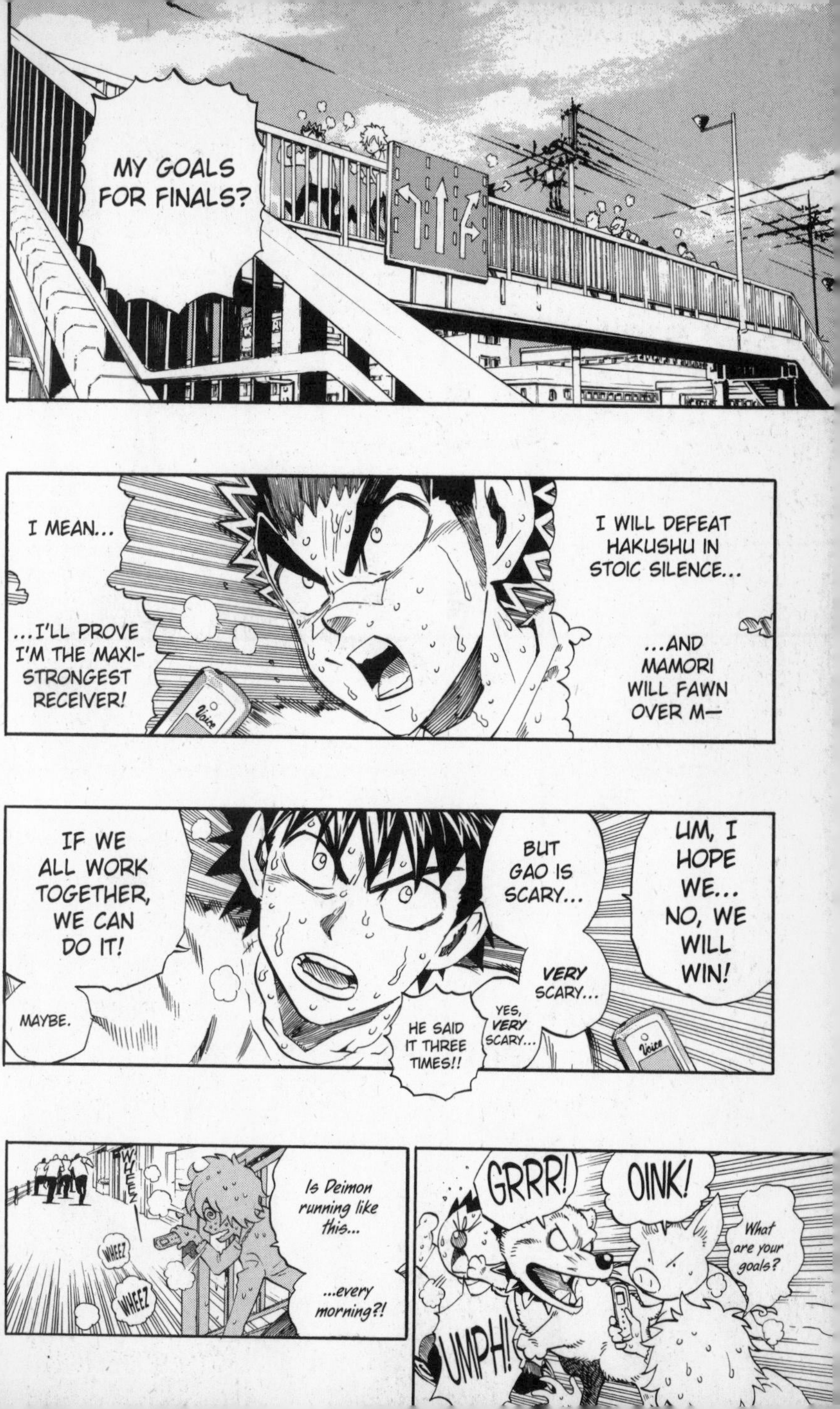
MY GOALS FOR FINALS?
I WILL DEFEAT HAKUSHU IN STOIC SILENCE...
...AND MAMORI WILL FAWN OVER M—
I MEAN...
...I'LL PROVE I'M THE MAXI-STRONGEST RECEIVER!
UM, I HOPE WE... NO, WE WILL WIN!
BUT GAO IS SCARY...
VERY SCARY...
YES, VERY SCARY...
HE SAID IT THREE TIMES!!
IF WE ALL WORK TOGETHER, WE CAN DO IT!
MAYBE.
OINK!
GRRR!
What are your goals?
UMPH!
Is Deimon running like this...
WHEEZ
WHEEZ
WHEEZ
...every morning?!

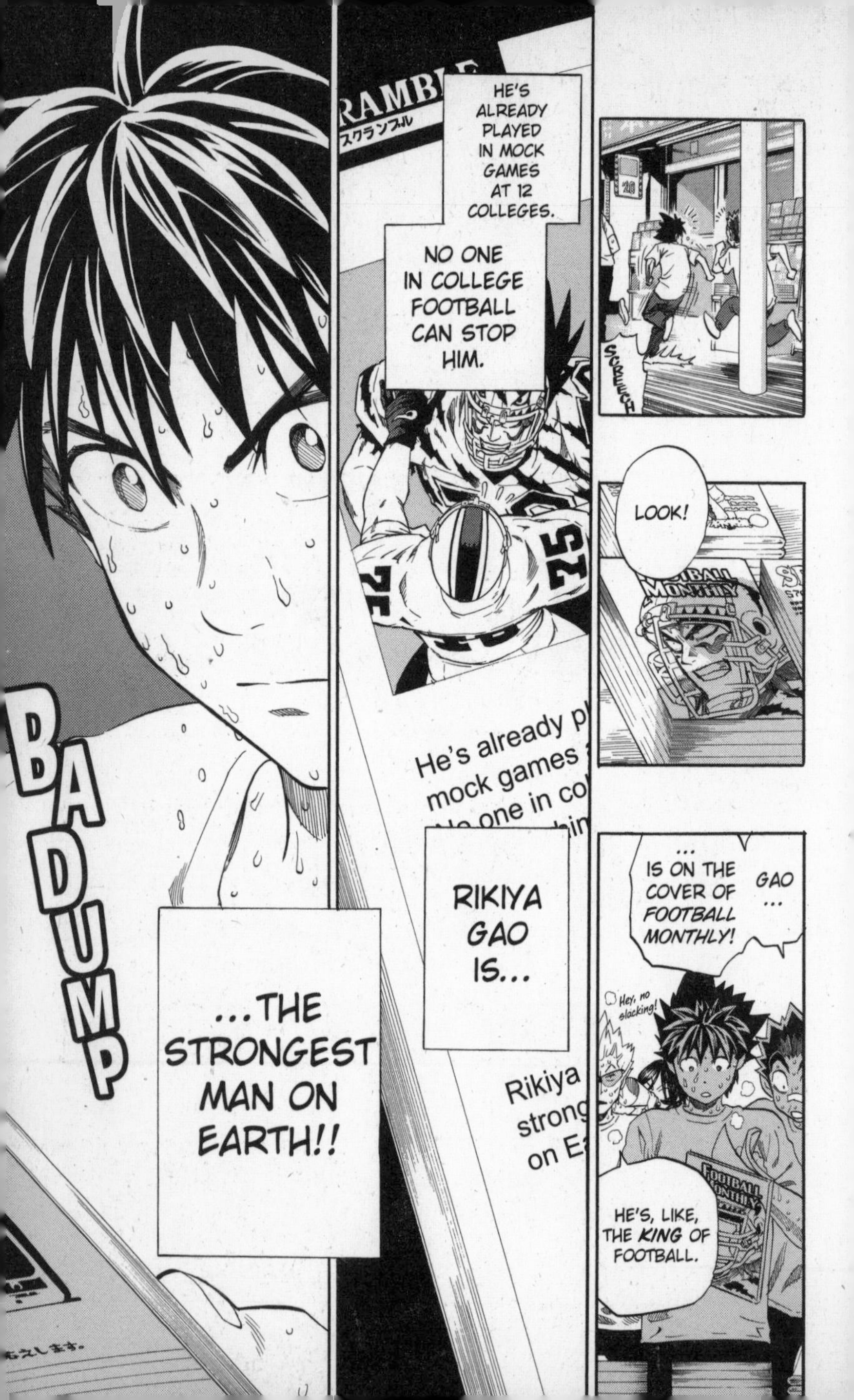
SCREECH
LOOK!
GAO ...
... IS ON THE COVER OF FOOTBALL MONTHLY!
Hey, no slacking!
HE'S, LIKE, THE KING OF FOOTBALL.
HE'S ALREADY PLAYED IN MOCK GAMES AT 12 COLLEGES.
NO ONE IN COLLEGE FOOTBALL CAN STOP HIM.
RIKIYA GAO IS...
... THE STRONGEST MAN ON EARTH!!
BADUMP

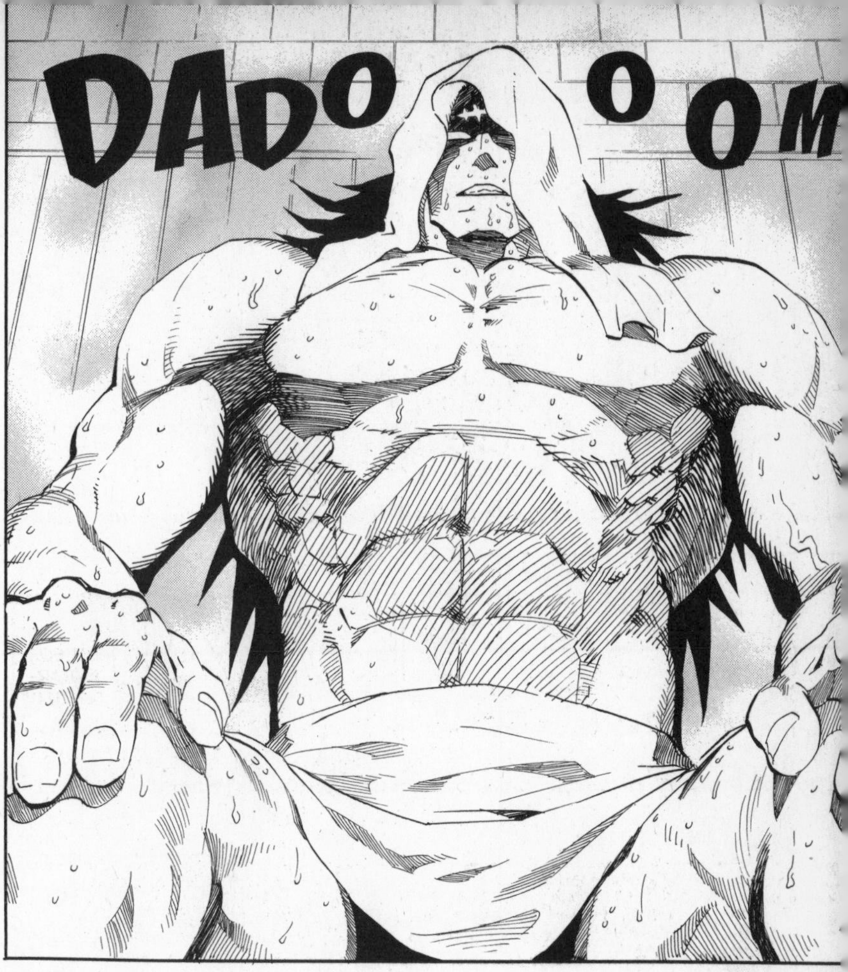
DADO O OM
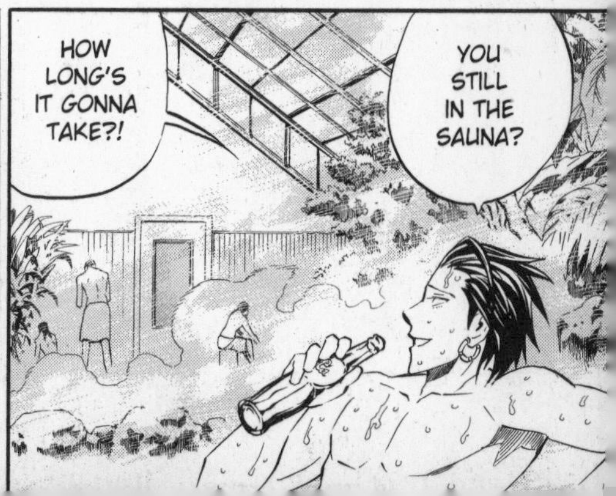
YOU STILL IN THE SAUNA?
HOW LONG'S IT GONNA TAKE?!
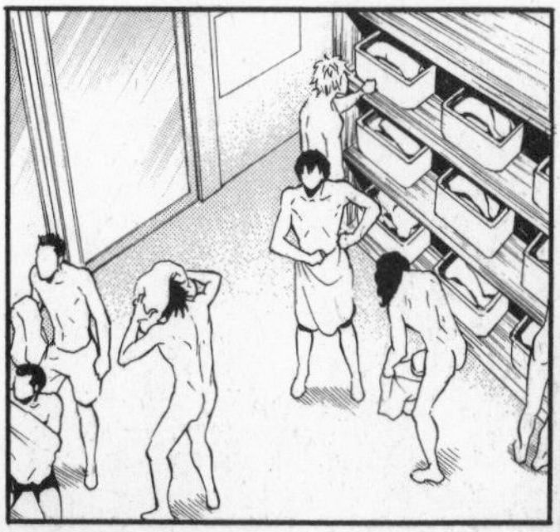

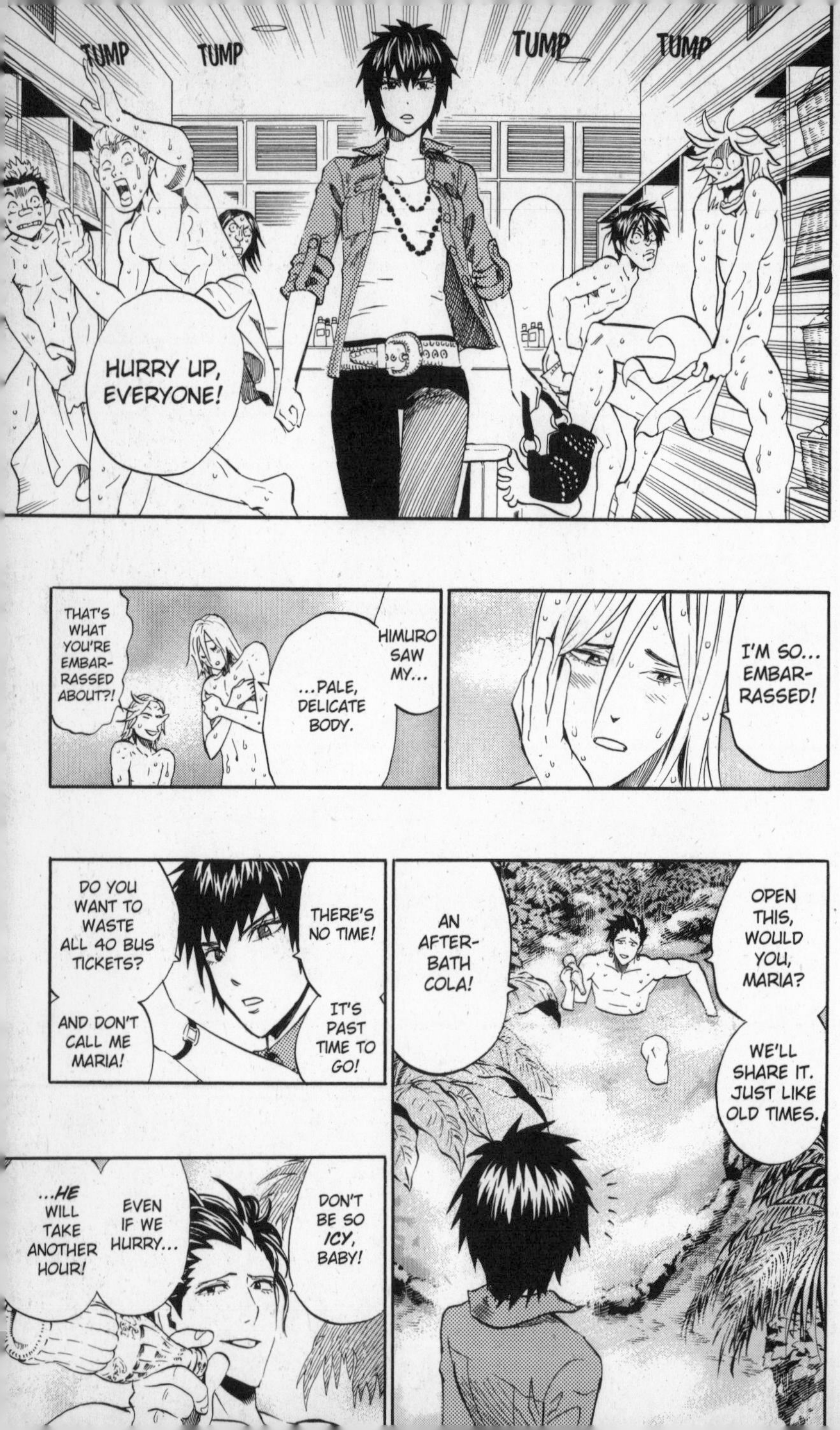
TUMP TUMP TUMP TUMP
HURRY UP, EVERYONE!
I'M SO... EMBARRASSED!
HIMURO SAW MY...
...PALE, DELICATE BODY.
THAT'S WHAT YOU'RE EMBARRASSED ABOUT?!
OPEN THIS, WOULD YOU, MARIA?
WE'LL SHARE IT. JUST LIKE OLD TIMES.
AN AFTER-BATH COLA!
THERE'S NO TIME!
IT'S PAST TIME TO GO!
DO YOU WANT TO WASTE ALL 40 BUS TICKETS?
AND DON'T CALL ME MARIA!
DON'T BE SO *ICY*, BABY!
EVEN IF WE HURRY...
...*HE* WILL TAKE ANOTHER HOUR!

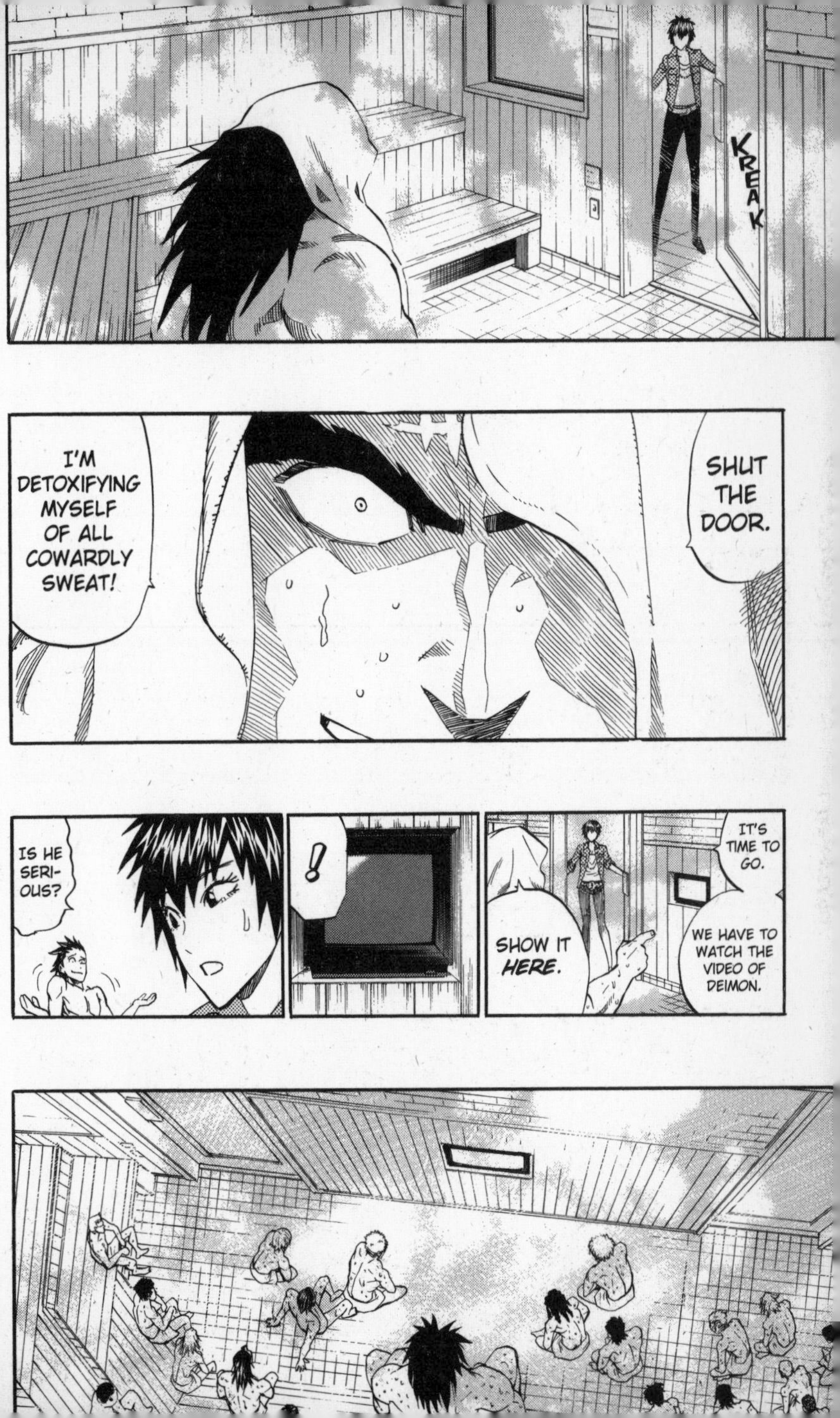
KREAK
SHUT THE DOOR.
I'M DETOXIFYING MYSELF OF ALL COWARDLY SWEAT!
IT'S TIME TO GO.
WE HAVE TO WATCH THE VIDEO OF DEIMON.
SHOW IT HERE.
!
IS HE SERI-OUS?

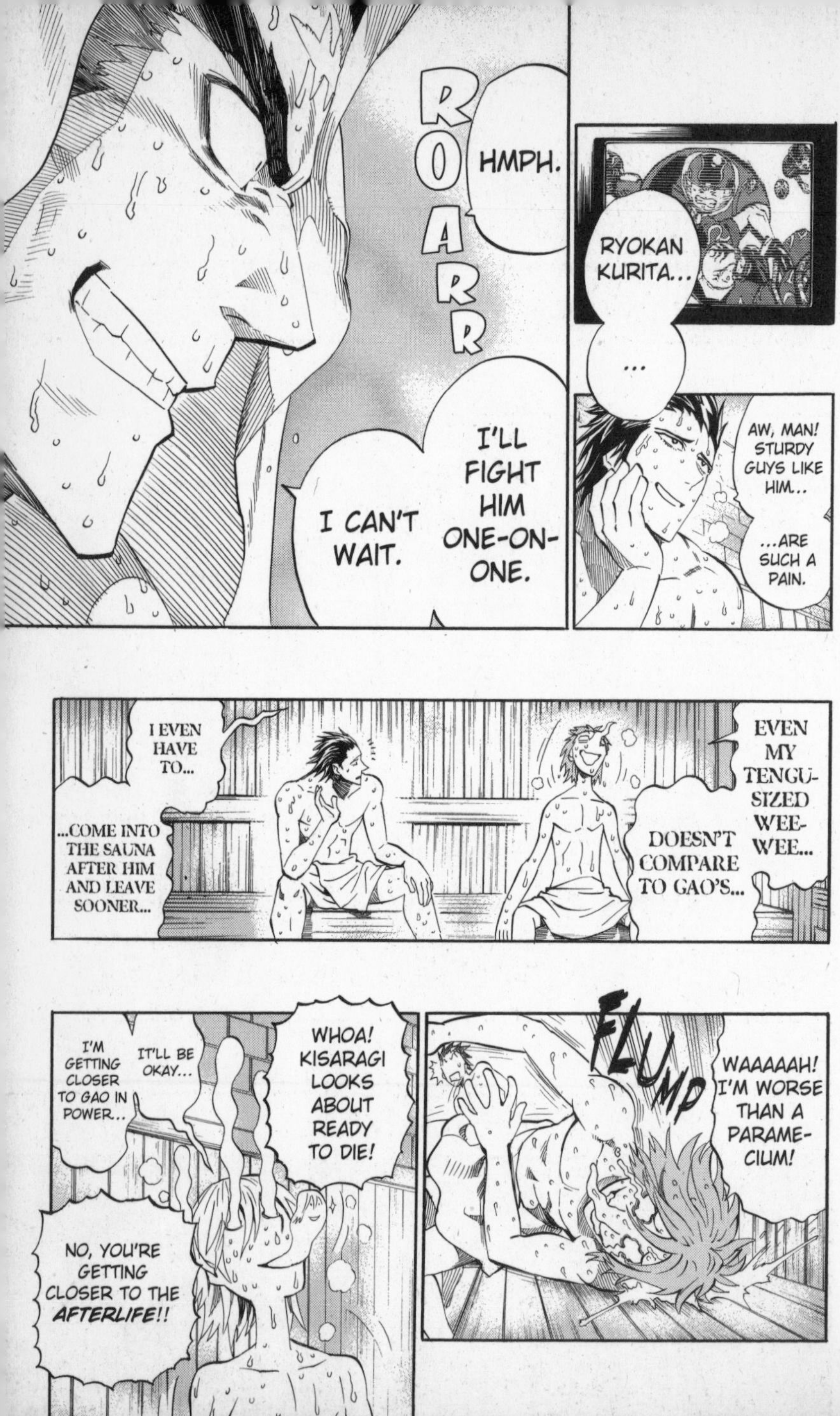
RYOKAN KURITA...
...
AW, MAN! STURDY GUYS LIKE HIM...
...ARE SUCH A PAIN.
HMPH.
ROARR
I'LL FIGHT HIM ONE-ON-ONE.
I CAN'T WAIT.
EVEN MY TENGU-SIZED WEE-WEE...
DOESN'T COMPARE TO GAO'S...
I EVEN HAVE TO...
...COME INTO THE SAUNA AFTER HIM AND LEAVE SOONER...
FLUMP
WAAAAAH! I'M WORSE THAN A PARAMECIUM!
WHOA! KISARAGI LOOKS ABOUT READY TO DIE!
IT'LL BE OKAY...
I'M GETTING CLOSER TO GAO IN POWER...
NO, YOU'RE GETTING CLOSER TO THE *AFTERLIFE*!!

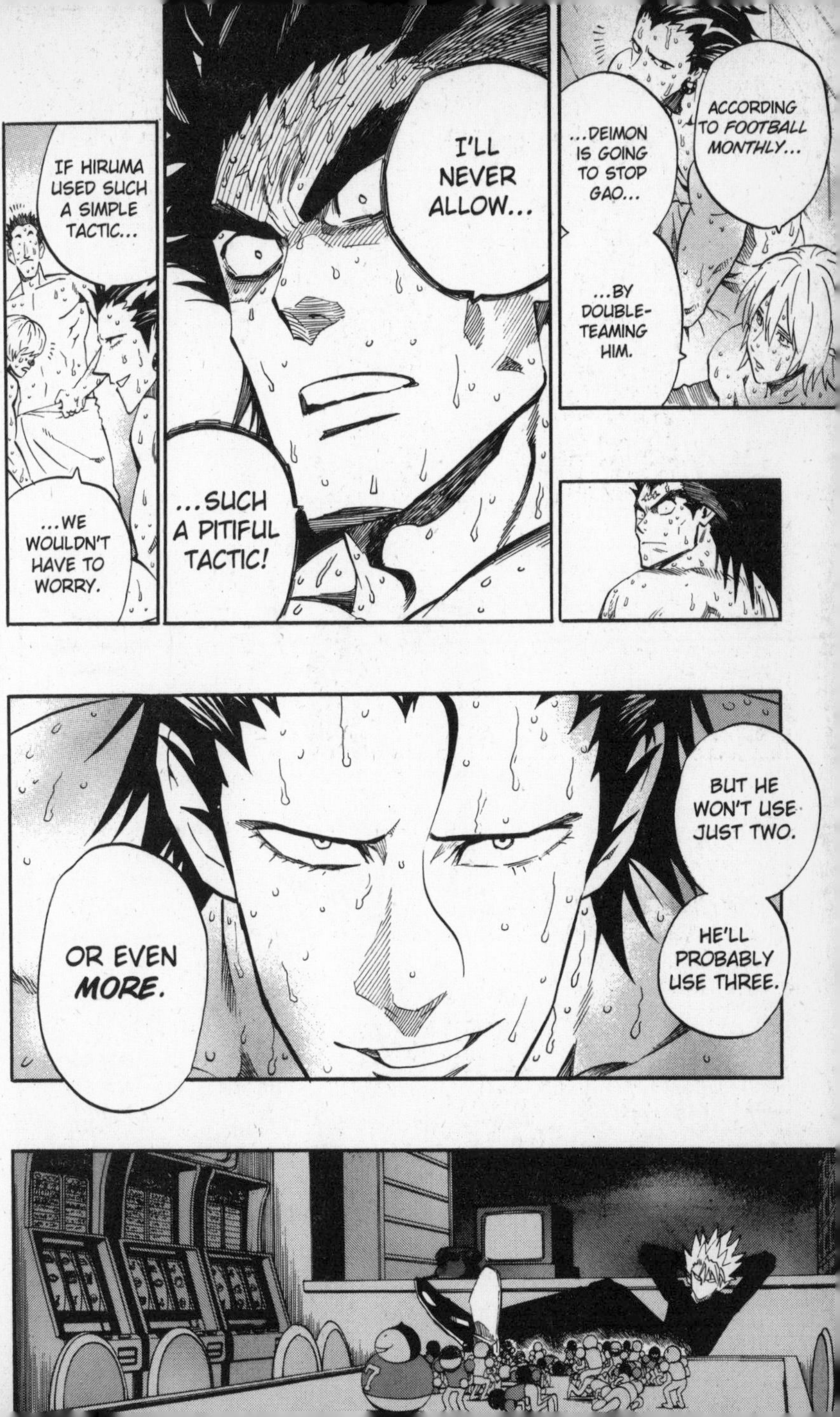
ACCORDING TO *FOOTBALL MONTHLY*...
...DEIMON IS GOING TO STOP GAO...
...BY DOUBLE-TEAMING HIM.
I'LL NEVER ALLOW...
...SUCH A PITIFUL TACTIC!
IF HIRUMA USED SUCH A SIMPLE TACTIC...
...WE WOULDN'T HAVE TO WORRY.
BUT HE WON'T USE JUST TWO.
HE'LL PROBABLY USE THREE.
OR EVEN ***MORE.***

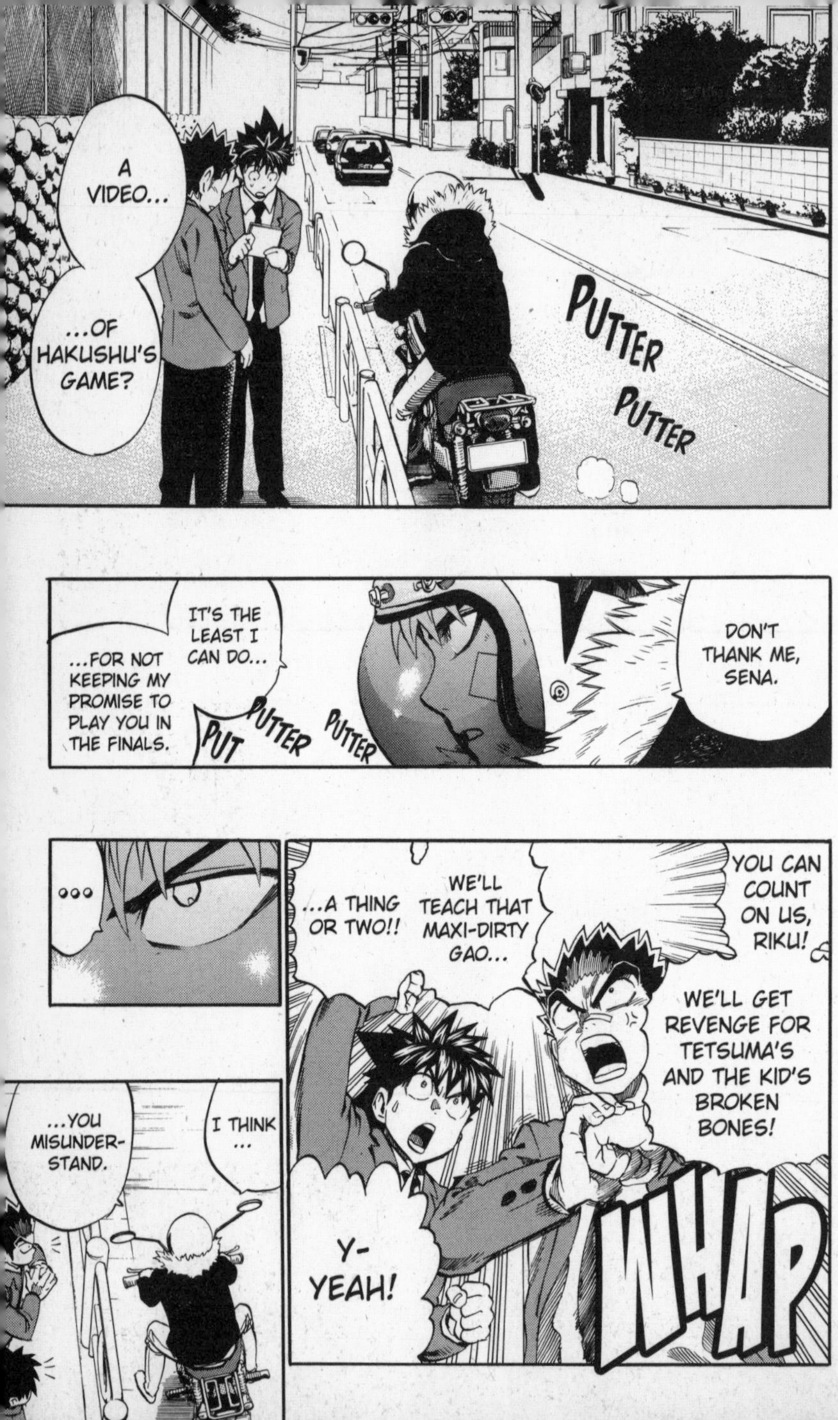
A VIDEO...
...OF HAKUSHU'S GAME?
PUTTER
PUTTER
DON'T THANK ME, SENA.
IT'S THE LEAST I CAN DO...
...FOR NOT KEEPING MY PROMISE TO PLAY YOU IN THE FINALS.
PUT
PUTTER
PUTTER
YOU CAN COUNT ON US, RIKU!
WE'LL TEACH THAT MAXI-DIRTY GAO...
...A THING OR TWO!!
WE'LL GET REVENGE FOR TETSUMA'S AND THE KID'S BROKEN BONES!
WHAP
Y-YEAH!
...
I THINK...
...YOU MISUNDERSTAND.

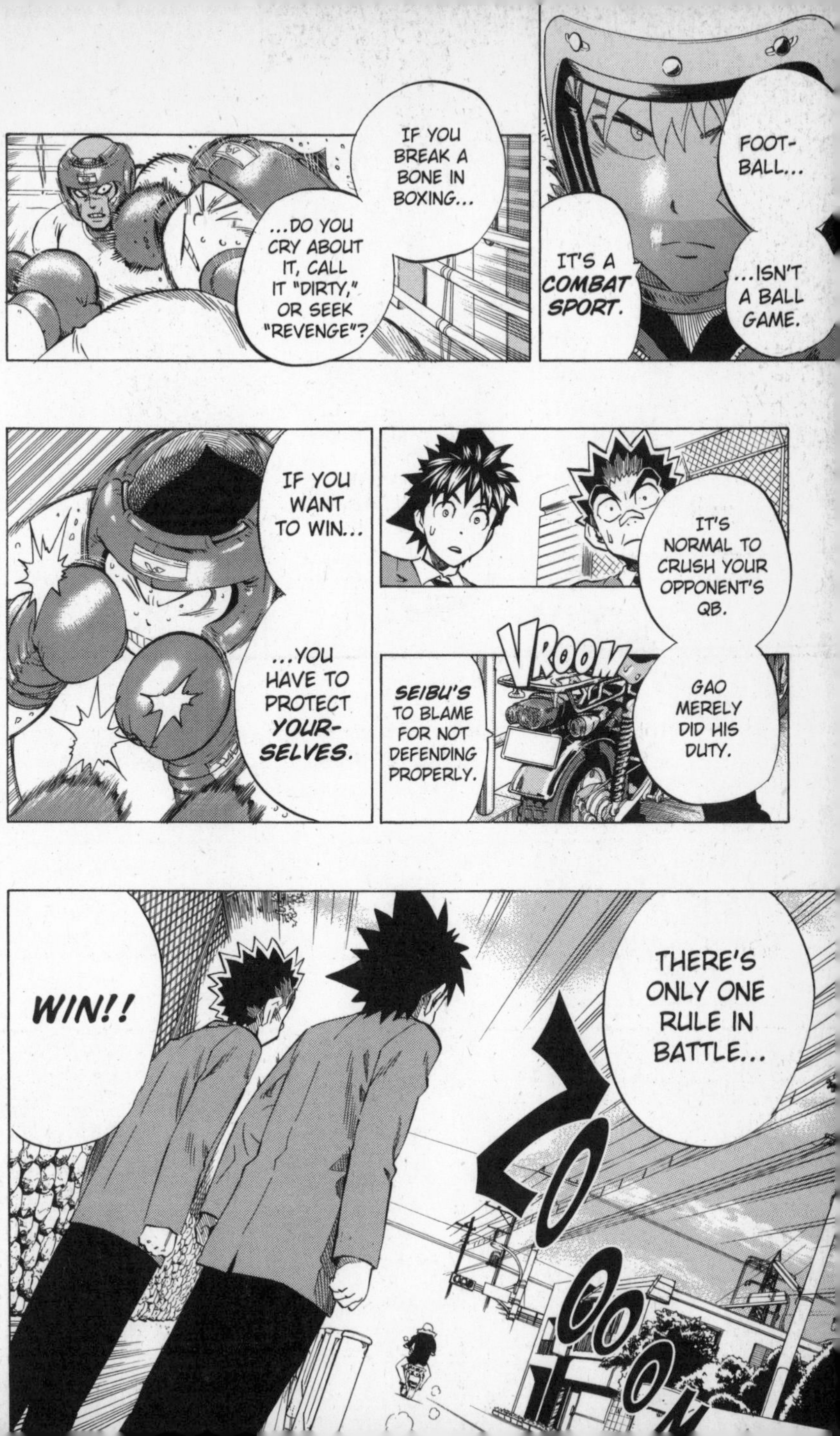
FOOT-BALL...
...ISN'T A BALL GAME.
IT'S A COMBAT SPORT.
IF YOU BREAK A BONE IN BOXING...
...DO YOU CRY ABOUT IT, CALL IT "DIRTY," OR SEEK "REVENGE"?
IT'S NORMAL TO CRUSH YOUR OPPONENT'S QB.
VROOM
GAO MERELY DID HIS DUTY.
SEIBU'S TO BLAME FOR NOT DEFENDING PROPERLY.
IF YOU WANT TO WIN...
...YOU HAVE TO PROTECT YOURSELVES.
THERE'S ONLY ONE RULE IN BATTLE...
WIN!!

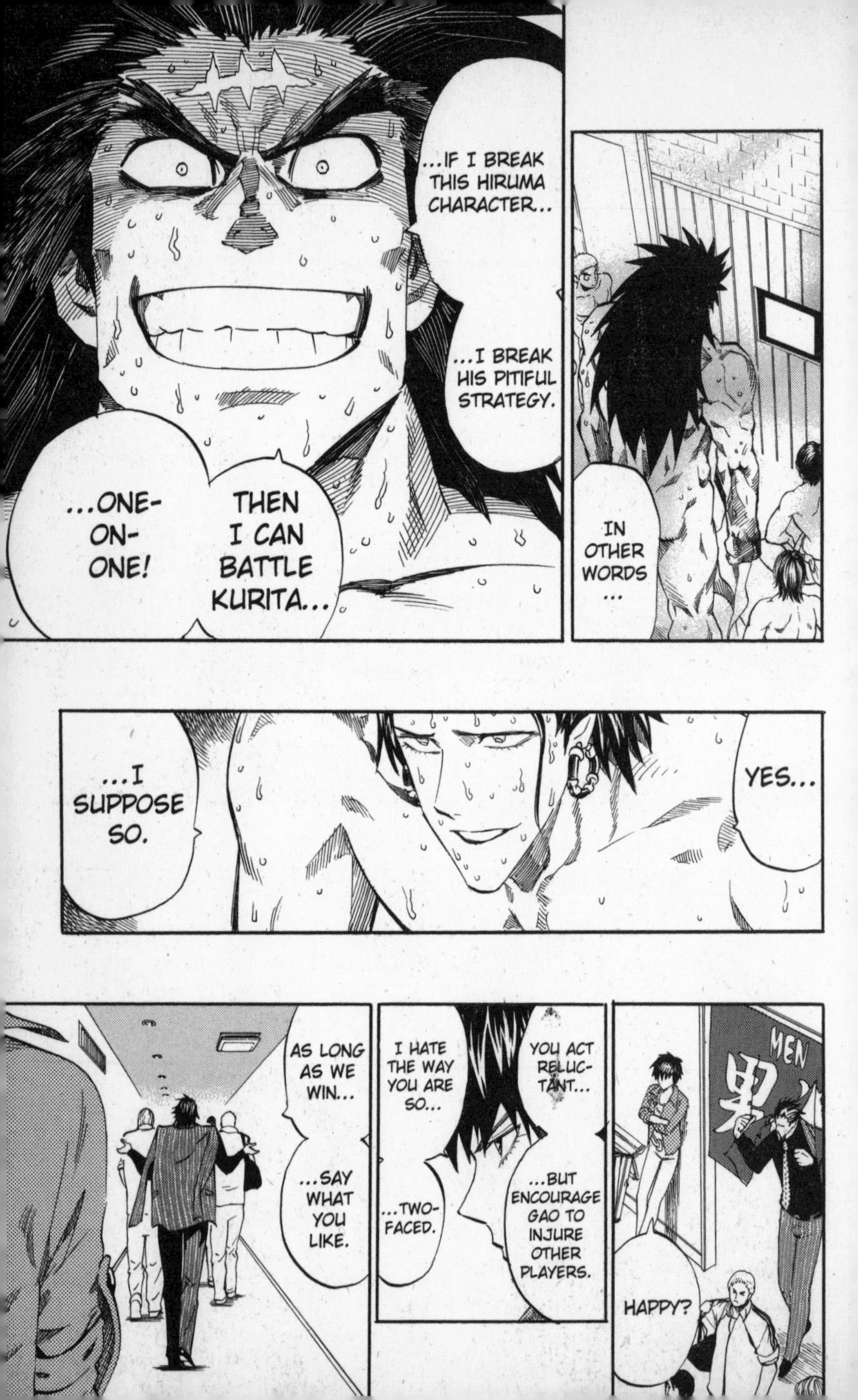
IN OTHER WORDS...
...IF I BREAK THIS HIRUMA CHARACTER...
...I BREAK HIS PITIFUL STRATEGY.
THEN I CAN BATTLE KURITA...
...ONE-ON-ONE!
YES...
...I SUPPOSE SO.
MEN
男
HAPPY?
YOU ACT RELUCTANT...
...BUT ENCOURAGE GAO TO INJURE OTHER PLAYERS.
I HATE THE WAY YOU ARE SO...
...TWO-FACED.
AS LONG AS WE WIN...
...SAY WHAT YOU LIKE.

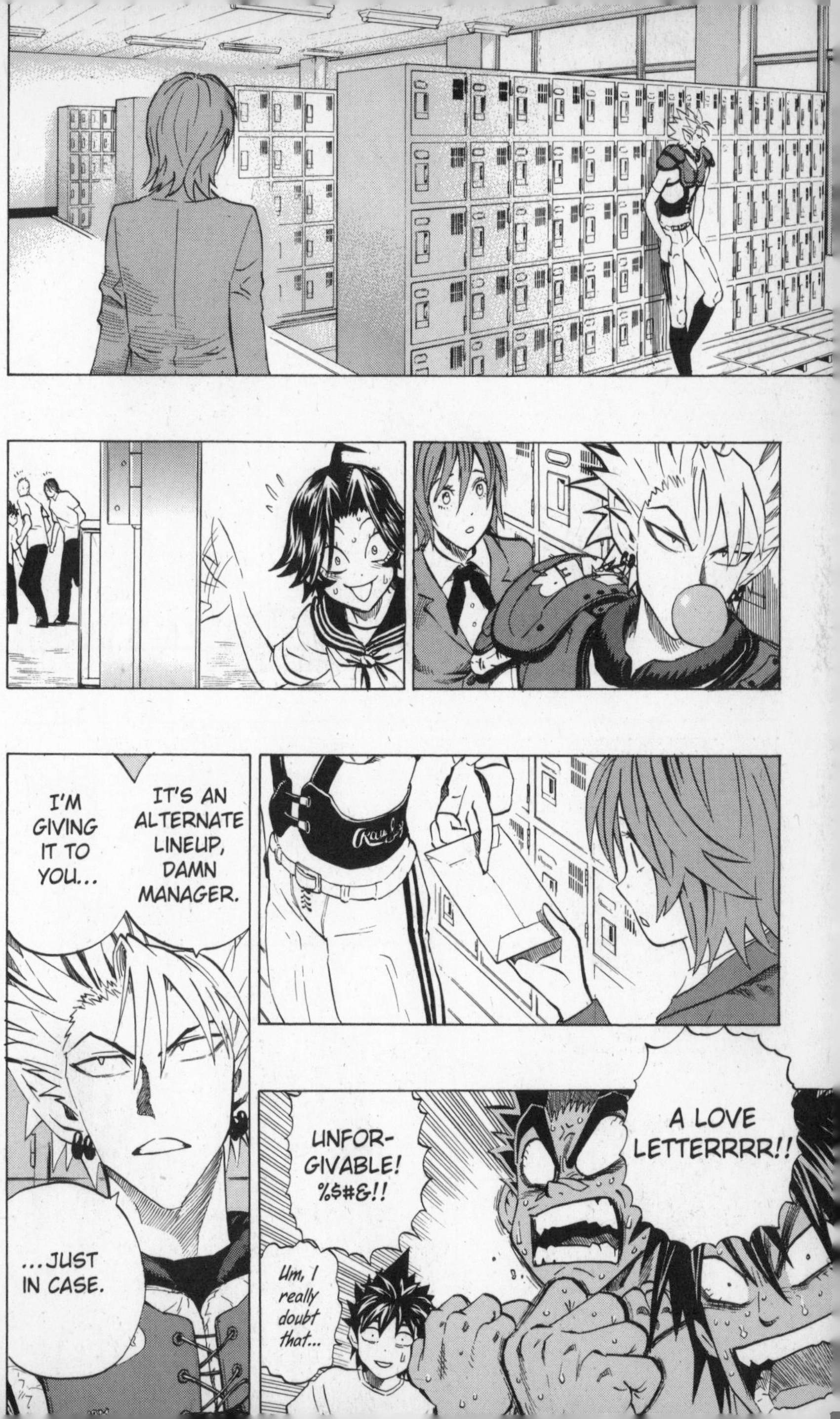
A LOVE LETTERRRR!!
UNFORGIVABLE! %$#&!!
Um, I really doubt that...
IT'S AN ALTERNATE LINEUP, DAMN MANAGER.
I'M GIVING IT TO YOU...
...JUST IN CASE.

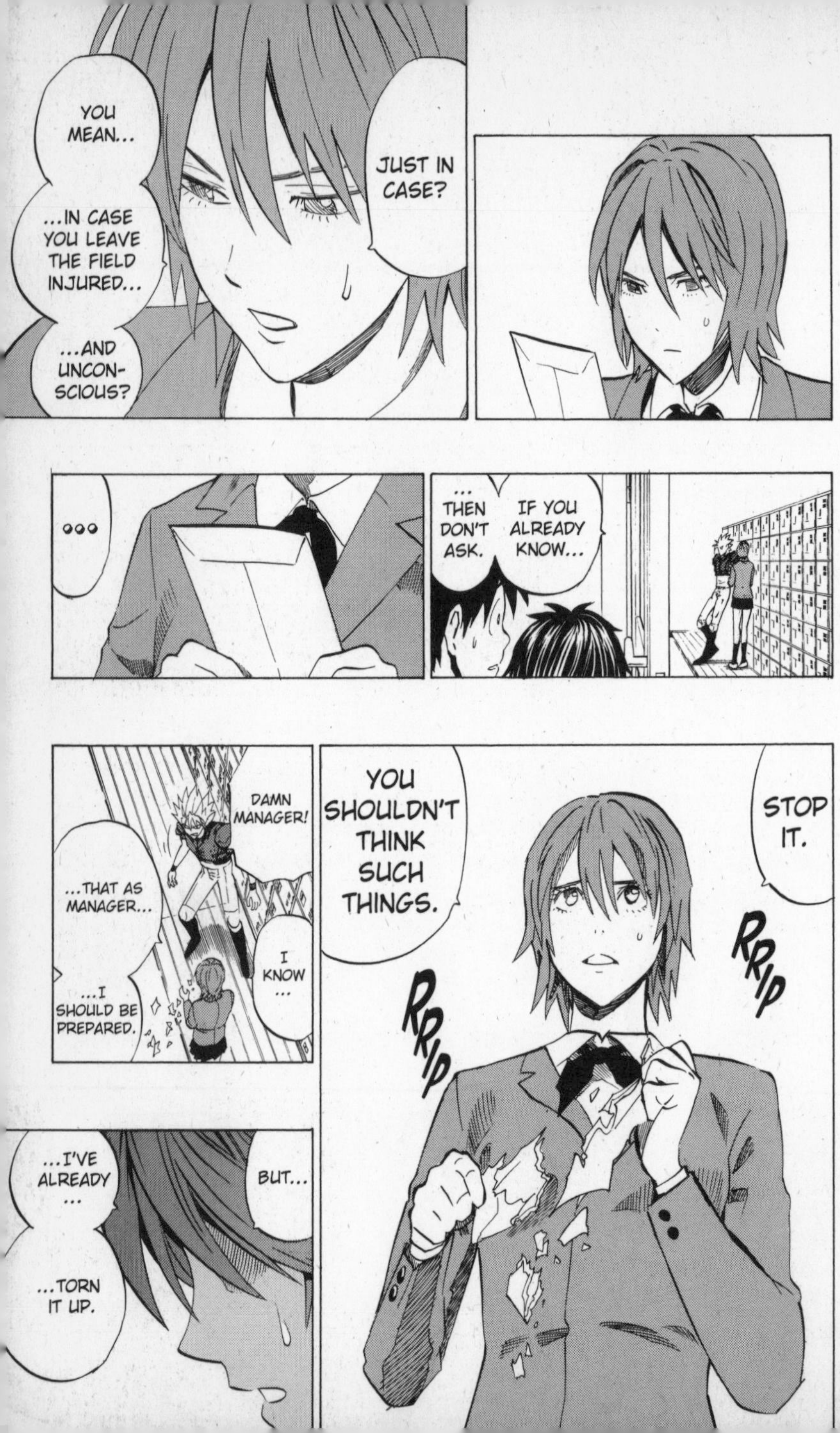
JUST IN CASE?
YOU MEAN...
...IN CASE YOU LEAVE THE FIELD INJURED...
...AND UNCONSCIOUS?
IF YOU ALREADY KNOW...
...THEN DON'T ASK.
...
STOP IT.
RRIP
YOU SHOULDN'T THINK SUCH THINGS.
RRIP
DAMN MANAGER!
I KNOW...
...THAT AS MANAGER...
...I SHOULD BE PREPARED.
BUT...
...I'VE ALREADY...
...TORN IT UP.

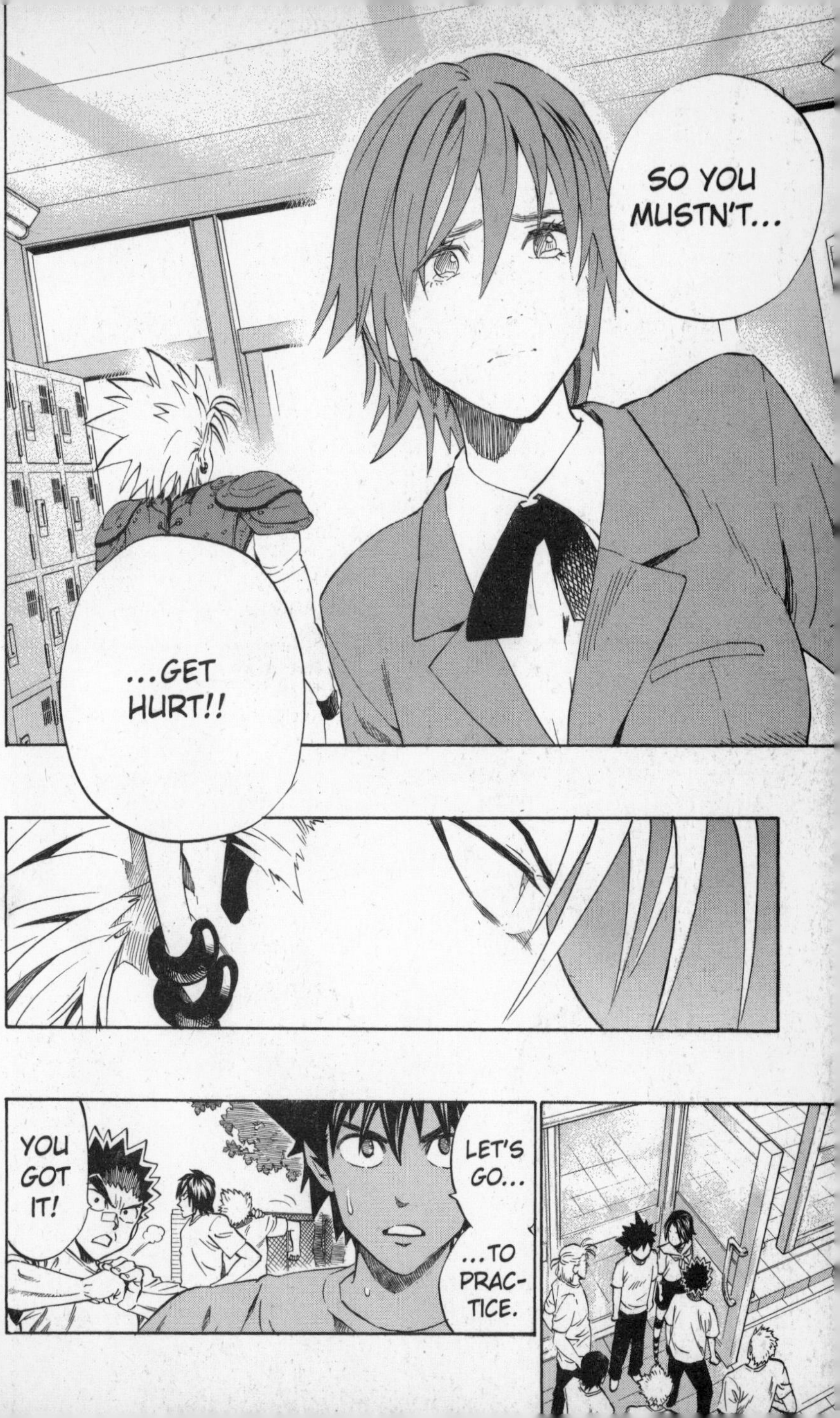
SO YOU MUSTN'T...
...GET HURT!!
LET'S GO...
...TO PRAC-TICE.
YOU GOT IT!

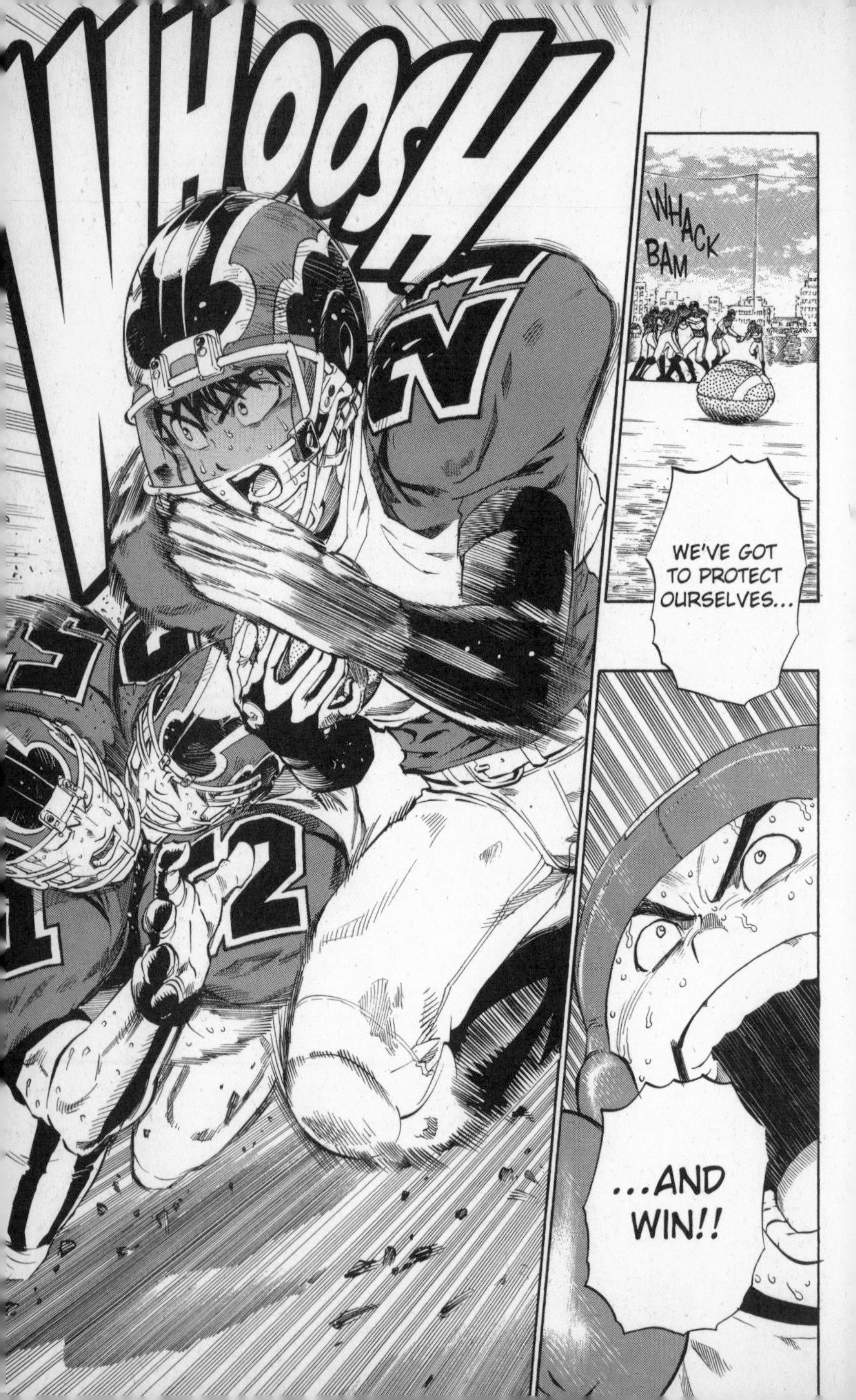
WHACK
BAM
WE'VE GOT TO PROTECT OURSELVES...
...AND WIN!!
WHOOSH

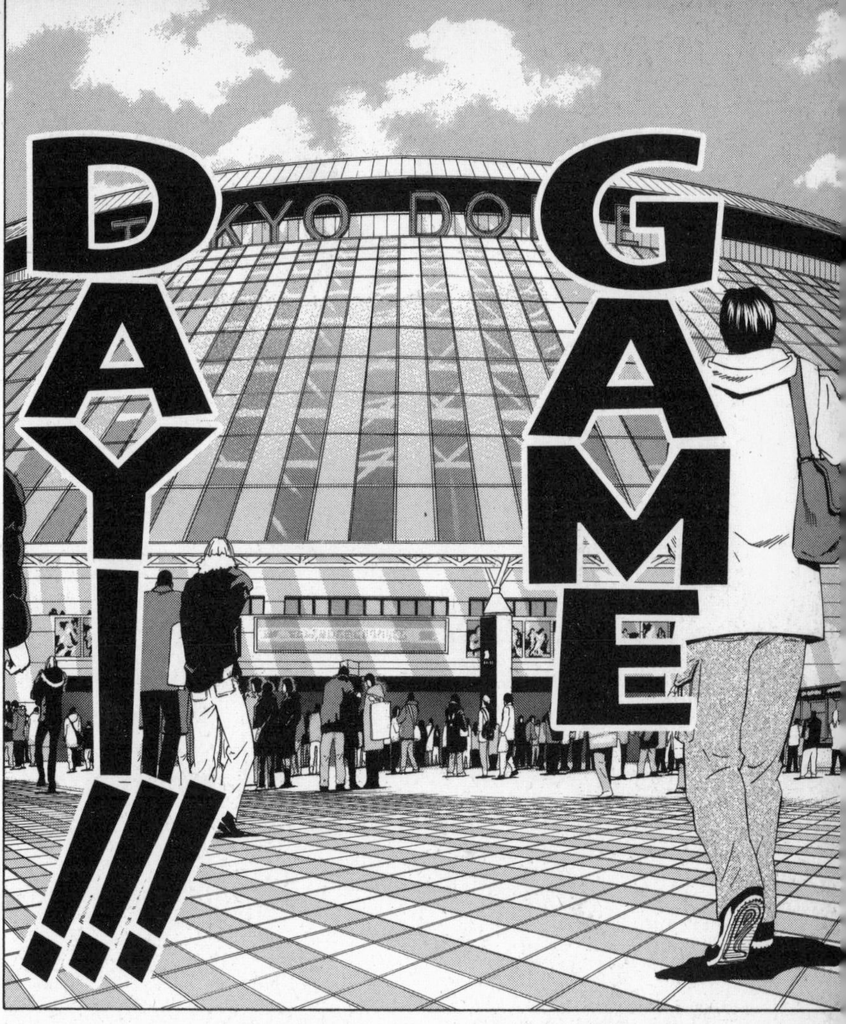
GAME
DAY!!!

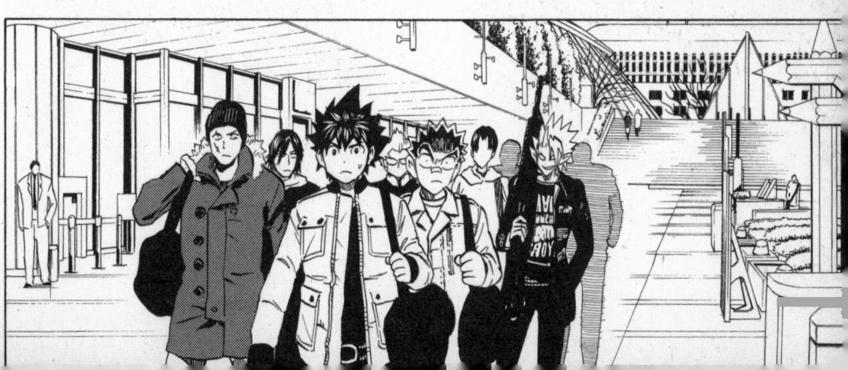

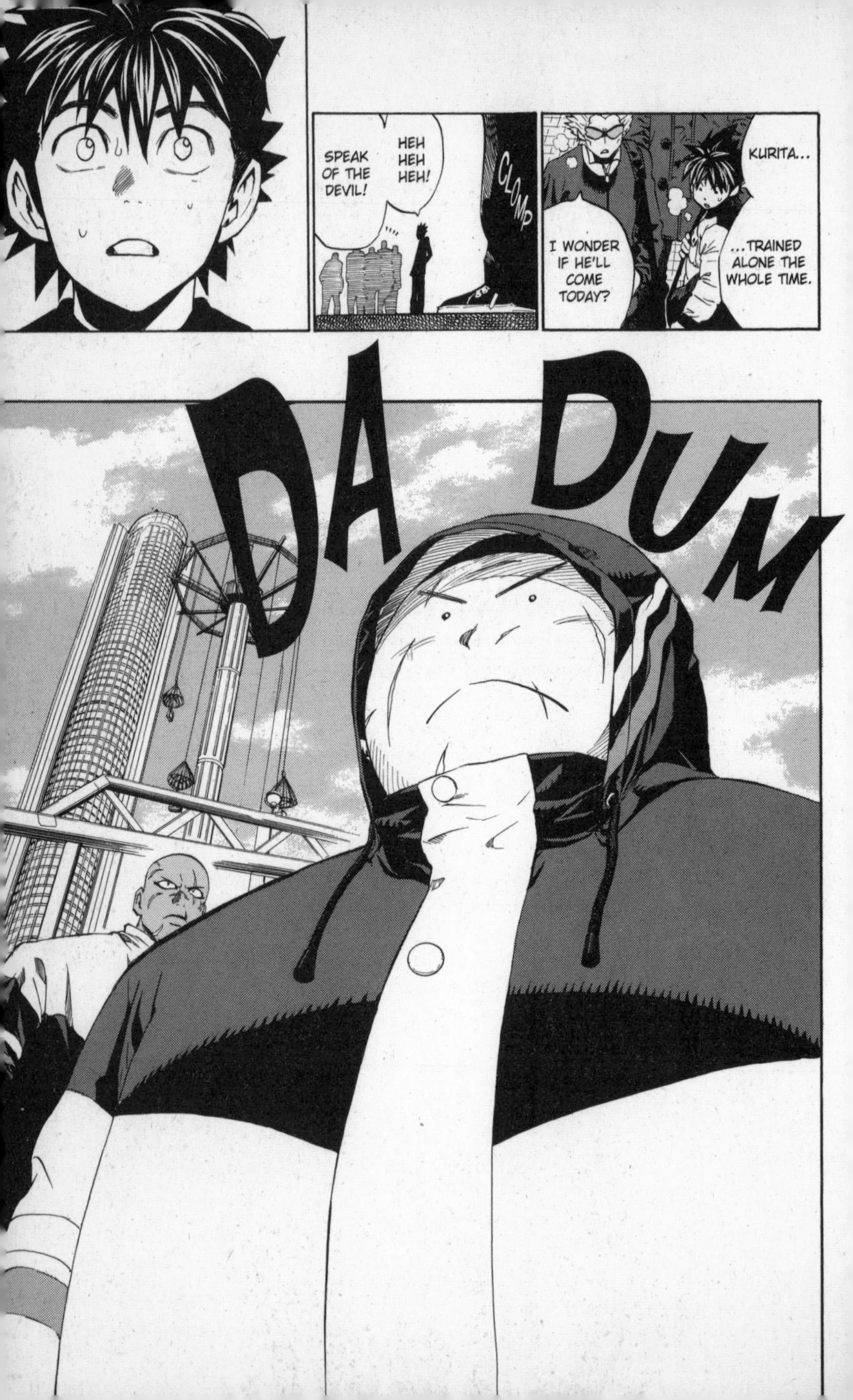

KURITA...
...TRAINED ALONE THE WHOLE TIME.
I WONDER IF HE'LL COME TODAY?
HEH HEH HEH!
SPEAK OF THE DEVIL!
CLOMP
DA DUM

Freshmen vs. Upperclassmen Dream Match Results!!

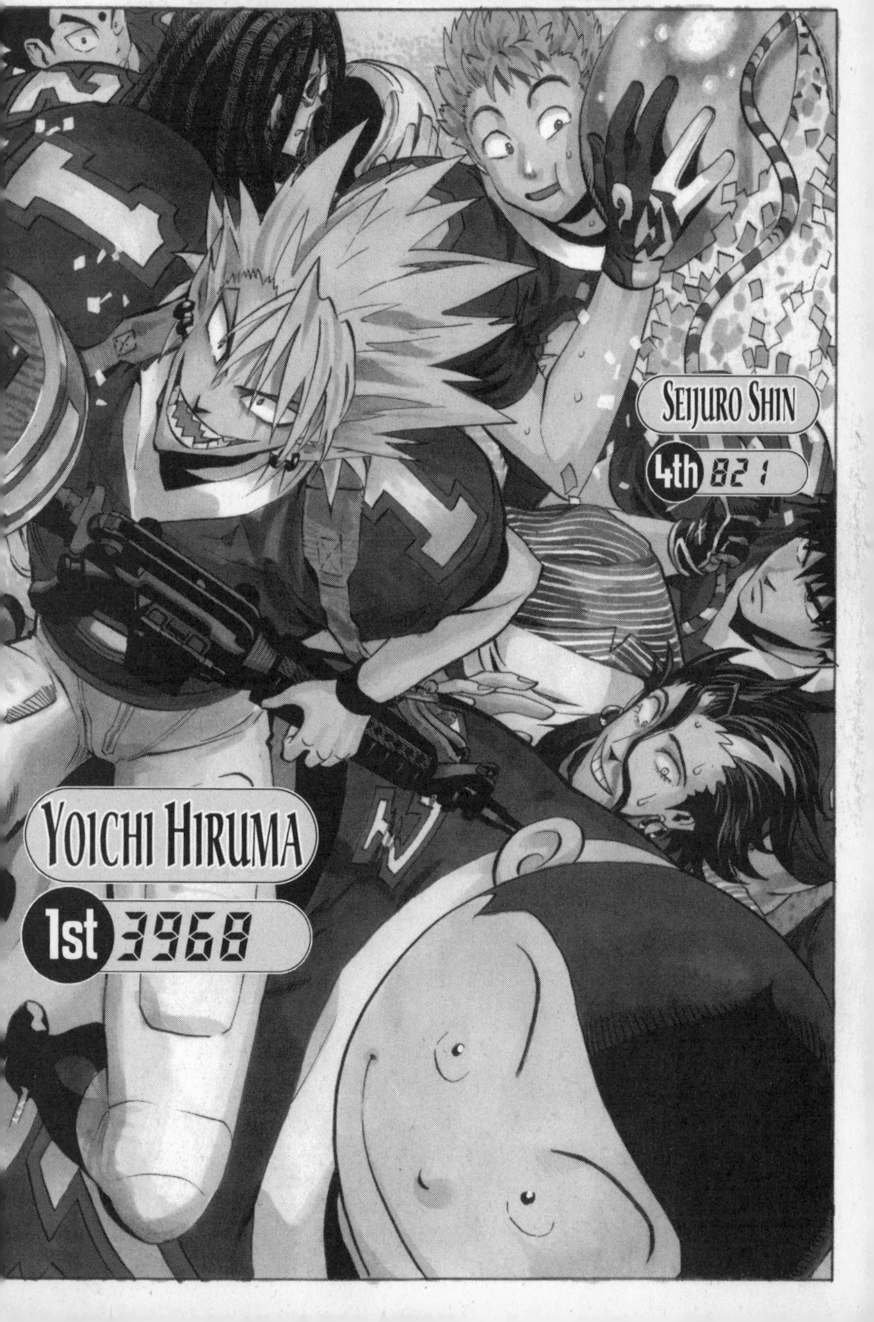
Seijuro Shin
4th 821
Yoichi Hiruma
1st 3968

Character Popularity Vote &

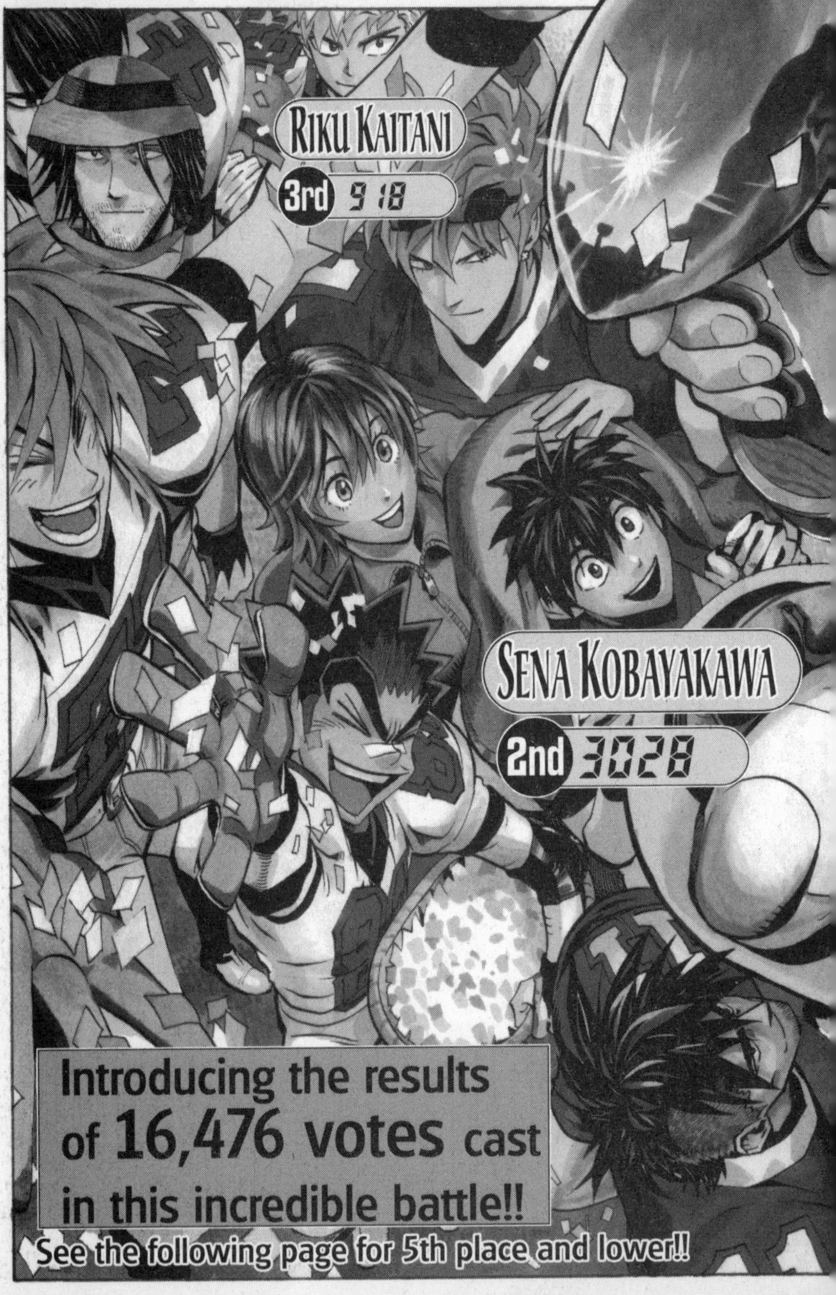

Riku Kaitani
3rd 918
Sena Kobayakawa
2nd 3028
Introducing the results of 16,476 votes cast in this incredible battle!!
See the following page for 5th place and lower!!

More results from the popularity vote!! Who did you vote for?!

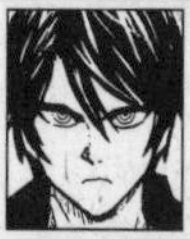
5th 605 Shun Kakei

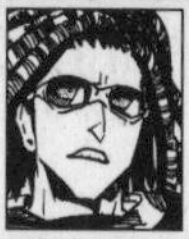
6th 596 Agon Kongo

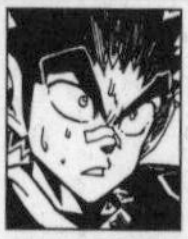
7th 529 Taro Raimon

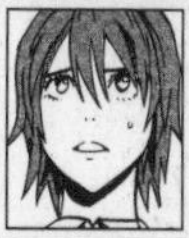
8th 520 Mamori Anezaki

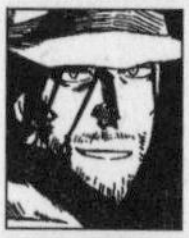
9th 520 The Kid

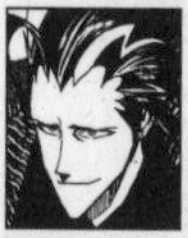
10th 436 Reiji Maruko

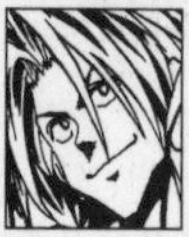
11th 427 Kengo Mizumachi

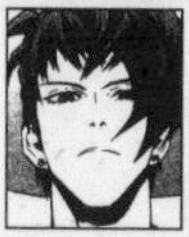
12th 400 Hayato Akaba

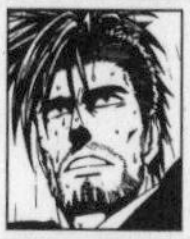
13th 354 Gen Takekura

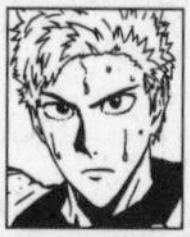
14th 337 Haruto Sakuraba

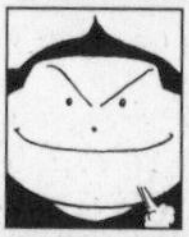
15th 307 Ryokan Kurita

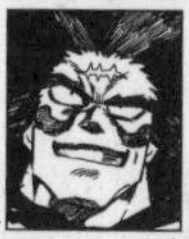
16th 290 Rikiya Gao

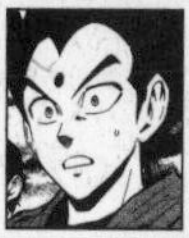
17th 277 Ikkyu Hosokawa

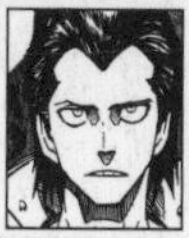
18th 252 Rui Habashira

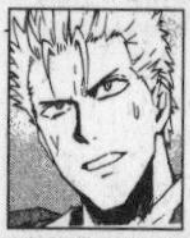
19th 224 Kazuki Jumonji

20th: Unsui Kongo 205
21st: Kotaro Sasaki 182
22nd: Jo Tetsuma 166
23rd: Patrick Spencer (Panther) 112
24th: Kiminari Harao 107
25th: Natsuhiko Taki 72
26th: Manabu Yukimitsu 61
27th: Hiromi Kisaragi 58
28th: Suzuna Taki 55
29th: Tetsuo Ishimaru 45
30th: Osamu Kobanzame 42
31st: Koji Kuroki 37
32nd: Ichiro Takami 34
33rd: Daikichi Komusubi 31
34th: Daigo Ikari 27
35th: Masaru Honjo 24
36th: Koharu Wakana 20
37th: Maruko Himuro 19
38th: Shozo Togano 18
39th: Hiroshi Onishi 15
40th: Hiroshi Ohira 13
41st: Cerberus 9
42nd: Doburoku Sakaki 7
43rd: Makoto Otawara 6
44th: Masayuki Seiten / Sosuke Ban 4
46th: Homer Fitzgerald / Sanzo 3
48th: Jo Arado / Kazuyoshi Inoue / Akira Onisawa / Toshiya Kondo 2
52nd: Gonzales (big brother) / Gonzales (little brother) / Ninobu Kasamatsu Keisuke Nekoyama / Juri Sawai / Love Sentoku / the Hiruma horse from Ben Ranch / Minta Hita 1

AND THE WINNER OF THE DREAM MATCH IS...

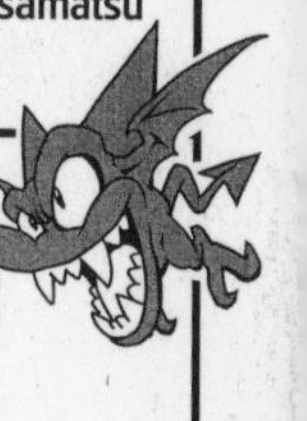

UPPERCLASSMEN: 8,674 FRESHMEN 6,845

THE UPPERCLASSMEN WIN!! YA-HA!!

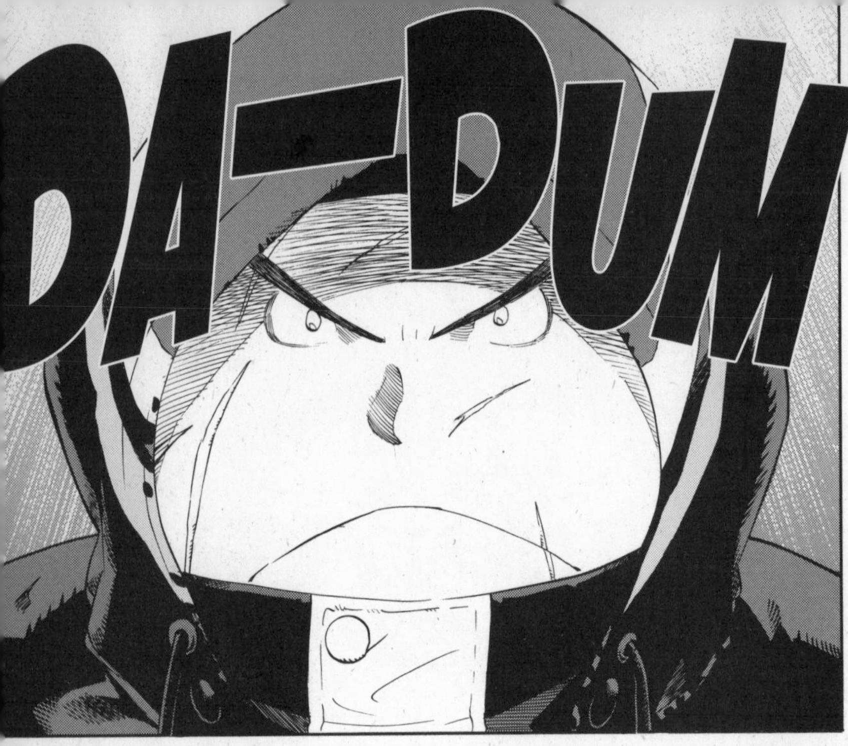
DA-DUM

Chapter 252 The Final

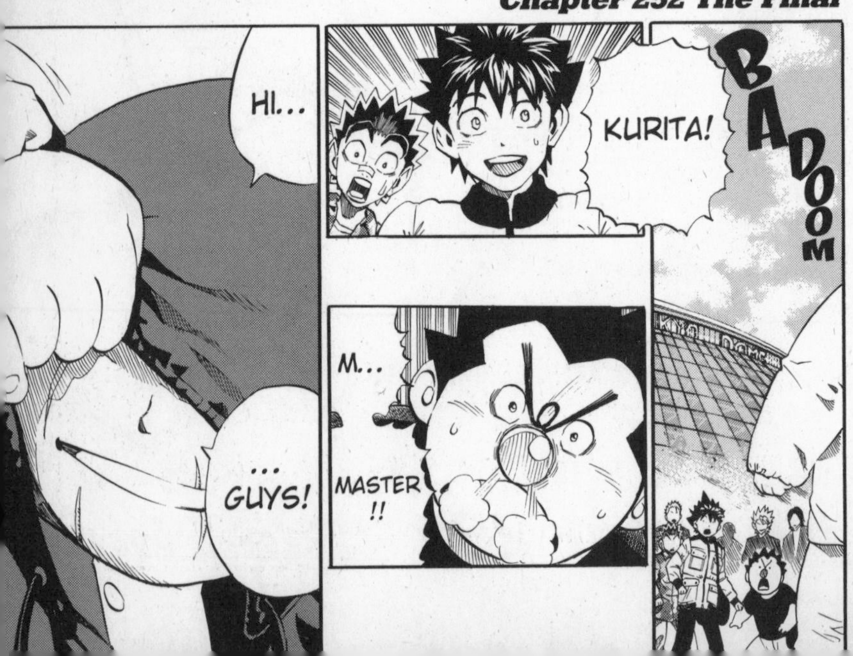
BADOOM
KURITA!
M...
MASTER !!
HI...
... GUYS!

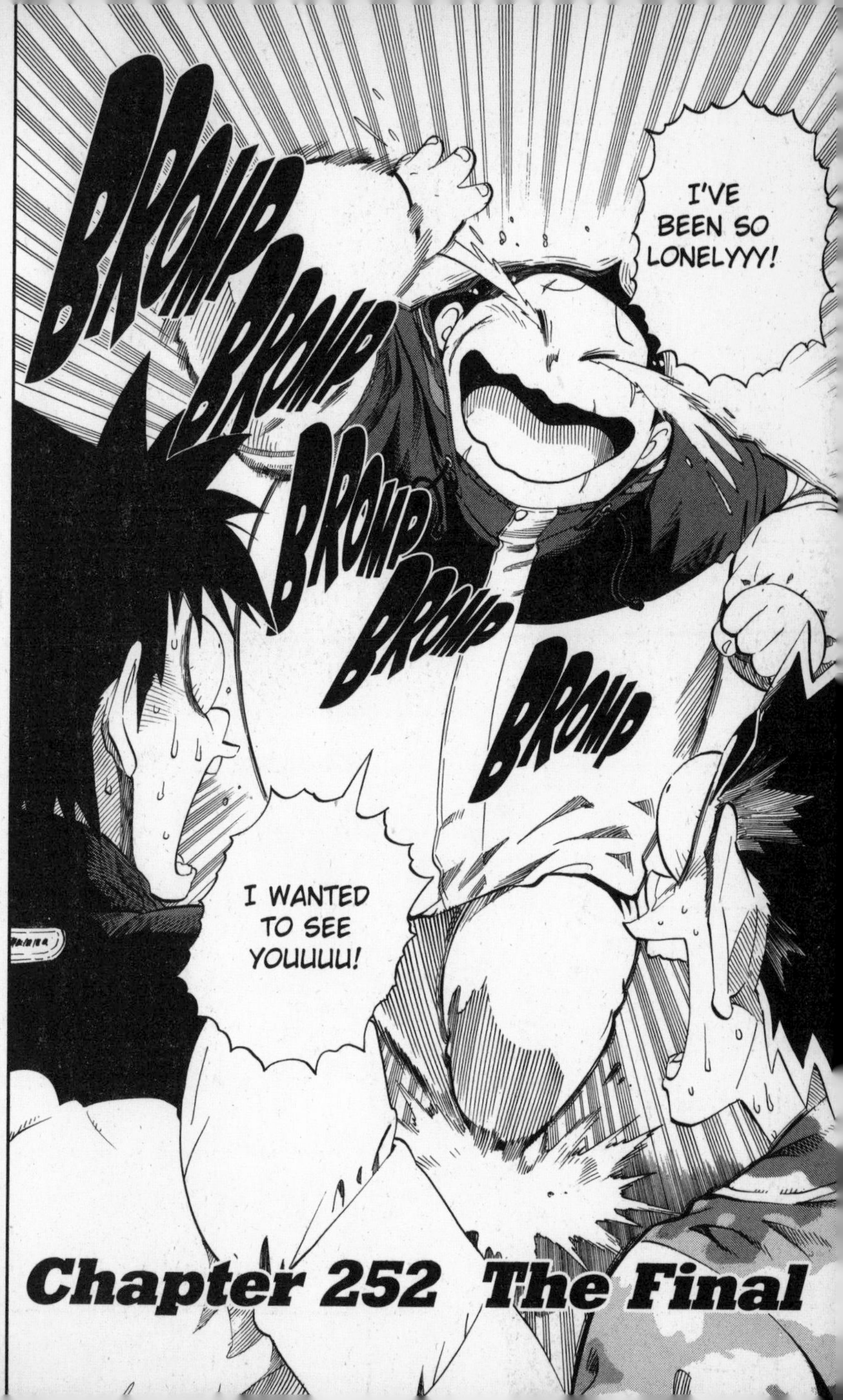
I'VE BEEN SO LONELYYY!
BROMP BROMP BROMP BROMP BROMP BROMP
I WANTED TO SEE YOUUUU!

Chapter 252 The Final

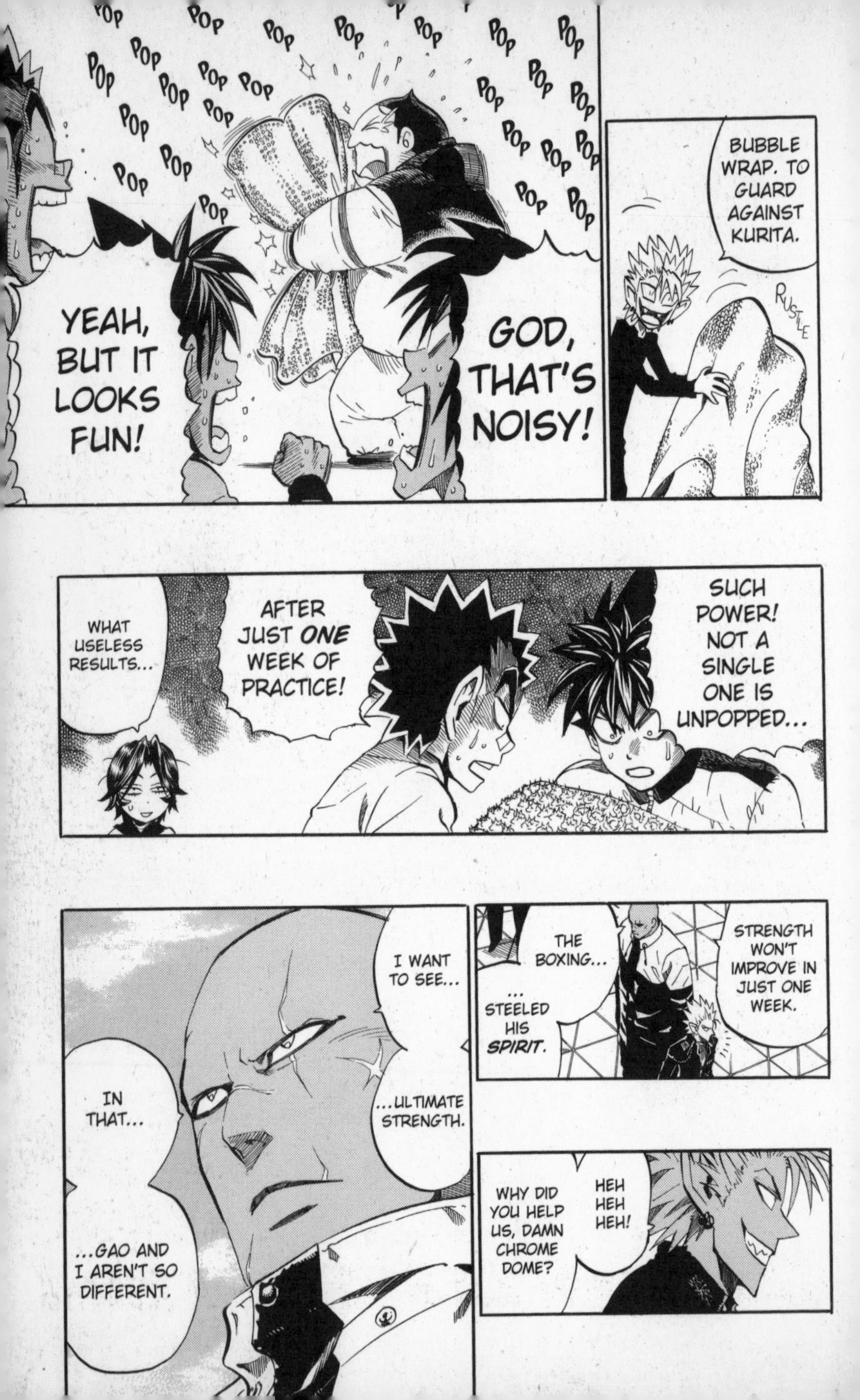

BUBBLE WRAP. TO GUARD AGAINST KURITA.
RUSTLE
POP POP POP POP POP POP POP POP POP POP POP POP POP POP POP POP POP POP POP POP POP POP
GOD, THAT'S NOISY!
YEAH, BUT IT LOOKS FUN!
SUCH POWER! NOT A SINGLE ONE IS UNPOPPED...
AFTER JUST *ONE* WEEK OF PRACTICE!
WHAT USELESS RESULTS...
STRENGTH WON'T IMPROVE IN JUST ONE WEEK.
THE BOXING...
...STEELED HIS *SPIRIT*.
HEH HEH HEH!
WHY DID YOU HELP US, DAMN CHROME DOME?
I WANT TO SEE...
...ULTIMATE STRENGTH.
IN THAT...
...GAO AND I AREN'T SO DIFFERENT.

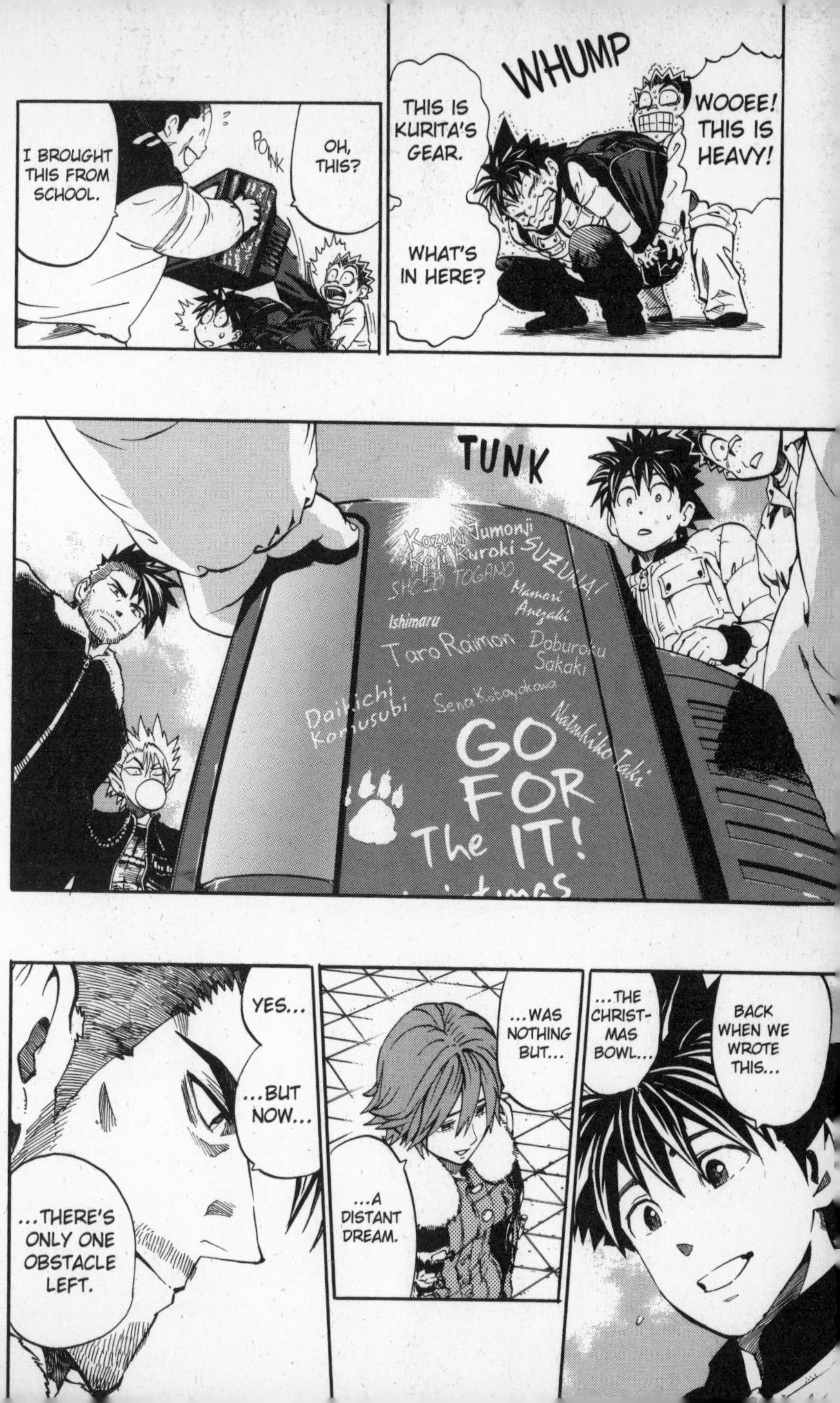
WOOEE! THIS IS HEAVY!
WHUMP
THIS IS KURITA'S GEAR.
WHAT'S IN HERE?
OH, THIS?
POINK
I BROUGHT THIS FROM SCHOOL.
TUNK
Kazuki Jumonji
Koji Kuroki
SUZUNA!
SHOZO TOGANO
Mamori Anezaki
Ishimaru
Taro Raimon
Doburoku Sakaki
Daikichi Komusubi
Sena Kobayakawa
Natsuhiko Taki
GO FOR The IT!
BACK WHEN WE WROTE THIS...
...THE CHRIST-MAS BOWL...
...WAS NOTHING BUT...
...A DISTANT DREAM.
YES...
...BUT NOW...
...THERE'S ONLY ONE OBSTACLE LEFT.

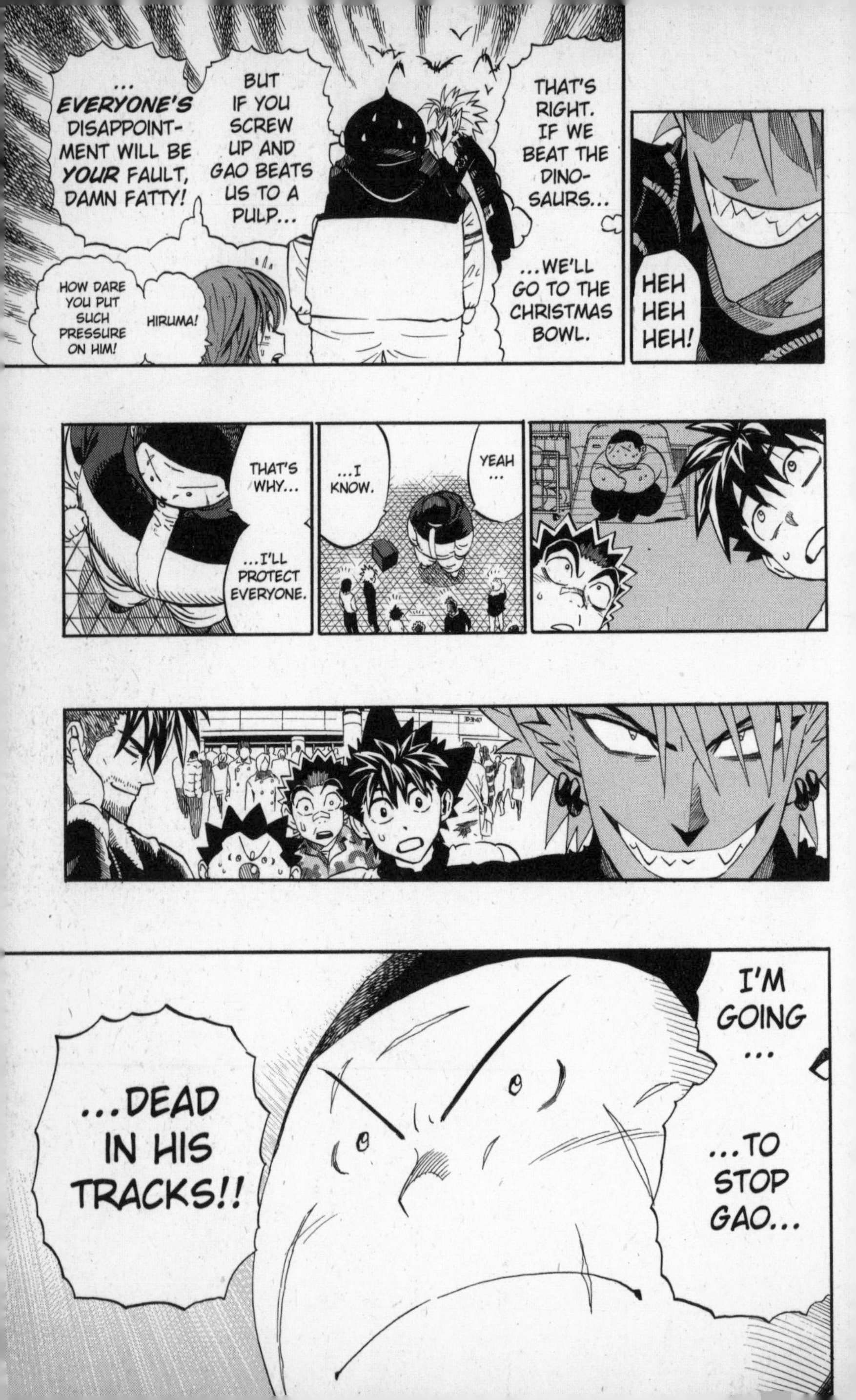
HEH HEH HEH!
THAT'S RIGHT. IF WE BEAT THE DINOSAURS...
...WE'LL GO TO THE CHRISTMAS BOWL.
BUT IF YOU SCREW UP AND GAO BEATS US TO A PULP...
...EVERYONE'S DISAPPOINTMENT WILL BE YOUR FAULT, DAMN FATTY!
HIRUMA!
HOW DARE YOU PUT SUCH PRESSURE ON HIM!
YEAH...
...I KNOW.
THAT'S WHY...
...I'LL PROTECT EVERYONE.
I'M GOING...
...TO STOP GAO...
...DEAD IN HIS TRACKS!!

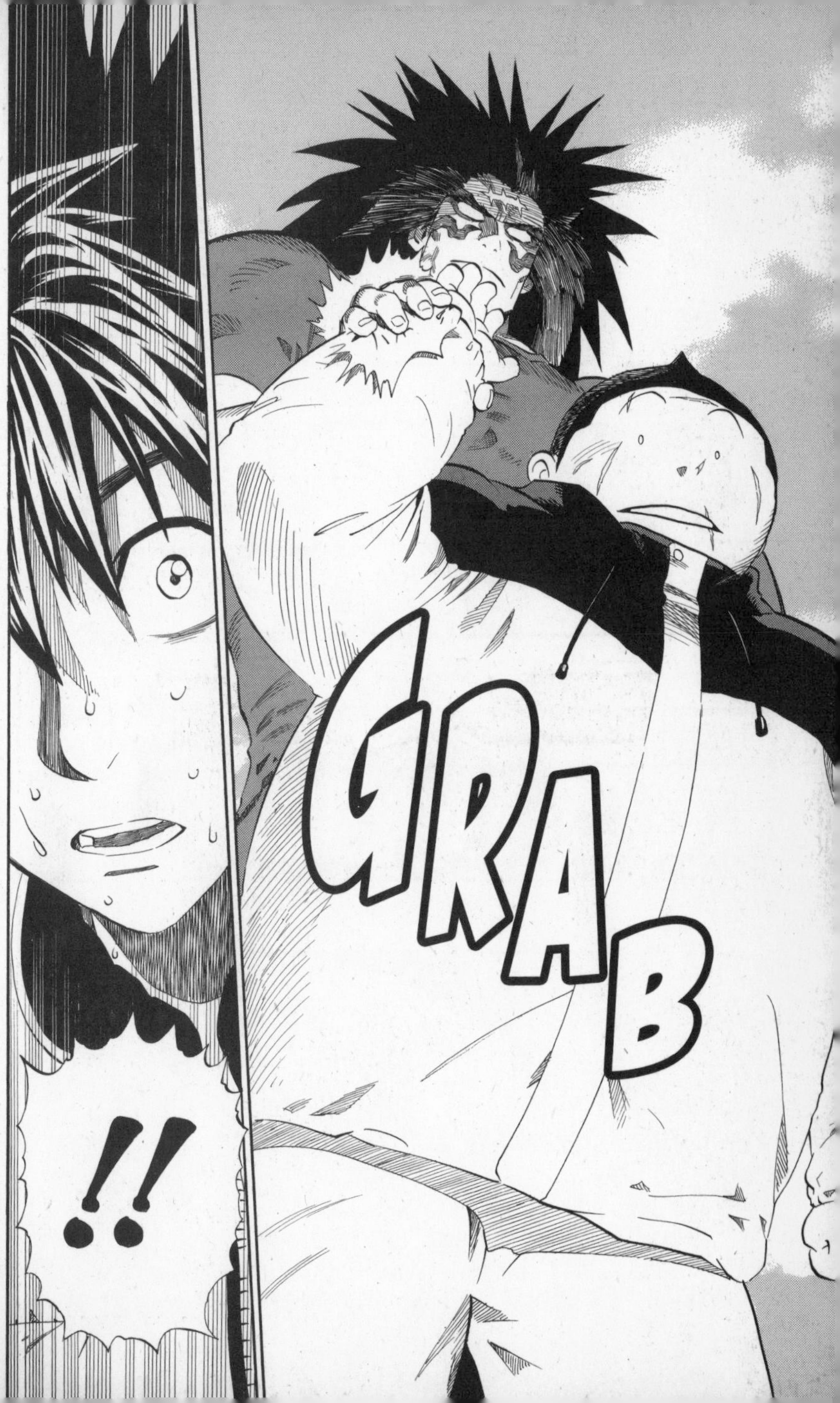
GRAB
!!

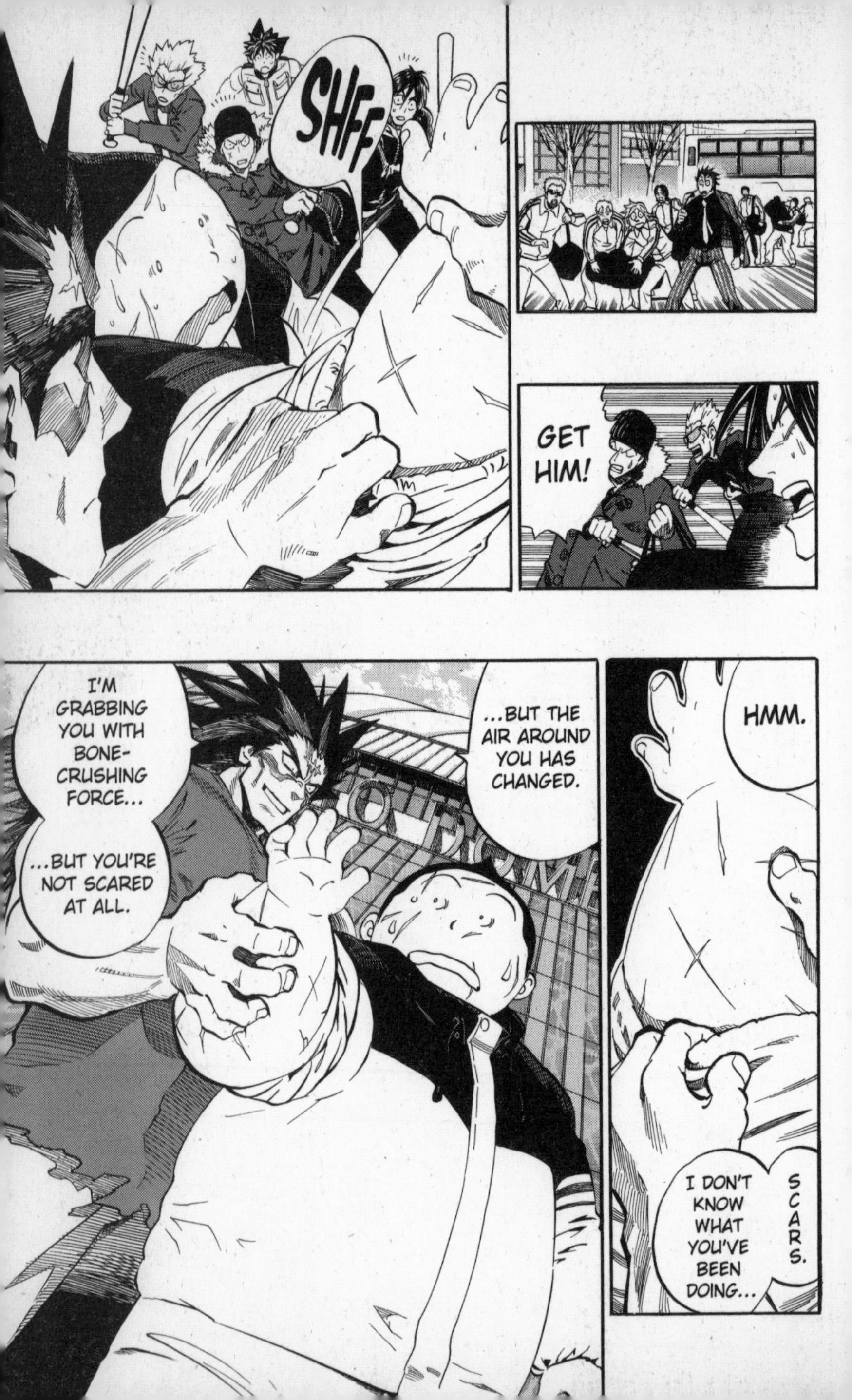
GET HIM!
SHFF
HMM.
I DON'T KNOW WHAT YOU'VE BEEN DOING...
SCARS.
...BUT THE AIR AROUND YOU HAS CHANGED.
I'M GRABBING YOU WITH BONE-CRUSHING FORCE...
...BUT YOU'RE NOT SCARED AT ALL.

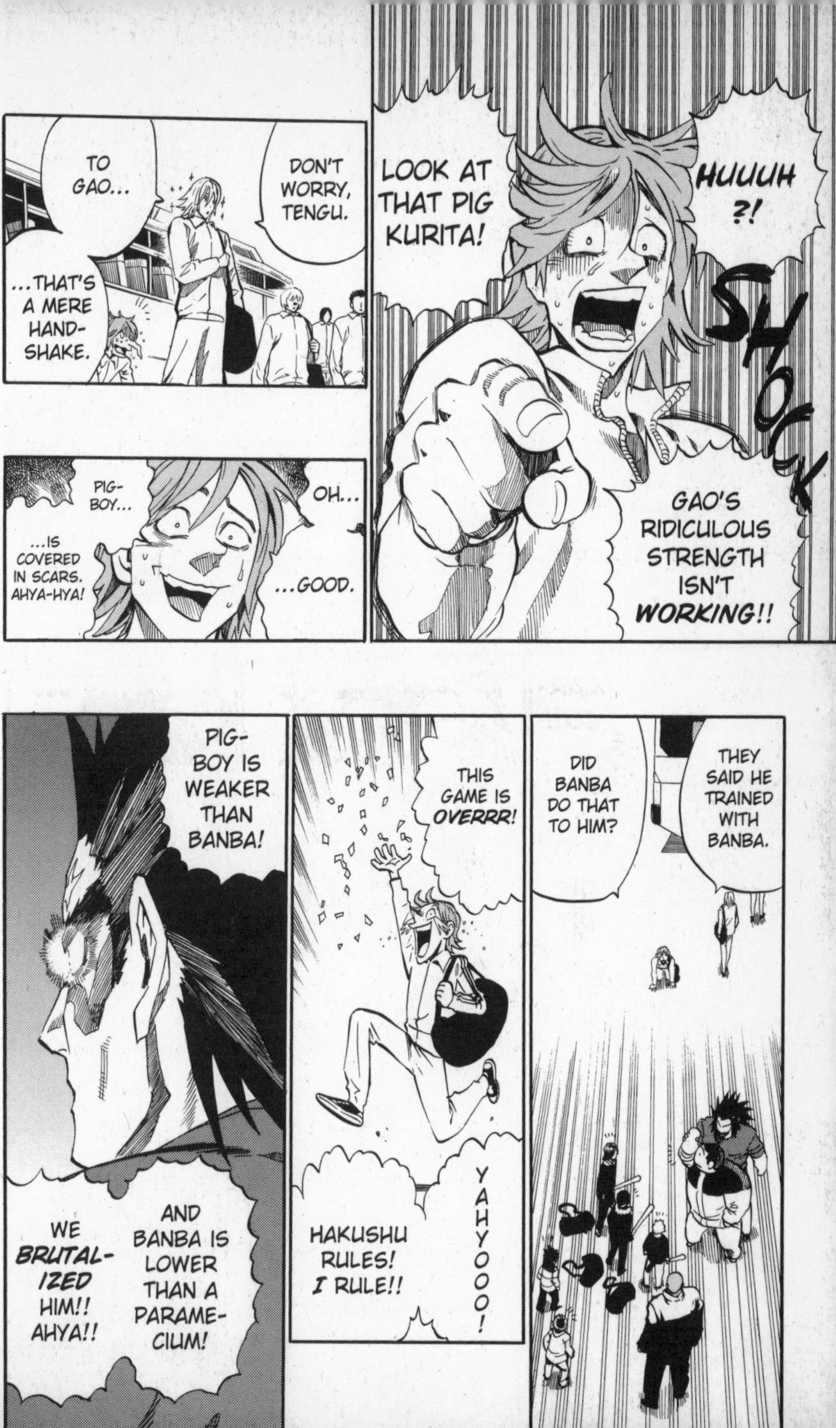
HUUUH ?!
LOOK AT THAT PIG KURITA!
SHOCK
GAO'S RIDICULOUS STRENGTH ISN'T WORKING!!
DON'T WORRY, TENGU.
TO GAO...
...THAT'S A MERE HANDSHAKE.
OH...
PIG-BOY...
...IS COVERED IN SCARS. AHYA-HYA!
...GOOD.
THEY SAID HE TRAINED WITH BANBA.
DID BANBA DO THAT TO HIM?
THIS GAME IS OVERRR!
YAHYOOOO!
HAKUSHU RULES! I RULE!!
PIG-BOY IS WEAKER THAN BANBA!
AND BANBA IS LOWER THAN A PARAMECIUM!
WE BRUTALIZED HIM!! AHYA!!

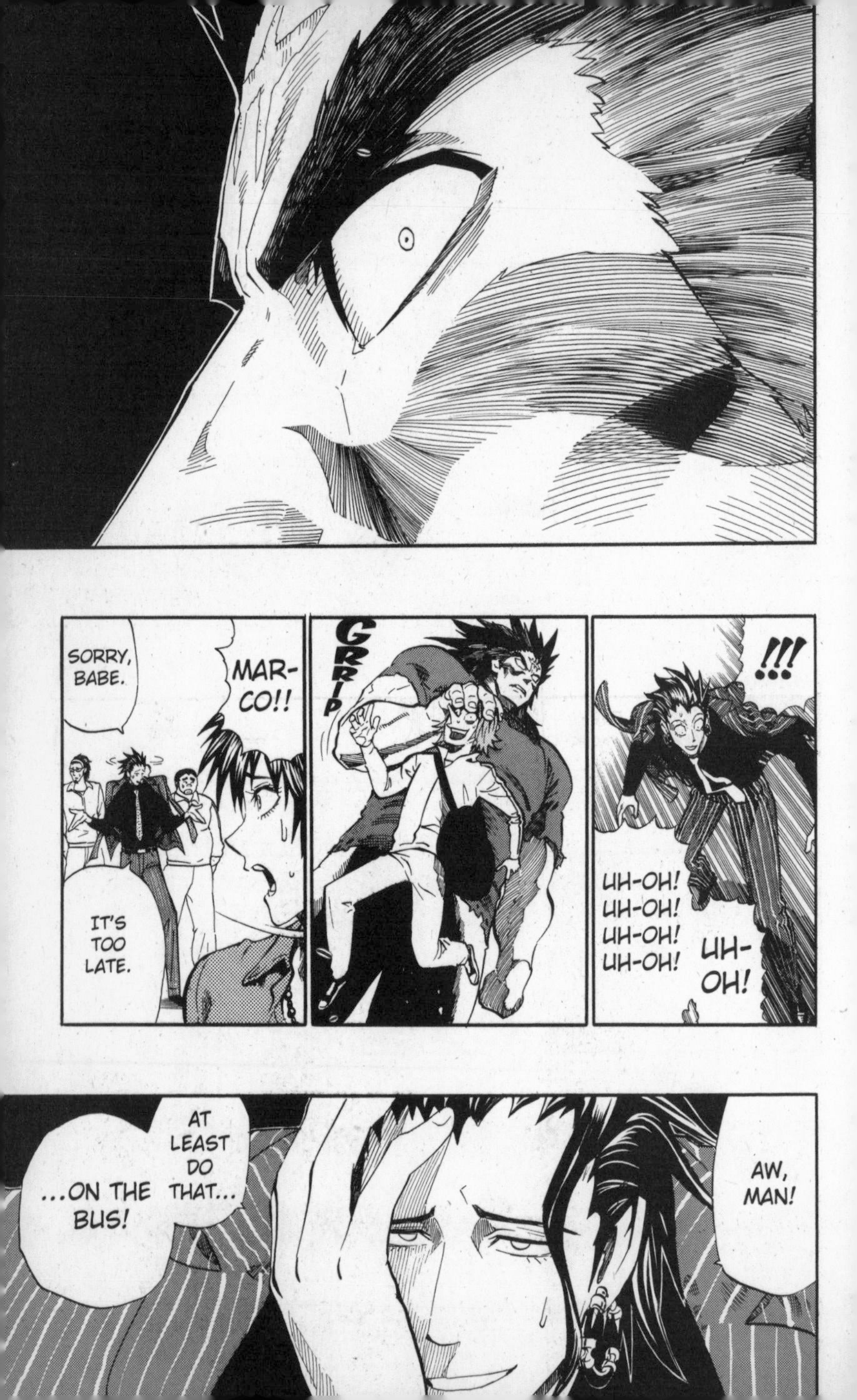
!!!
UH-OH! UH-OH! UH-OH! UH-OH!
UH-OH!
GRRIP
MAR-CO!!
SORRY, BABE.
IT'S TOO LATE.
AW, MAN!
AT LEAST DO THAT...
...ON THE BUS!

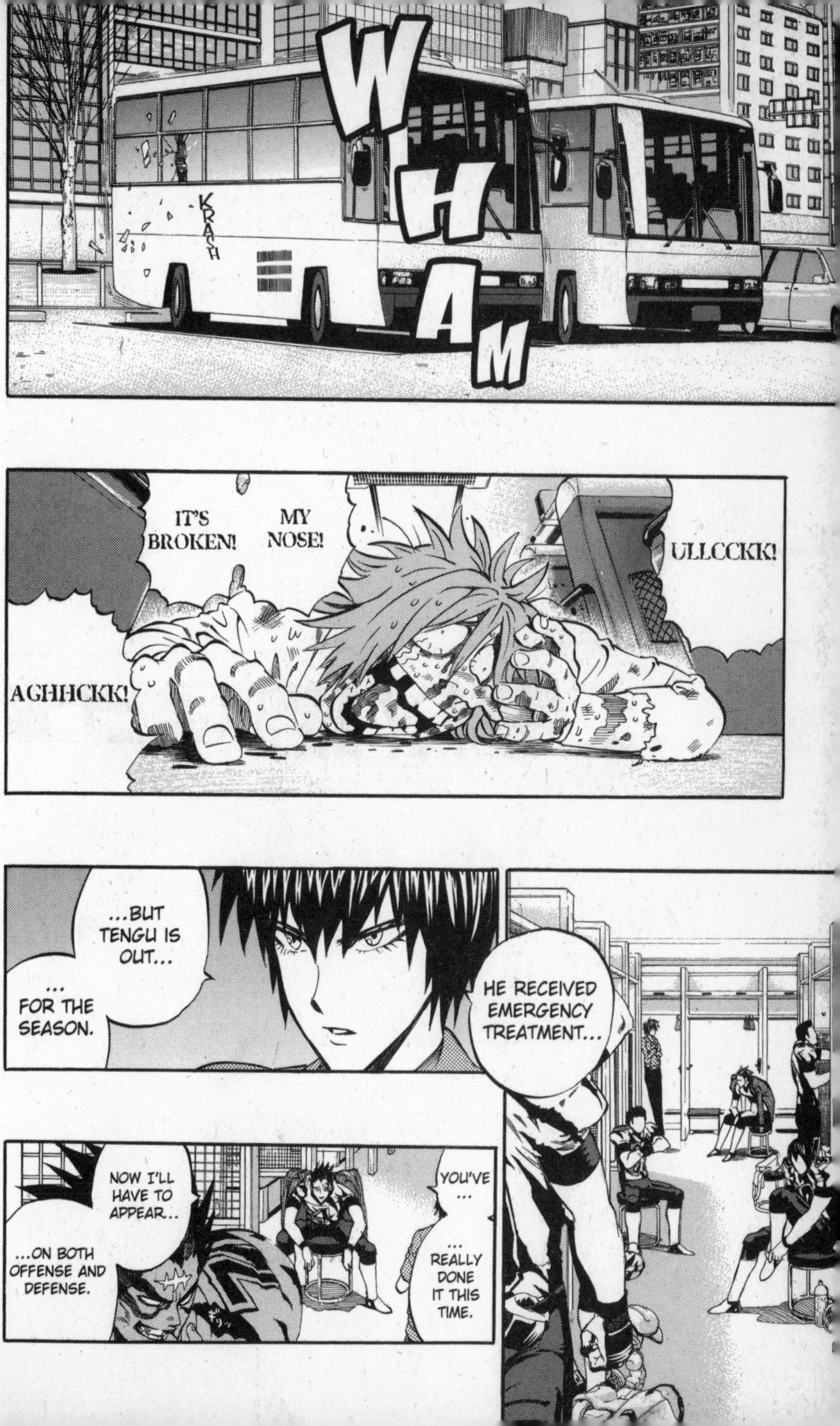
WHAM
KRASH
ULLCCKK!
MY NOSE!
IT'S BROKEN!
AGHHCKK!
HE RECEIVED EMERGENCY TREATMENT...
...BUT TENGU IS OUT...
... FOR THE SEASON.
YOU'VE ...
... REALLY DONE IT THIS TIME.
NOW I'LL HAVE TO APPEAR...
...ON BOTH OFFENSE AND DEFENSE.

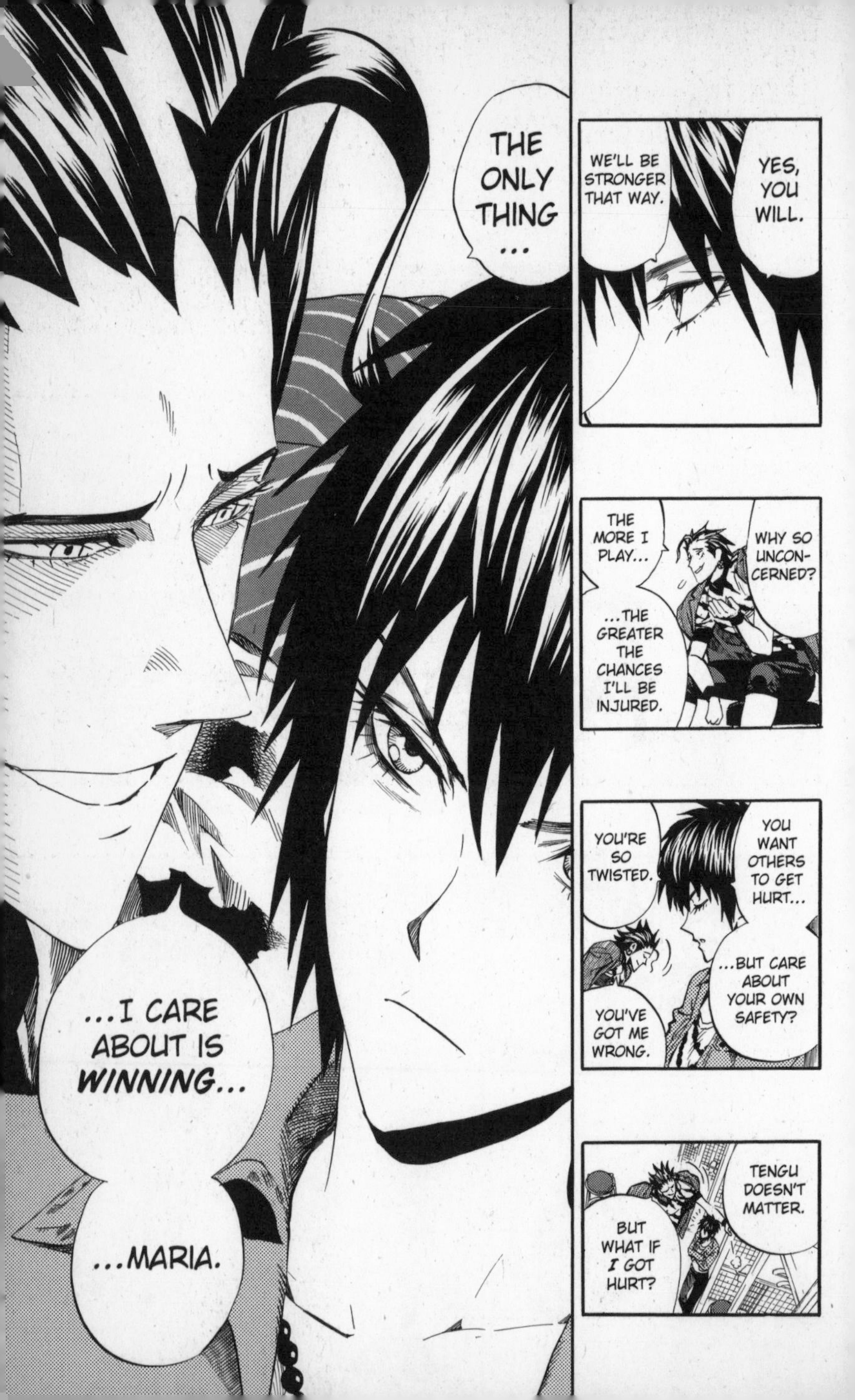
YES, YOU WILL.
WE'LL BE STRONGER THAT WAY.
WHY SO UNCONCERNED?
THE MORE I PLAY...
...THE GREATER THE CHANCES I'LL BE INJURED.
YOU WANT OTHERS TO GET HURT...
YOU'RE SO TWISTED.
...BUT CARE ABOUT YOUR OWN SAFETY?
YOU'VE GOT ME WRONG.
TENGU DOESN'T MATTER.
BUT WHAT IF *I* GOT HURT?
THE ONLY THING...
...I CARE ABOUT IS *WINNING*...
...MARIA.

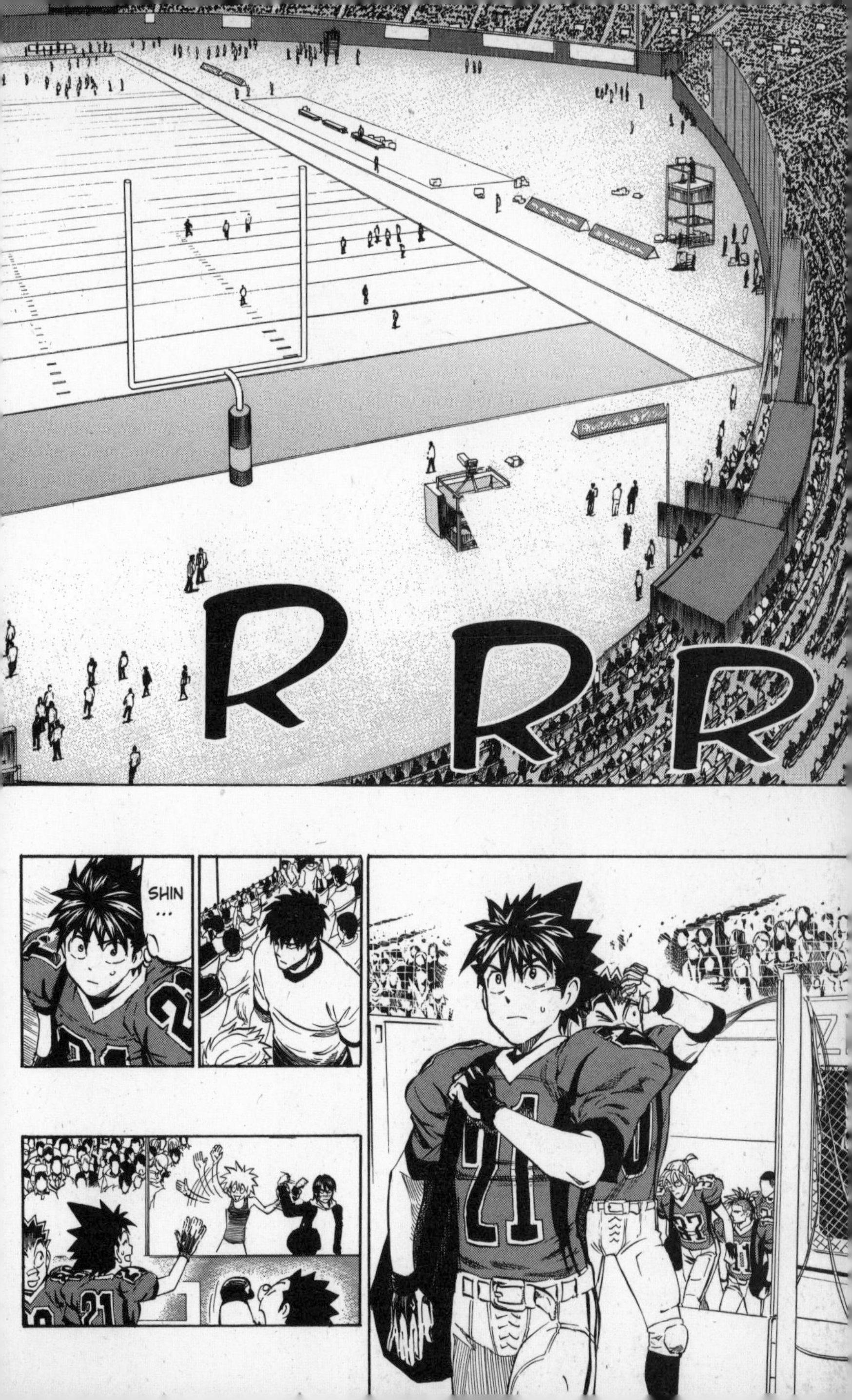
R R R
SHIN ...

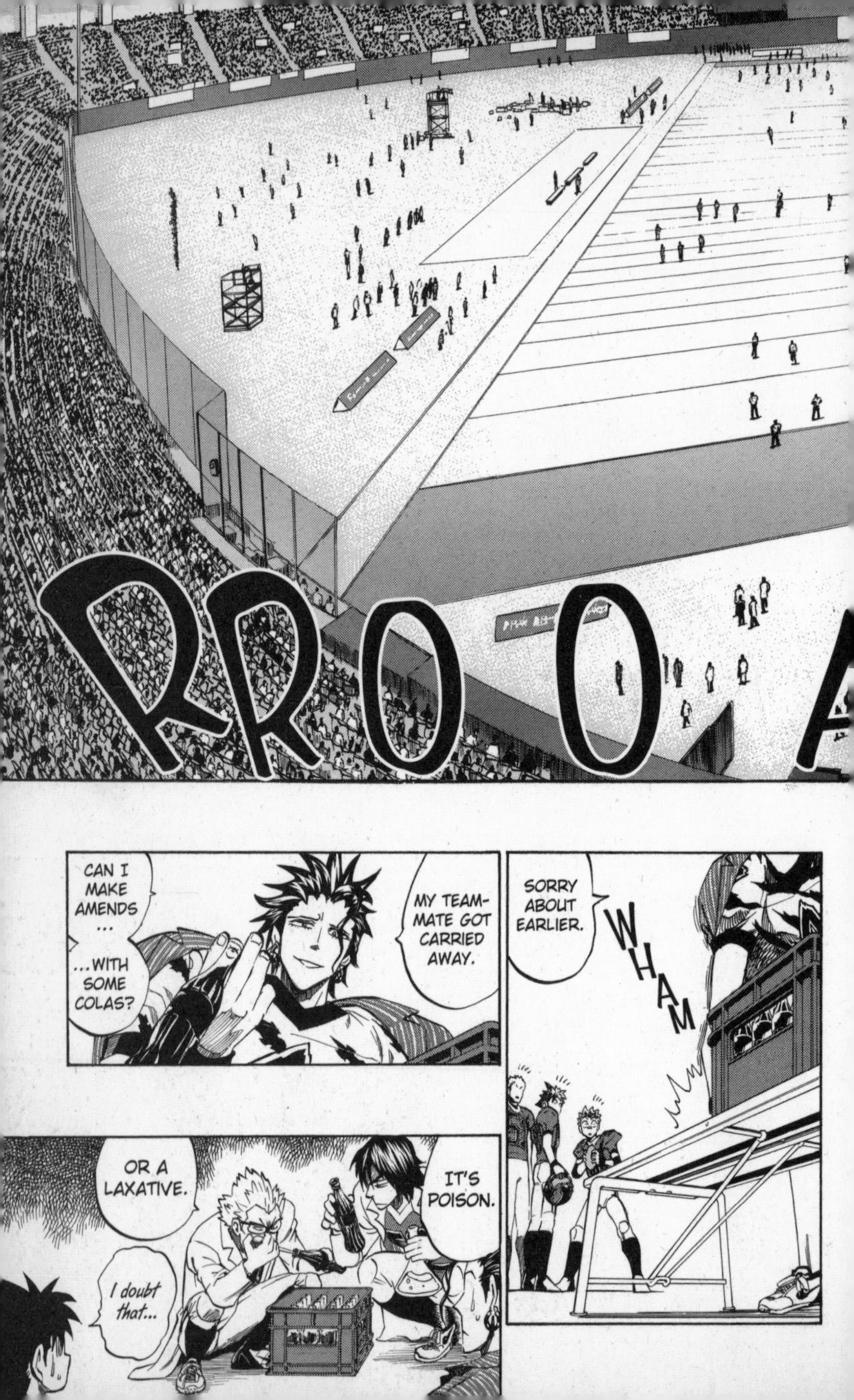
RRO O A
SORRY ABOUT EARLIER.
WHAM
MY TEAM-MATE GOT CARRIED AWAY.
CAN I MAKE AMENDS...
...WITH SOME COLAS?
IT'S POISON.
OR A LAXATIVE.
I doubt that...

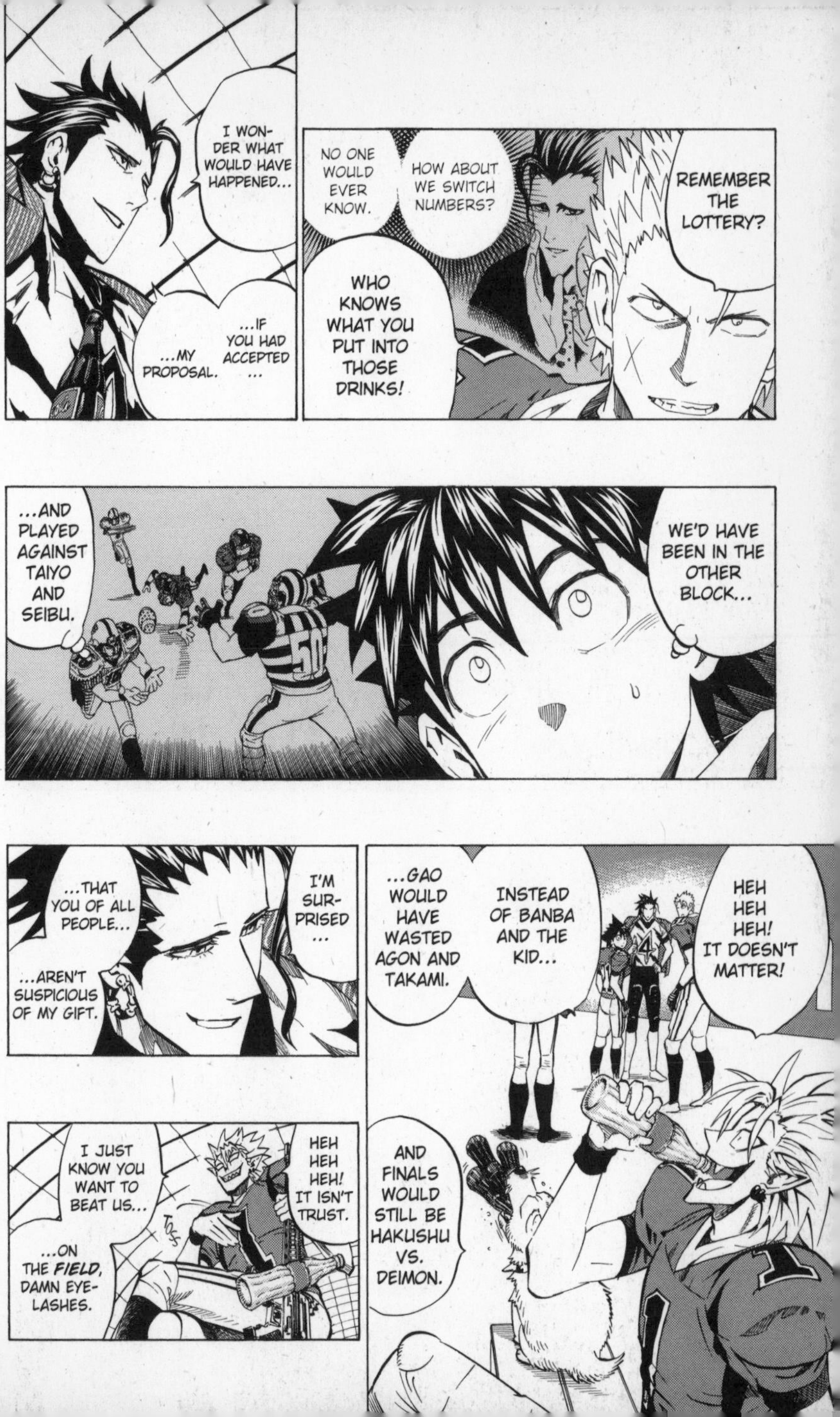
REMEMBER THE LOTTERY?
HOW ABOUT WE SWITCH NUMBERS?
NO ONE WOULD EVER KNOW.
WHO KNOWS WHAT YOU PUT INTO THOSE DRINKS!
I WONDER WHAT WOULD HAVE HAPPENED...
...IF YOU HAD ACCEPTED...
...MY PROPOSAL.
WE'D HAVE BEEN IN THE OTHER BLOCK...
...AND PLAYED AGAINST TAIYO AND SEIBU.
HEH HEH HEH! IT DOESN'T MATTER!
INSTEAD OF BANBA AND THE KID...
...GAO WOULD HAVE WASTED AGON AND TAKAMI.
AND FINALS WOULD STILL BE HAKUSHU VS. DEIMON.
I'M SURPRISED...
...THAT YOU OF ALL PEOPLE...
...AREN'T SUSPICIOUS OF MY GIFT.
HEH HEH HEH! IT ISN'T TRUST.
I JUST KNOW YOU WANT TO BEAT US...
TOSS
...ON THE *FIELD*, DAMN EYE-LASHES.

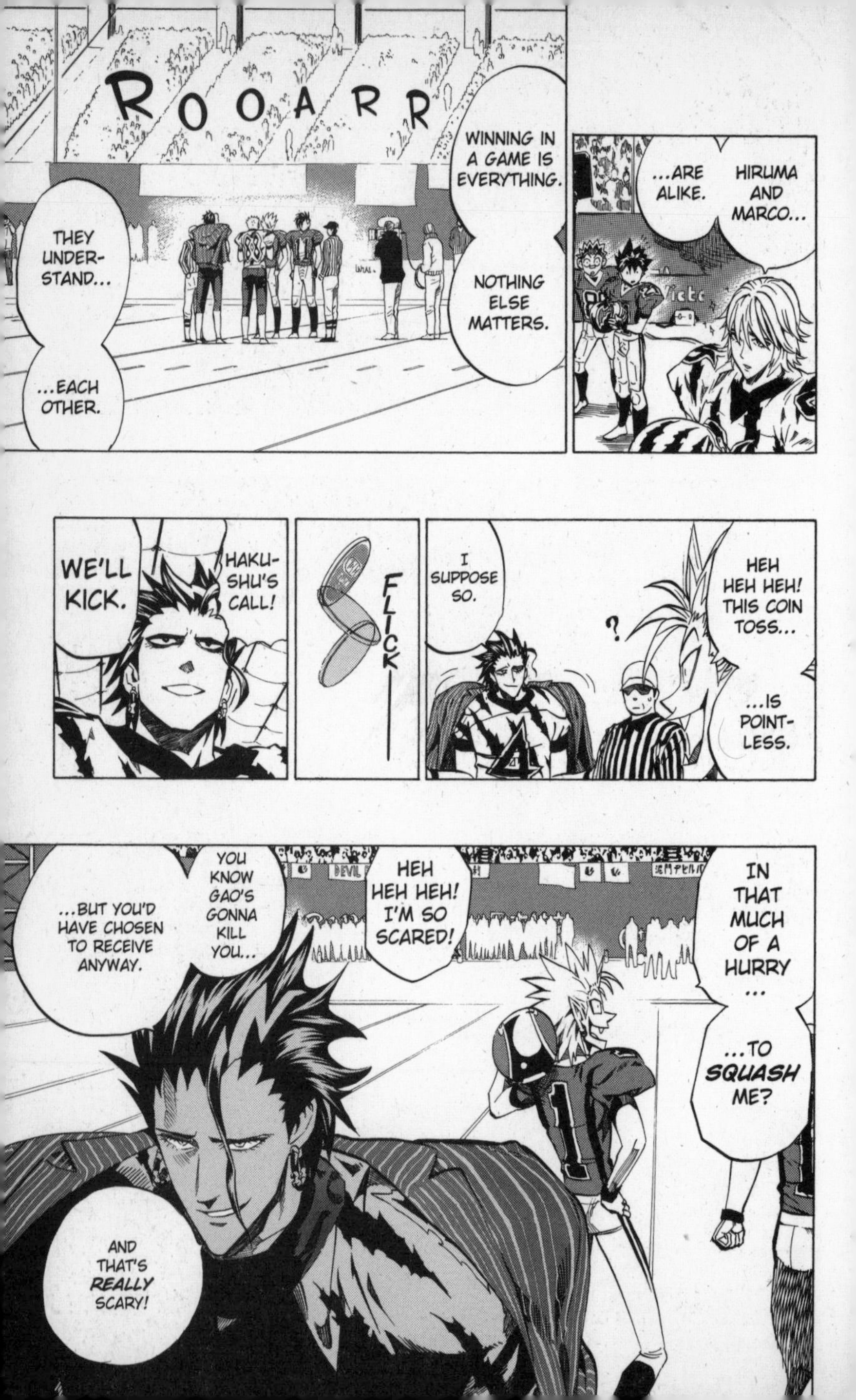
HIRUMA AND MARCO...
...ARE ALIKE.
ROOARR
WINNING IN A GAME IS EVERYTHING.
NOTHING ELSE MATTERS.
THEY UNDERSTAND...
...EACH OTHER.
HEH HEH HEH! THIS COIN TOSS...
...IS POINTLESS.
?
I SUPPOSE SO.
FLICK
HAKUSHU'S CALL!
WE'LL KICK.
IN THAT MUCH OF A HURRY...
...TO *SQUASH* ME?
HEH HEH HEH! I'M SO SCARED!
YOU KNOW GAO'S GONNA KILL YOU...
...BUT YOU'D HAVE CHOSEN TO RECEIVE ANYWAY.
AND THAT'S *REALLY* SCARY!

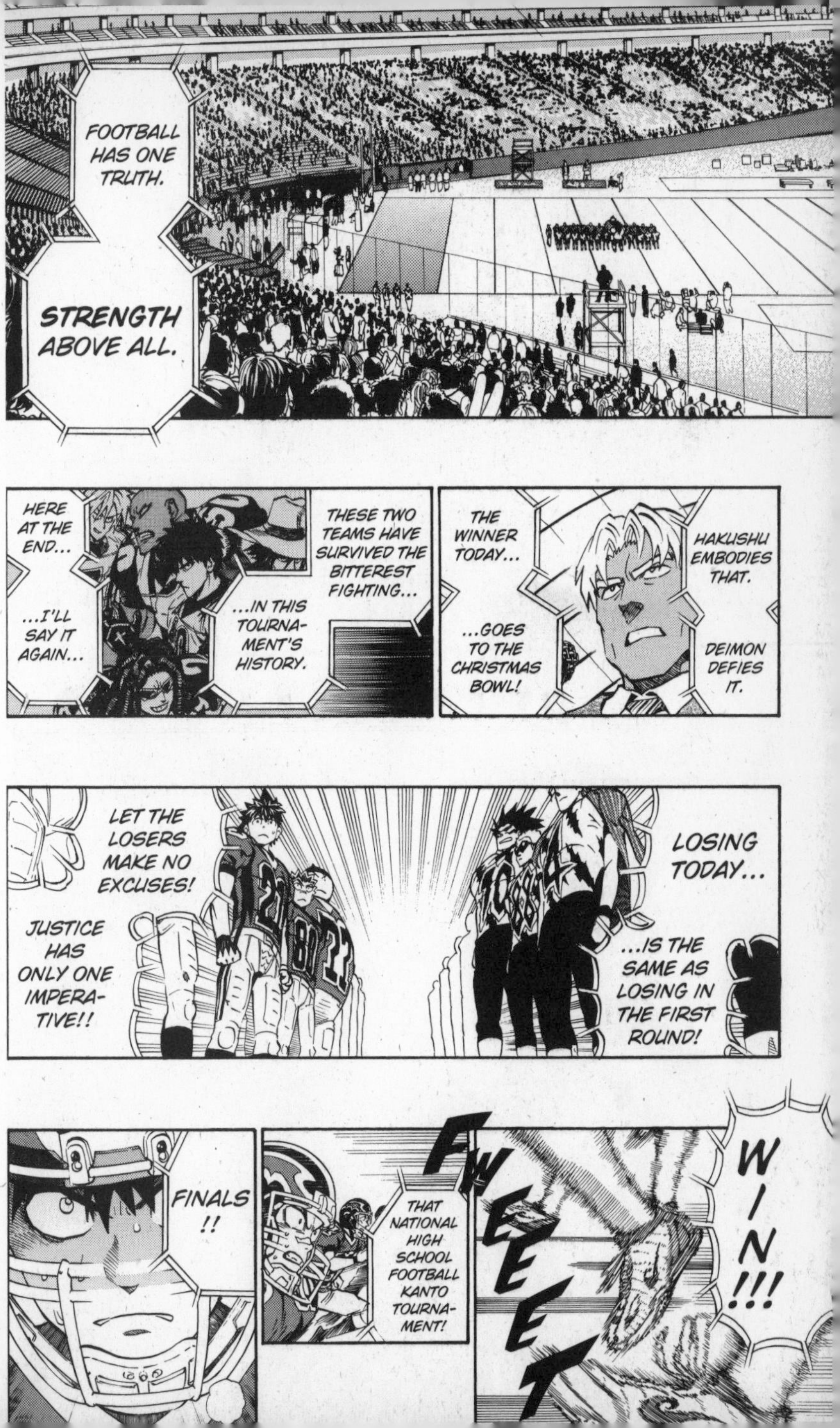
FOOTBALL HAS ONE TRUTH.
STRENGTH ABOVE ALL.
HAKUSHU EMBODIES THAT.
DEIMON DEFIES IT.
THE WINNER TODAY...
...GOES TO THE CHRISTMAS BOWL!
THESE TWO TEAMS HAVE SURVIVED THE BITTEREST FIGHTING...
...IN THIS TOURNA-MENT'S HISTORY.
HERE AT THE END...
...I'LL SAY IT AGAIN...
LOSING TODAY...
...IS THE SAME AS LOSING IN THE FIRST ROUND!
LET THE LOSERS MAKE NO EXCUSES!
JUSTICE HAS ONLY ONE IMPERA-TIVE!!
WIN!!!
FWEEEET
THAT NATIONAL HIGH SCHOOL FOOTBALL KANTO TOURNA-MENT!
FINALS!!

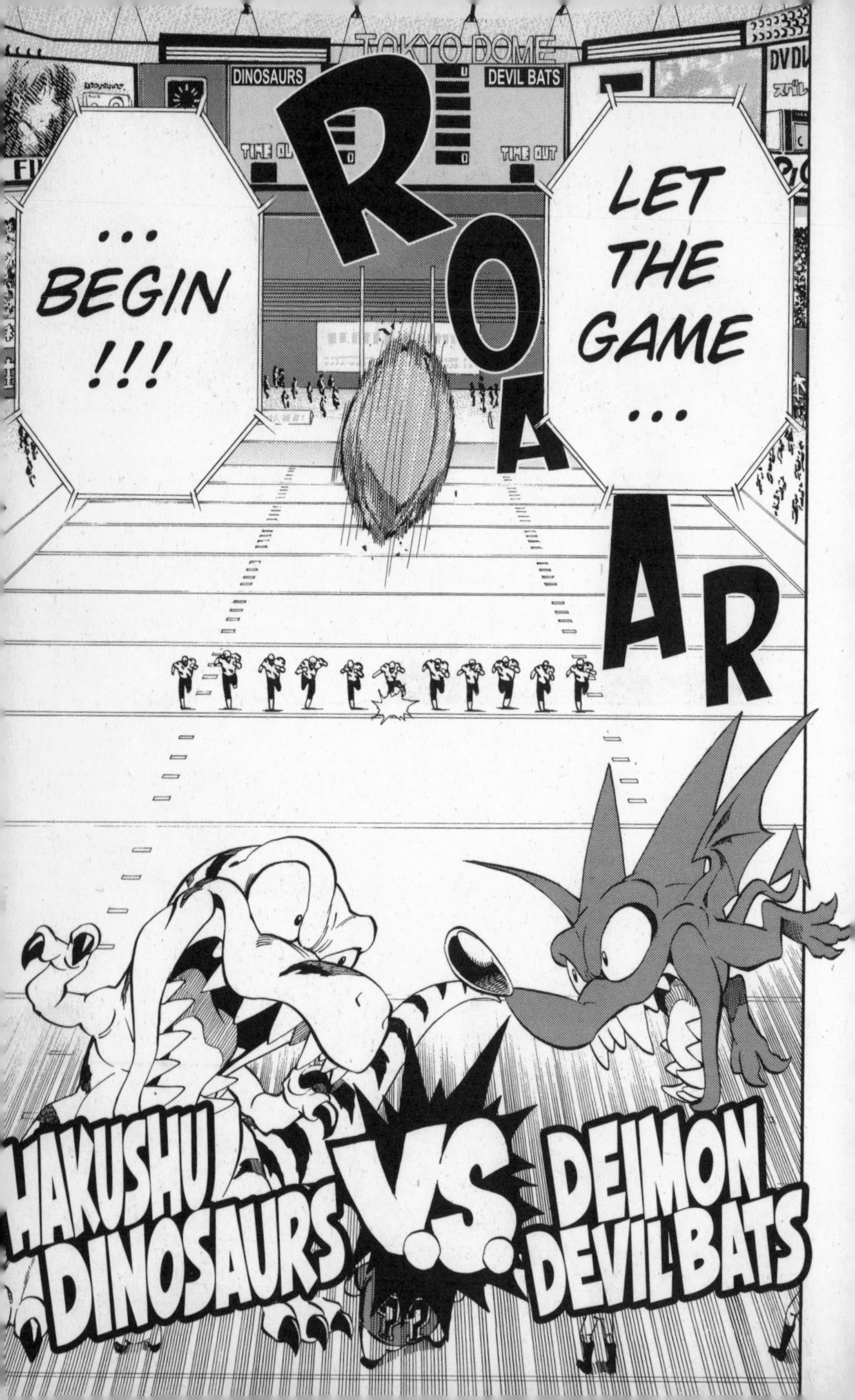
TOKYO DOME
DEVIL BATS
DINOSAURS
TIME OUT
LET THE GAME ...
... BEGIN !!!
ROAAR
DEIMON DEVIL BATS
V.S.
HAKUSHU DINOSAURS

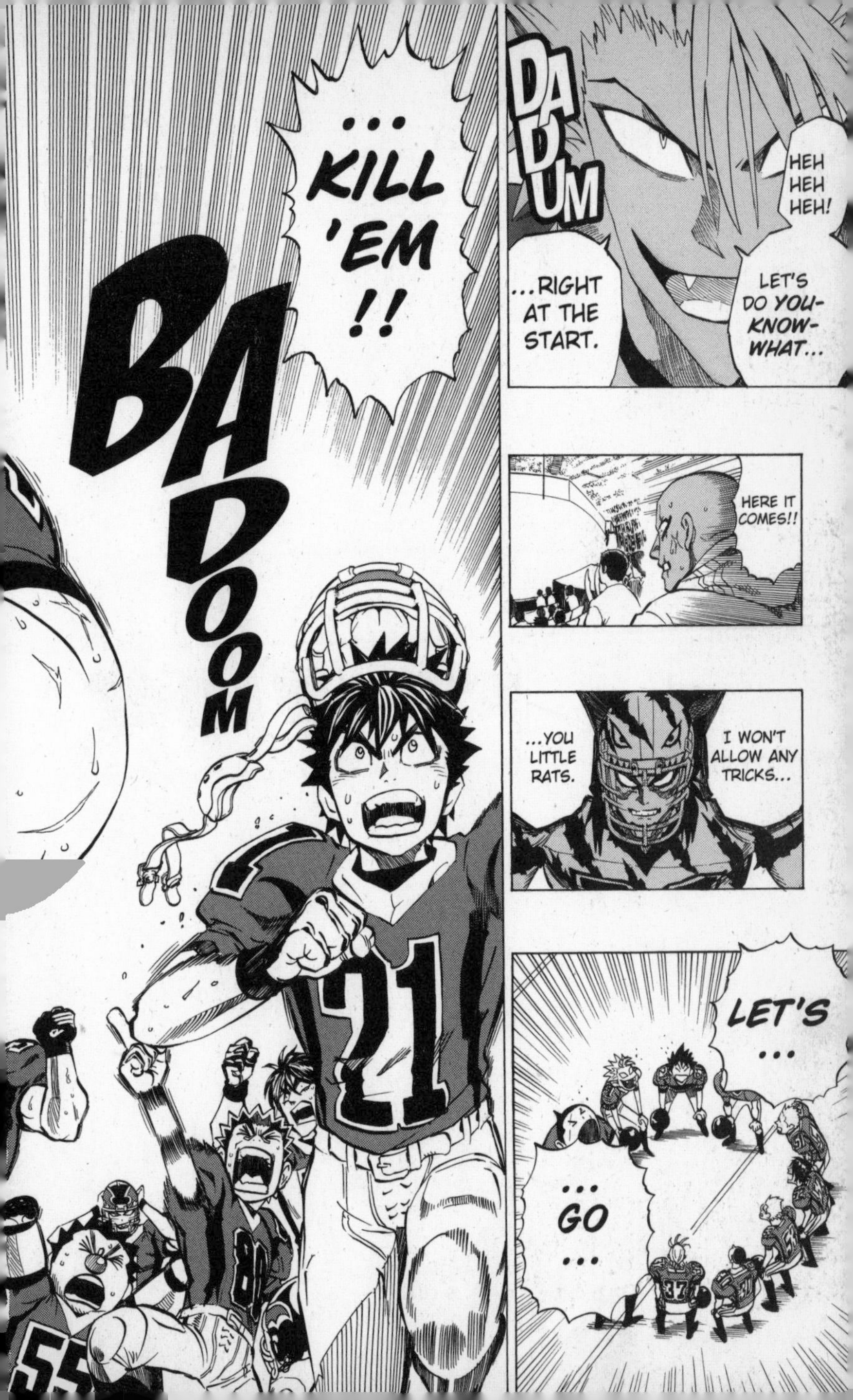

HEH HEH HEH!
DADUM
LET'S DO YOU-KNOW-WHAT...
...RIGHT AT THE START.
HERE IT COMES!!
I WON'T ALLOW ANY TRICKS...
...YOU LITTLE RATS.
LET'S...
...GO...
...KILL 'EM!!
BADOOM

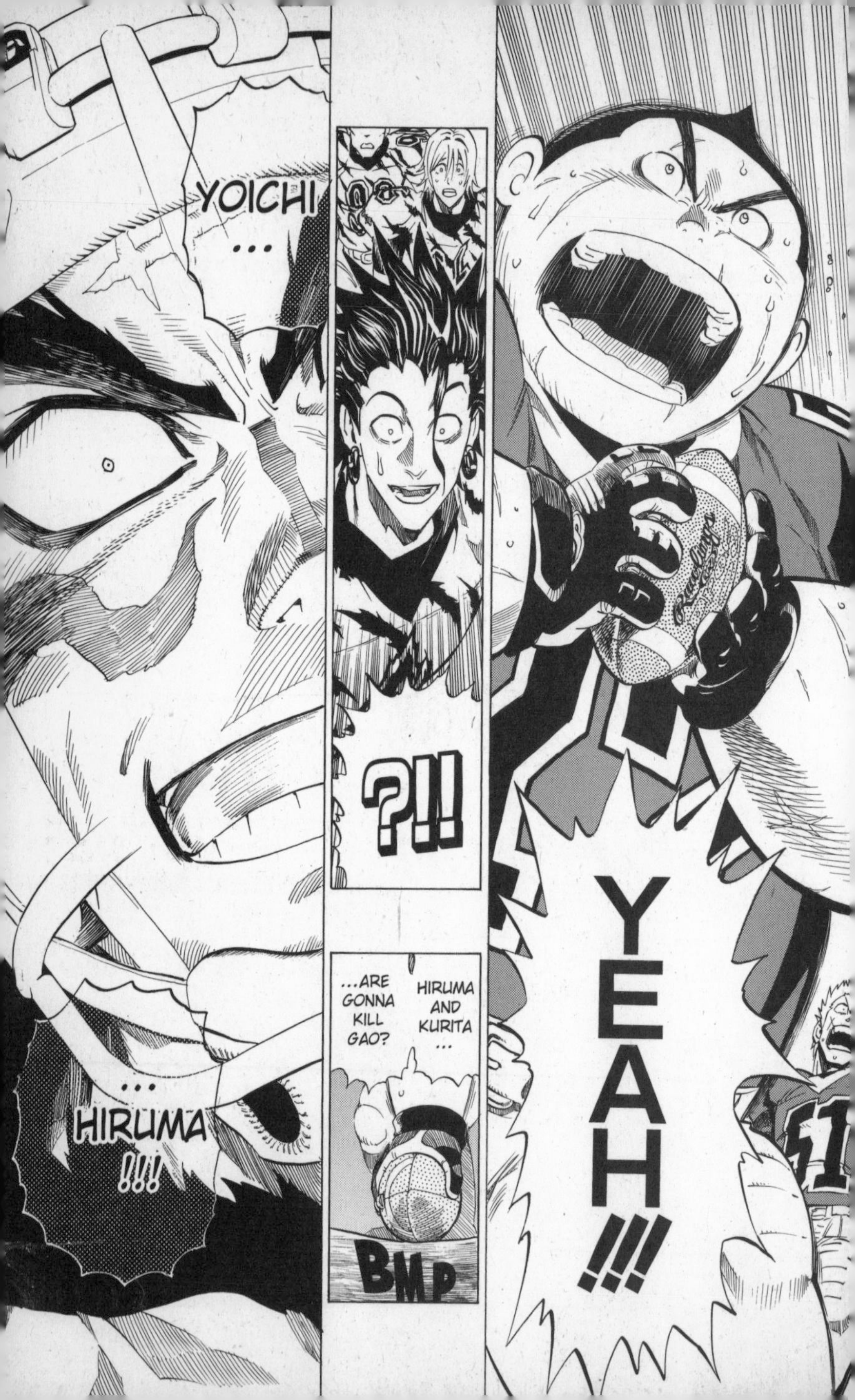
YEAH!!!
?!!
HIRUMA AND KURITA ...
...ARE GONNA KILL GAO?
BMP
YOICHI ...
... HIRUMA !!!

DEIMON & HAKUSHU CELL PHONE WALLPAPER CHECK!

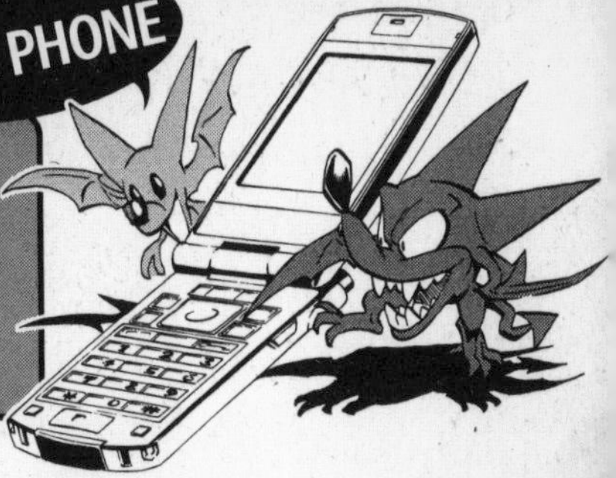

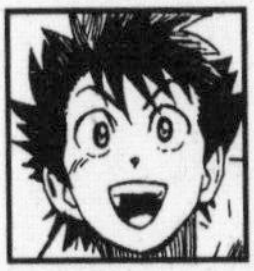

Sena

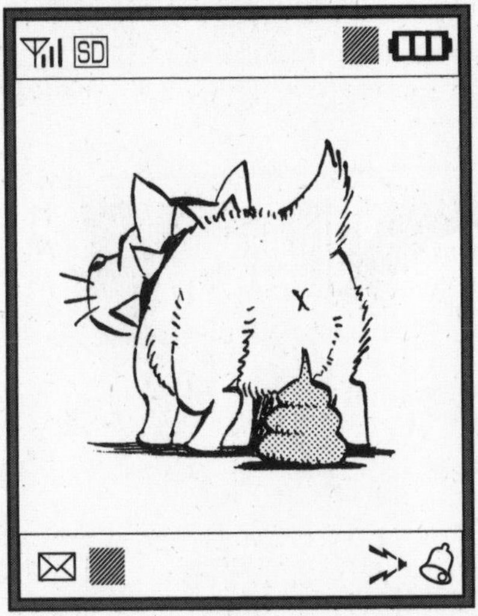

WHAT THE HECK?!

THE HAH BROTHERS SET THIS AS A TRICK YESTERDAY AND SENA DOESN'T KNOW HOW TO CHANGE IT! POOR HIM...

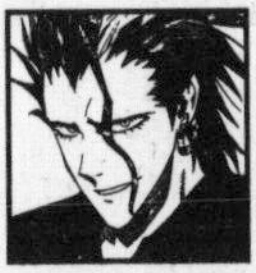

Marco

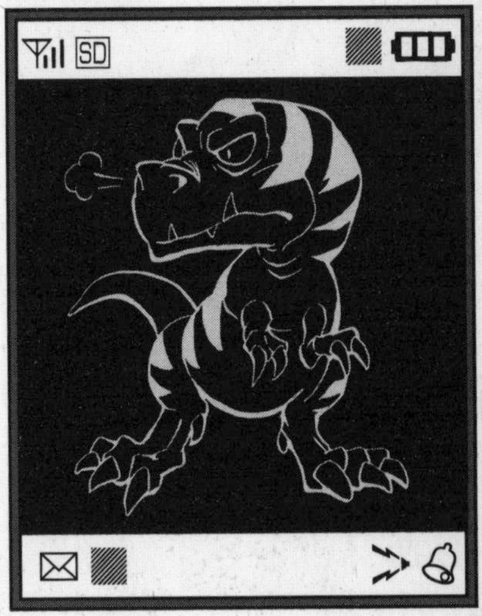

HE PLACED A PRIVACY FILTER OVER THE SCREEN SO IT CAN'T BE SEEN FROM AN ANGLE. IT'S PITCH BLACK...

HE'S SECRETIVE ABOUT EVERYTHING. HE'S VERY CAUTIOUS...

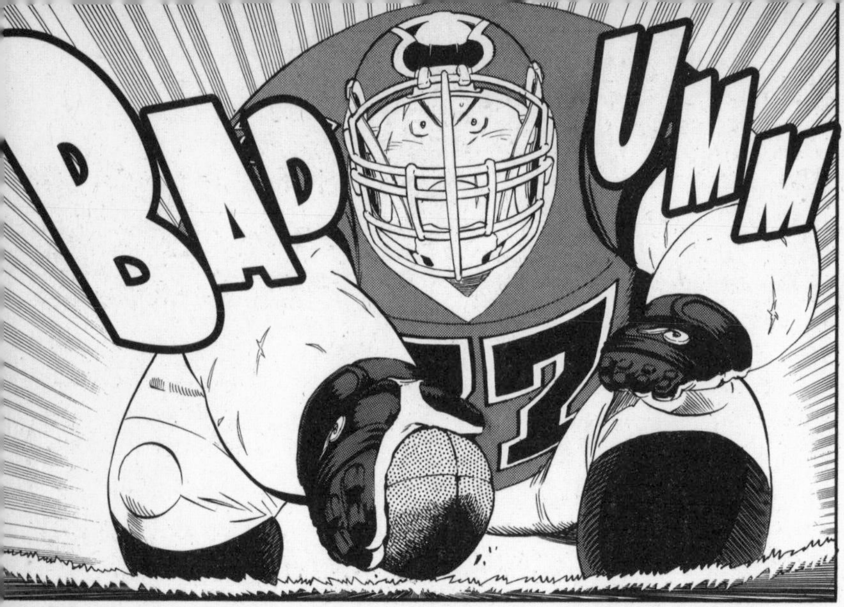
BADUMMM

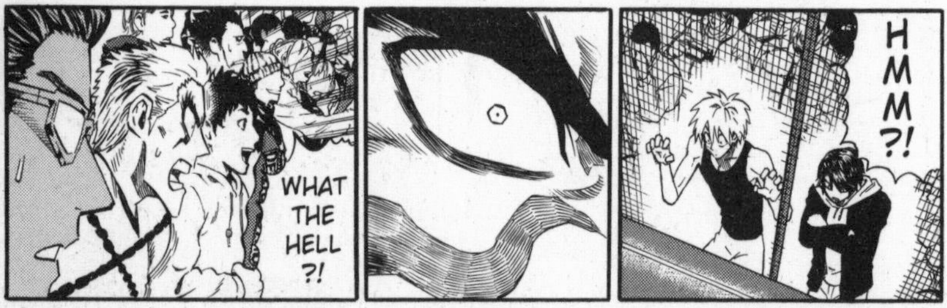
HMM?!
WHAT THE HELL?!

Chapter 253 A Lone Warrior on the Battlefield

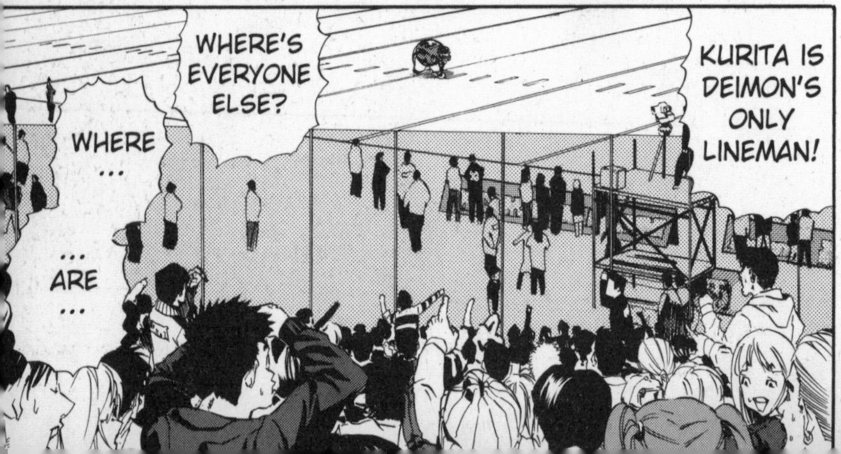
KURITA IS DEIMON'S ONLY LINEMAN!
WHERE'S EVERYONE ELSE?
WHERE...
...ARE...

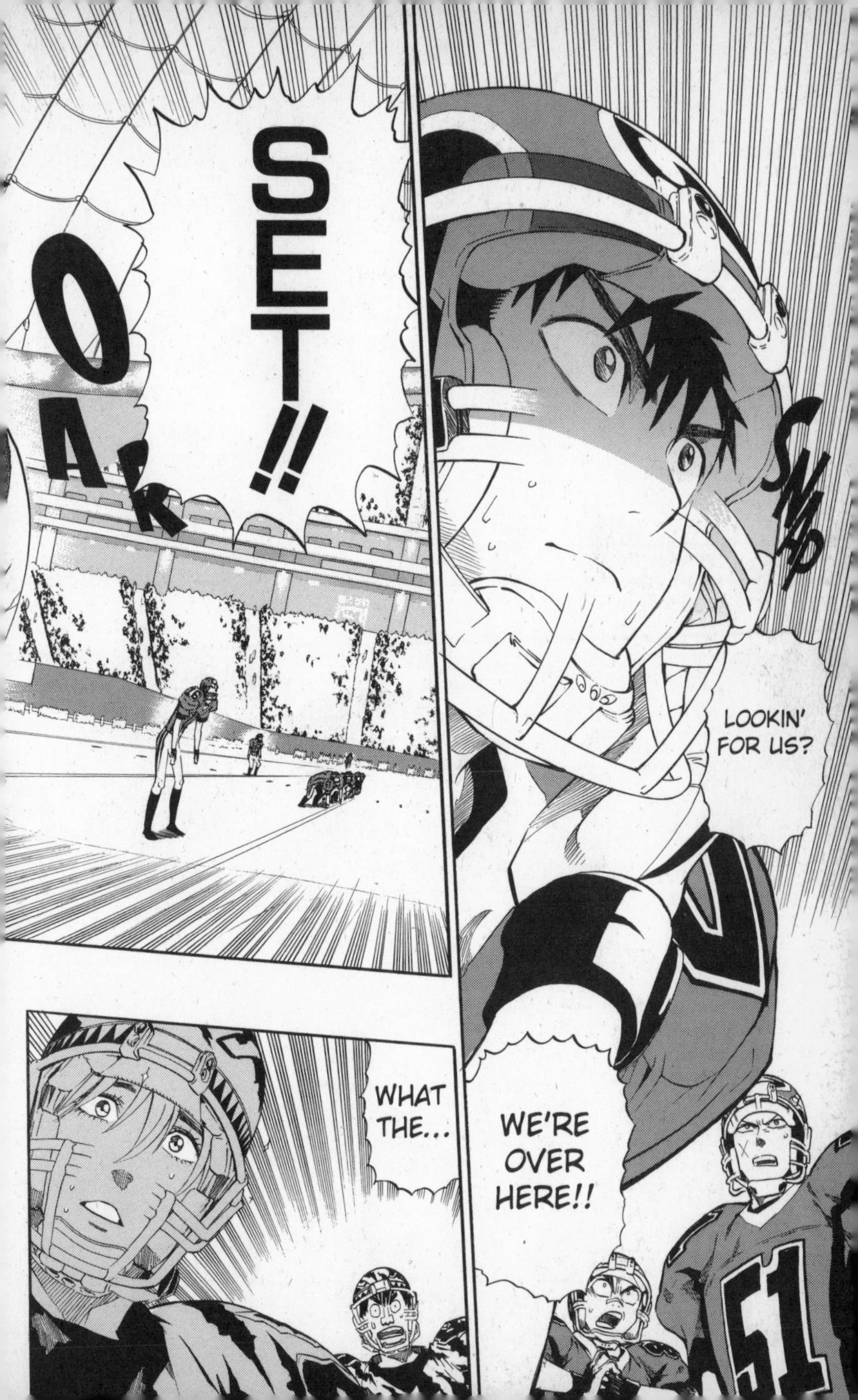

SNAP
LOOKIN' FOR US?
WE'RE OVER HERE!!
SET!!
OAK
WHAT THE...

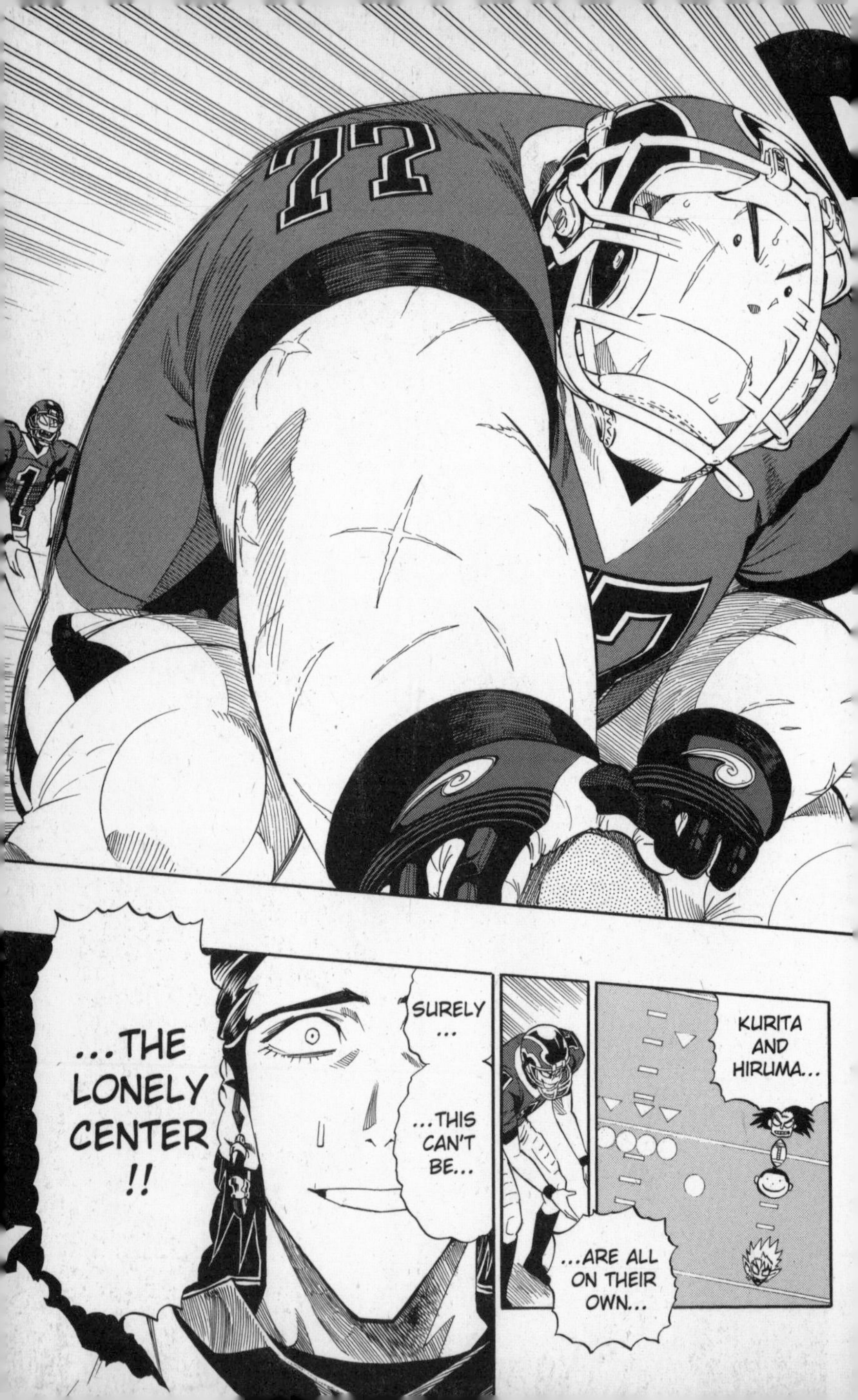
KURITA AND HIRUMA...
...ARE ALL ON THEIR OWN...
SURELY...
...THIS CAN'T BE...
...THE LONELY CENTER!!

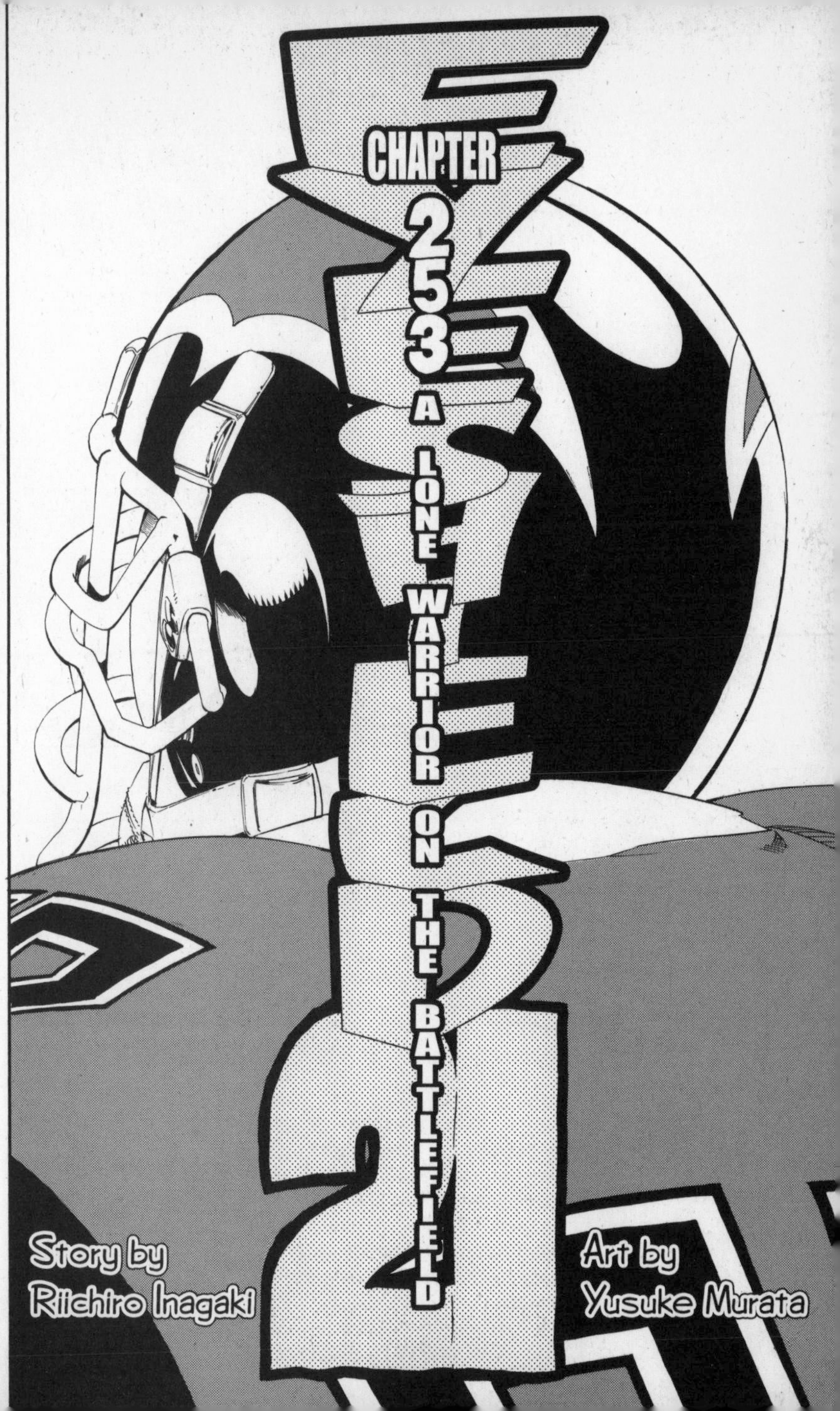
CHAPTER 253
A LONE WARRIOR ON THE BATTLEFIELD
Story by
Riichiro Inagaki
Art by
Yusuke Murata

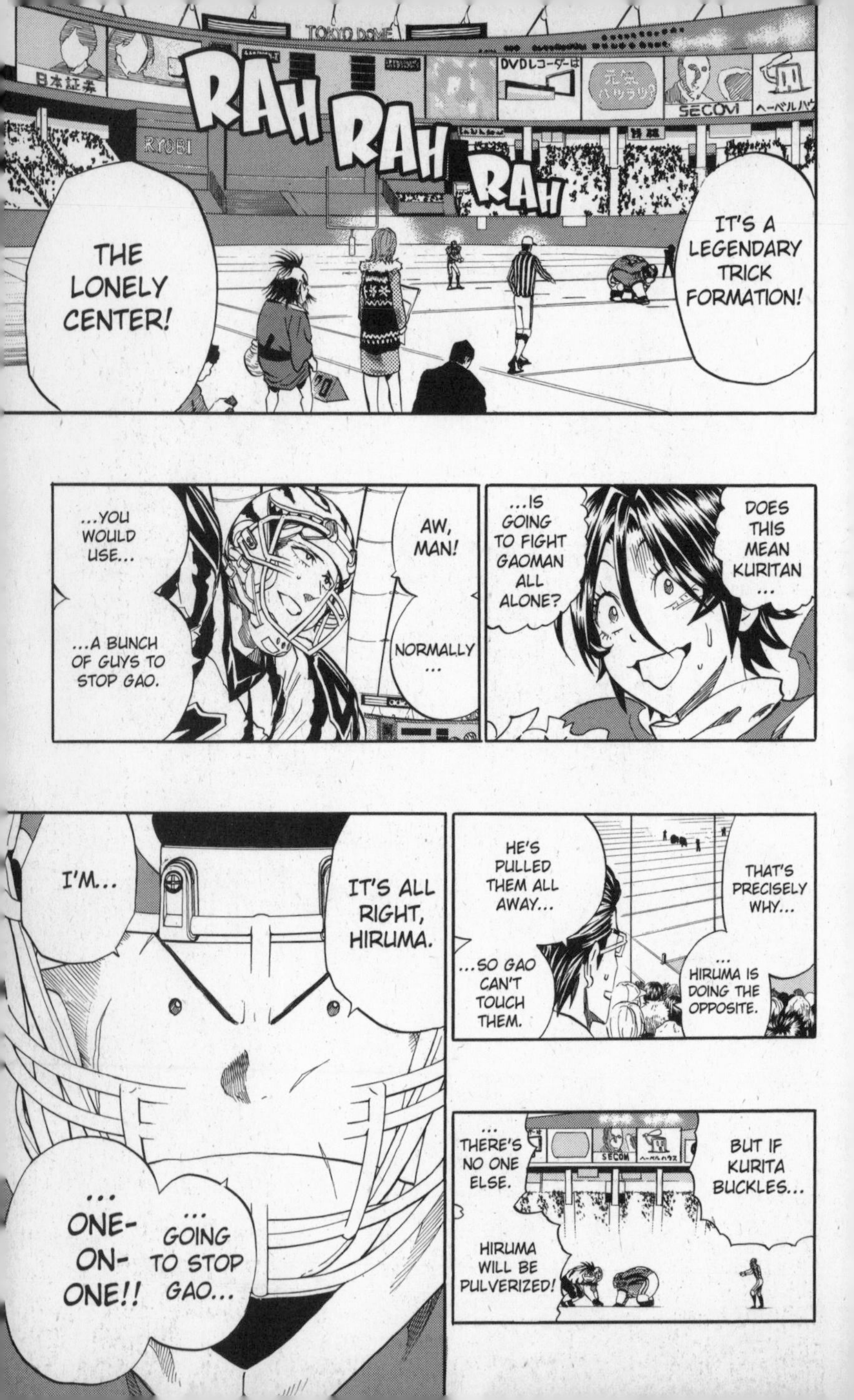
TOKYO DOME
日本証券
DVDレコーダーは
SECOM
ヘーベルハウ
RYOBI
RAH RAH RAH
IT'S A LEGENDARY TRICK FORMATION!
THE LONELY CENTER!
DOES THIS MEAN KURITAN...
...IS GOING TO FIGHT GAOMAN ALL ALONE?
AW, MAN!
NORMALLY...
...YOU WOULD USE...
...A BUNCH OF GUYS TO STOP GAO.
THAT'S PRECISELY WHY...
...HIRUMA IS DOING THE OPPOSITE.
HE'S PULLED THEM ALL AWAY...
...SO GAO CAN'T TOUCH THEM.
BUT IF KURITA BUCKLES...
...THERE'S NO ONE ELSE.
SECOM
ヘーベルハウス
HIRUMA WILL BE PULVERIZED!
IT'S ALL RIGHT, HIRUMA.
I'M...
...GOING TO STOP GAO...
...ONE-ON-ONE!!

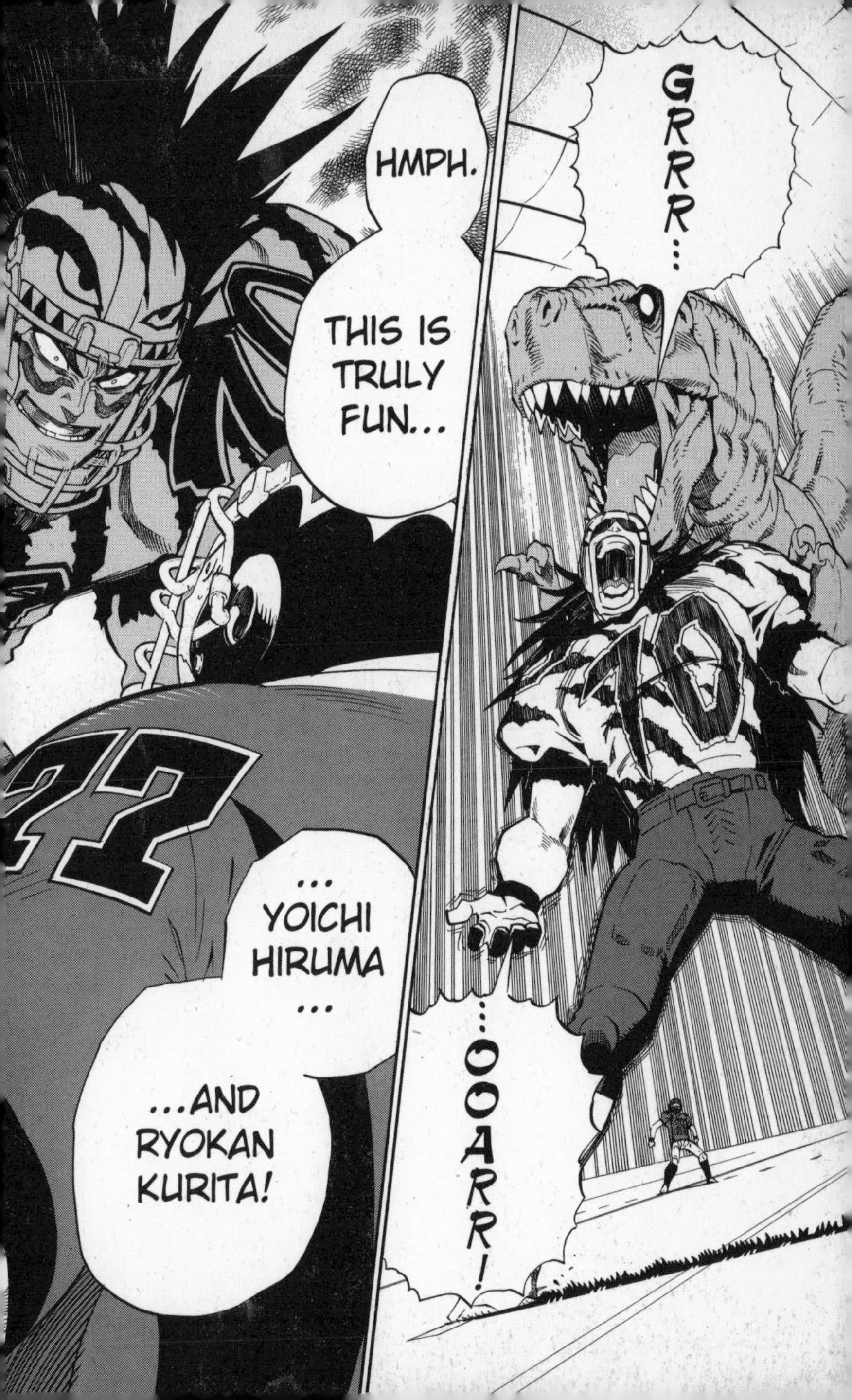
GRRR...
...OOARR!
HMPH.
THIS IS TRULY FUN...
...YOICHI HIRUMA...
...AND RYOKAN KURITA!

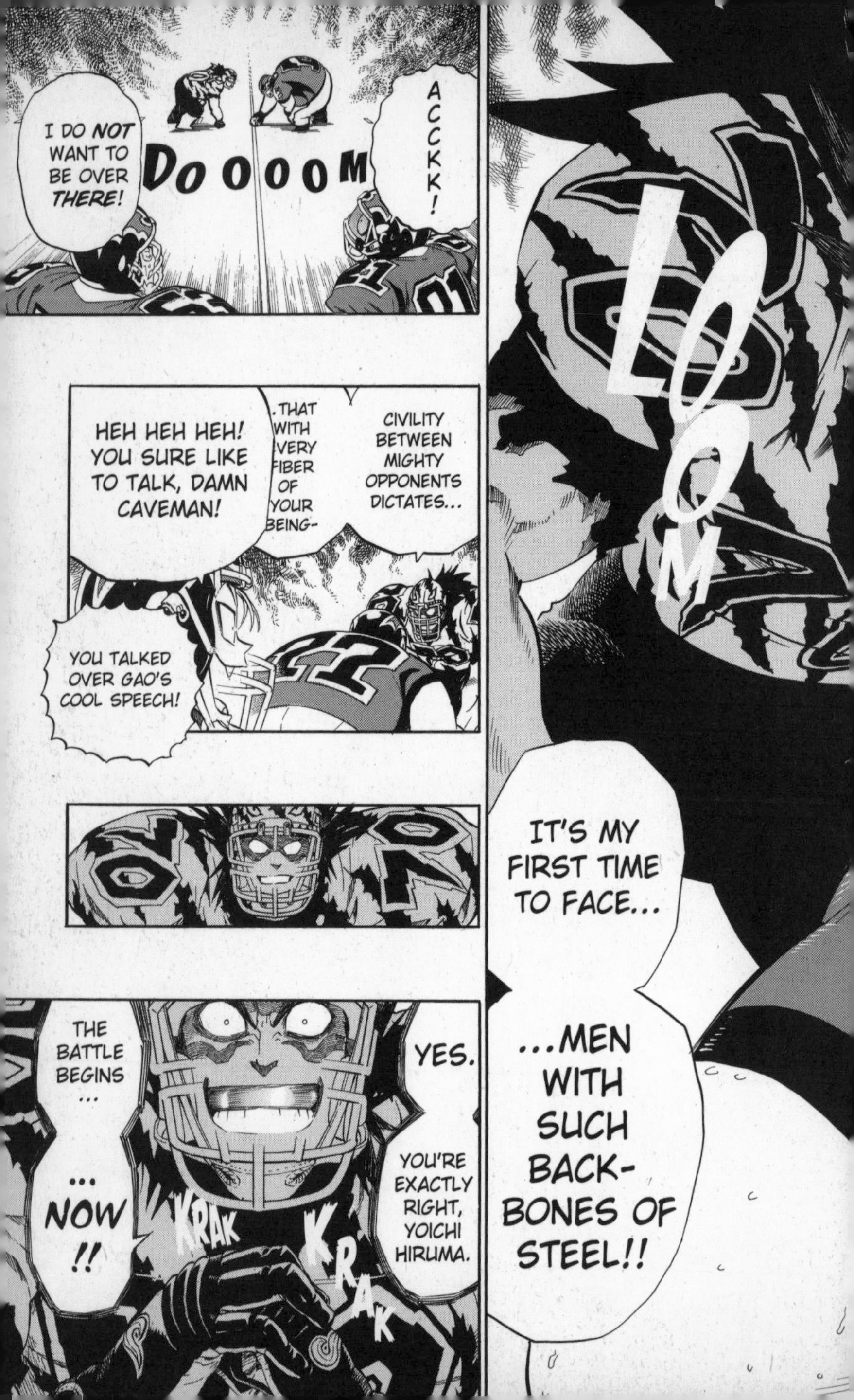
LOOM
IT'S MY FIRST TIME TO FACE...
...MEN WITH SUCH BACK-BONES OF STEEL!!
ACCKK!
DOOOOM
I DO NOT WANT TO BE OVER THERE!
CIVILITY BETWEEN MIGHTY OPPONENTS DICTATES...
.THAT WITH VERY FIBER OF YOUR BEING-
HEH HEH HEH! YOU SURE LIKE TO TALK, DAMN CAVEMAN!
YOU TALKED OVER GAO'S COOL SPEECH!
YES.
YOU'RE EXACTLY RIGHT, YOICHI HIRUMA.
KRAK
KRAK
THE BATTLE BEGINS...
...NOW!!

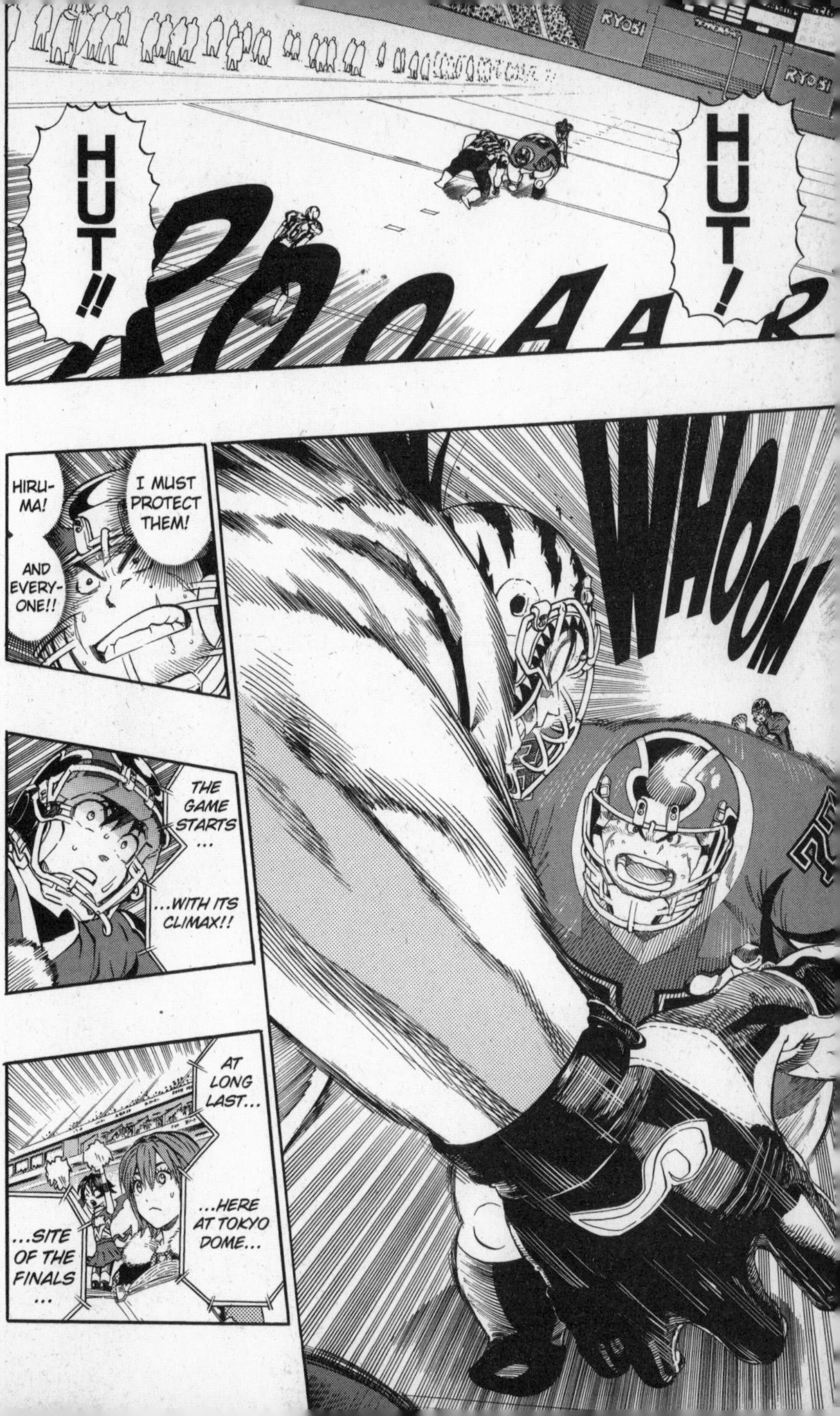
HUT!
HUT!!
WHOOM
I MUST PROTECT THEM!
HIRUMA!
AND EVERYONE!!
THE GAME STARTS...
...WITH ITS CLIMAX!!
AT LONG LAST...
...HERE AT TOKYO DOME...
...SITE OF THE FINALS...

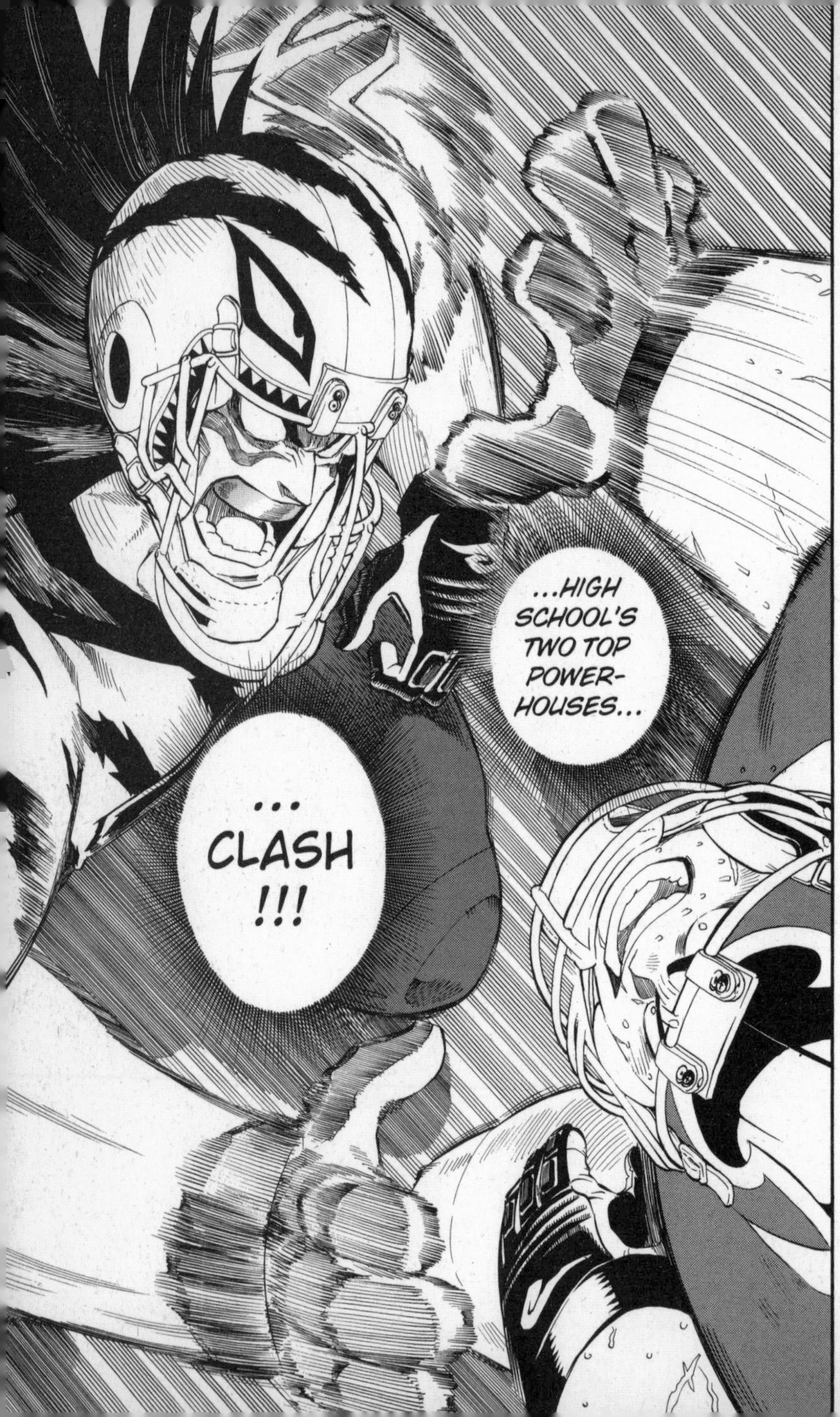
...HIGH SCHOOL'S TWO TOP POWER-HOUSES...
... CLASH !!!

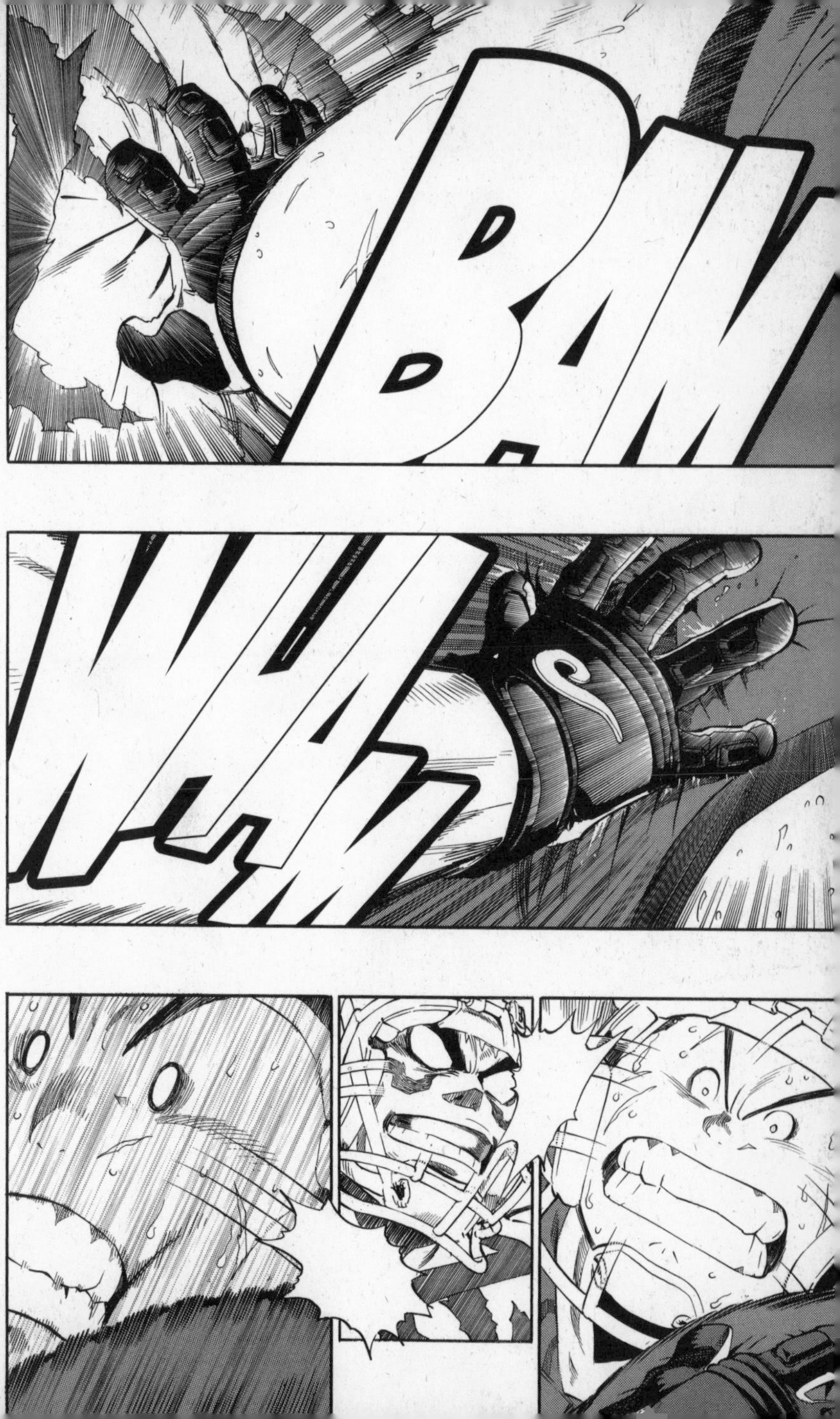
BAM
WHAM

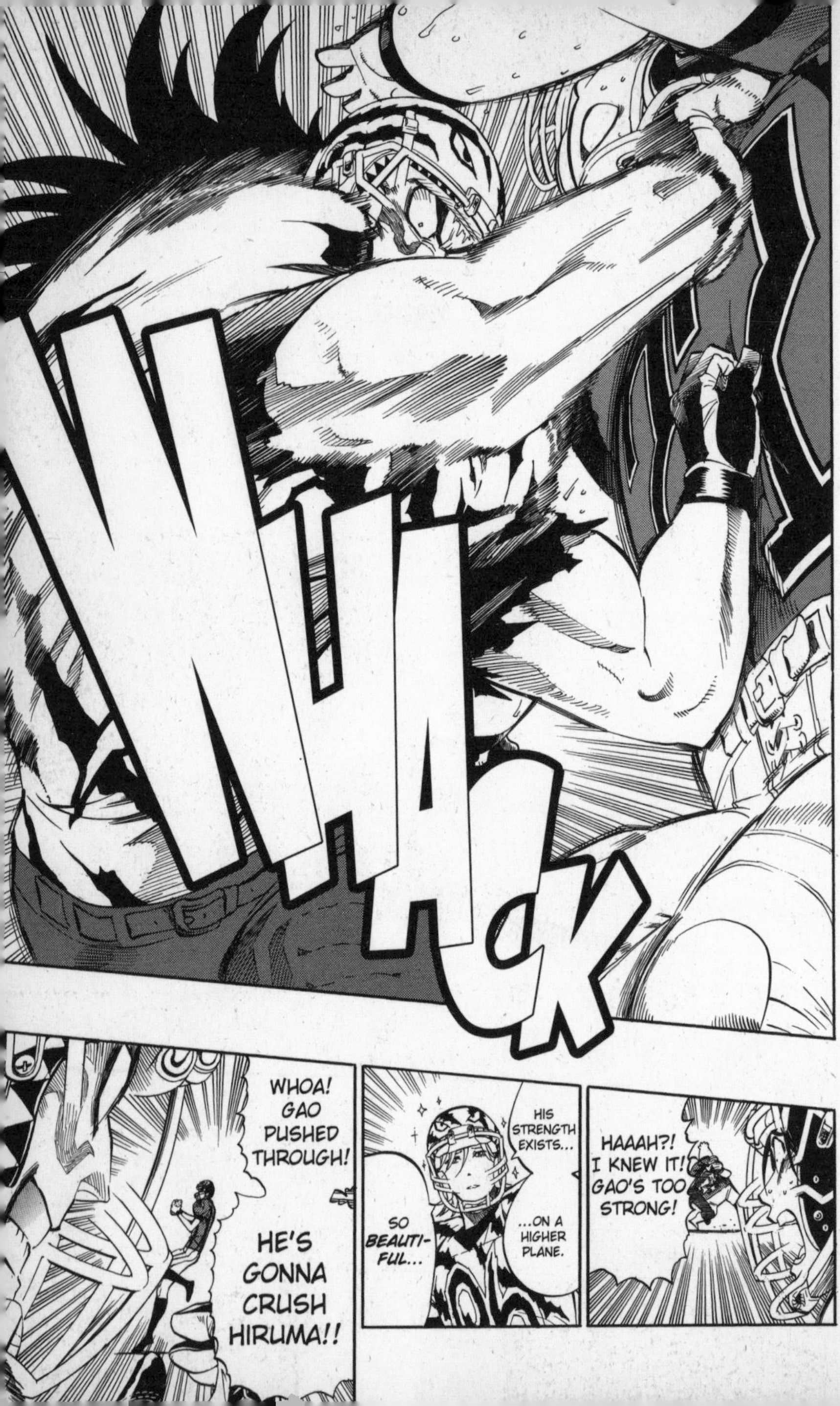
WHACK
HAAAH?! I KNEW IT! GAO'S TOO STRONG!
HIS STRENGTH EXISTS...
...ON A HIGHER PLANE.
SO *BEAUTIFUL*...
WHOA! GAO PUSHED THROUGH!
HE'S GONNA CRUSH HIRUMA!!

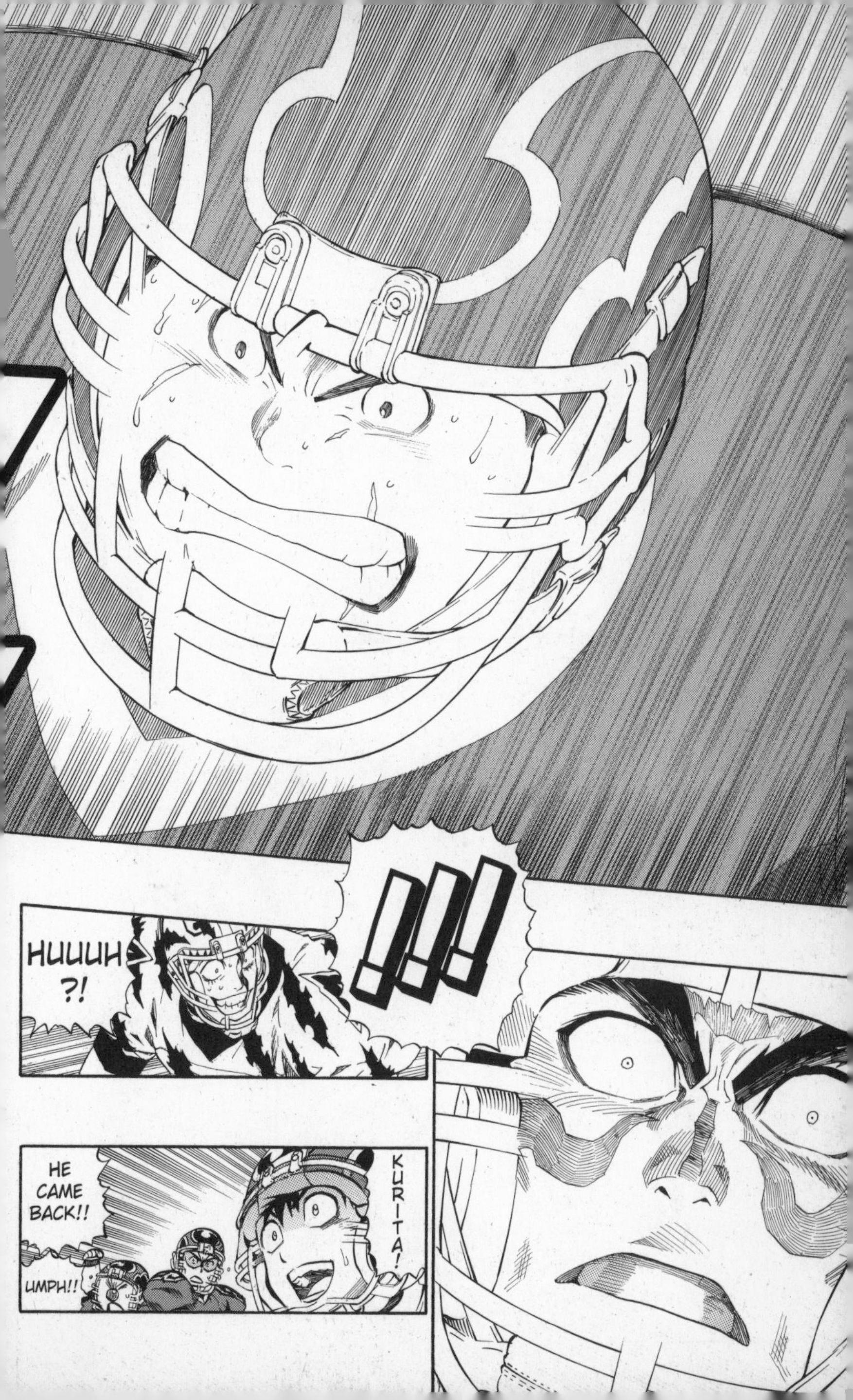
!!!
HUUUH ?!
KURITA!
HE CAME BACK!!
UMPH!!

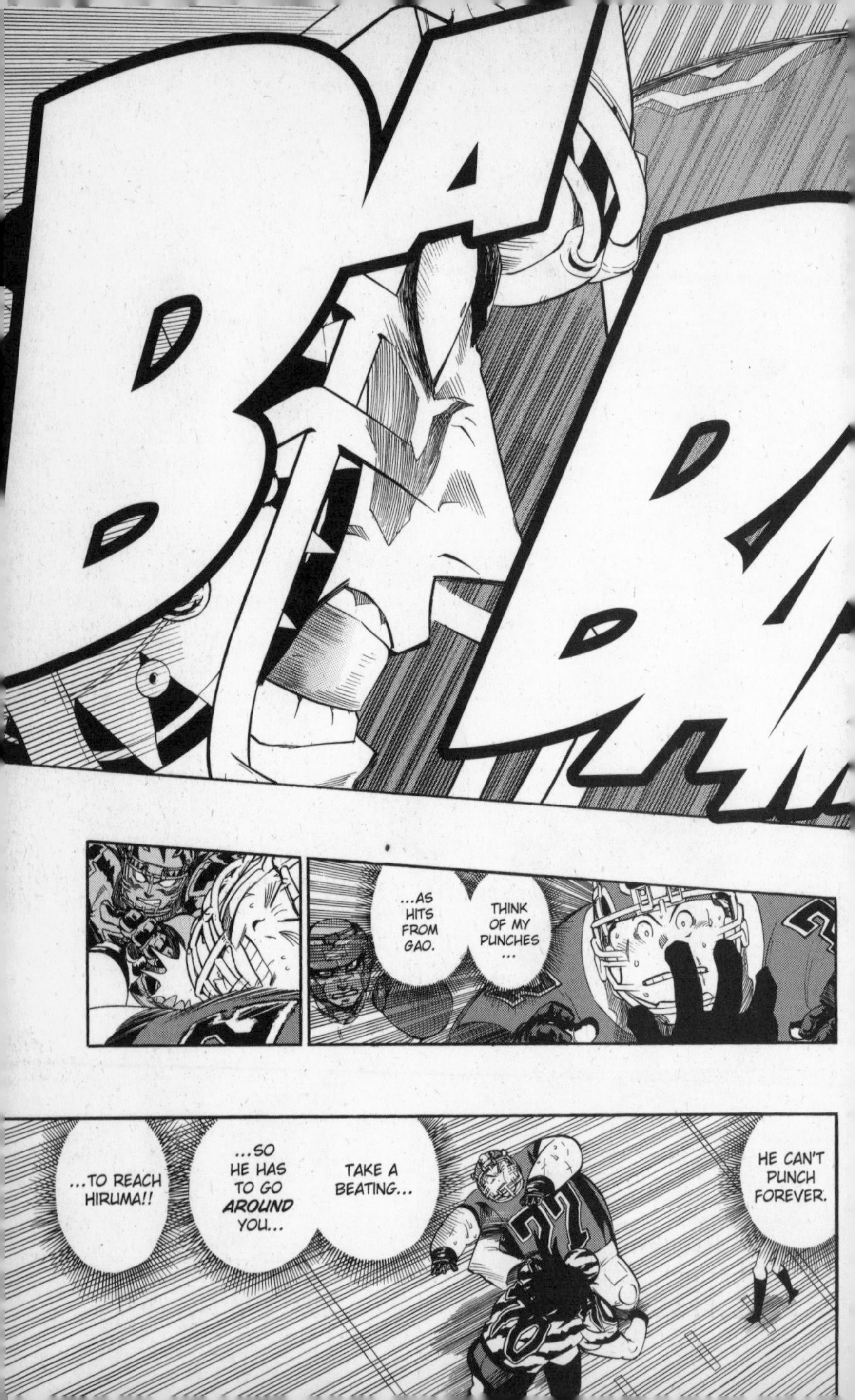
THINK OF MY PUNCHES...
...AS HITS FROM GAO.
HE CAN'T PUNCH FOREVER.
TAKE A BEATING...
...SO HE HAS TO GO **AROUND** YOU...
...TO REACH HIRUMA!!

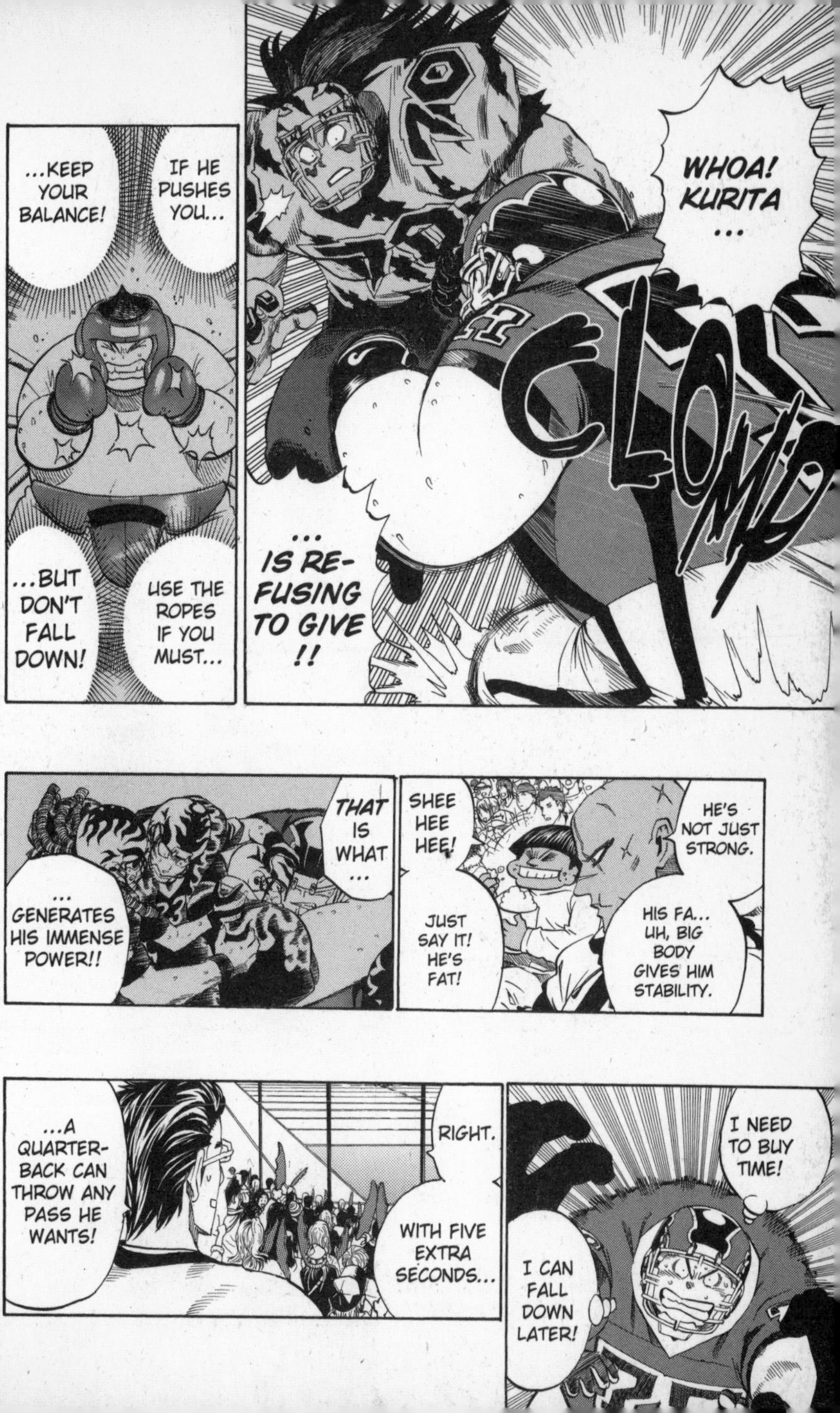
WHOA! KURITA ...
... IS RE-FUSING TO GIVE !!
IF HE PUSHES YOU...
...KEEP YOUR BALANCE!
USE THE ROPES IF YOU MUST...
...BUT DON'T FALL DOWN!
HE'S NOT JUST STRONG.
HIS FA... UH, BIG BODY GIVES HIM STABILITY.
SHEE HEE HEE!
JUST SAY IT! HE'S FAT!
THAT IS WHAT ...
... GENERATES HIS IMMENSE POWER!!
I NEED TO BUY TIME!
I CAN FALL DOWN LATER!
RIGHT.
WITH FIVE EXTRA SECONDS...
...A QUARTER-BACK CAN THROW ANY PASS HE WANTS!

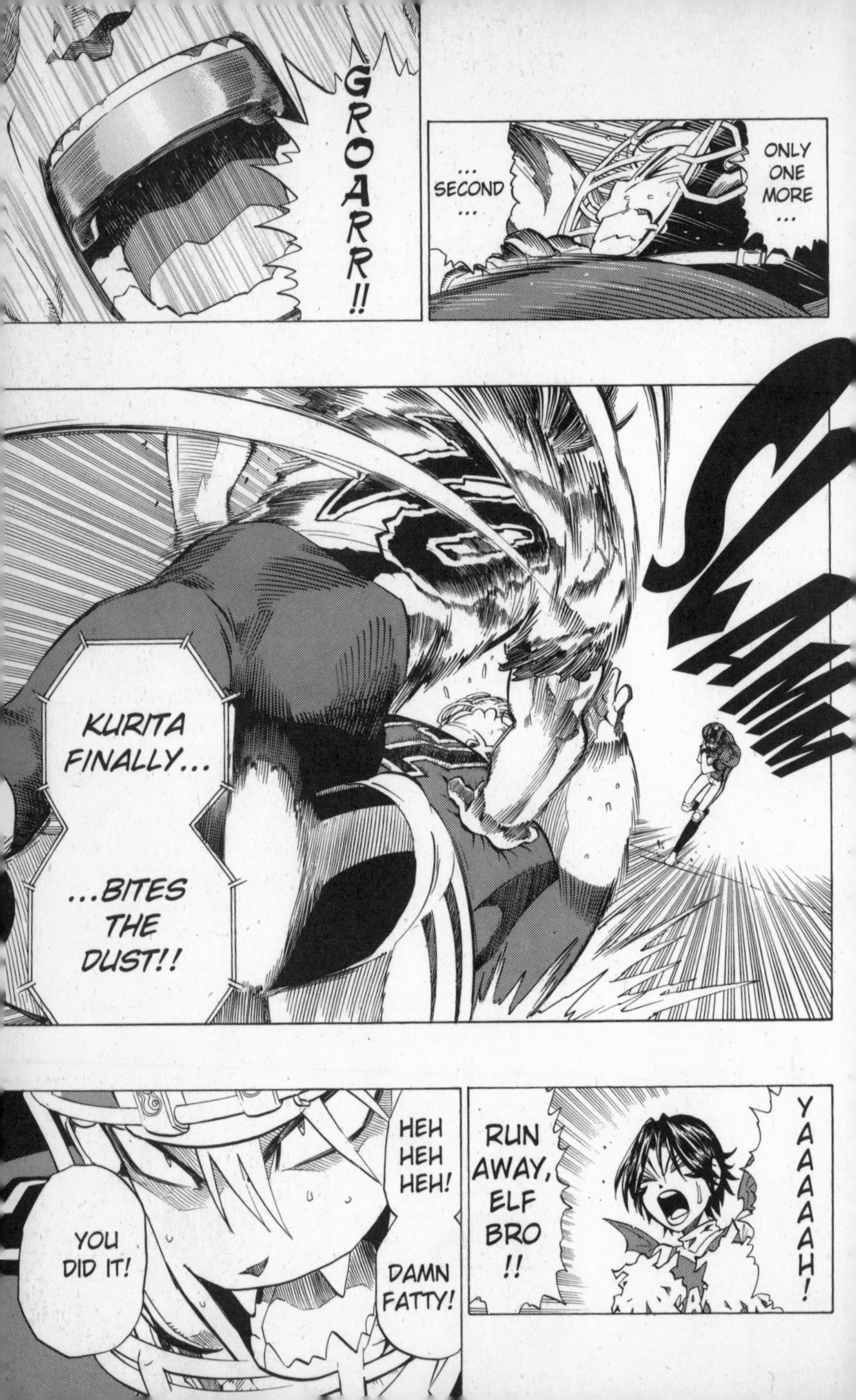
ONLY ONE MORE...
...SECOND...
GROARR!!
SLAMM
KURITA FINALLY...
...BITES THE DUST!!
YAAAAAH!
RUN AWAY, ELF BRO!!
HEH HEH HEH!
DAMN FATTY!
YOU DID IT!

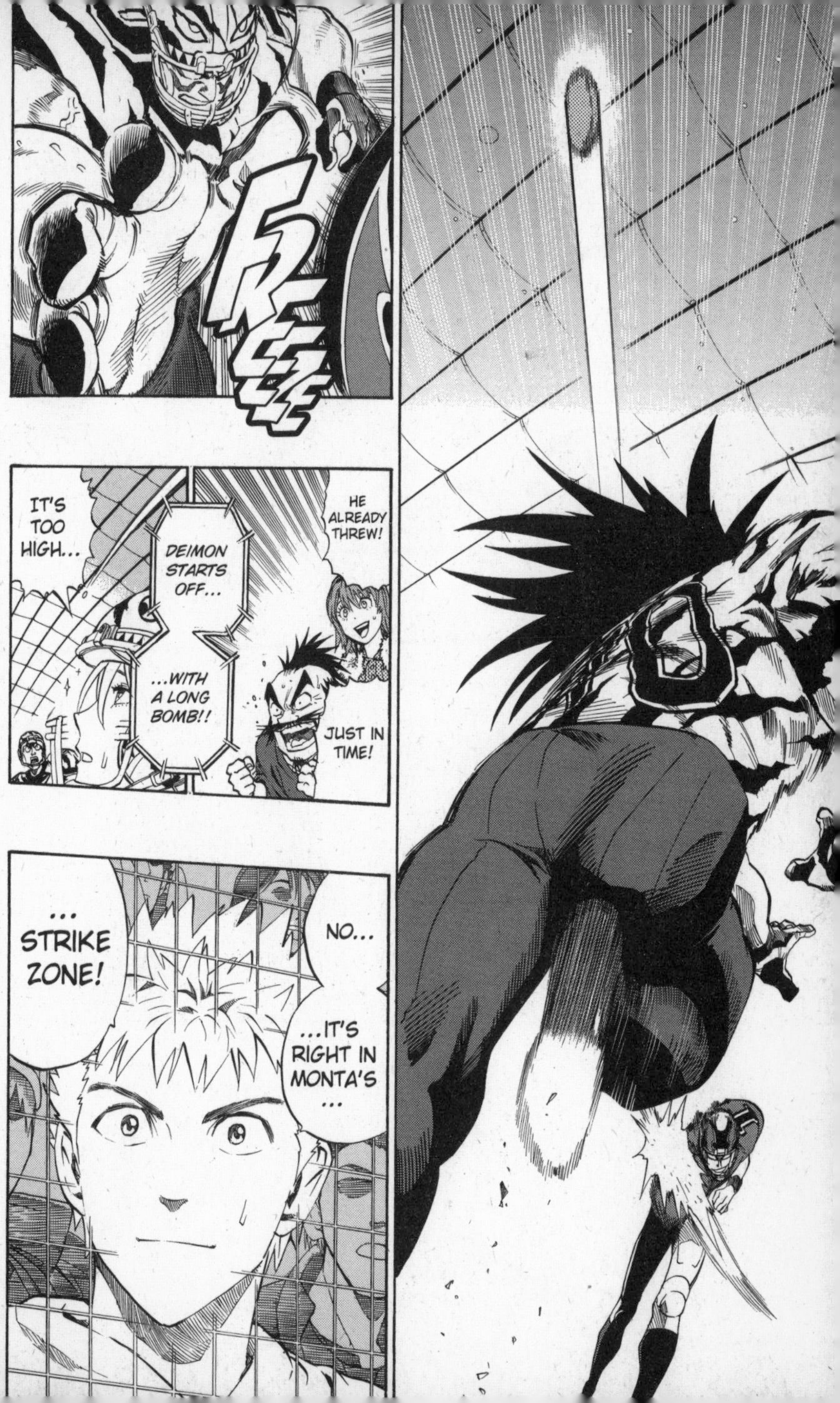
HE ALREADY THREW!
DEIMON STARTS OFF...
IT'S TOO HIGH...
JUST IN TIME!
...WITH A LONG BOMB!!
NO...
...IT'S RIGHT IN MONTA'S ...
... STRIKE ZONE!

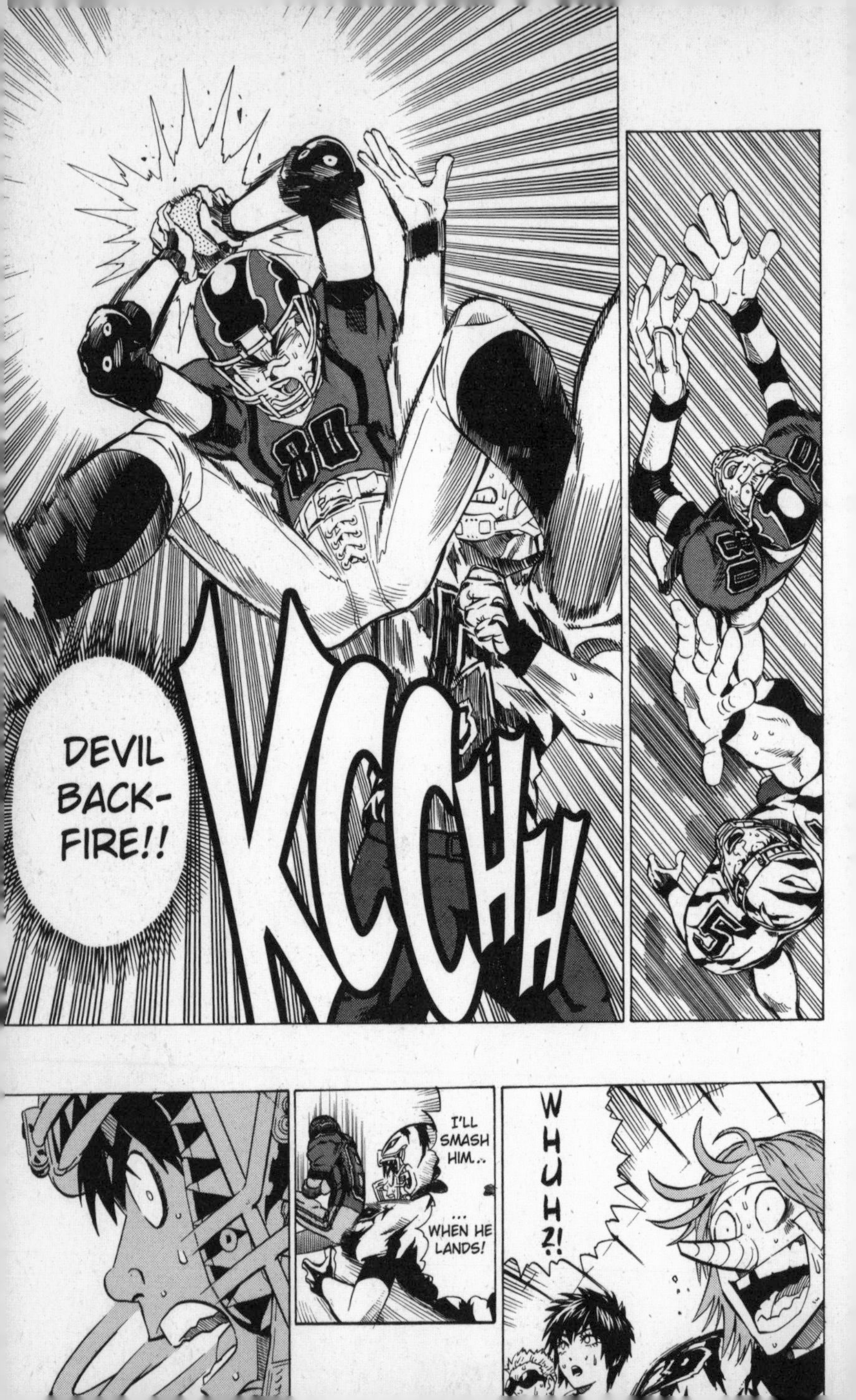
DEVIL BACK-FIRE!!
KCCHH
WHUH?!
I'LL SMASH HIM...
... WHEN HE LANDS!

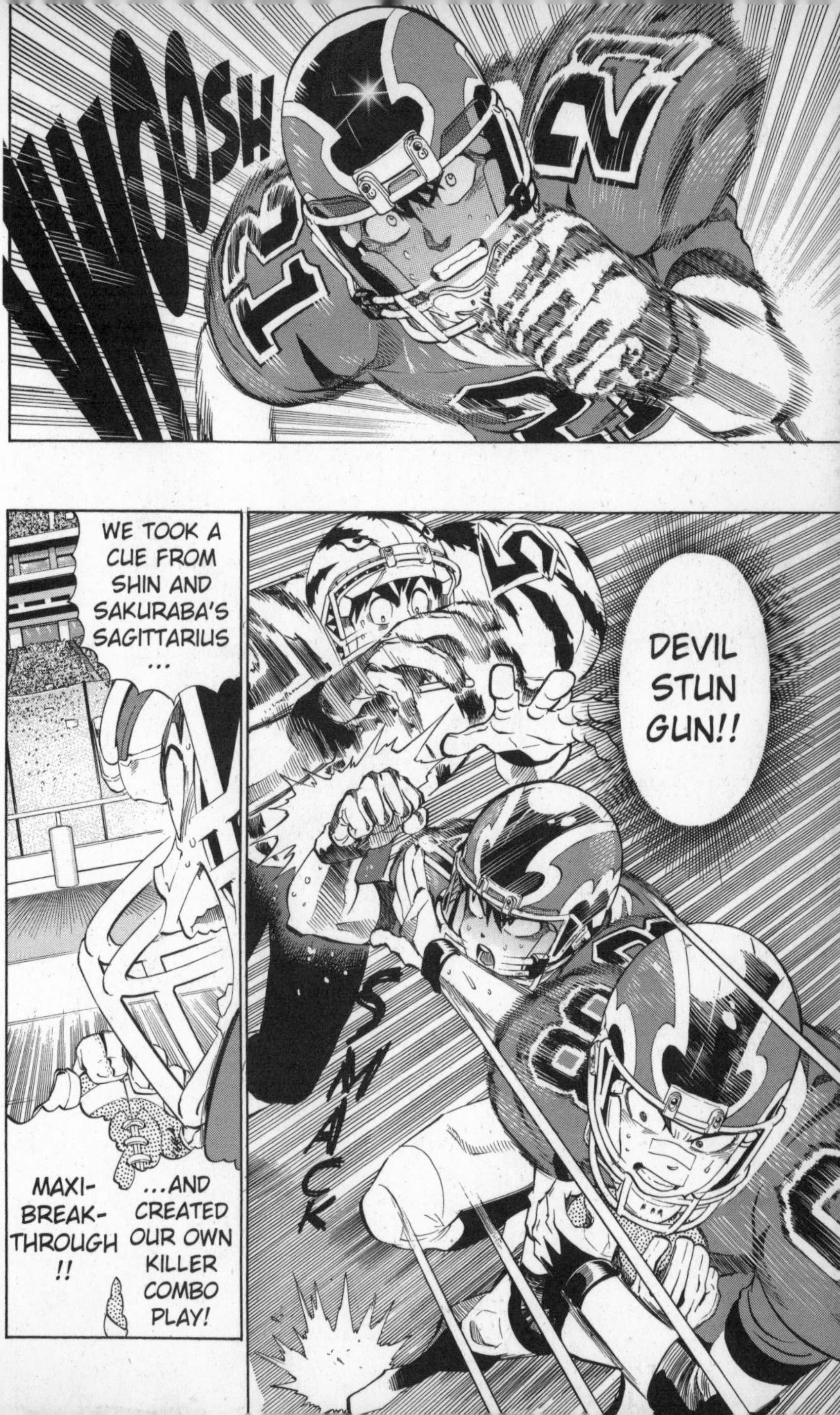
WHOOSH
DEVIL STUN GUN!!
SMACK
WE TOOK A CUE FROM SHIN AND SAKURABA'S SAGITTARIUS ...
...AND CREATED OUR OWN KILLER COMBO PLAY!
MAXI-BREAK-THROUGH !!

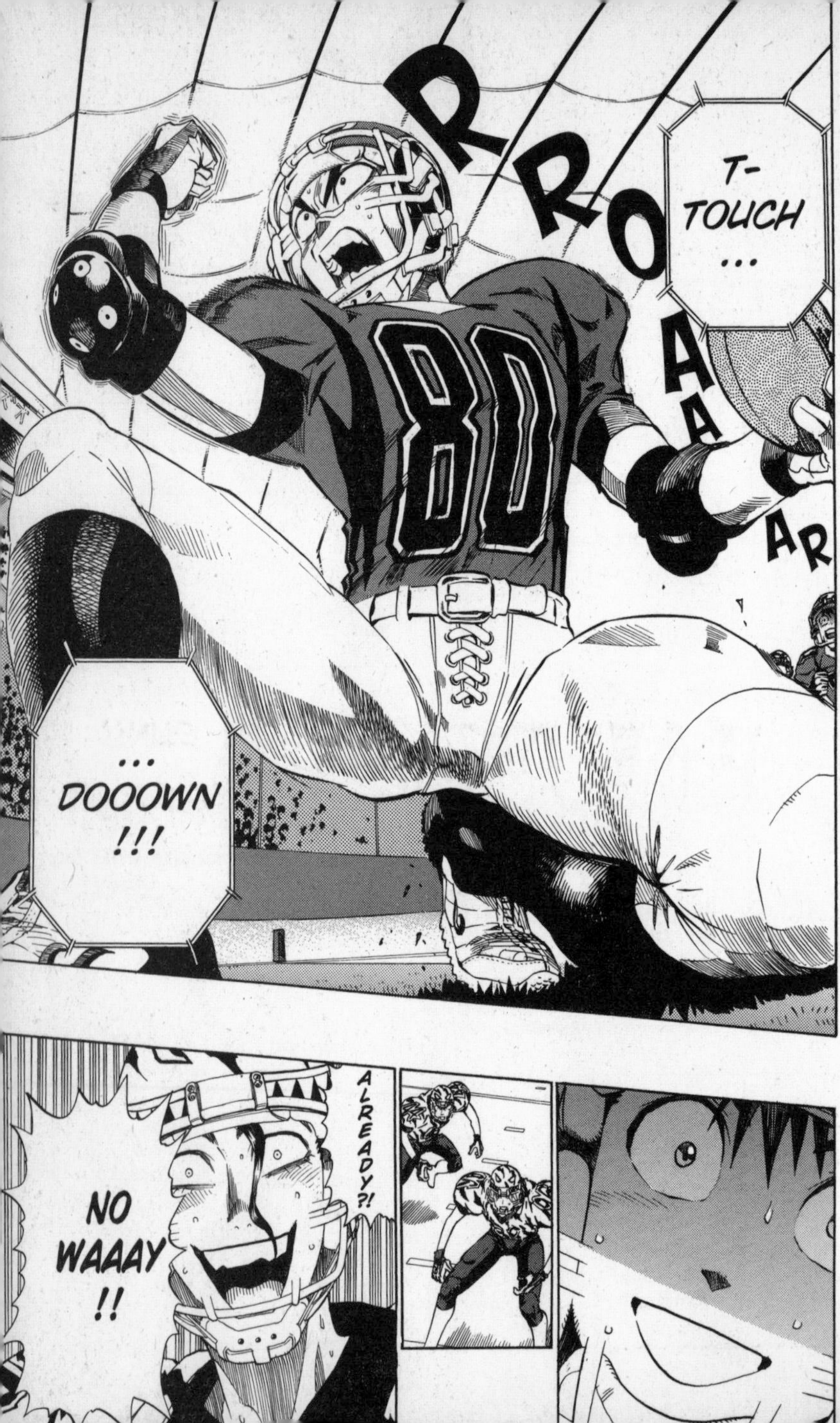
T-TOUCH...
RROOAAAAR
...DOOOWN!!!
ALREADY?!
NO WAAAY!!

DEIMON & HAKUSHU CELL PHONE

WALLPAPER CHECK!

 ## Monta

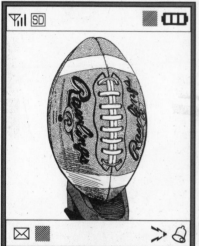

 I THOUGHT MONTA WOULD HAVE A PICTURE OF MAMORI!

HE'S SERIOUS ABOUT THINGS LIKE THIS.

 ## Kisaragi

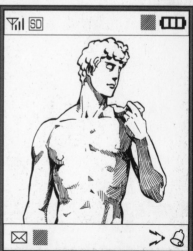

 WHAT IS...THIS?

 A BEAUTIFUL BODY OR SOMETHING LIKE THAT...

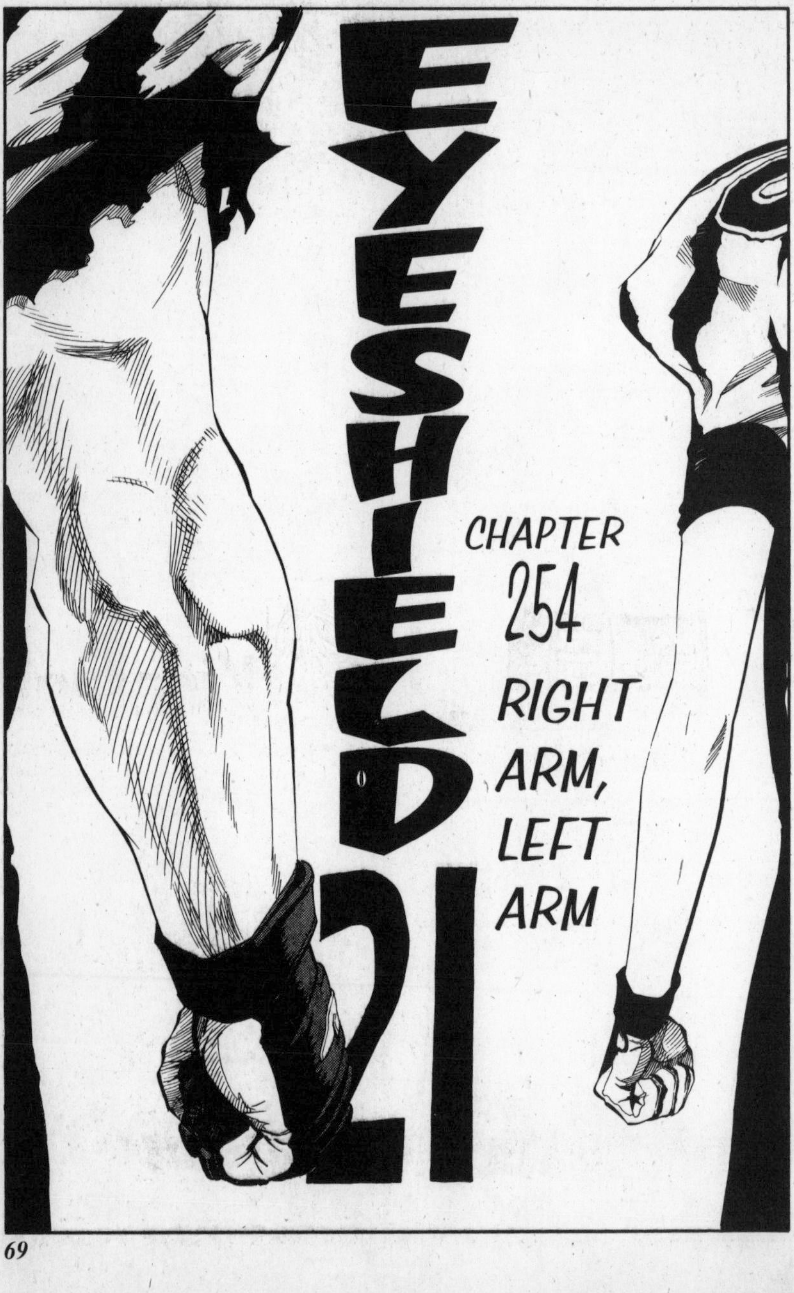
EYESHIELD 21
CHAPTER 254
RIGHT ARM, LEFT ARM

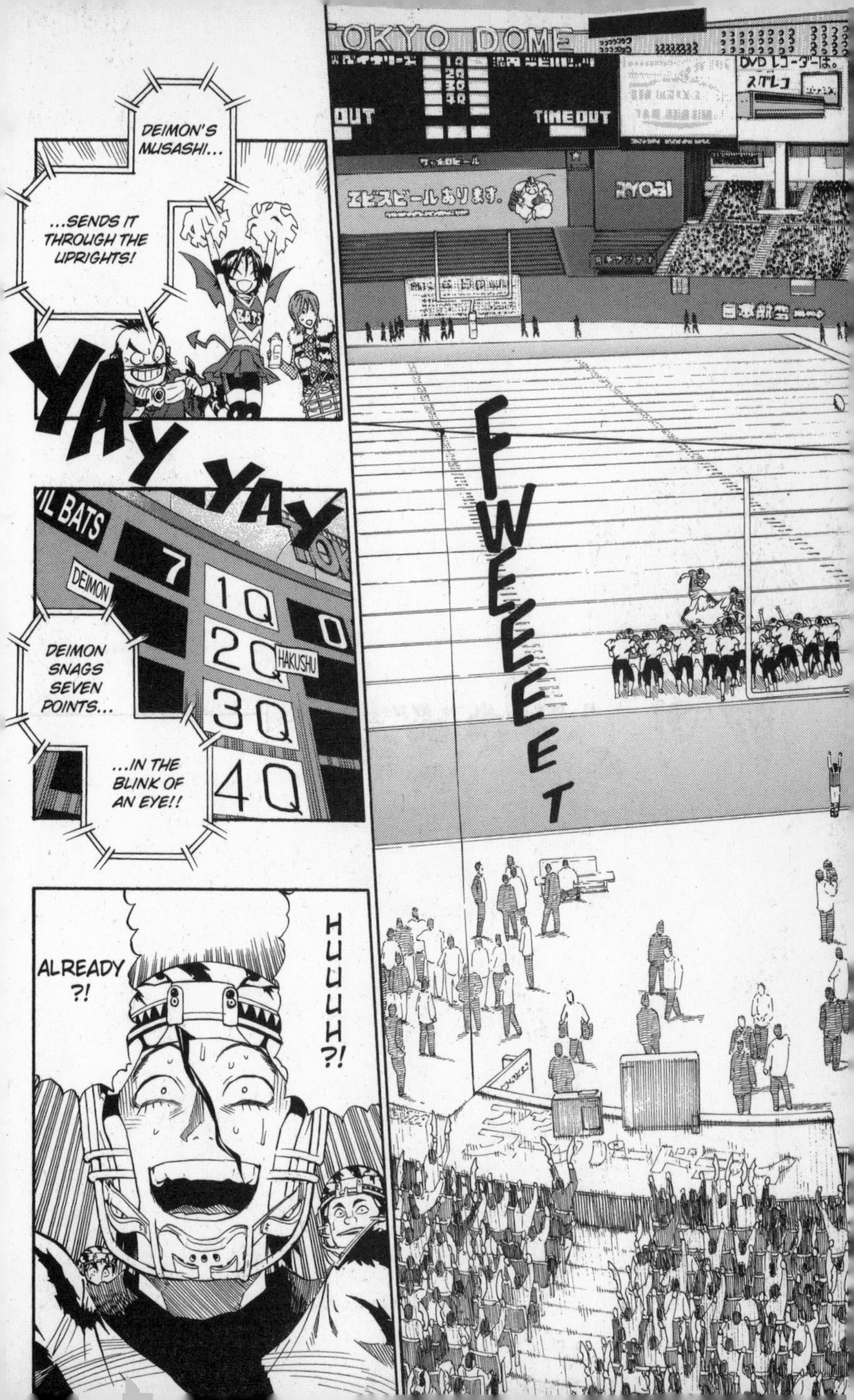
TOKYO DOME
DVD レコーダーは。
スグレコ
OUT
TIME OUT
エビスビールあります。
RYOBI
FWEEEEET
DEIMON'S MUSASHI...
...SENDS IT THROUGH THE UPRIGHTS!
YAY YAY
DEIMON
7
1Q
2Q
3Q
4Q
HAKUSHU
0
DEIMON SNAGS SEVEN POINTS...
...IN THE BLINK OF AN EYE!!
HUUUUH?!
ALREADY?!

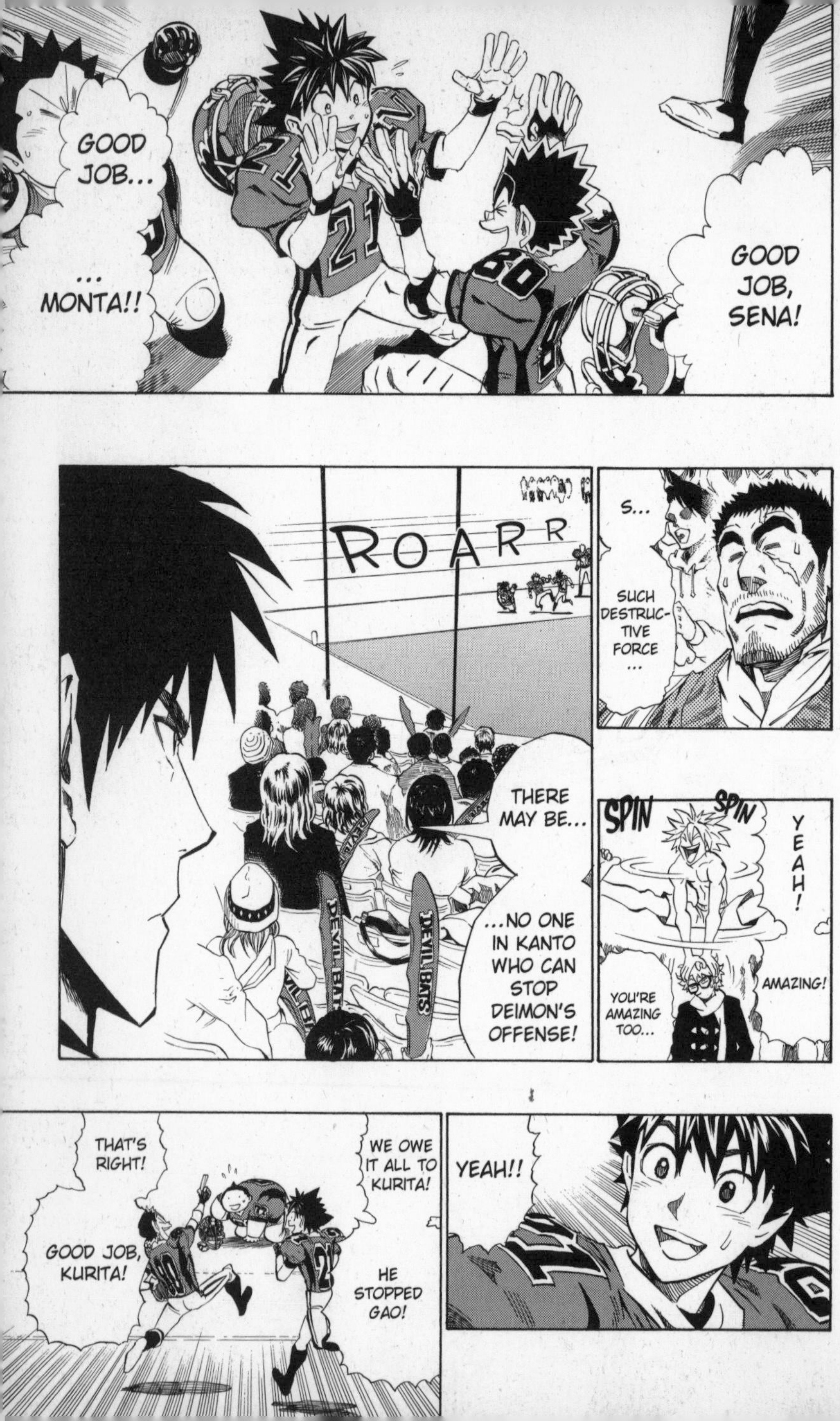
GOOD JOB, SENA!
GOOD JOB...
...MONTA!!
S...
SUCH DESTRUCTIVE FORCE...
SPIN
SPIN
YEAH!
AMAZING!
YOU'RE AMAZING TOO...
ROARR
THERE MAY BE...
...NO ONE IN KANTO WHO CAN STOP DEIMON'S OFFENSE!
DEVIL BATS
DEVIL BATS
YEAH!!
WE OWE IT ALL TO KURITA!
THAT'S RIGHT!
HE STOPPED GAO!
GOOD JOB, KURITA!

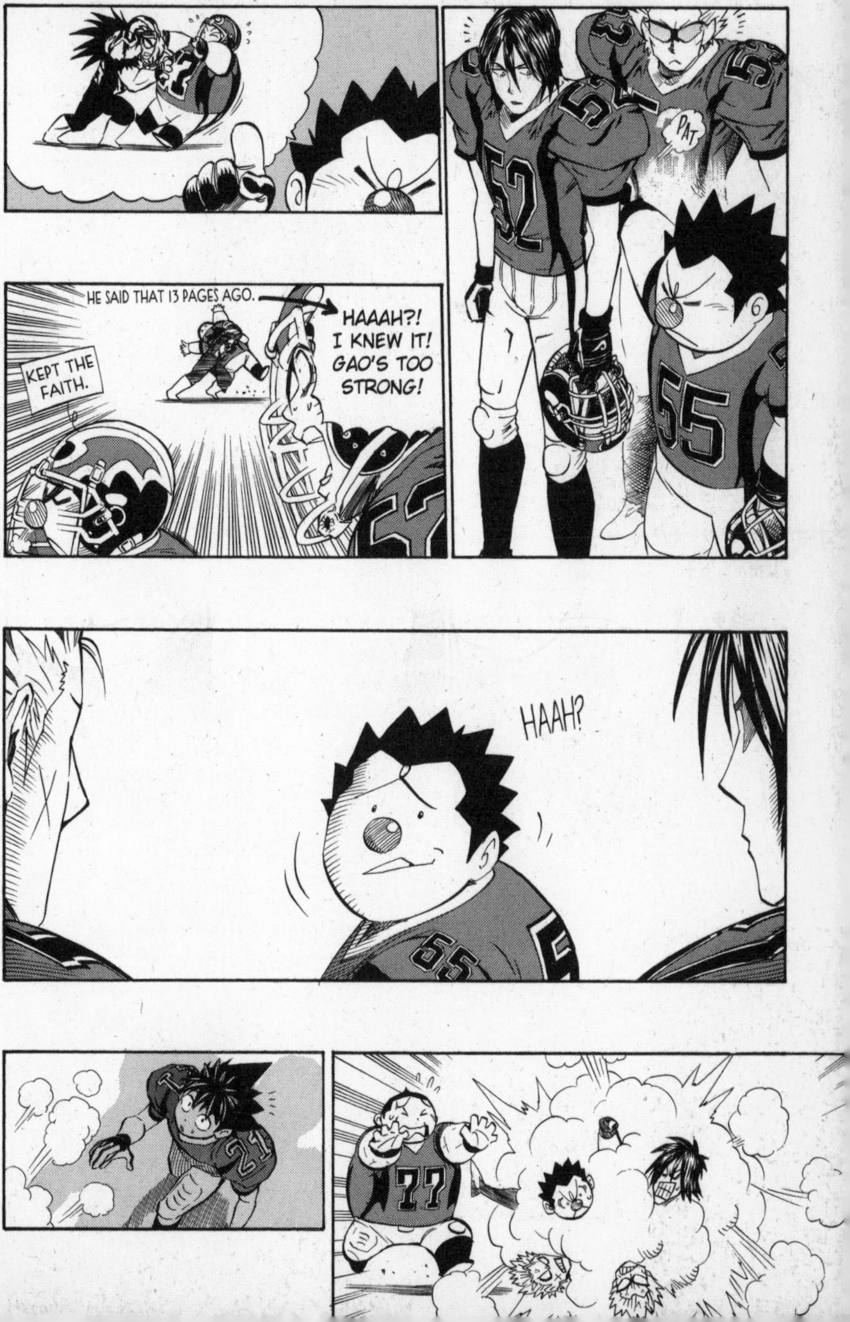
PAT
HAAAH?! I KNEW IT! GAO'S TOO STRONG!
HE SAID THAT 13 PAGES AGO.
KEPT THE FAITH.
HAAH?

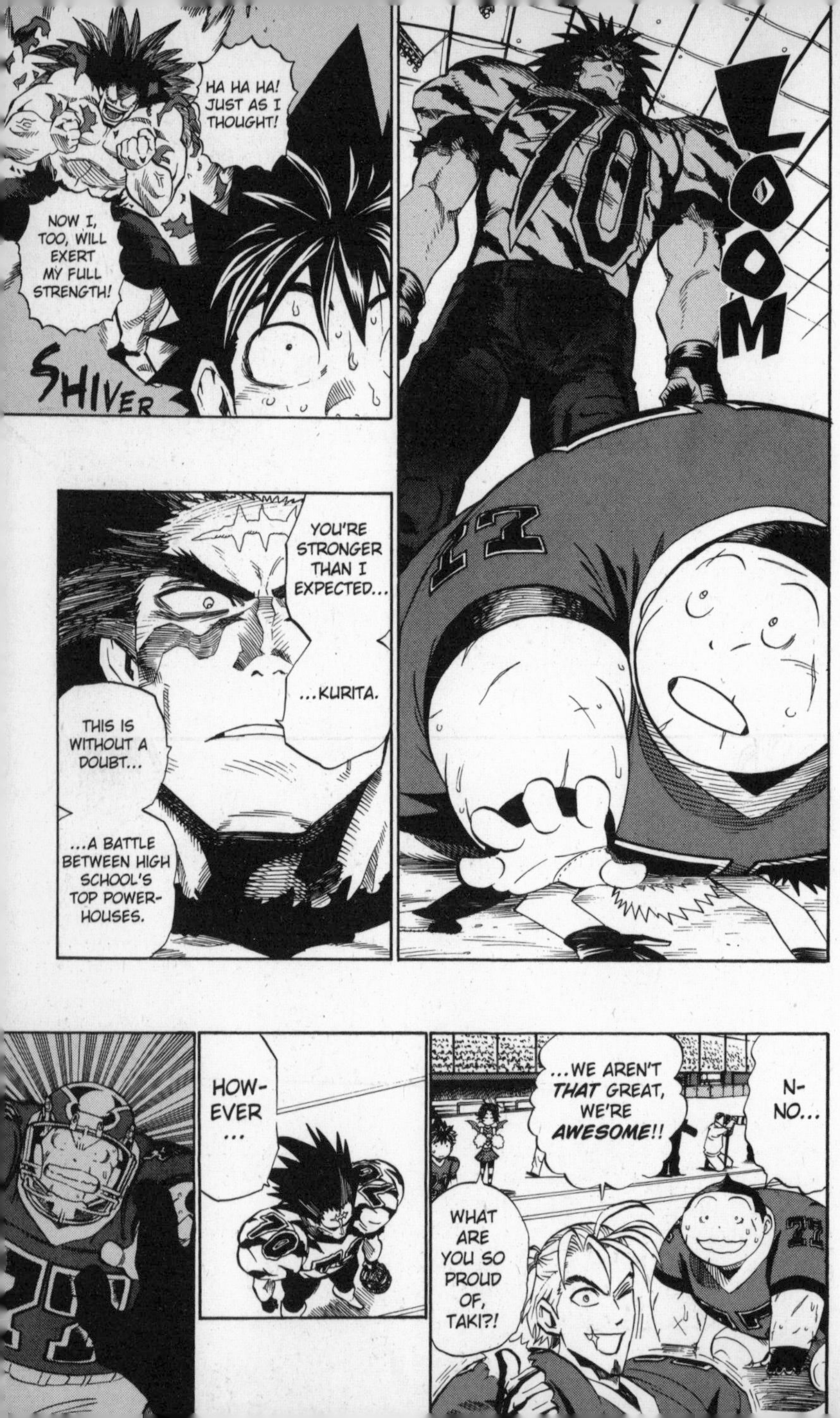
LOOM
HA HA HA! JUST AS I THOUGHT!
NOW I, TOO, WILL EXERT MY FULL STRENGTH!
SHIVER
YOU'RE STRONGER THAN I EXPECTED...
...KURITA.
THIS IS WITHOUT A DOUBT...
...A BATTLE BETWEEN HIGH SCHOOL'S TOP POWER-HOUSES.
N-NO...
...WE AREN'T *THAT* GREAT, WE'RE ***AWESOME***!!
WHAT ARE YOU SO PROUD OF, TAKI?!
HOW-EVER...

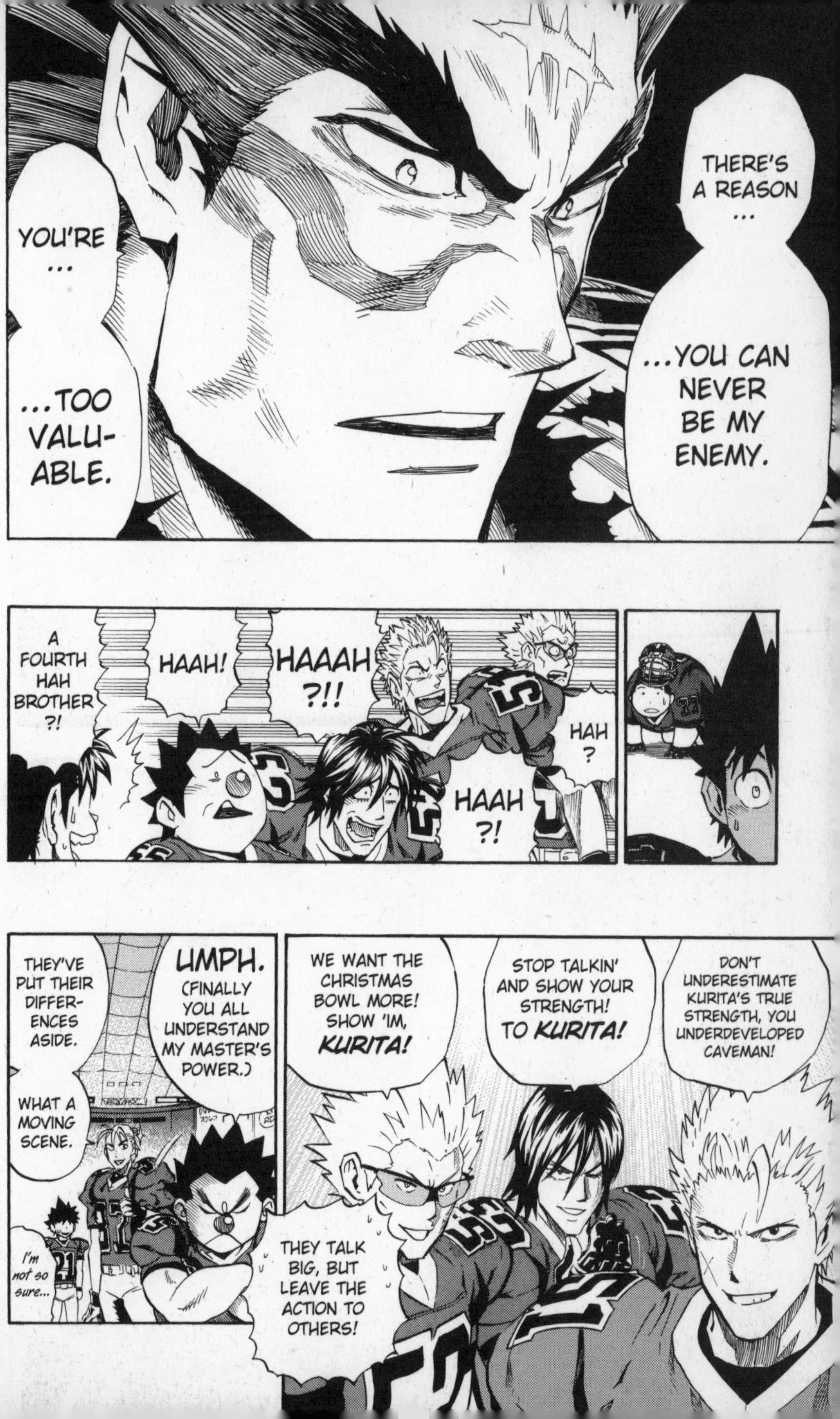
THERE'S A REASON ...
...YOU CAN NEVER BE MY ENEMY.
YOU'RE ...
...TOO VALUABLE.
HAH?
HAAH?!
HAAAH?!!
HAAH!
A FOURTH HAH BROTHER?!
DON'T UNDERESTIMATE KURITA'S TRUE STRENGTH, YOU UNDERDEVELOPED CAVEMAN!
STOP TALKIN' AND SHOW YOUR STRENGTH! TO KURITA!
WE WANT THE CHRISTMAS BOWL MORE! SHOW 'IM, KURITA!
THEY TALK BIG, BUT LEAVE THE ACTION TO OTHERS!
UMPH. (FINALLY YOU ALL UNDERSTAND MY MASTER'S POWER.)
THEY'VE PUT THEIR DIFFERENCES ASIDE.
WHAT A MOVING SCENE.
I'm not so sure...

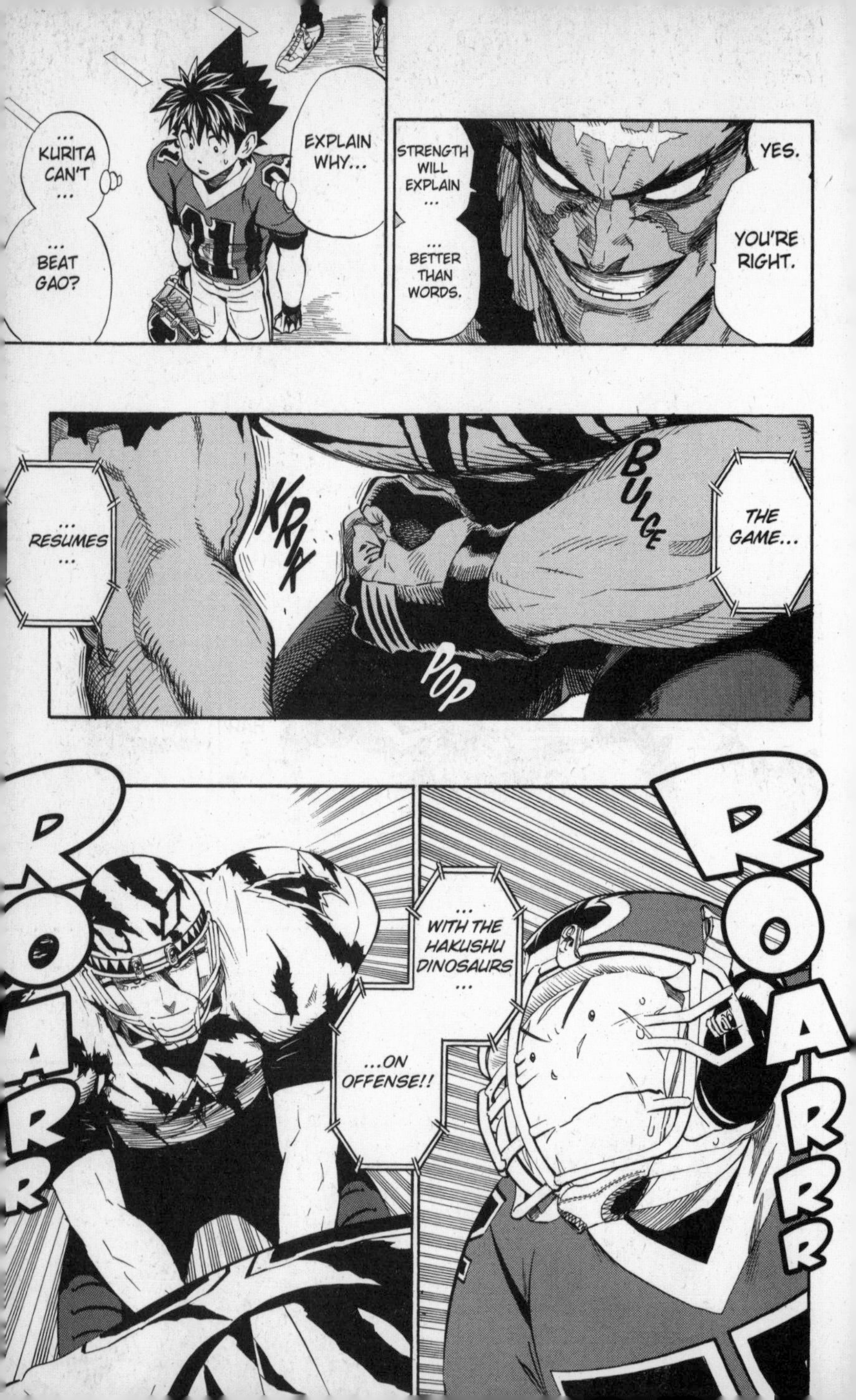
YES.
YOU'RE RIGHT.
STRENGTH WILL EXPLAIN ...
... BETTER THAN WORDS.
EXPLAIN WHY...
... KURITA CAN'T ...
... BEAT GAO?
THE GAME...
BULGE
KRIK
... RESUMES ...
POP
ROARRR
... WITH THE HAKUSHU DINOSAURS ...
...ON OFFENSE!!
ROARR

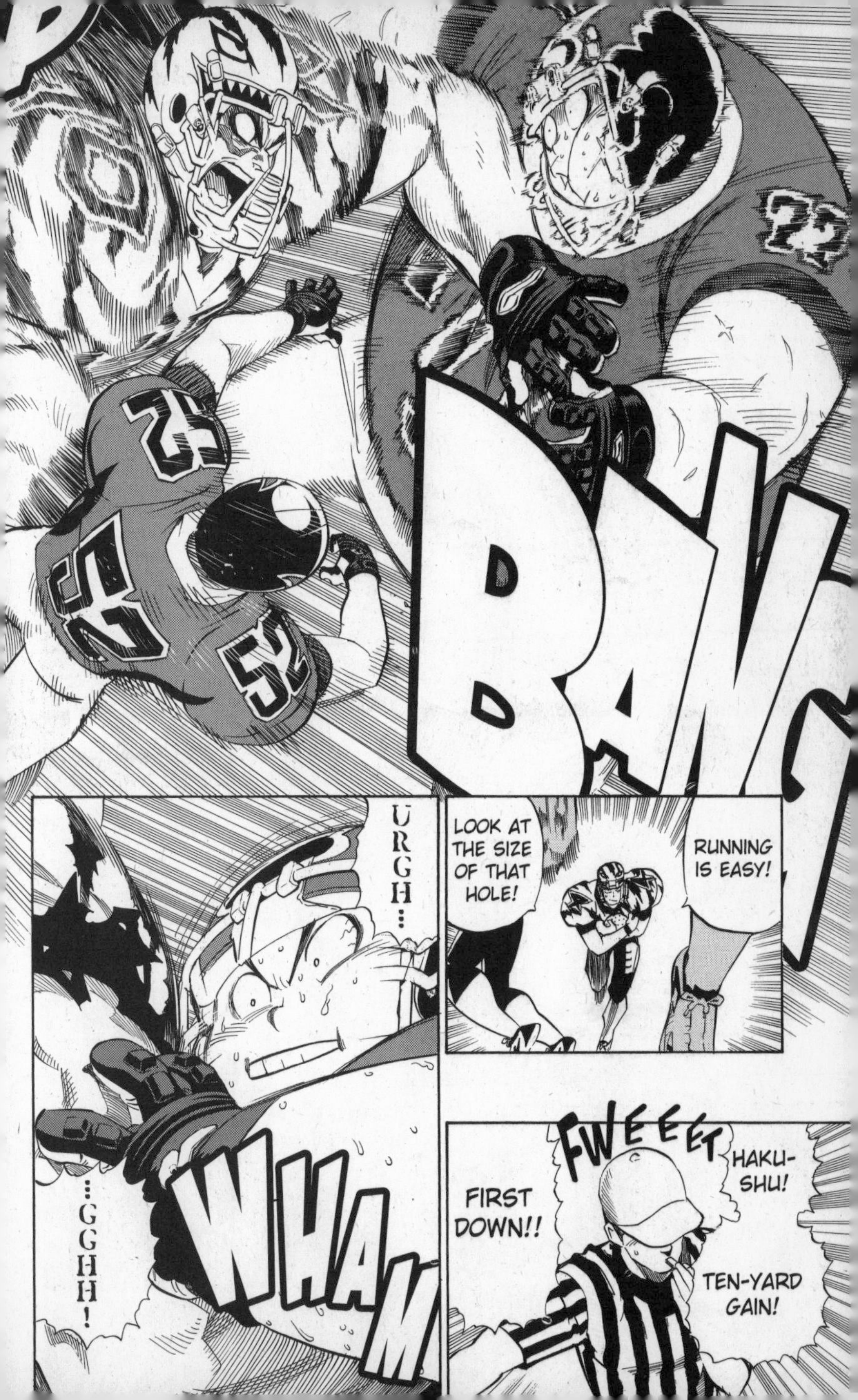

BAM
RUNNING IS EASY!
LOOK AT THE SIZE OF THAT HOLE!
FWEEET
HAKU-SHU!
TEN-YARD GAIN!
FIRST DOWN!!
URGH...
WHAM
...GGHH!

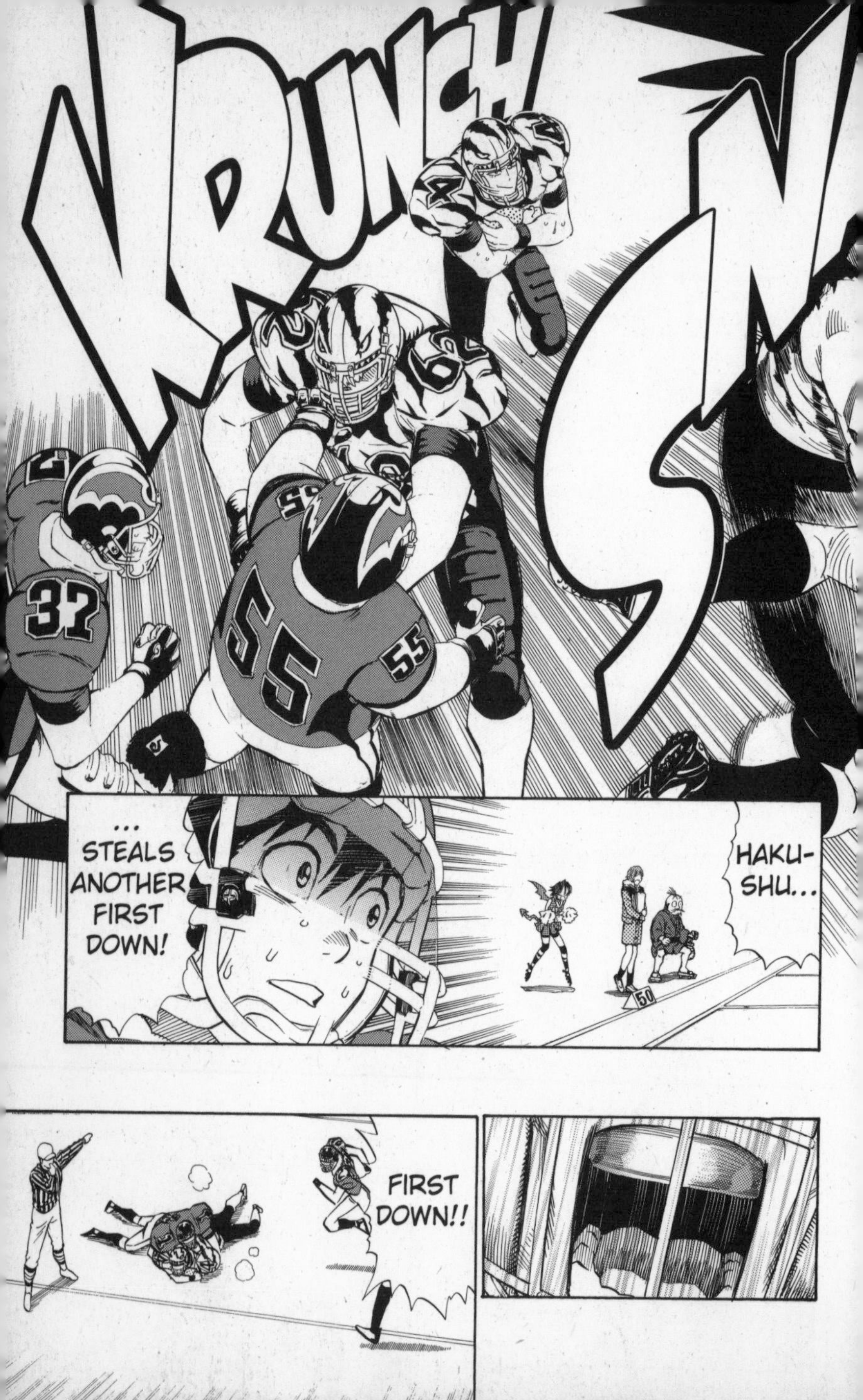
HAKU-SHU...
... STEALS ANOTHER FIRST DOWN!
FIRST DOWN!!

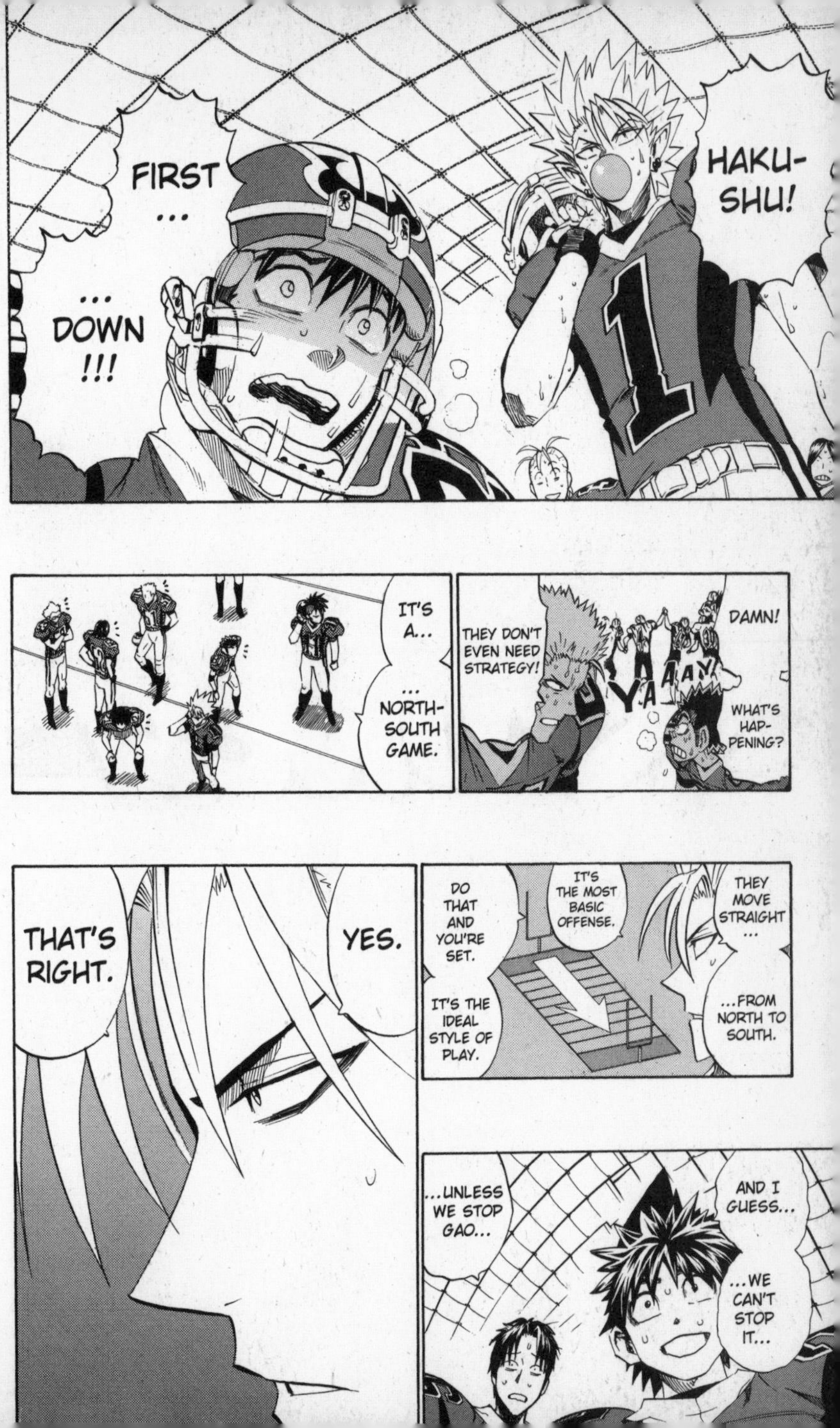
HAKU-SHU!
FIRST ...
... DOWN !!!
DAMN!
WHAT'S HAP-PENING?
THEY DON'T EVEN NEED STRATEGY!
IT'S A...
... NORTH-SOUTH GAME.
THEY MOVE STRAIGHT ...
...FROM NORTH TO SOUTH.
IT'S THE MOST BASIC OFFENSE.
DO THAT AND YOU'RE SET.
IT'S THE IDEAL STYLE OF PLAY.
AND I GUESS...
...WE CAN'T STOP IT...
...UNLESS WE STOP GAO...
YES.
THAT'S RIGHT.

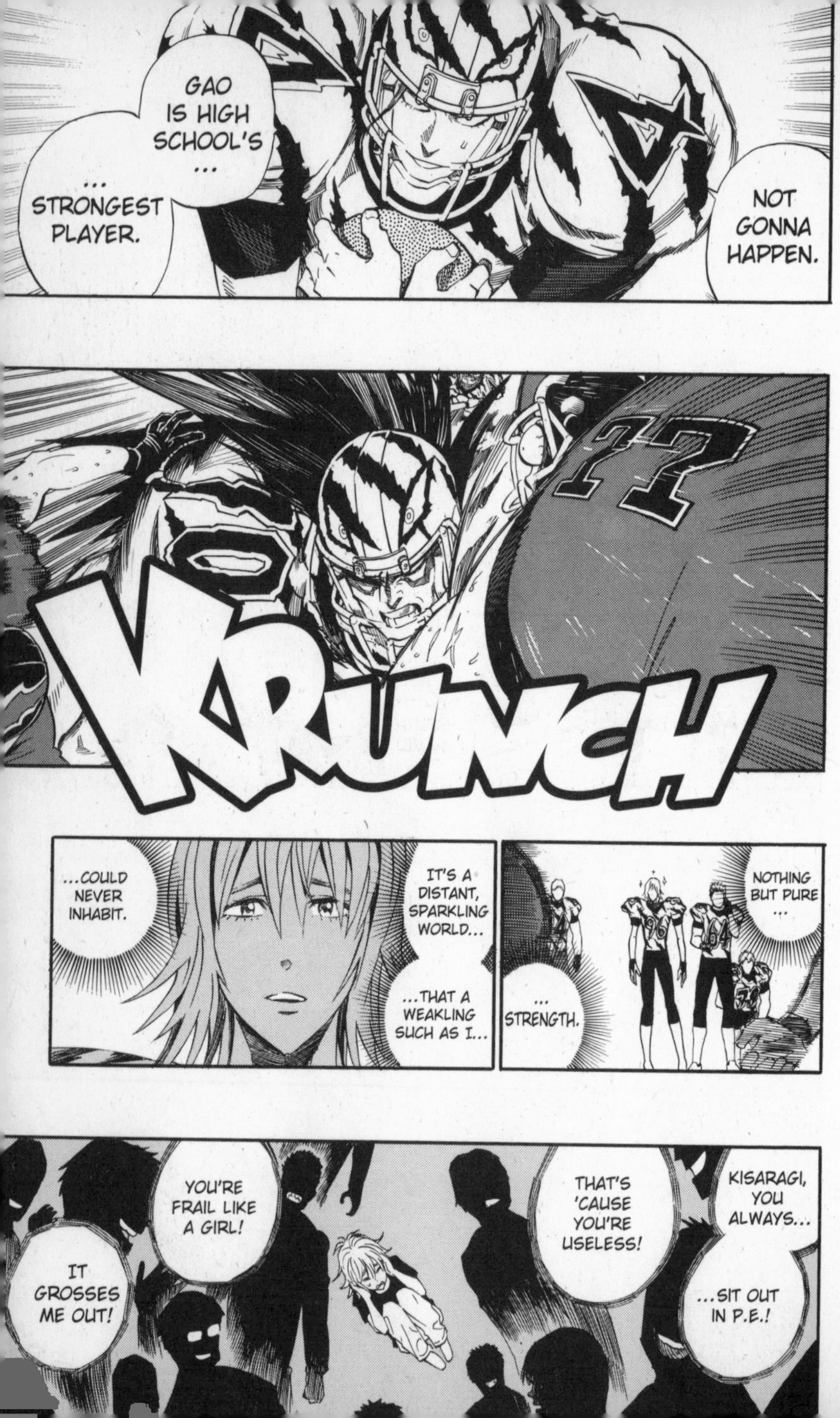
GAO IS HIGH SCHOOL'S ...
... STRONGEST PLAYER.
NOT GONNA HAPPEN.
KRUNCH
NOTHING BUT PURE ...
... STRENGTH.
IT'S A DISTANT, SPARKLING WORLD...
...THAT A WEAKLING SUCH AS I...
...COULD NEVER INHABIT.
KISARAGI, YOU ALWAYS...
...SIT OUT IN P.E.!
THAT'S 'CAUSE YOU'RE USELESS!
YOU'RE FRAIL LIKE A GIRL!
IT GROSSES ME OUT!

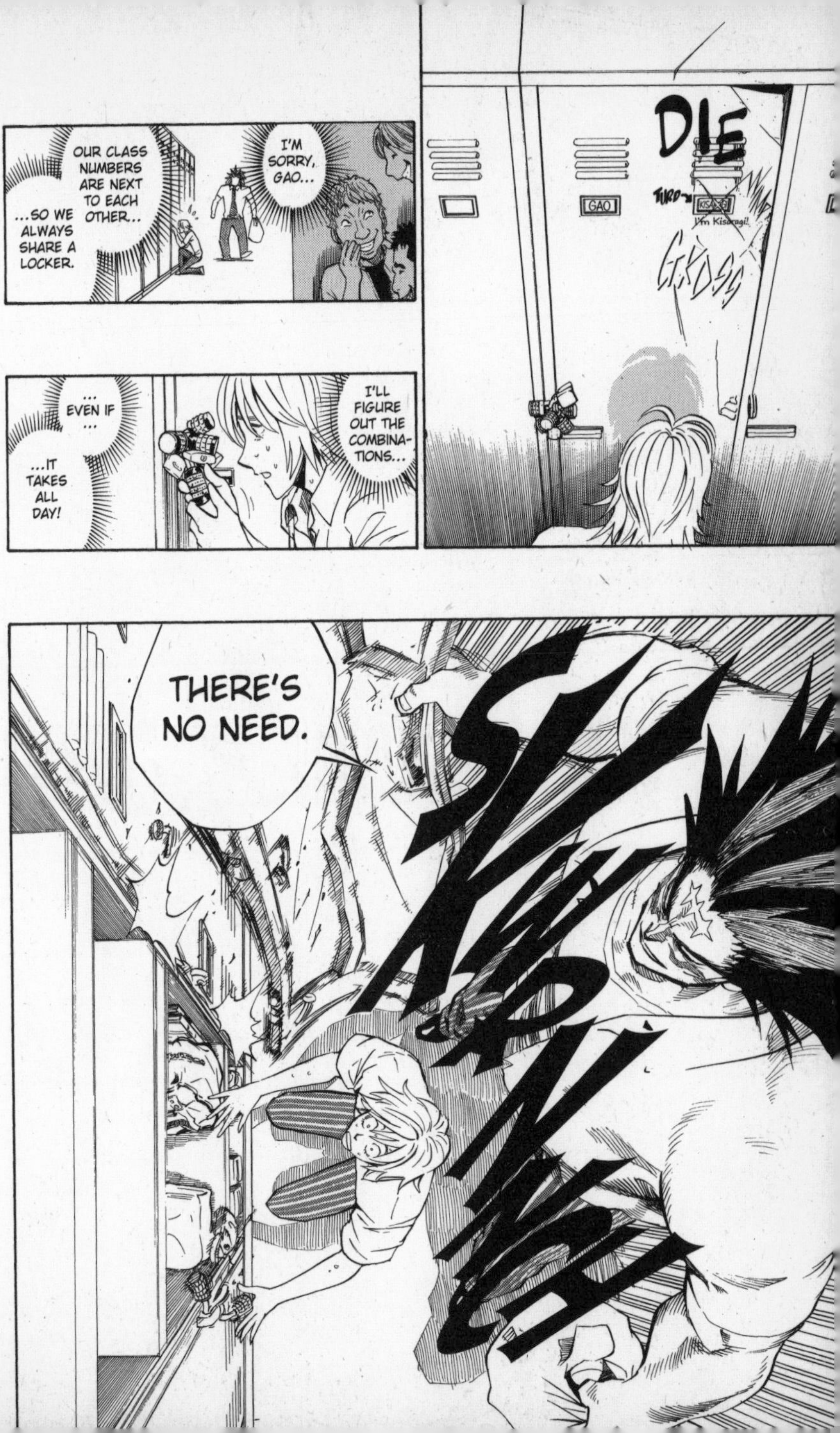
DIE
GAO
TURD
I'm Kisaragi!
...SO WE ALWAYS SHARE A LOCKER.
OUR CLASS NUMBERS ARE NEXT TO EACH OTHER...
I'M SORRY, GAO...
I'LL FIGURE OUT THE COMBINATIONS...
... EVEN IF ...
...IT TAKES ALL DAY!
THERE'S NO NEED.

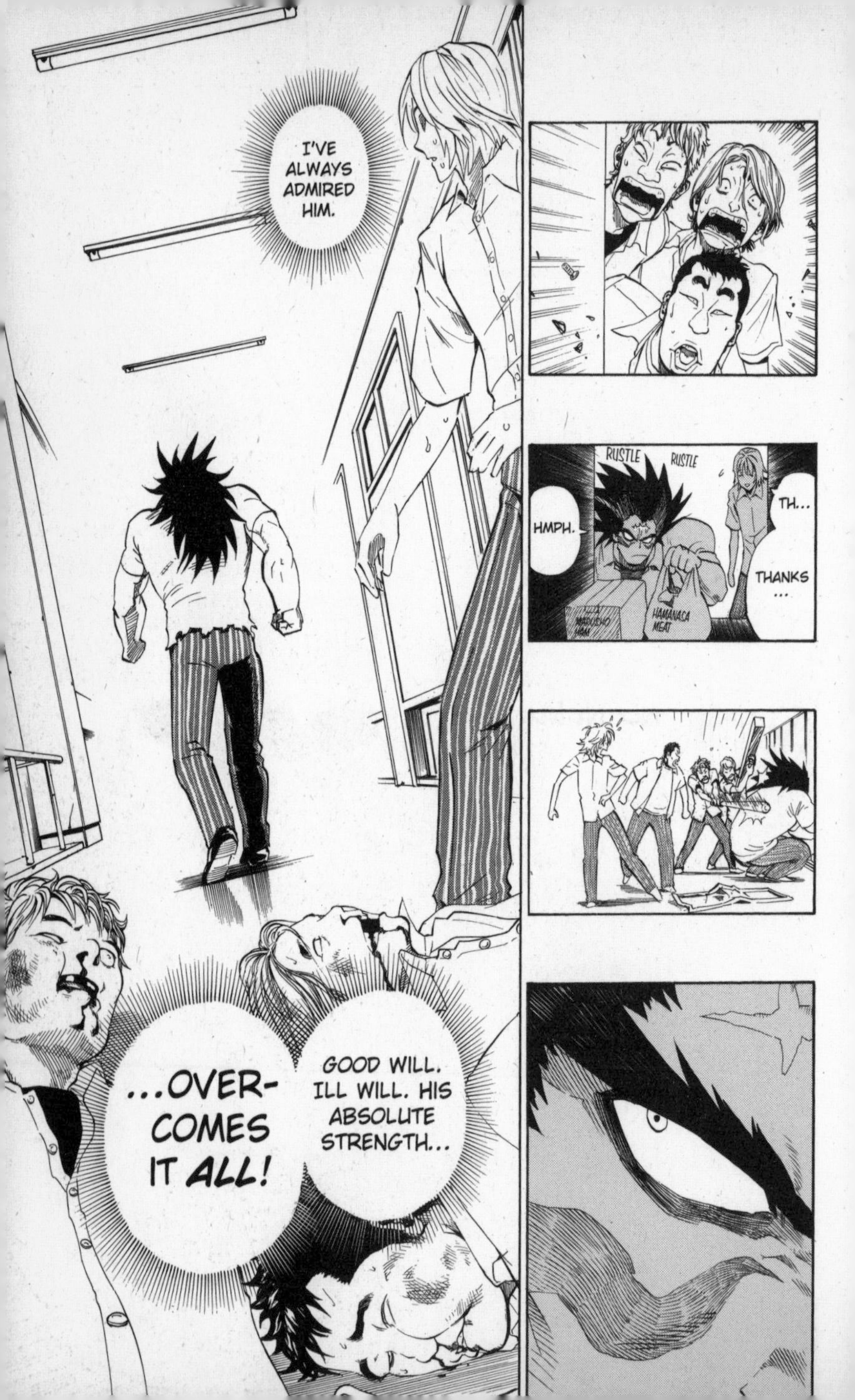
RUSTLE
RUSTLE
TH...
THANKS...
HAMANACA MEAT
MARUSHO HAM
HMPH.
I'VE ALWAYS ADMIRED HIM.
GOOD WILL. ILL WILL. HIS ABSOLUTE STRENGTH...
...OVER-COMES IT ALL!

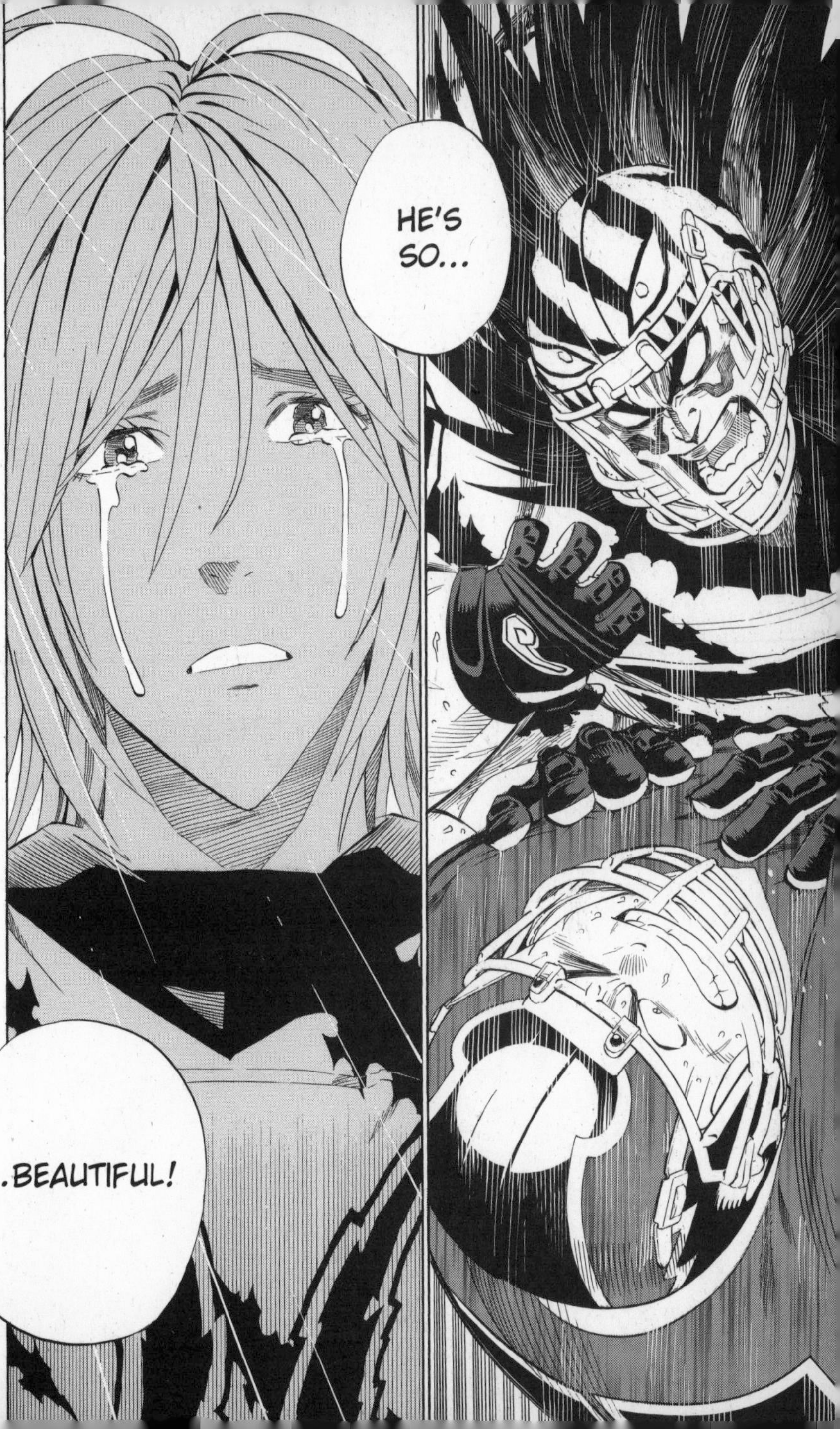
HE'S SO...
...BEAUTIFUL!

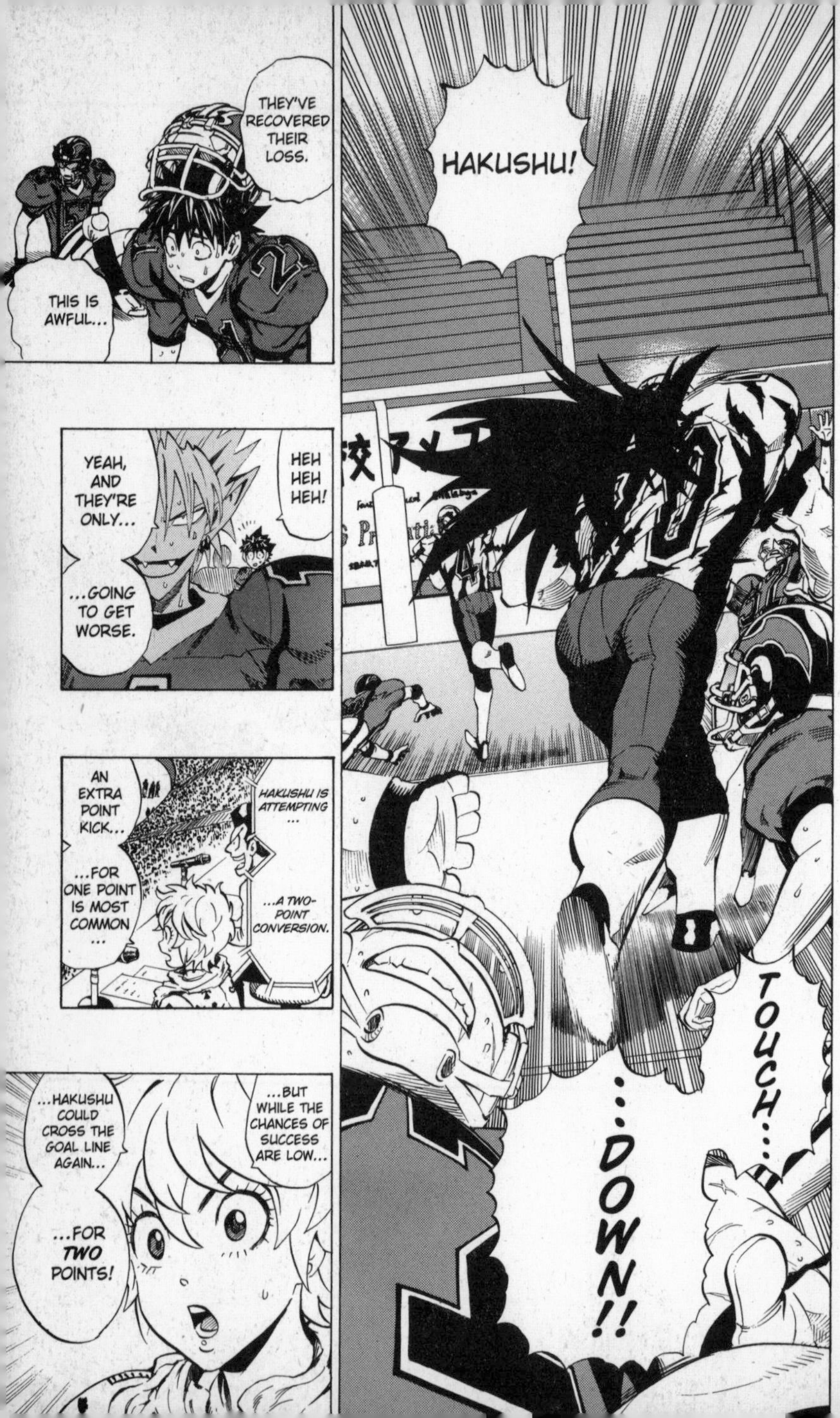
HAKUSHU!
TOUCH...
...DOWN!!
THEY'VE RECOVERED THEIR LOSS.
THIS IS AWFUL...
HEH HEH HEH!
YEAH, AND THEY'RE ONLY...
...GOING TO GET WORSE.
HAKUSHU IS ATTEMPTING ...
...A TWO-POINT CONVERSION.
AN EXTRA POINT KICK...
...FOR ONE POINT IS MOST COMMON ...
...BUT WHILE THE CHANCES OF SUCCESS ARE LOW...
...HAKUSHU COULD CROSS THE GOAL LINE AGAIN...
...FOR *TWO* POINTS!

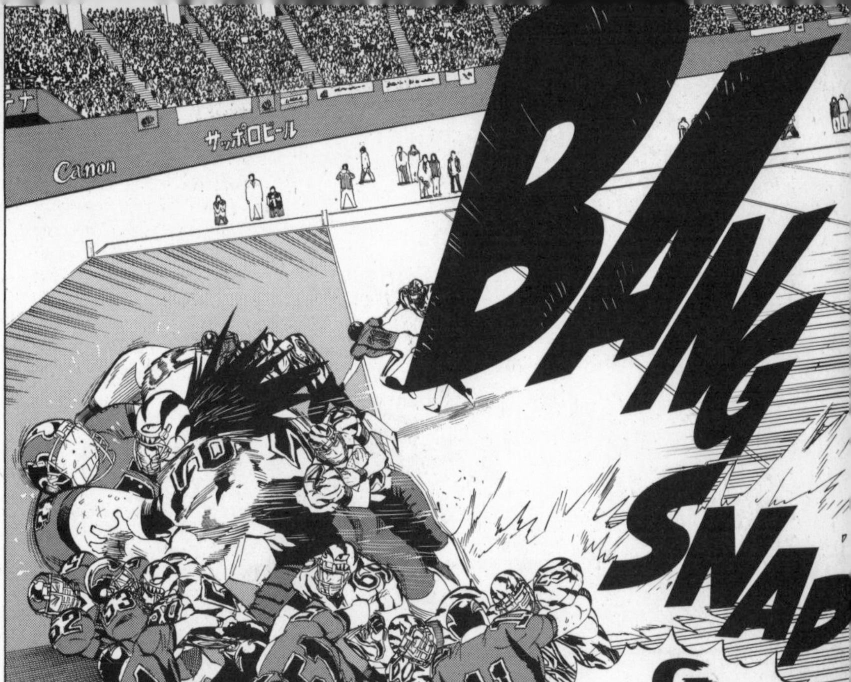
Canon
サッポロビール
BANG
SNAP
GRRAAH!!!
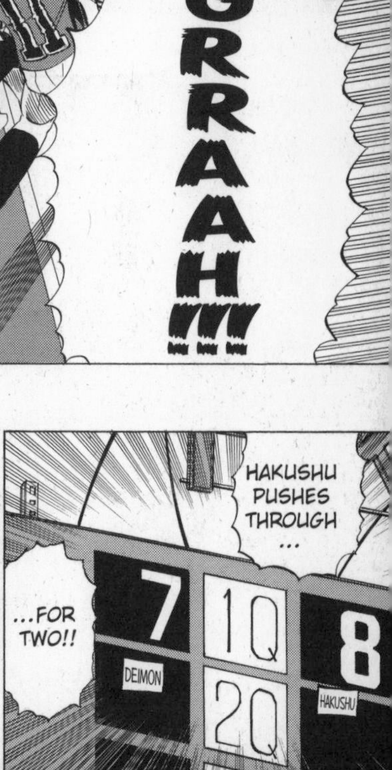
HAKUSHU PUSHES THROUGH...
...FOR TWO!!
7
DEIMON
1Q
2Q
8
HAKUSHU
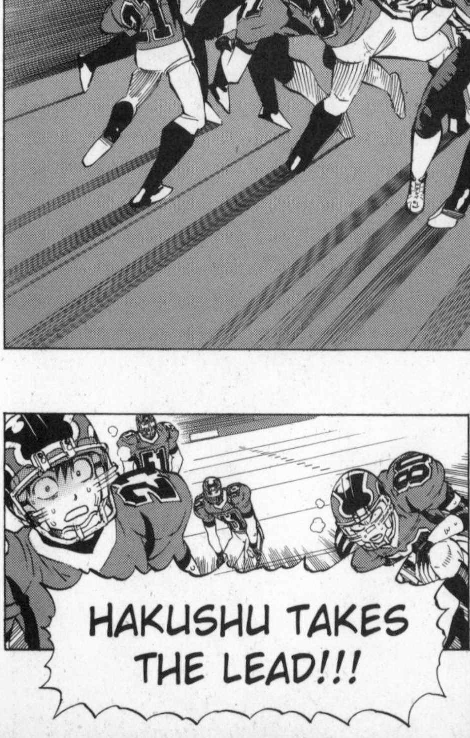
HAKUSHU TAKES THE LEAD!!!

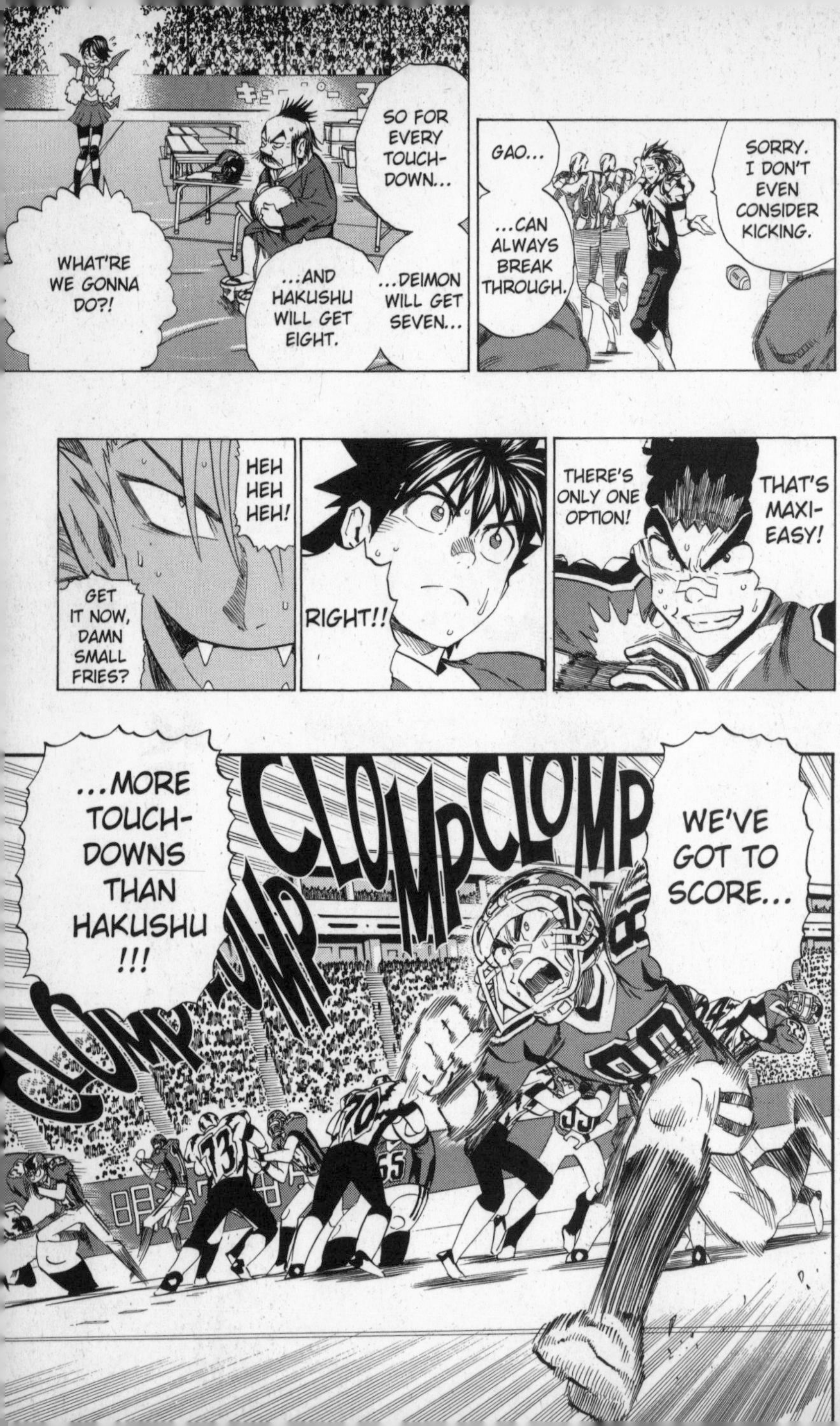
SORRY. I DON'T EVEN CONSIDER KICKING.
GAO...
...CAN ALWAYS BREAK THROUGH.
SO FOR EVERY TOUCH-DOWN...
...DEIMON WILL GET SEVEN...
...AND HAKUSHU WILL GET EIGHT.
WHAT'RE WE GONNA DO?!
THAT'S MAXI-EASY!
THERE'S ONLY ONE OPTION!
RIGHT!!
HEH HEH HEH!
GET IT NOW, DAMN SMALL FRIES?
WE'VE GOT TO SCORE...
CLOMPCLOMP
CLOMP
...MORE TOUCH-DOWNS THAN HAKUSHU!!!
CLOMPCLOMP

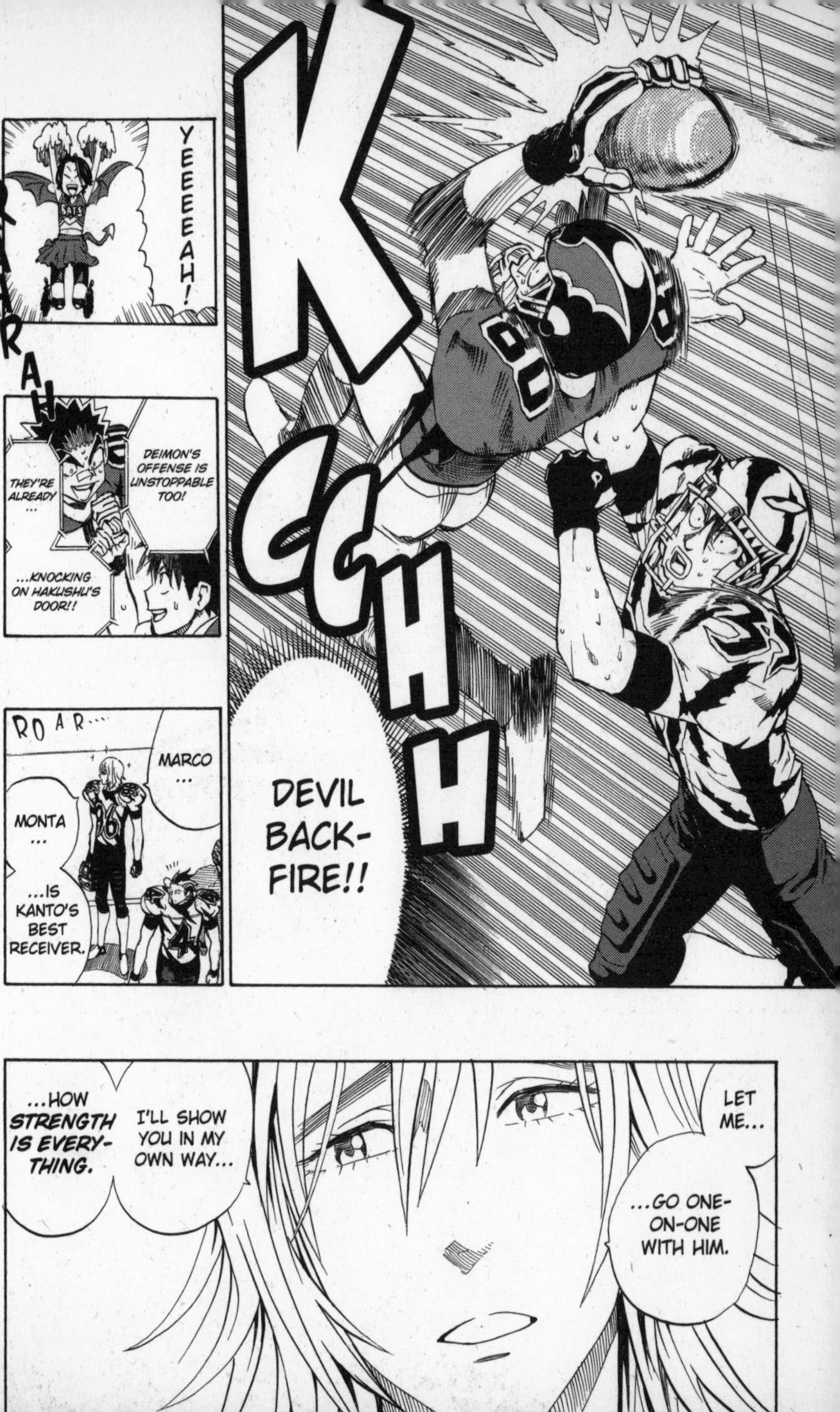
KCCHH
DEVIL BACKFIRE!!
YEEEEAH!
RAHRAH
DEIMON'S OFFENSE IS UNSTOPPABLE TOO!
THEY'RE ALREADY...
...KNOCKING ON HAKUSHU'S DOOR!!
ROAR...
MARCO...
MONTA...
...IS KANTO'S BEST RECEIVER.
LET ME...
...GO ONE-ON-ONE WITH HIM.
I'LL SHOW YOU IN MY OWN WAY...
...HOW **STRENGTH IS EVERYTHING.**

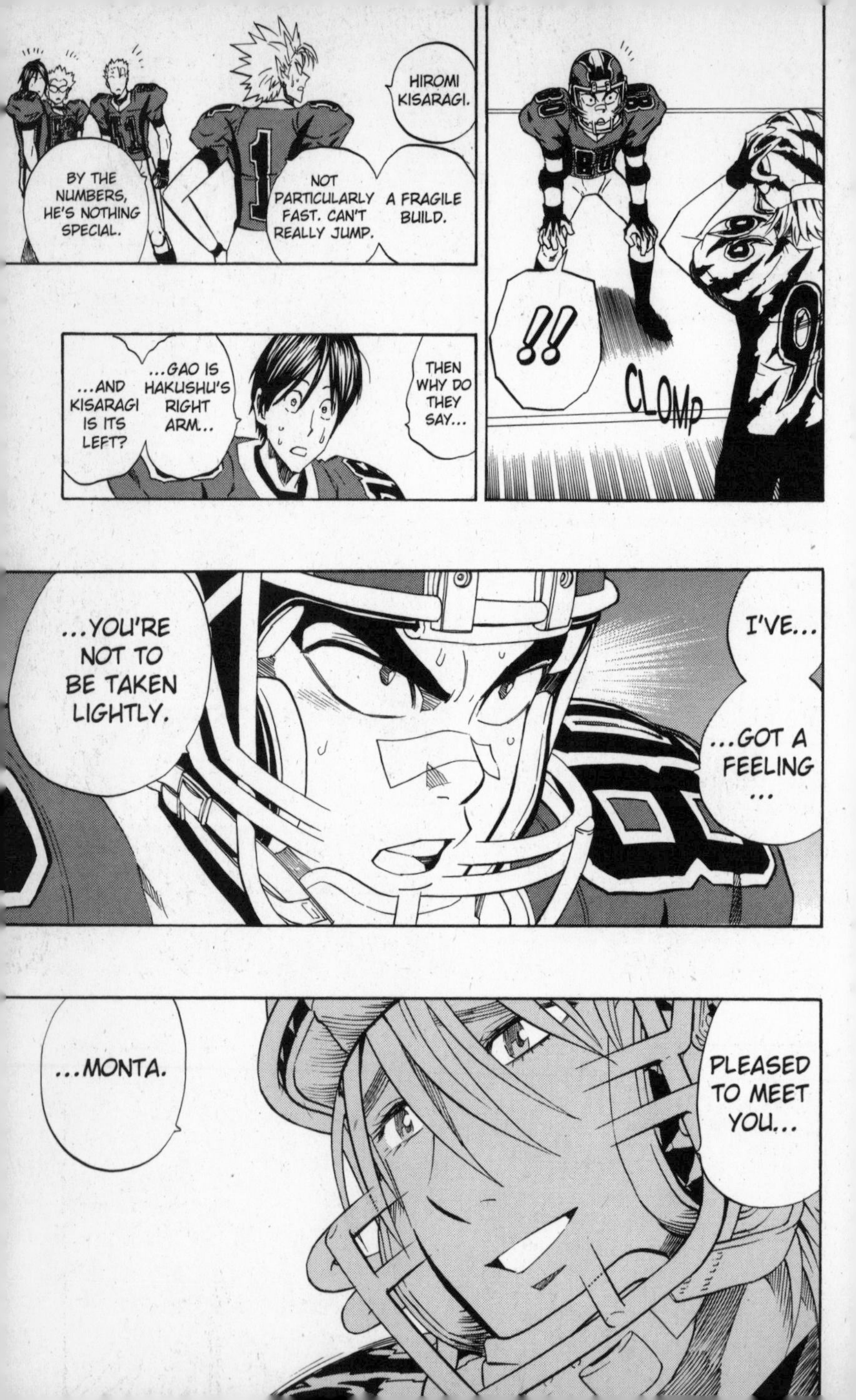
!!
CLOMP
HIROMI KISARAGI.
A FRAGILE BUILD.
NOT PARTICULARLY FAST. CAN'T REALLY JUMP.
BY THE NUMBERS, HE'S NOTHING SPECIAL.
THEN WHY DO THEY SAY...
...GAO IS HAKUSHU'S RIGHT ARM...
...AND KISARAGI IS ITS LEFT?
I'VE...
...GOT A FEELING...
...YOU'RE NOT TO BE TAKEN LIGHTLY.
PLEASED TO MEET YOU...
...MONTA.

DEIMON & HAKUSHU CELL PHONE WALLPAPER CHECK!

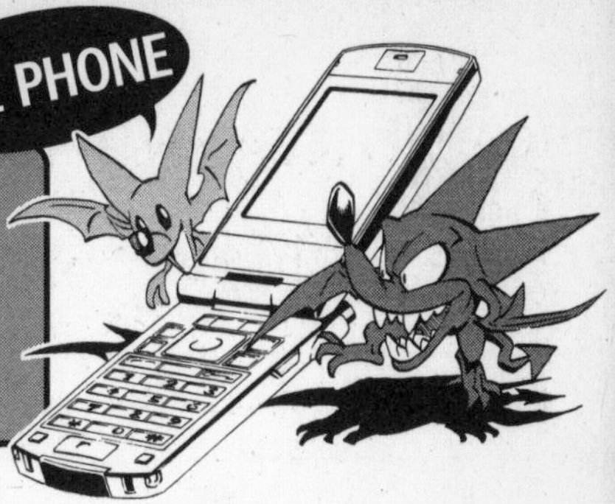

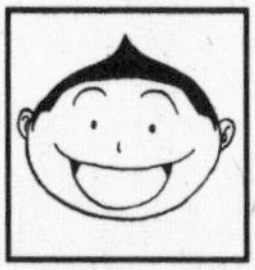

Kurita

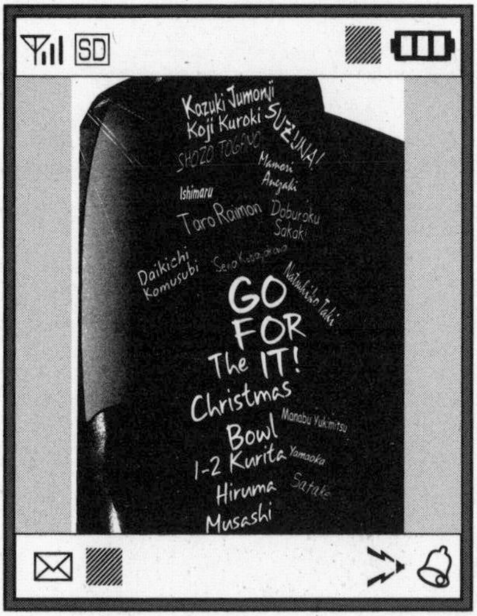
SD
Kazuki Jumonji
Koji Kuroki
SUZUNA!
SHOZO TOGANO
Mamori Anezaki
Ishimaru
Taro Raimon
Doburoku Sakaki
Daikichi Komusubi
Natsuhiko Taki
GO FOR The IT! Christmas Bowl
Manabu Yukimitsu
1-2 Kurita
Yamaoka
Hiruma
Satake
Musashi

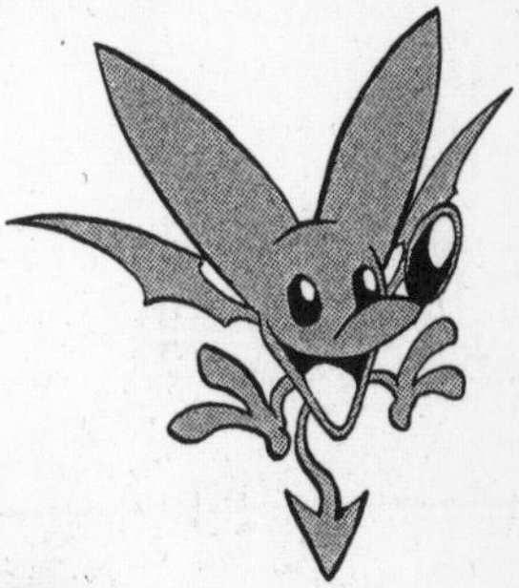

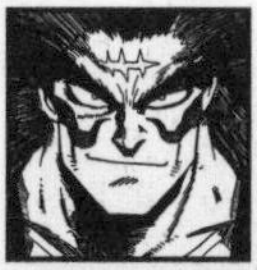

Gao

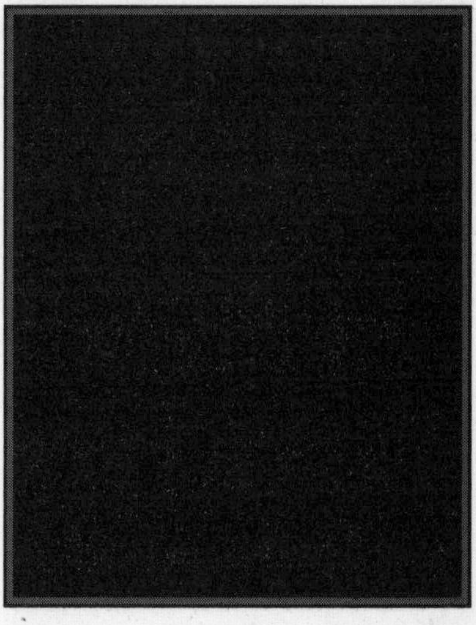

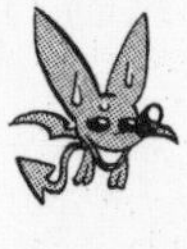

WHOA! GAO'S GOT A PRIVACY FILTER ON IT SO YOU CAN'T SEE ANYTHING AT ALL!

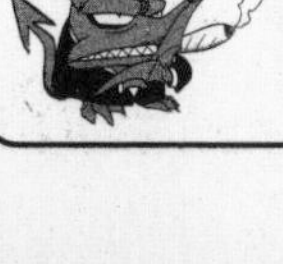

NO, MARCO MADE HIM HAVE A PHONE, BUT HE DOESN'T USE IT, SO THE POWER'S ALWAYS GONE.

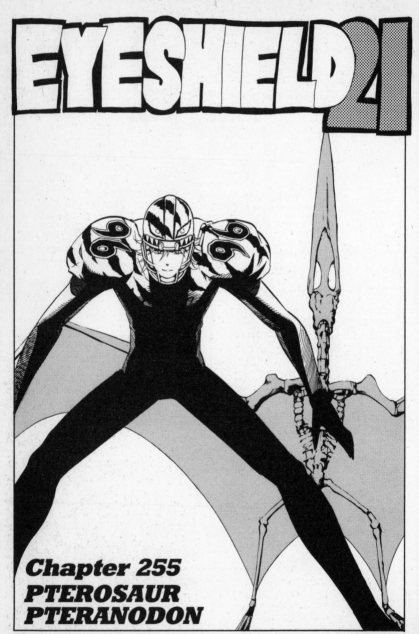

EYESHIELD 21

Chapter 255
PTEROSAUR
PTERANODON

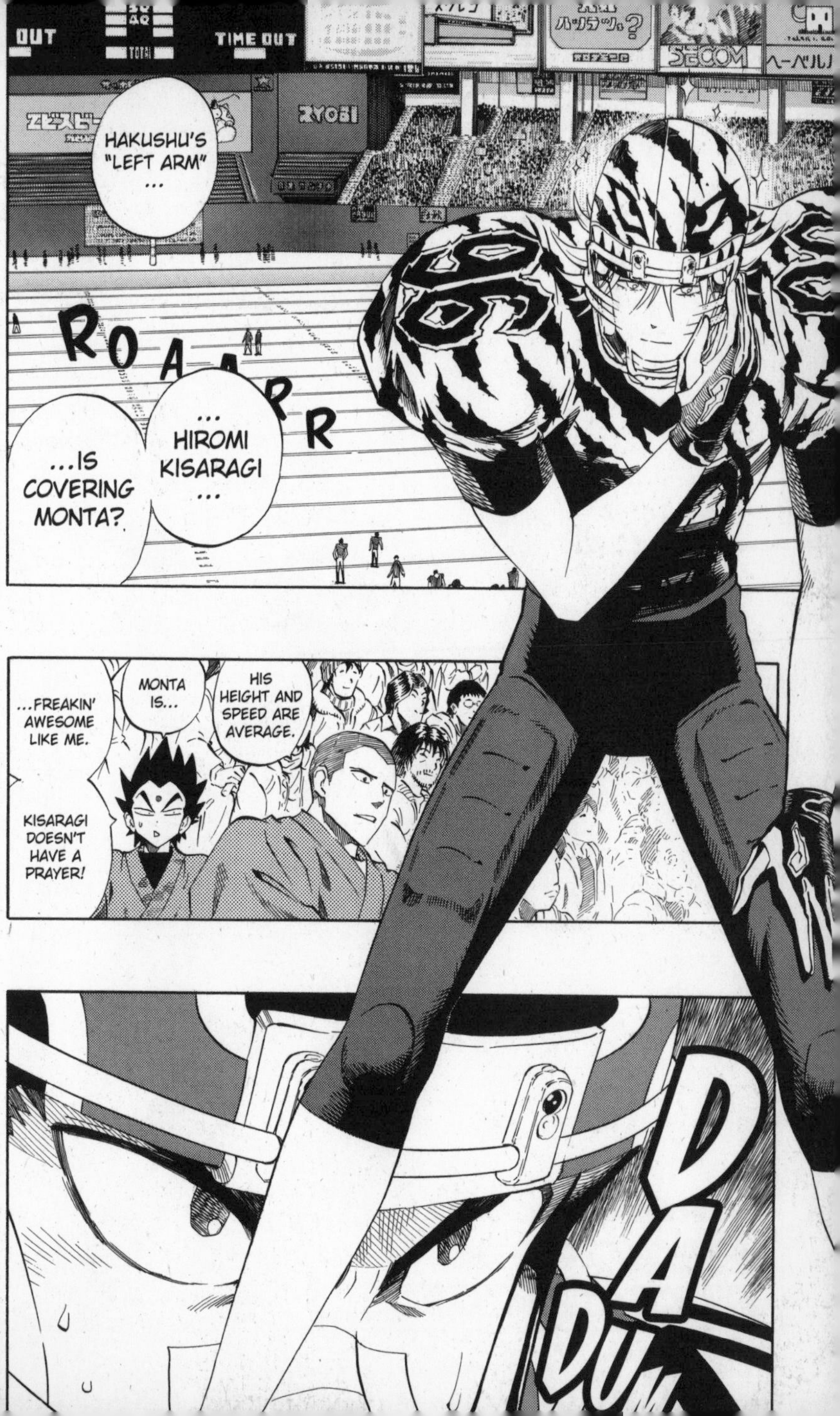
OUT
TIME OUT
RYOBI
SECOM
HAKUSHU'S "LEFT ARM" ...
ROAARR
... HIROMI KISARAGI ...
...IS COVERING MONTA?
HIS HEIGHT AND SPEED ARE AVERAGE.
MONTA IS...
...FREAKIN' AWESOME LIKE ME.
KISARAGI DOESN'T HAVE A PRAYER!
DA
DU

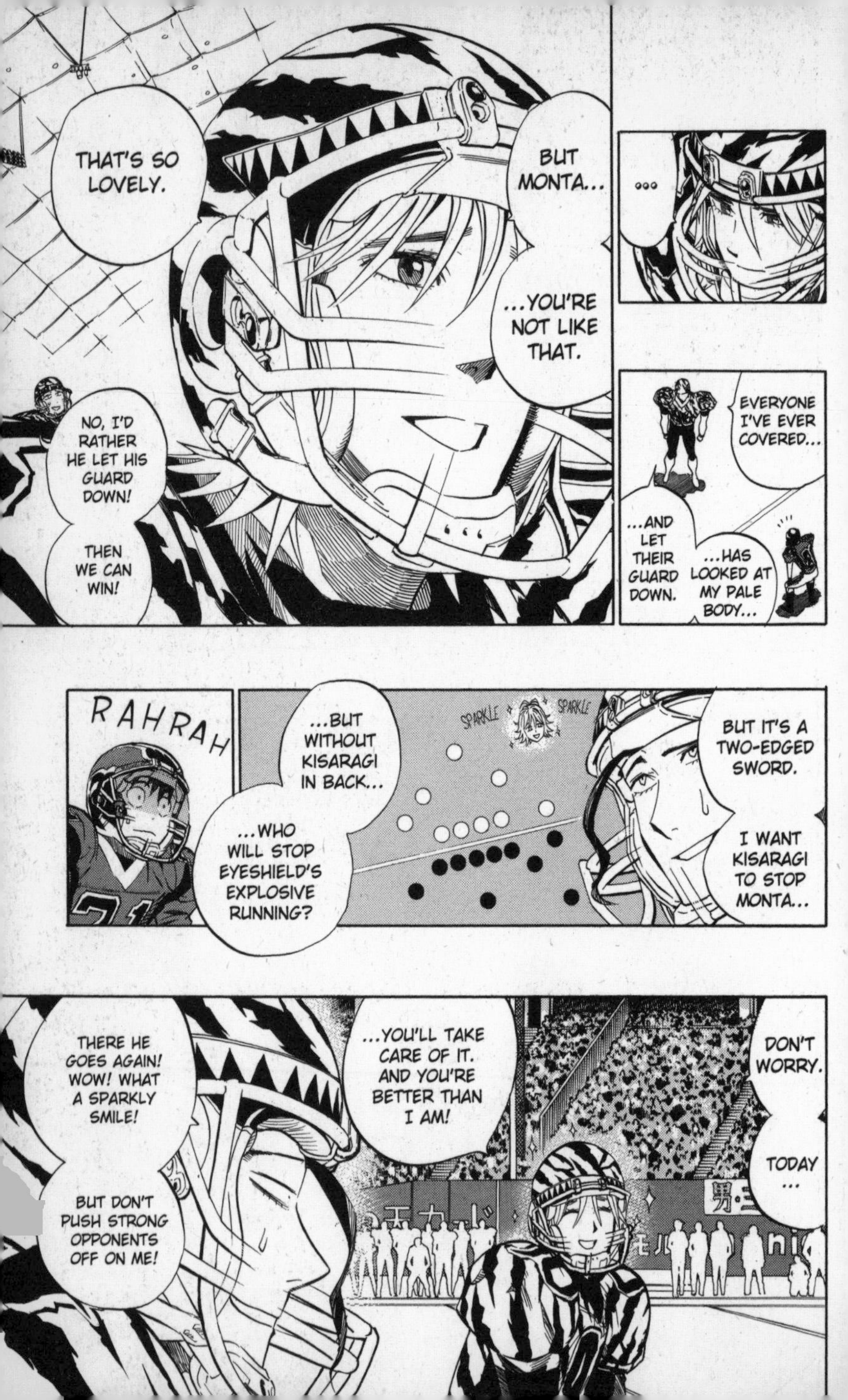
...
EVERYONE I'VE EVER COVERED...
...HAS LOOKED AT MY PALE BODY...
...AND LET THEIR GUARD DOWN.
BUT MONTA...
...YOU'RE NOT LIKE THAT.
THAT'S SO LOVELY.
NO, I'D RATHER HE LET HIS GUARD DOWN!
THEN WE CAN WIN!
BUT IT'S A TWO-EDGED SWORD.
I WANT KISARAGI TO STOP MONTA...
SPARKLE
SPARKLE
...BUT WITHOUT KISARAGI IN BACK...
...WHO WILL STOP EYESHIELD'S EXPLOSIVE RUNNING?
RAHRAH
DON'T WORRY.
TODAY...
...YOU'LL TAKE CARE OF IT. AND YOU'RE BETTER THAN I AM!
THERE HE GOES AGAIN! WOW! WHAT A SPARKLY SMILE!
BUT DON'T PUSH STRONG OPPONENTS OFF ON ME!

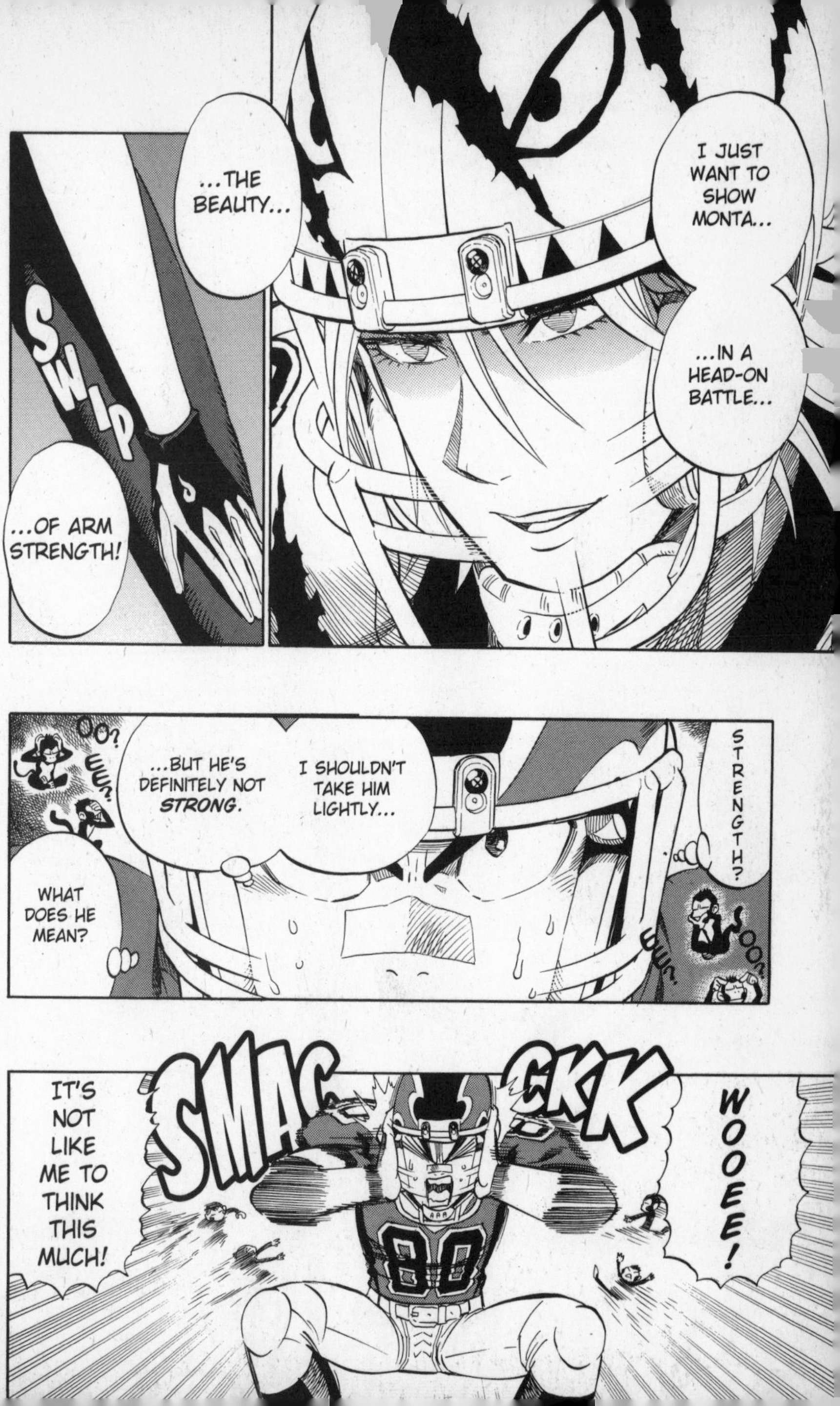
I JUST WANT TO SHOW MONTA...
...IN A HEAD-ON BATTLE...
...THE BEAUTY...
SWIP
...OF ARM STRENGTH!
STRENGTH?
I SHOULDN'T TAKE HIM LIGHTLY...
...BUT HE'S DEFINITELY NOT STRONG.
OO? EE?
WHAT DOES HE MEAN?
WOOOEE!
SMAC CKK
IT'S NOT LIKE ME TO THINK THIS MUCH!

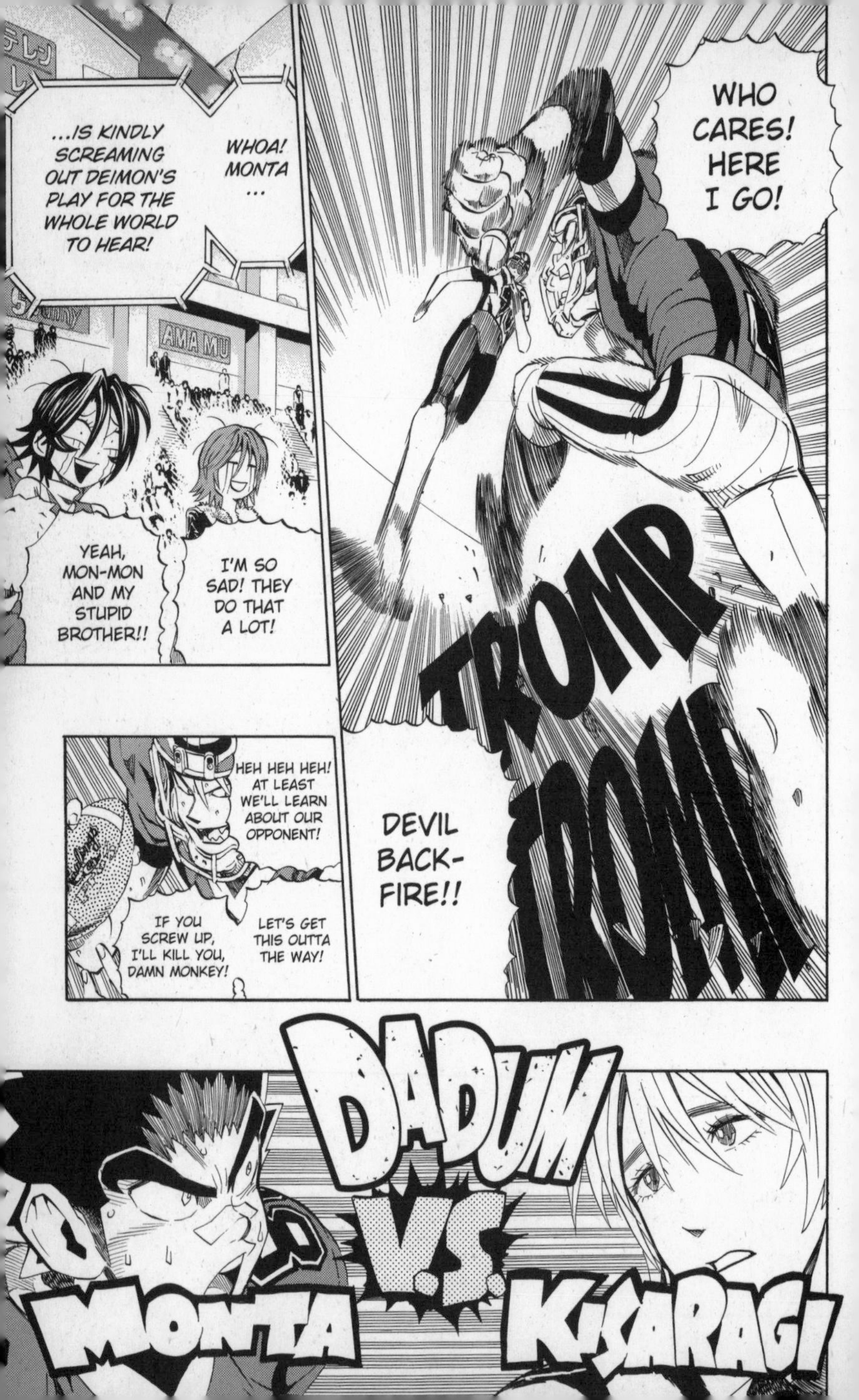
WHO CARES! HERE I GO!
TROMP
TROMP
DEVIL BACK-FIRE!!
WHOA! MONTA ...
...IS KINDLY SCREAMING OUT DEIMON'S PLAY FOR THE WHOLE WORLD TO HEAR!
AMA MU
I'M SO SAD! THEY DO THAT A LOT!
YEAH, MON-MON AND MY STUPID BROTHER!!
HEH HEH HEH! AT LEAST WE'LL LEARN ABOUT OUR OPPONENT!
LET'S GET THIS OUTTA THE WAY!
IF YOU SCREW UP, I'LL KILL YOU, DAMN MONKEY!
DADUM
MONTA V.S. KISARAGI!

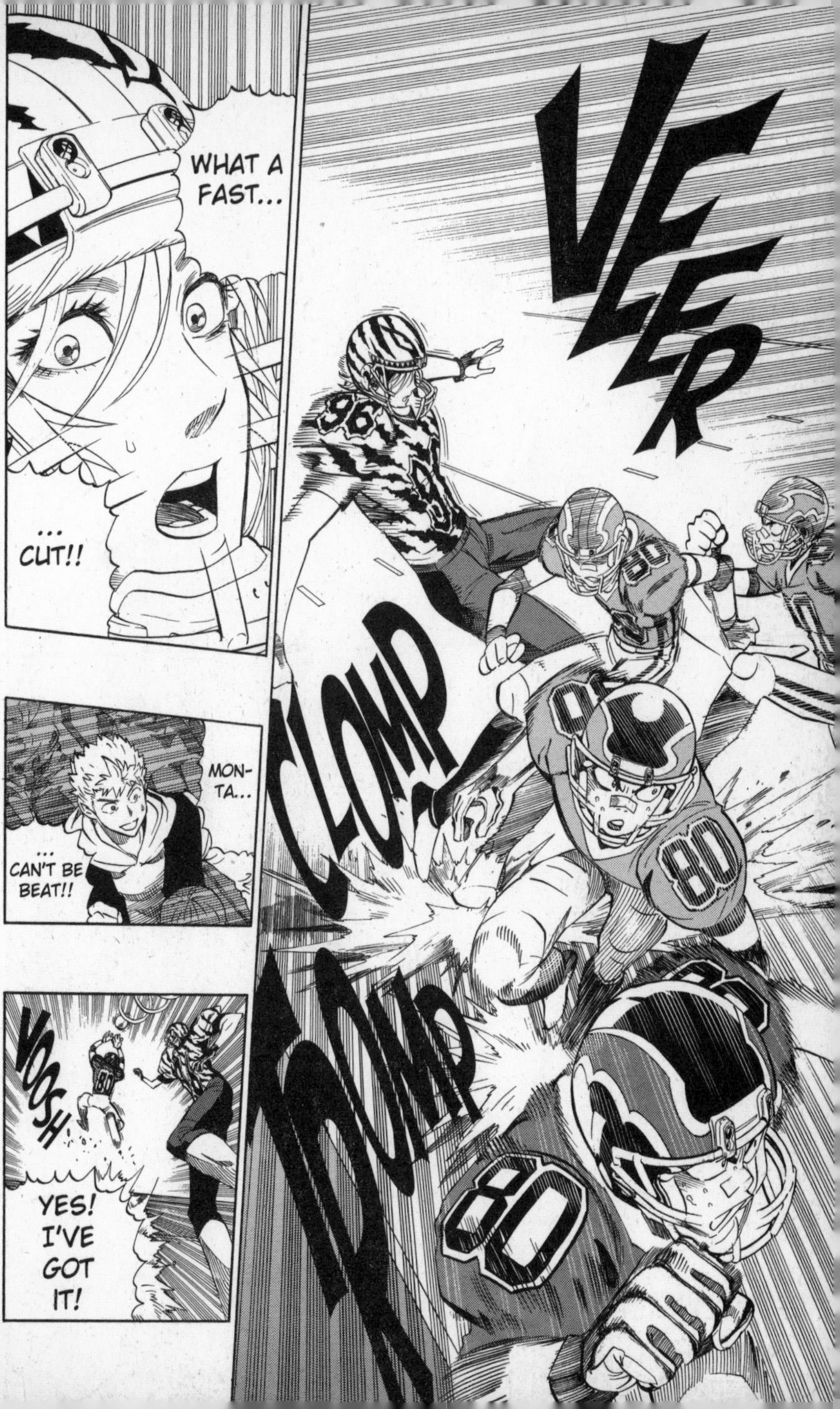
VEER
CLOMP
CLOMP
WHAT A FAST...
...CUT!!
MON-TA...
...CAN'T BE BEAT!!
VOOSH
YES! I'VE GOT IT!

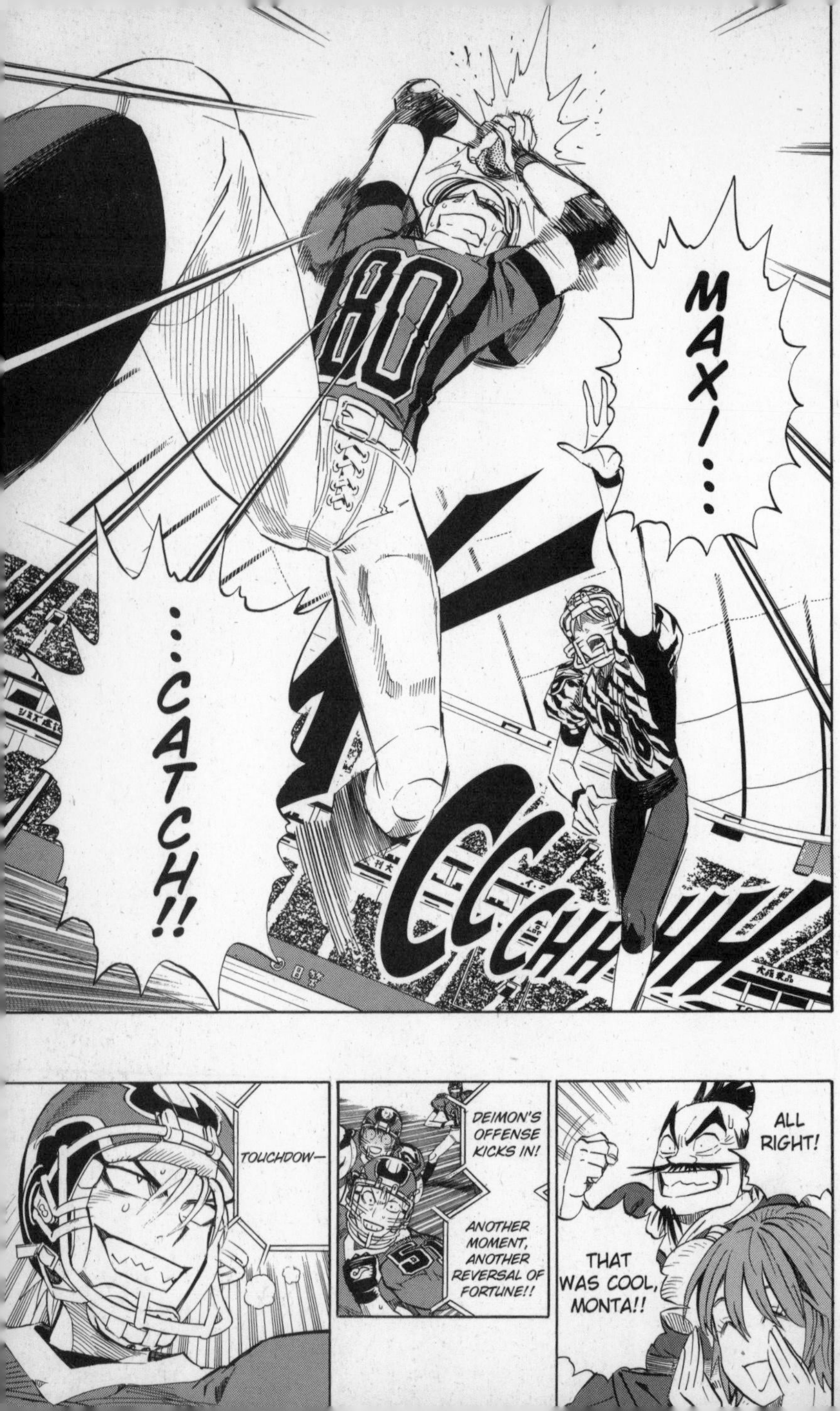
MAX!...
...CATCH!!
CCCHHHH
ALL RIGHT!
THAT WAS COOL, MONTA!!
DEIMON'S OFFENSE KICKS IN!
ANOTHER MOMENT, ANOTHER REVERSAL OF FORTUNE!!
TOUCHDOW—

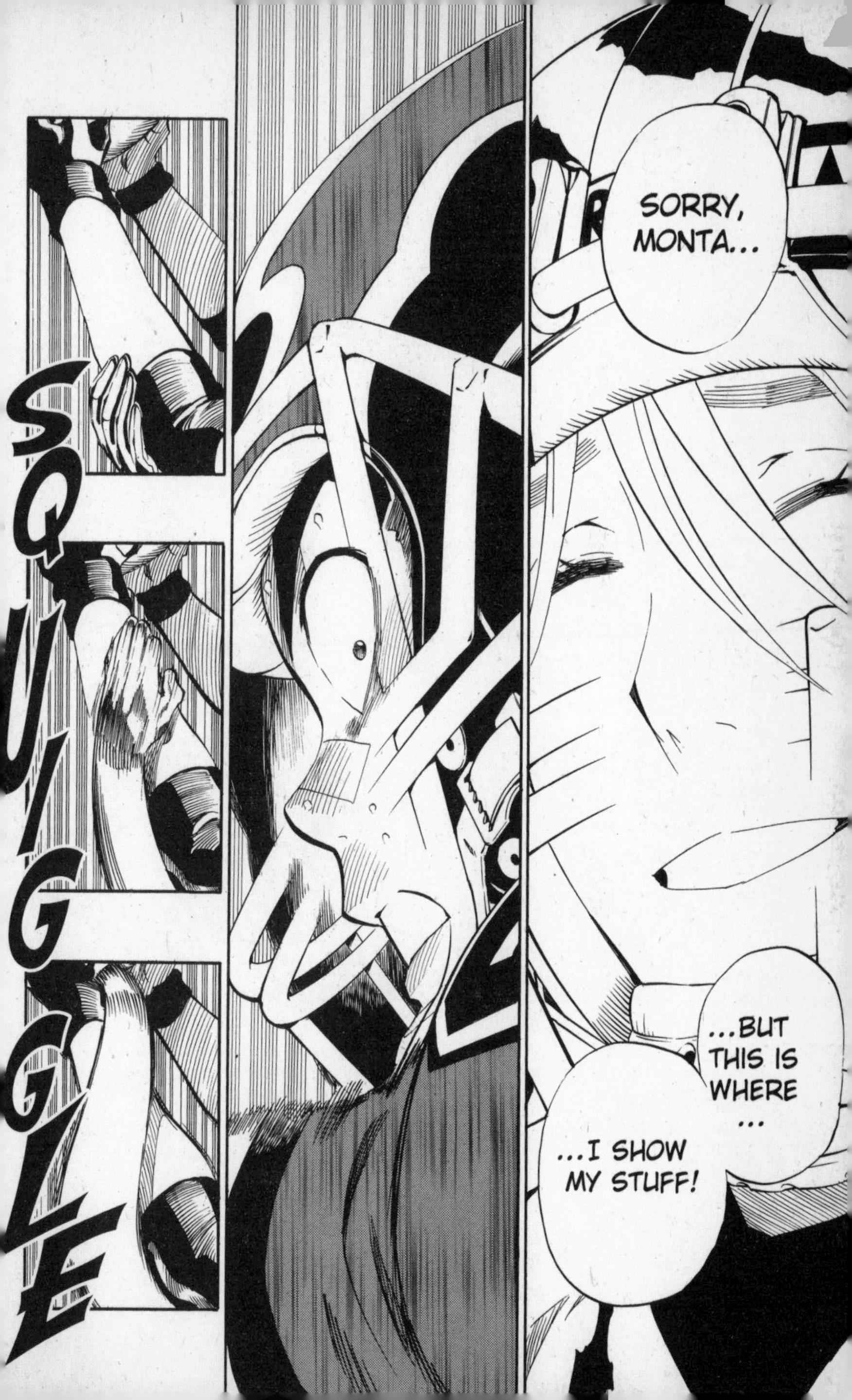
SORRY, MONTA...
...BUT THIS IS WHERE ...
...I SHOW MY STUFF!
SQUIGGLE

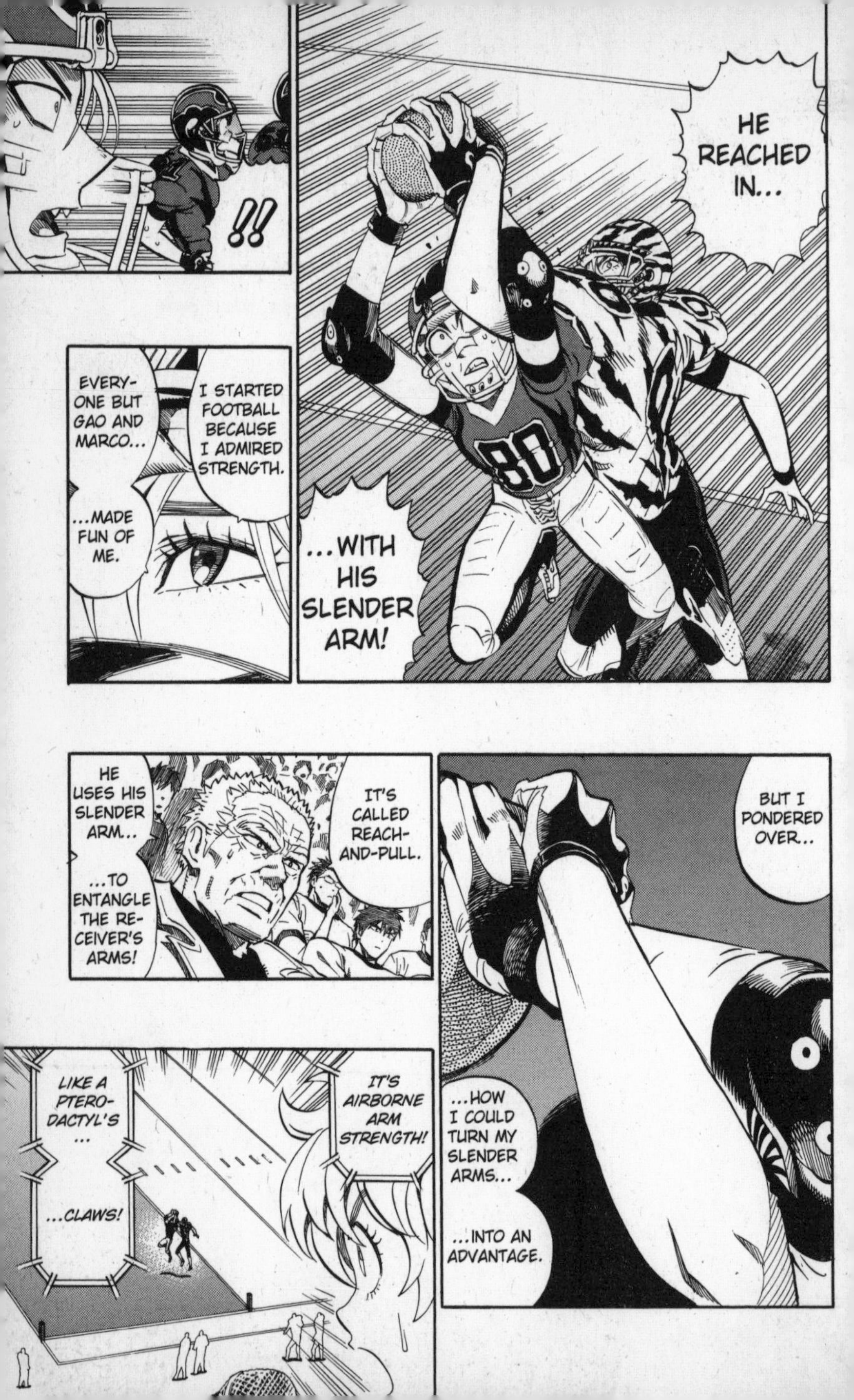
HE REACHED IN...
...WITH HIS SLENDER ARM!
!!
I STARTED FOOTBALL BECAUSE I ADMIRED STRENGTH.
EVERY-ONE BUT GAO AND MARCO...
...MADE FUN OF ME.
BUT I PONDERED OVER...
...HOW I COULD TURN MY SLENDER ARMS...
...INTO AN ADVANTAGE.
IT'S CALLED REACH-AND-PULL.
HE USES HIS SLENDER ARM...
...TO ENTANGLE THE RE-CEIVER'S ARMS!
IT'S AIRBORNE ARM STRENGTH!
LIKE A PTERO-DACTYL'S...
...CLAWS!

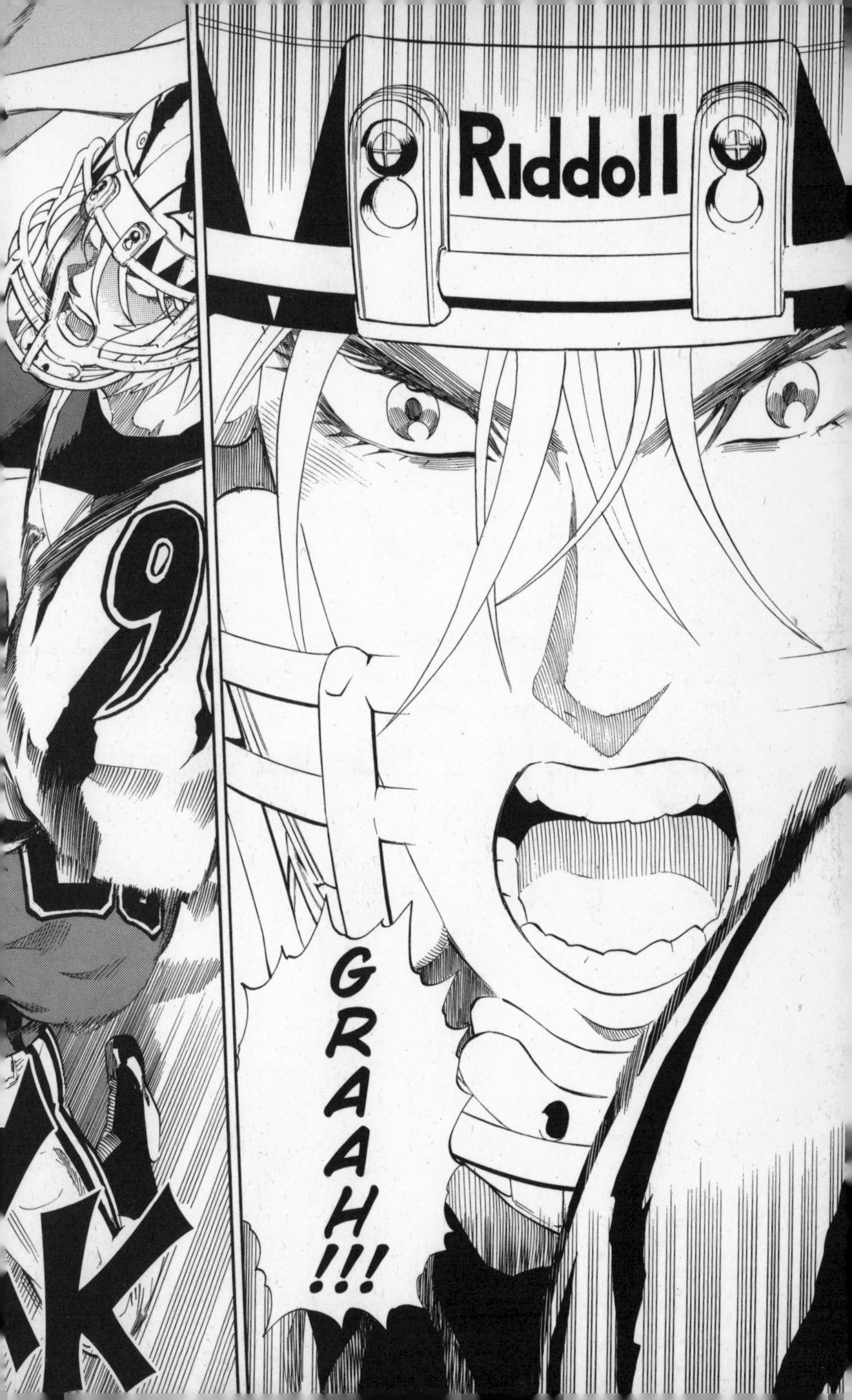
Riddoll
GRAAH!!!

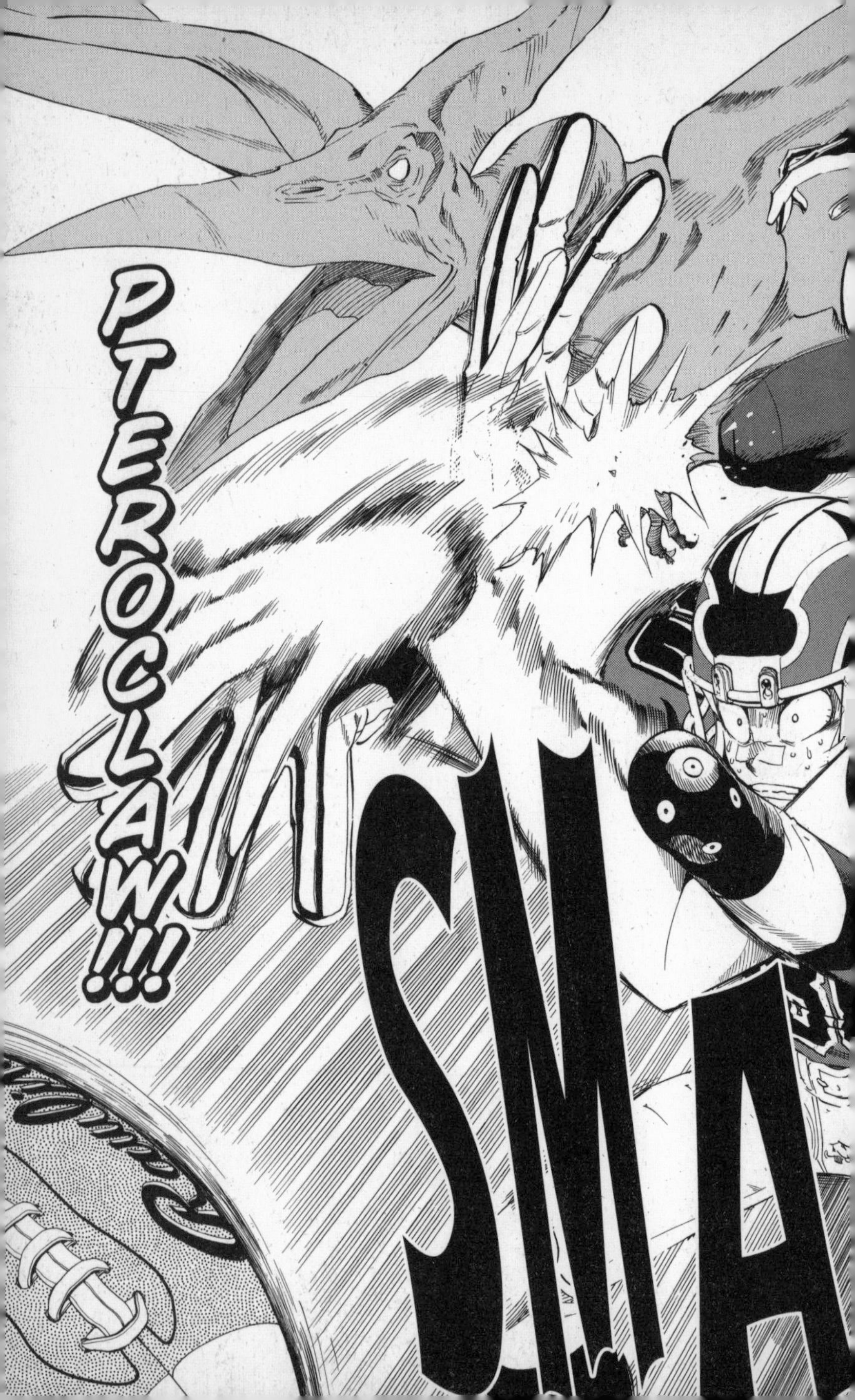
PTEROCLAW!!!
SMA

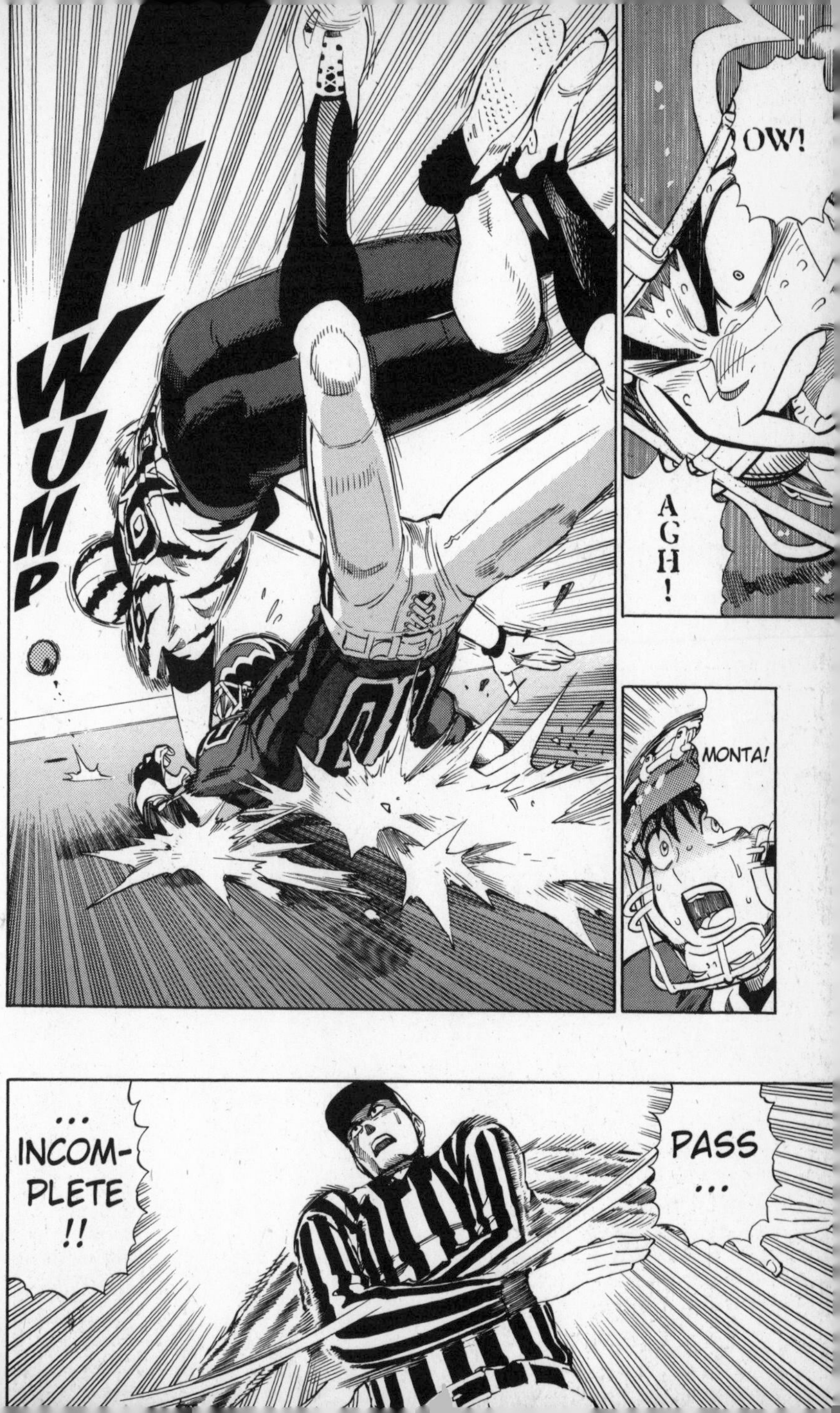
OW!
AGH!
MONTA!
WUMP
PASS ...
... INCOMPLETE !!

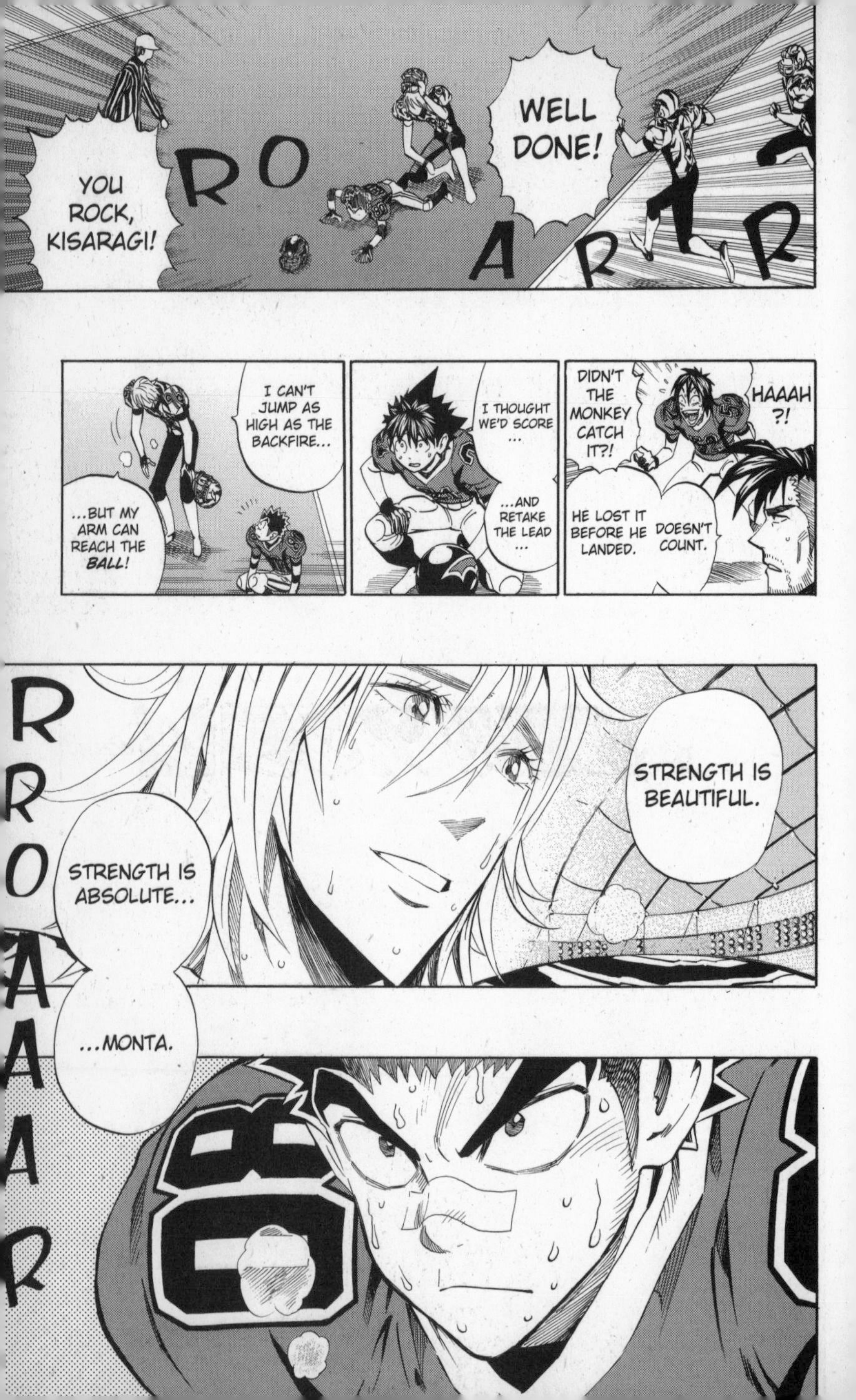
WELL DONE!
YOU ROCK, KISARAGI!
ROARR
HAAAH ?!
DIDN'T THE MONKEY CATCH IT?!
HE LOST IT BEFORE HE LANDED. DOESN'T COUNT.
I THOUGHT WE'D SCORE ...
...AND RETAKE THE LEAD ...
I CAN'T JUMP AS HIGH AS THE BACKFIRE...
...BUT MY ARM CAN REACH THE BALL!
STRENGTH IS BEAUTIFUL.
STRENGTH IS ABSOLUTE...
...MONTA.
RROAAAAR

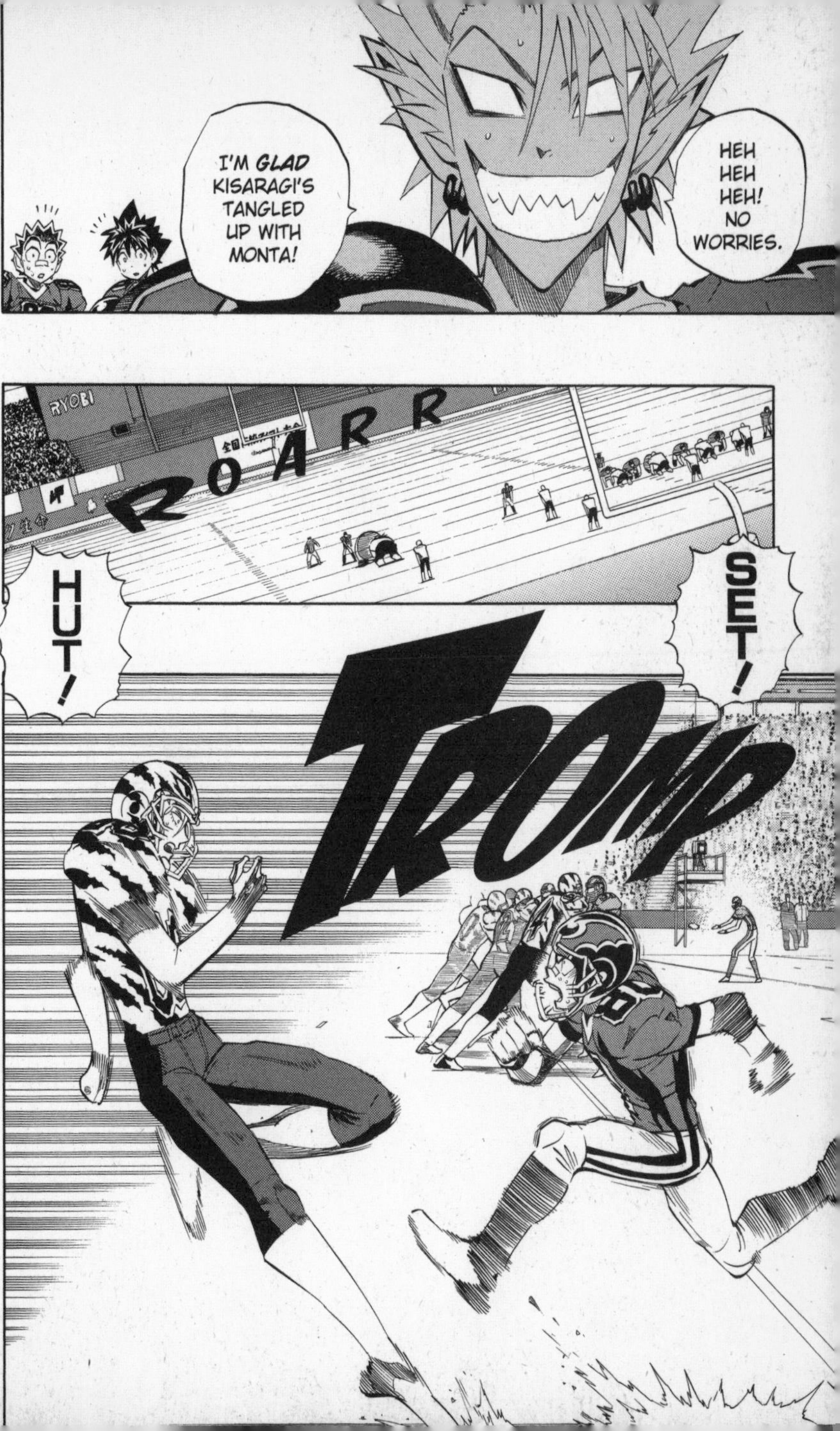
HEH HEH HEH! NO WORRIES.
I'M GLAD KISARAGI'S TANGLED UP WITH MONTA!
RYOBI
ROARR
SET!
HUT!
TROMP

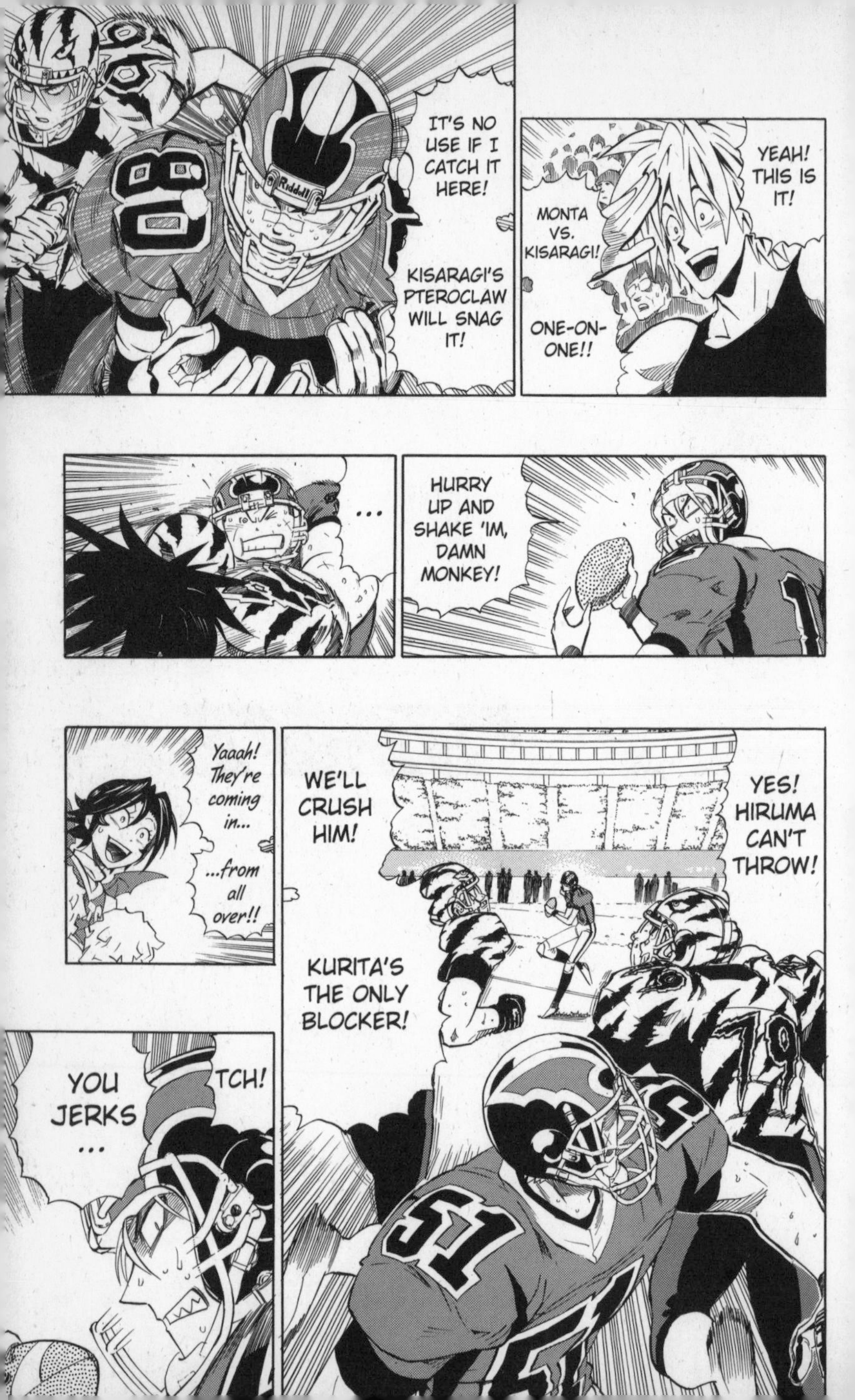
YEAH! THIS IS IT!
MONTA VS. KISARAGI!
ONE-ON-ONE!!
IT'S NO USE IF I CATCH IT HERE!
KISARAGI'S PTEROCLAW WILL SNAG IT!
HURRY UP AND SHAKE 'IM, DAMN MONKEY!
...
YES! HIRUMA CAN'T THROW!
WE'LL CRUSH HIM!
KURITA'S THE ONLY BLOCKER!
Yaaah! They're coming in...
...from all over!!
TCH!
YOU JERKS...

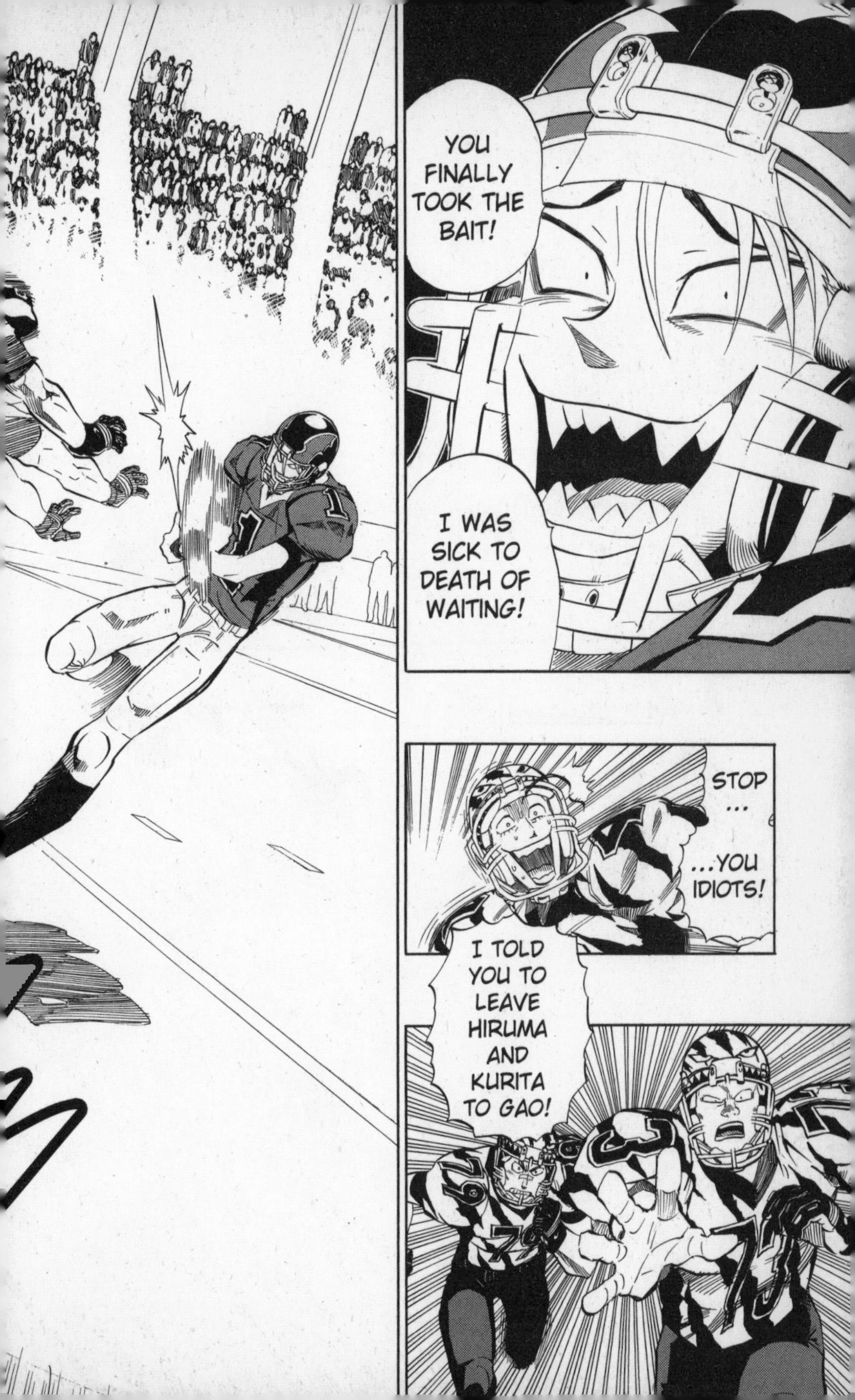
YOU FINALLY TOOK THE BAIT!
I WAS SICK TO DEATH OF WAITING!
STOP ...
...YOU IDIOTS!
I TOLD YOU TO LEAVE HIRUMA AND KURITA TO GAO!

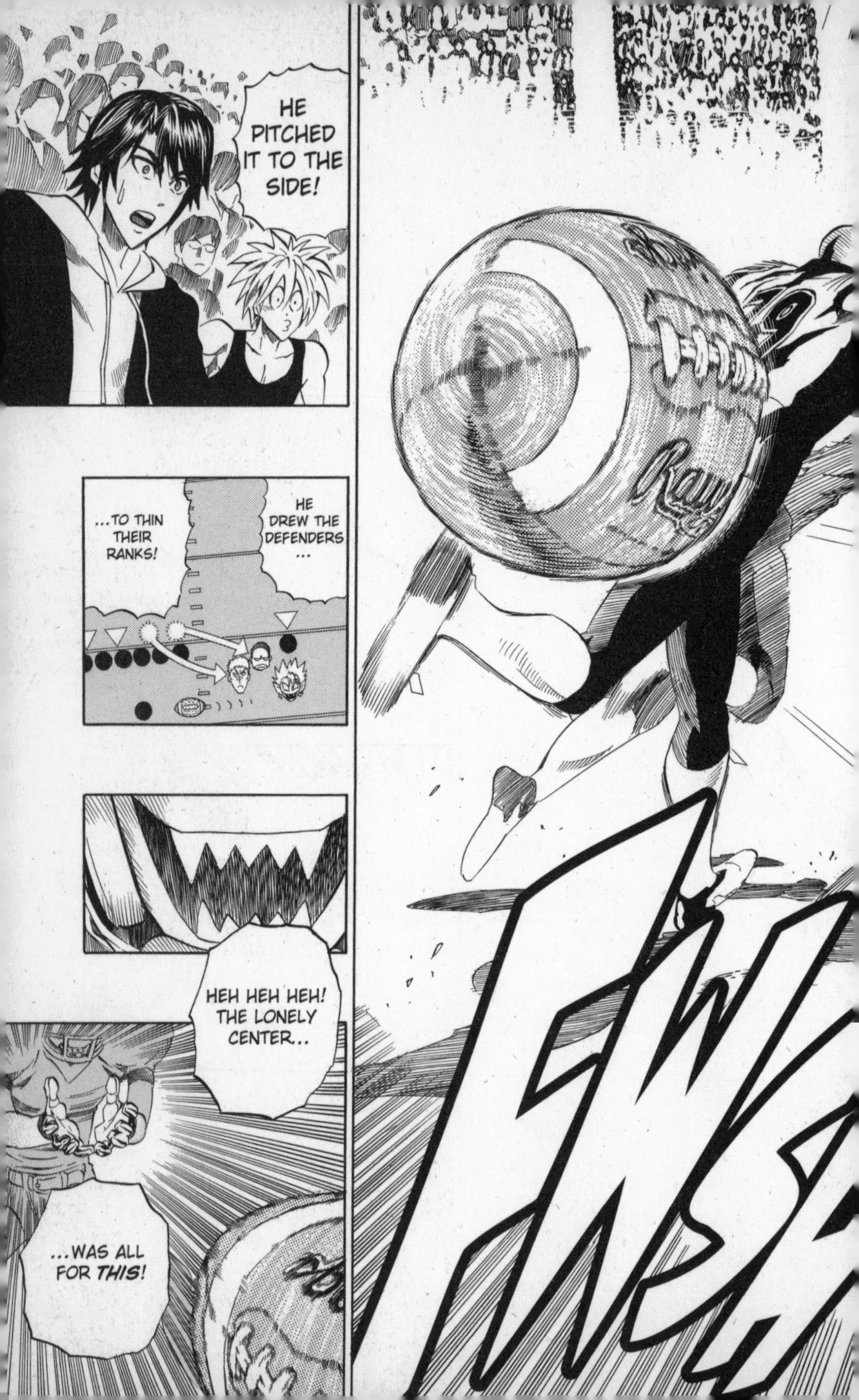
HE PITCHED IT TO THE SIDE!
HE DREW THE DEFENDERS...
...TO THIN THEIR RANKS!
HEH HEH HEH! THE LONELY CENTER...
...WAS ALL FOR *THIS*!

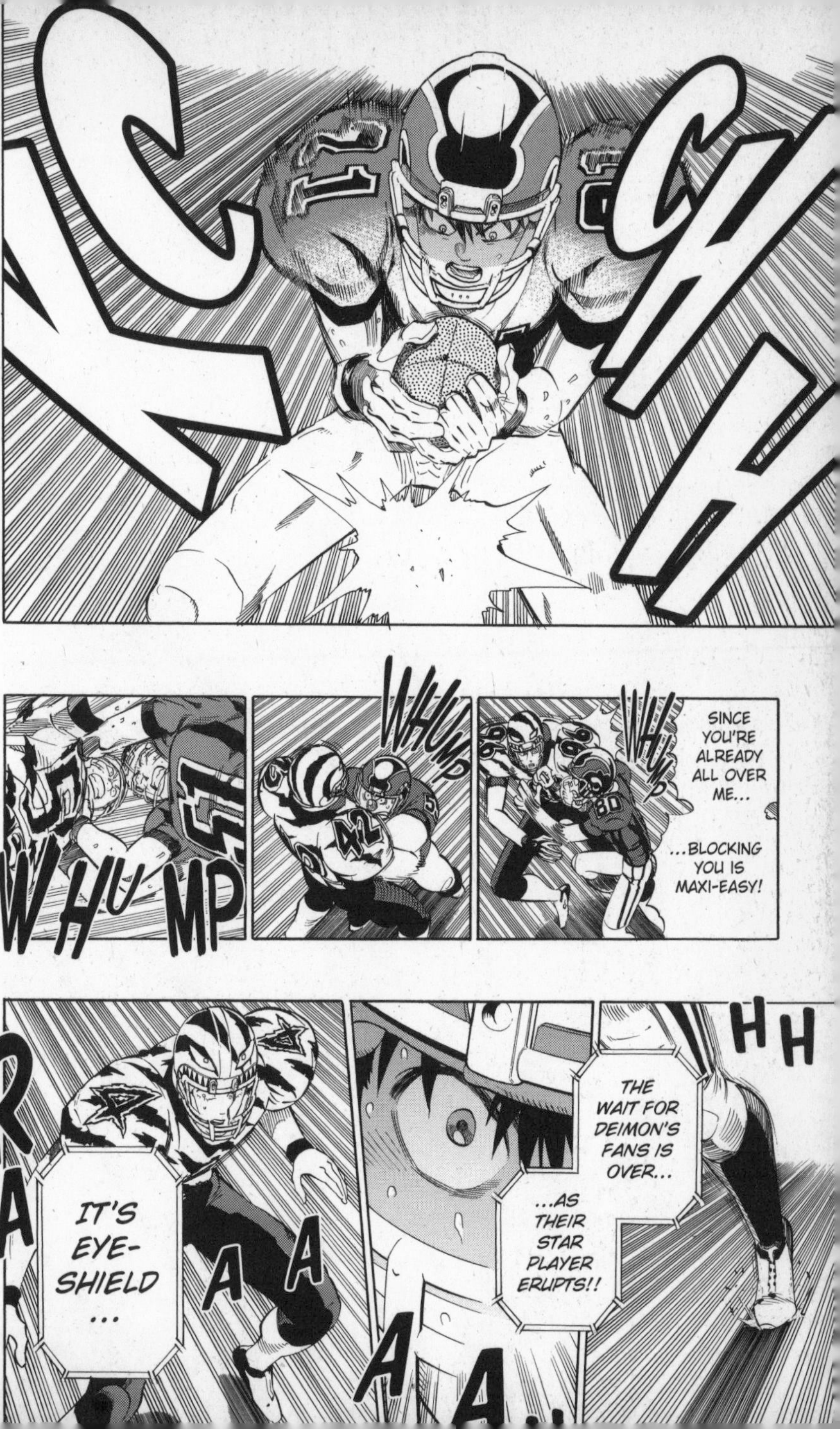
WHUMP
SINCE YOU'RE ALREADY ALL OVER ME...
...BLOCKING YOU IS MAXI-EASY!
WHUMP
WHUMP
HH
THE WAIT FOR DEIMON'S FANS IS OVER...
...AS THEIR STAR PLAYER ERUPTS!!
IT'S EYE-SHIELD...
RAAAAA..

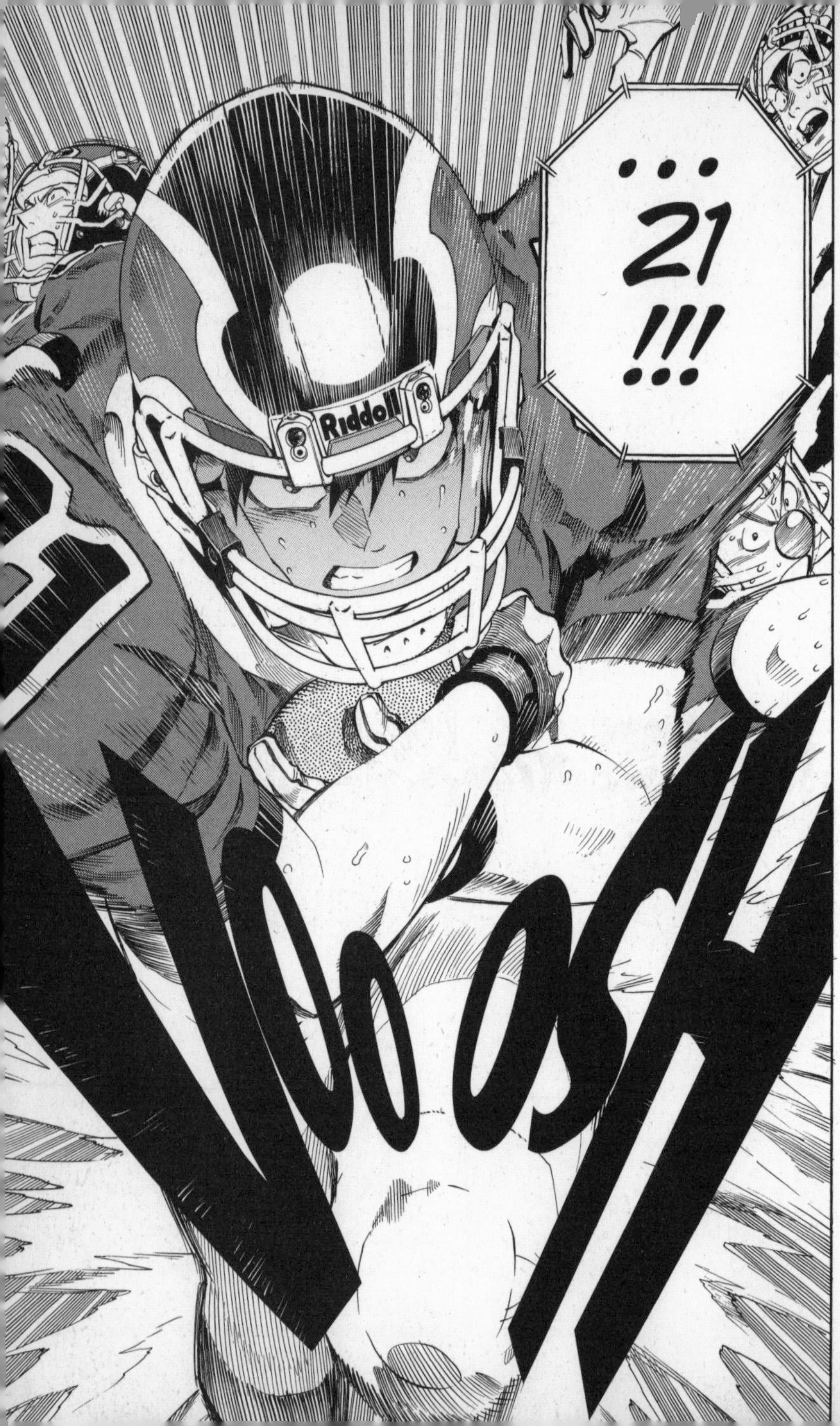
...21!!!
WHOOSH

DEIMON & HAKUSHU  CELL PHONE
WALLPAPER CHECK!

  Mamori & Suzuna

 YEAH, BABY!!
THE REST OF YOU CHUMPS SHOULD LEARN FROM THIS! YA-HA!!

 **Maruko**

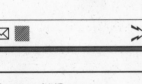 HUH?
IN THIS PICTURE IT LOOKS LIKE MARUKO AND MARCO WERE STILL GETTING ALONG.

  YEAH. THINGS CHANGE.

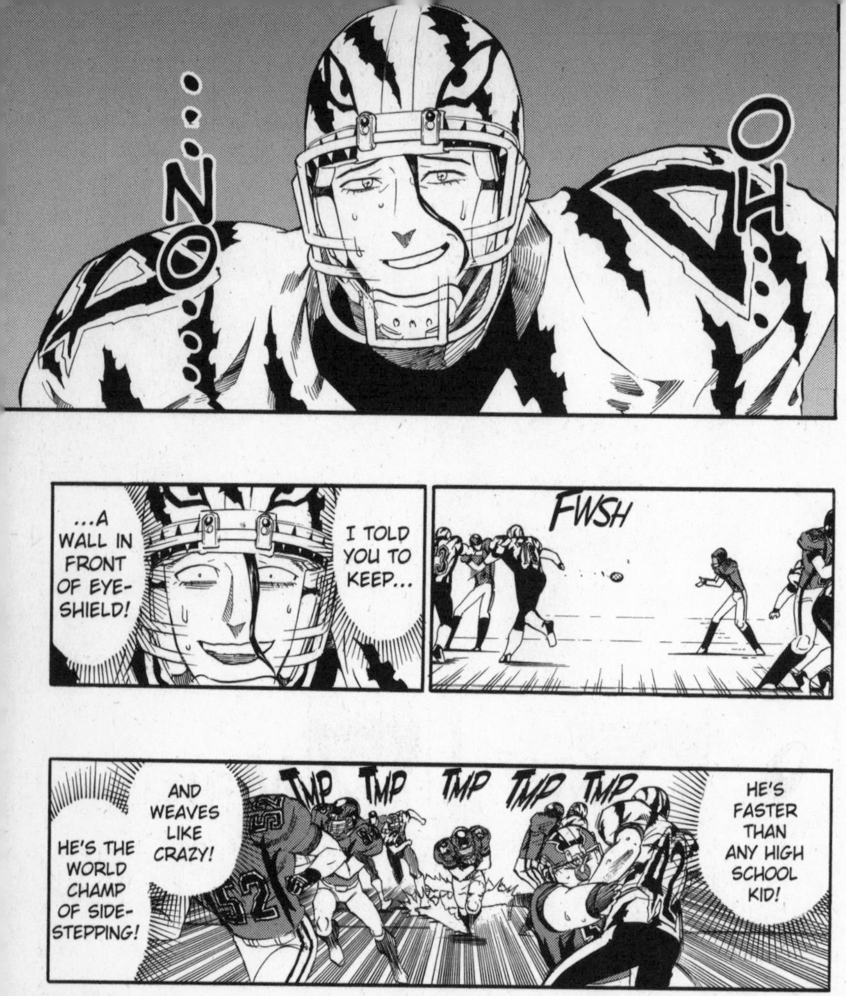
OH...
NO...
FWSH
I TOLD YOU TO KEEP...
...A WALL IN FRONT OF EYE-SHIELD!
HE'S FASTER THAN ANY HIGH SCHOOL KID!
TMP TMP TMP TMP TMP
AND WEAVES LIKE CRAZY!
HE'S THE WORLD CHAMP OF SIDE-STEPPING!

Chapter 256 The Cunning Hunter

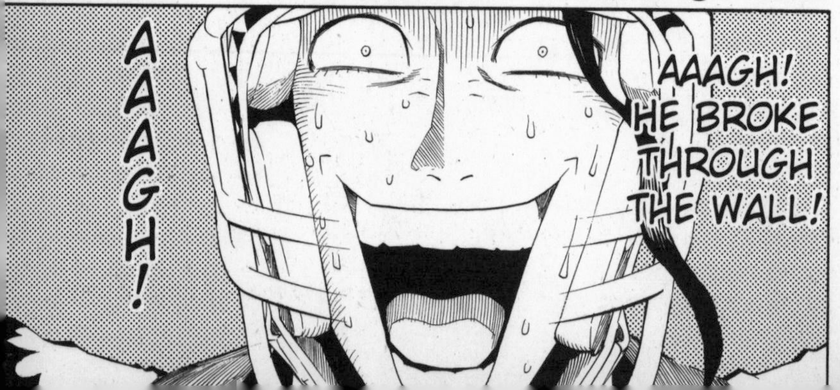
AAAGH! HE BROKE THROUGH THE WALL!
AAAAGH!

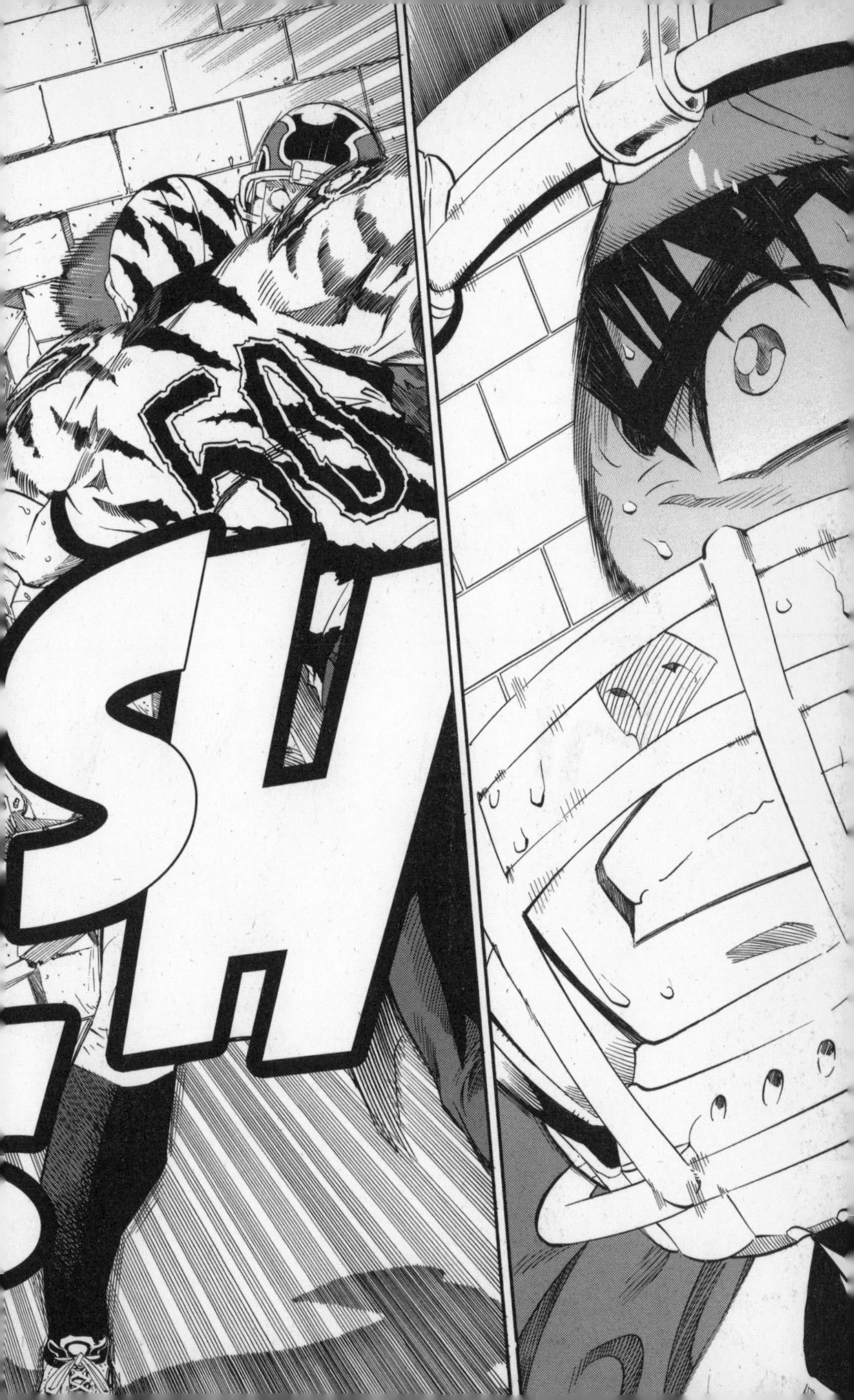
SH

Chapter 256
The Cunning Hunter

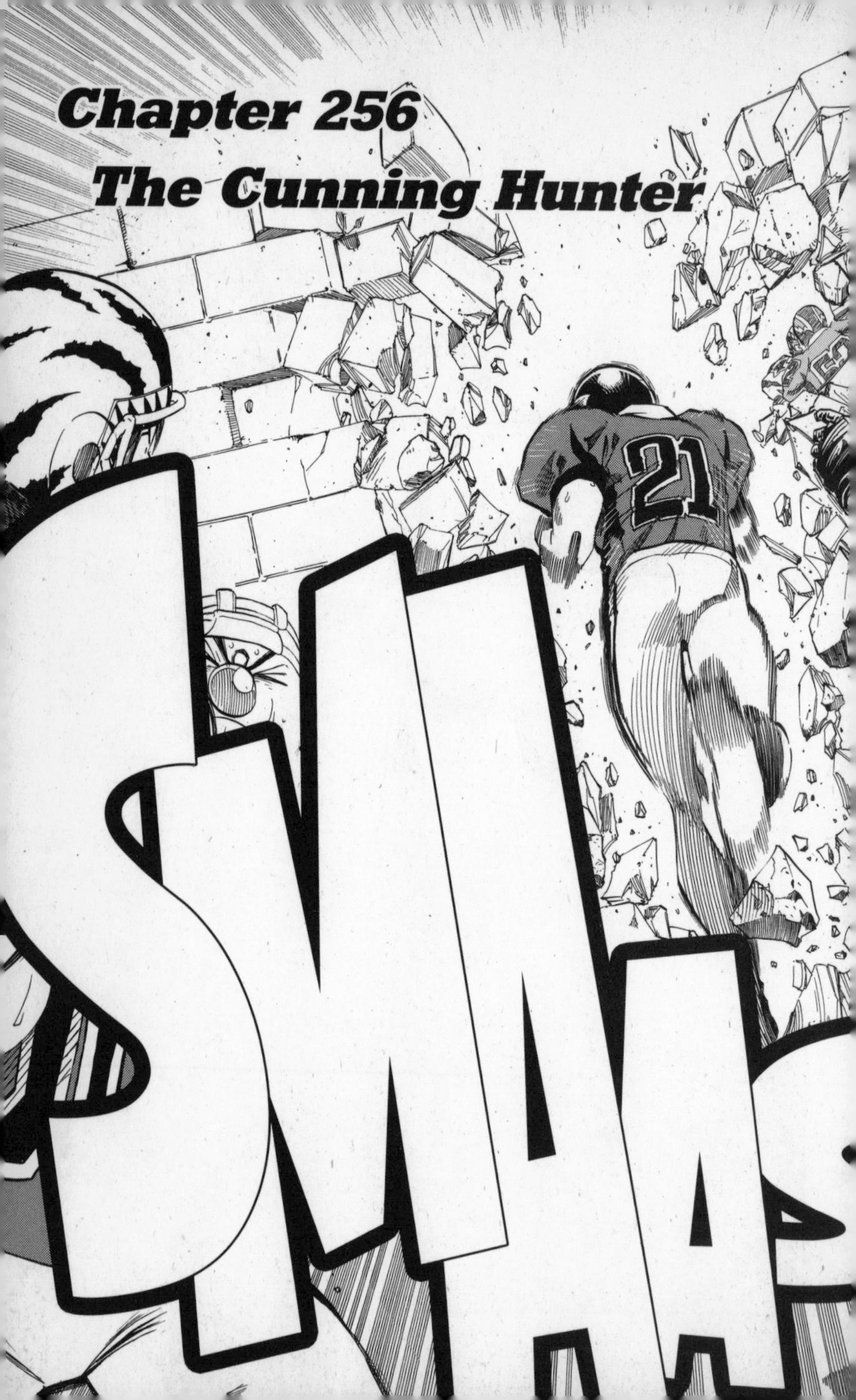
SMAS

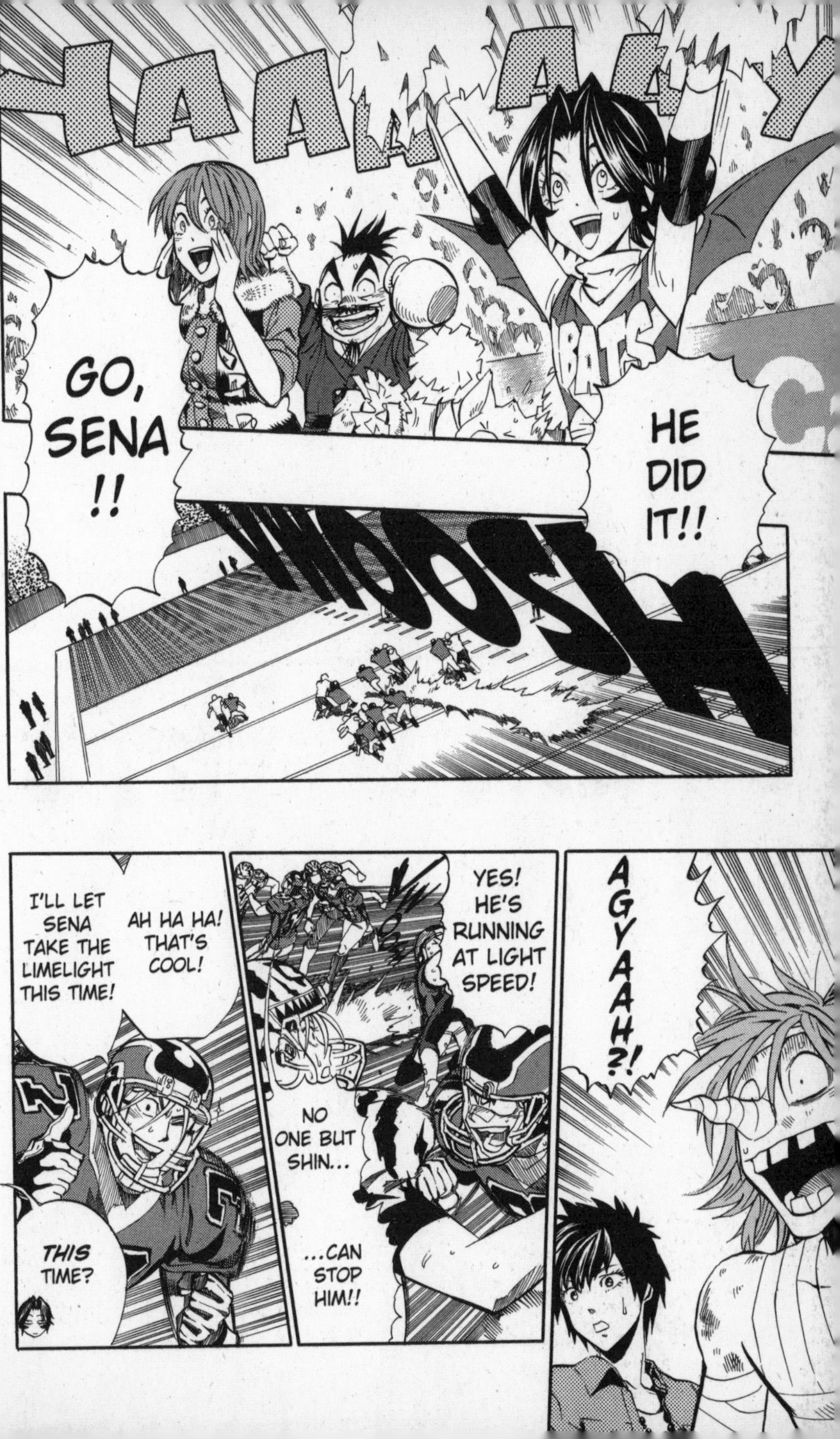
YAAAAAY
HE DID IT!!
GO, SENA!!
WHOOSH
AGYAAAH?!
YES! HE'S RUNNING AT LIGHT SPEED!
NO ONE BUT SHIN...
...CAN STOP HIM!!
AH HA HA! THAT'S COOL!
I'LL LET SENA TAKE THE LIMELIGHT THIS TIME!
THIS TIME?

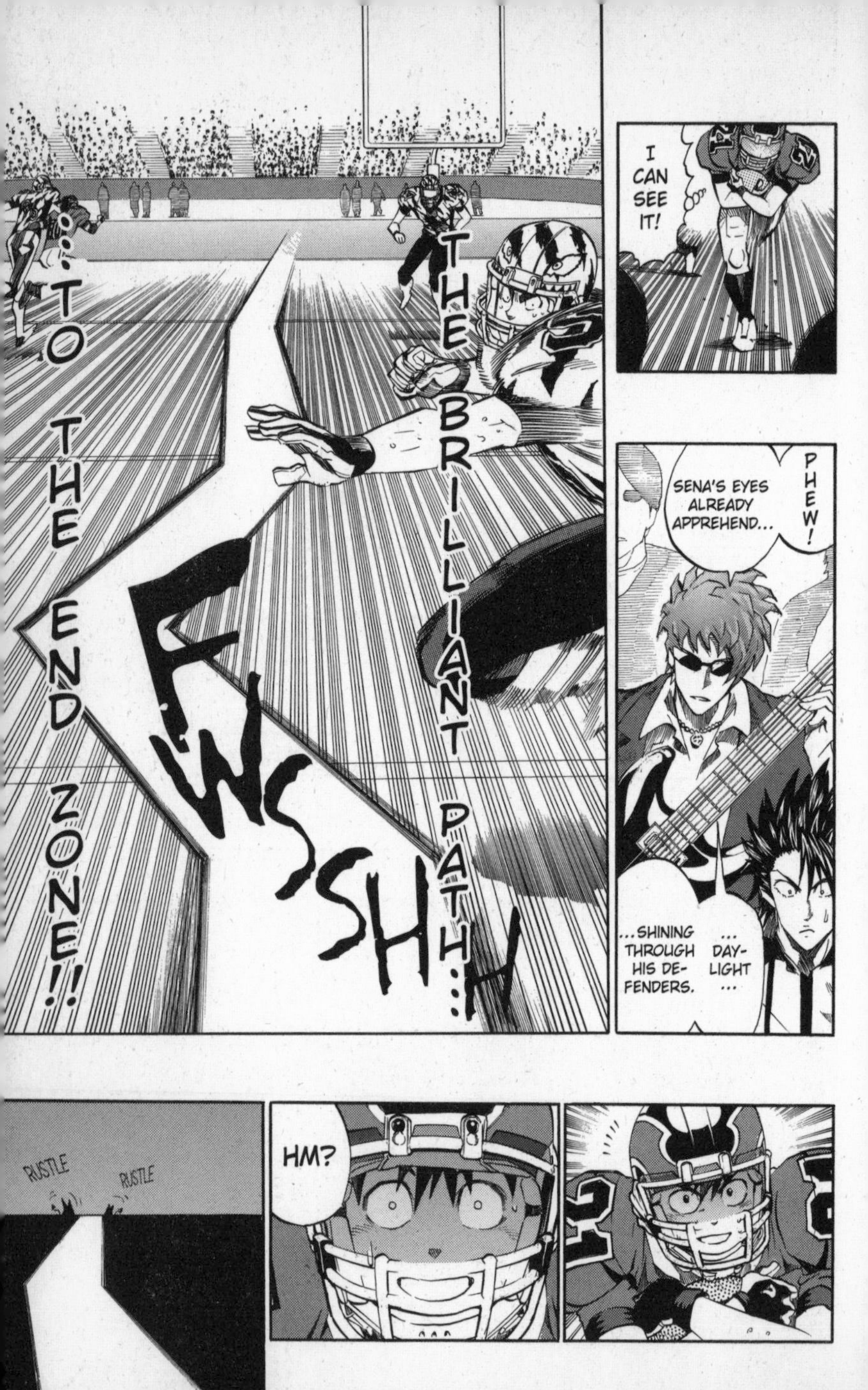
I CAN SEE IT!
PHEW!
SENA'S EYES ALREADY APPREHEND...
...DAY-LIGHT...
...SHINING THROUGH HIS DE-FENDERS.
THE BRILLIANT PATH...
FWSSHH
...TO THE END ZONE!!
HM?
RUSTLE
RUSTLE

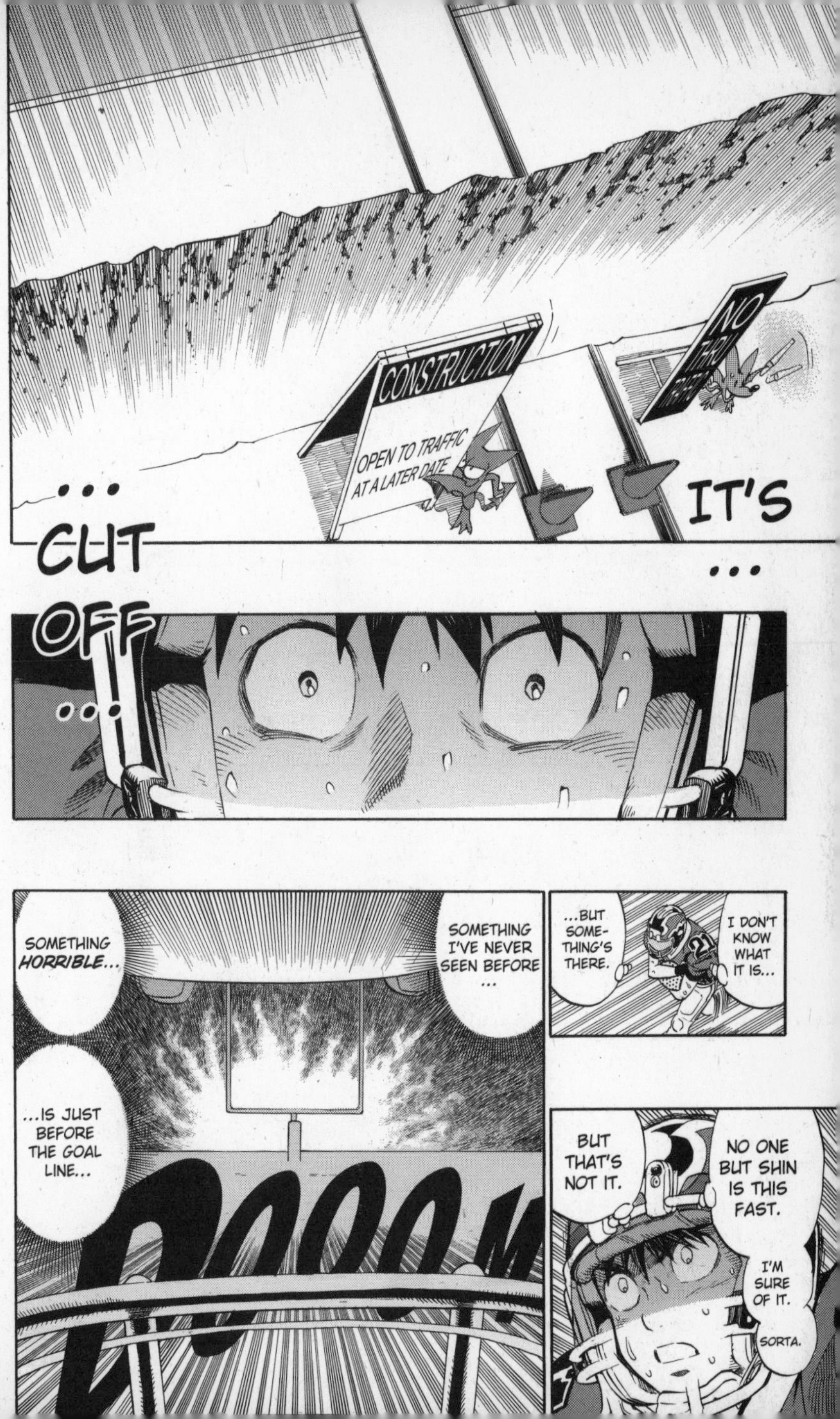
IT'S ...
... CUT OFF ...
CONSTRUCTION
OPEN TO TRAFFIC AT A LATER DATE
I DON'T KNOW WHAT IT IS...
...BUT SOME-THING'S THERE.
NO ONE BUT SHIN IS THIS FAST.
BUT THAT'S NOT IT.
I'M SURE OF IT.
SORTA.
SOMETHING I'VE NEVER SEEN BEFORE ...
SOMETHING *HORRIBLE*...
...IS JUST BEFORE THE GOAL LINE...
DOOOM

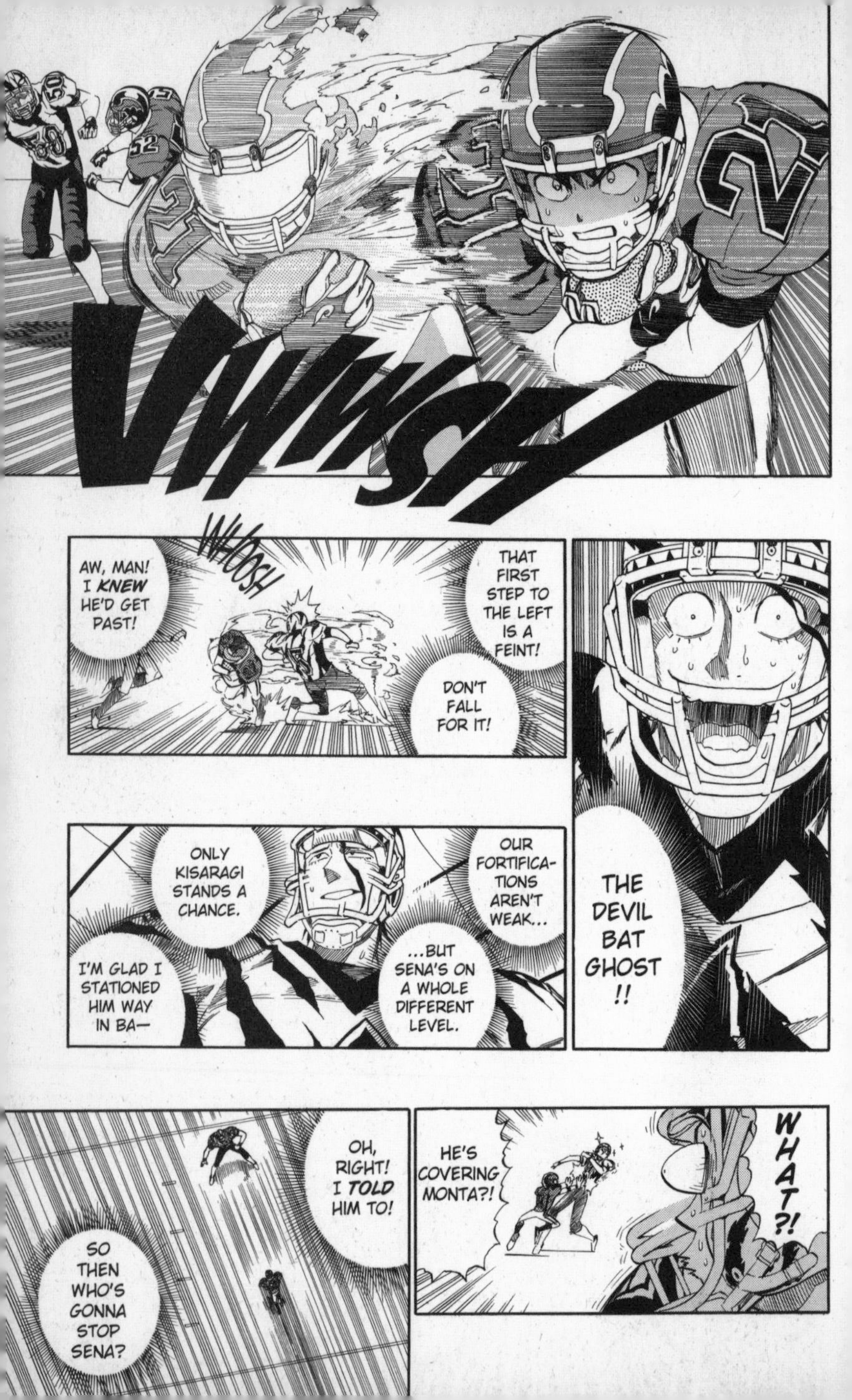
VWISH
THE DEVIL BAT GHOST !!
THAT FIRST STEP TO THE LEFT IS A FEINT!
DON'T FALL FOR IT!
WHOOSH
AW, MAN! I *KNEW* HE'D GET PAST!
OUR FORTIFICATIONS AREN'T WEAK...
...BUT SENA'S ON A WHOLE DIFFERENT LEVEL.
ONLY KISARAGI STANDS A CHANCE.
I'M GLAD I STATIONED HIM WAY IN BA—
WHAT?!
HE'S COVERING MONTA?!
OH, RIGHT! I *TOLD* HIM TO!
SO THEN WHO'S GONNA STOP SENA?

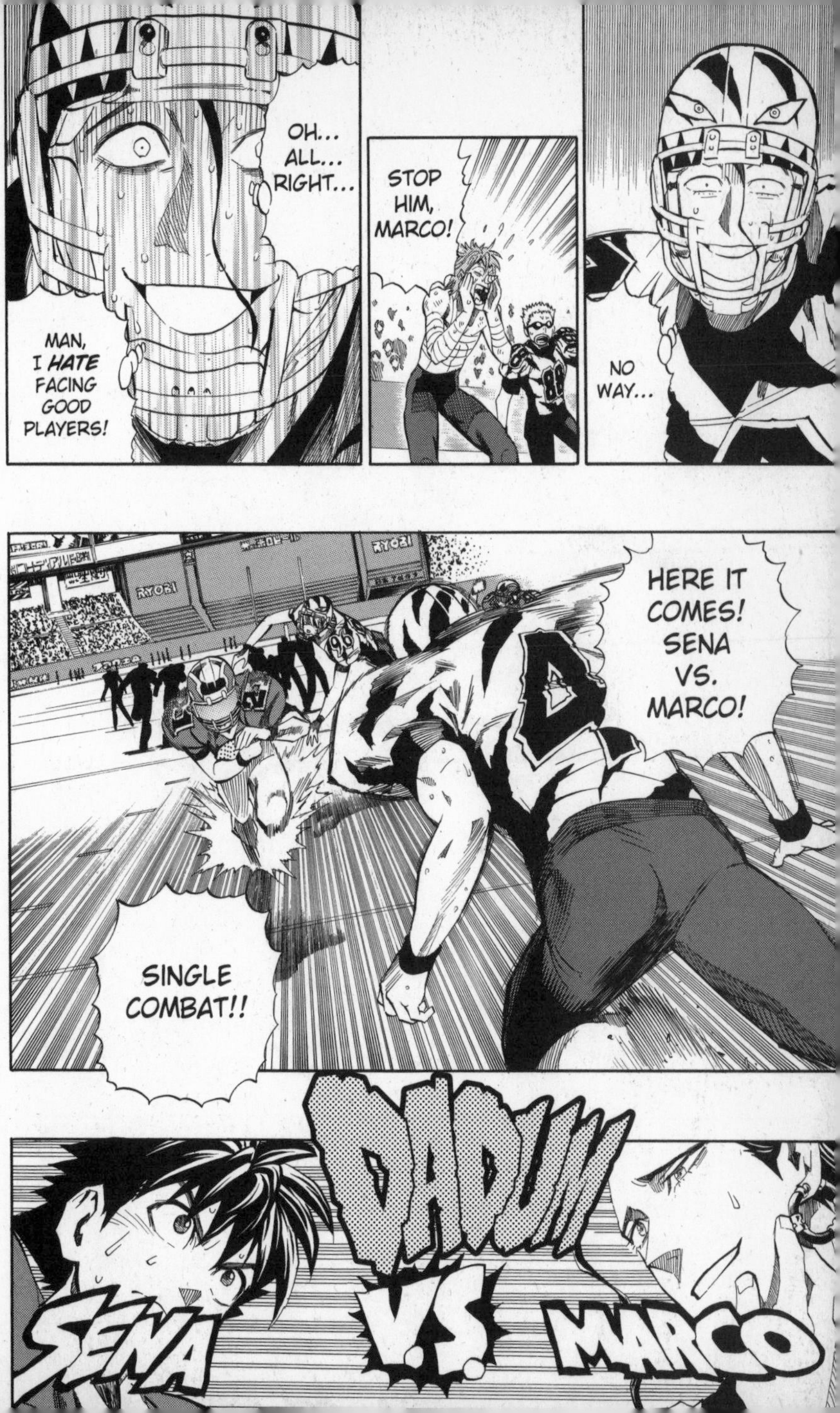
NO WAY...
STOP HIM, MARCO!
OH... ALL... RIGHT...
MAN, I HATE FACING GOOD PLAYERS!
HERE IT COMES! SENA VS. MARCO!
SINGLE COMBAT!!
DADUM
SENA V.S. MARCO

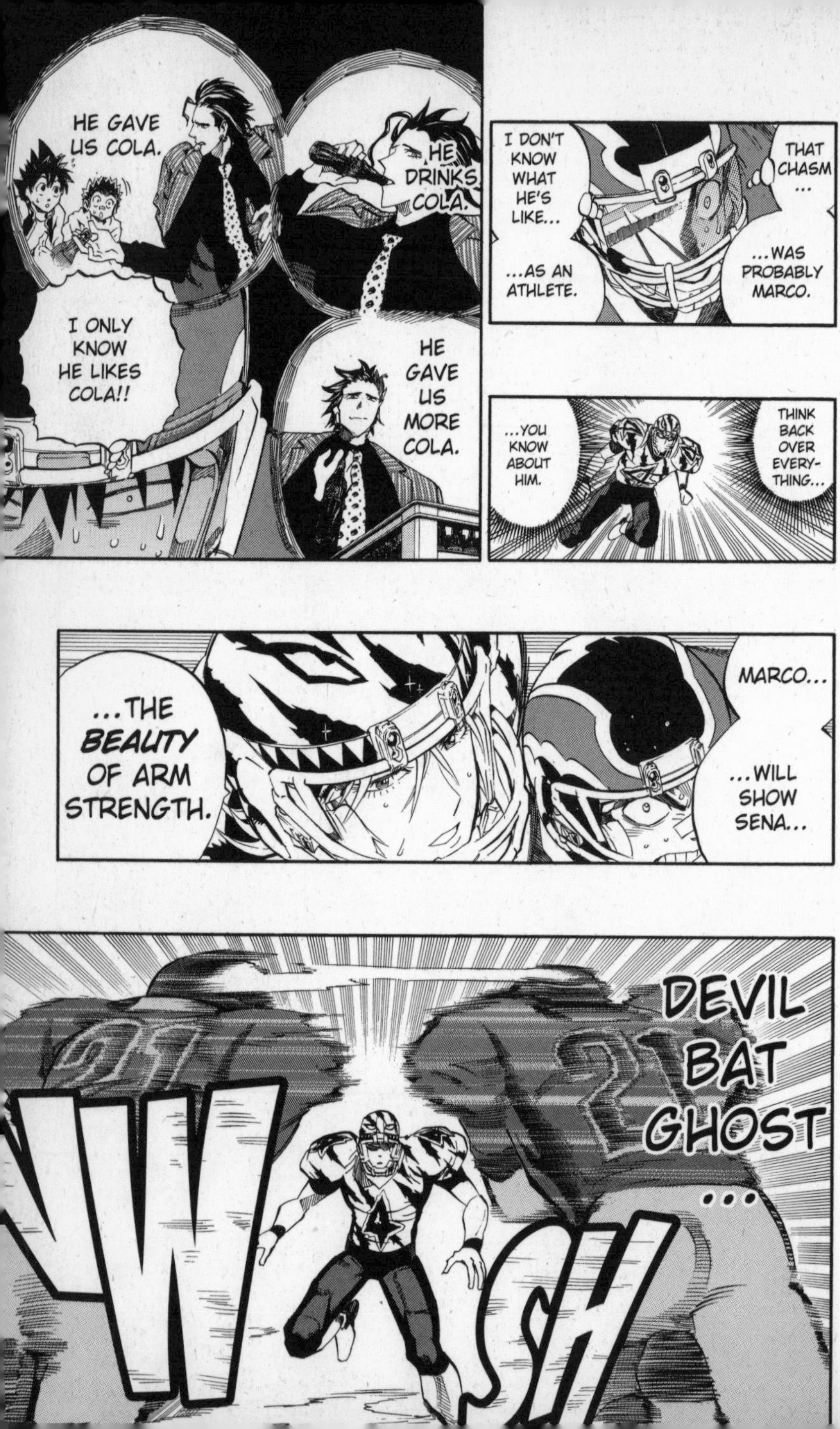
THAT CHASM...
...WAS PROBABLY MARCO.
I DON'T KNOW WHAT HE'S LIKE...
...AS AN ATHLETE.
THINK BACK OVER EVERYTHING...
...YOU KNOW ABOUT HIM.
HE DRINKS COLA.
HE GAVE US COLA.
HE GAVE US MORE COLA.
I ONLY KNOW HE LIKES COLA!!
MARCO...
...WILL SHOW SENA...
...THE BEAUTY OF ARM STRENGTH.
DEVIL BAT GHOST...
W
SH

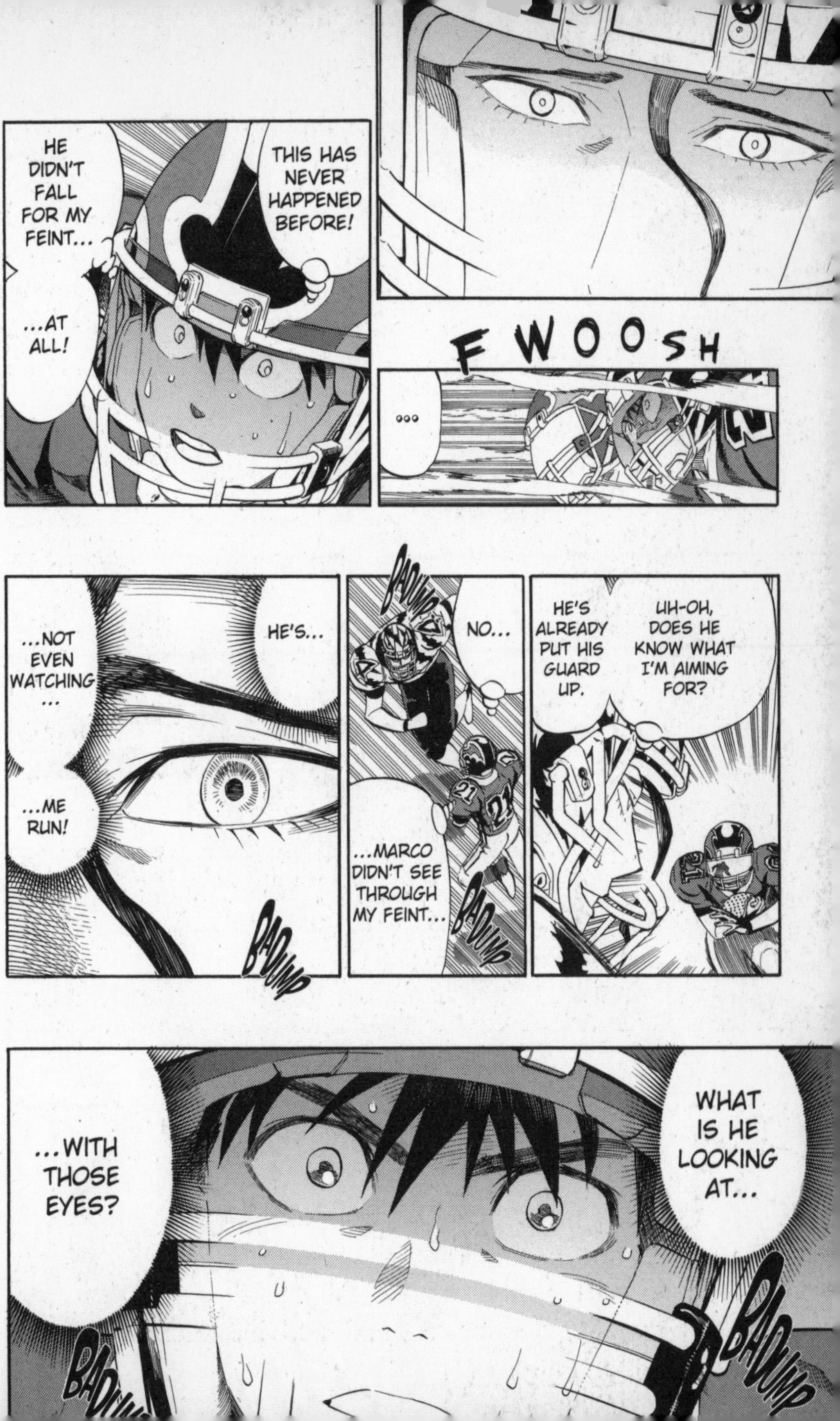
FWOOSH
...
THIS HAS NEVER HAPPENED BEFORE!
HE DIDN'T FALL FOR MY FEINT...
...AT ALL!
UH-OH, DOES HE KNOW WHAT I'M AIMING FOR?
HE'S ALREADY PUT HIS GUARD UP.
BADUMP
NO...
...MARCO DIDN'T SEE THROUGH MY FEINT...
BADUMP
HE'S...
...NOT EVEN WATCHING...
...ME RUN!
BADUMP
WHAT IS HE LOOKING AT...
...WITH THOSE EYES?
BADUMP
BADUMP

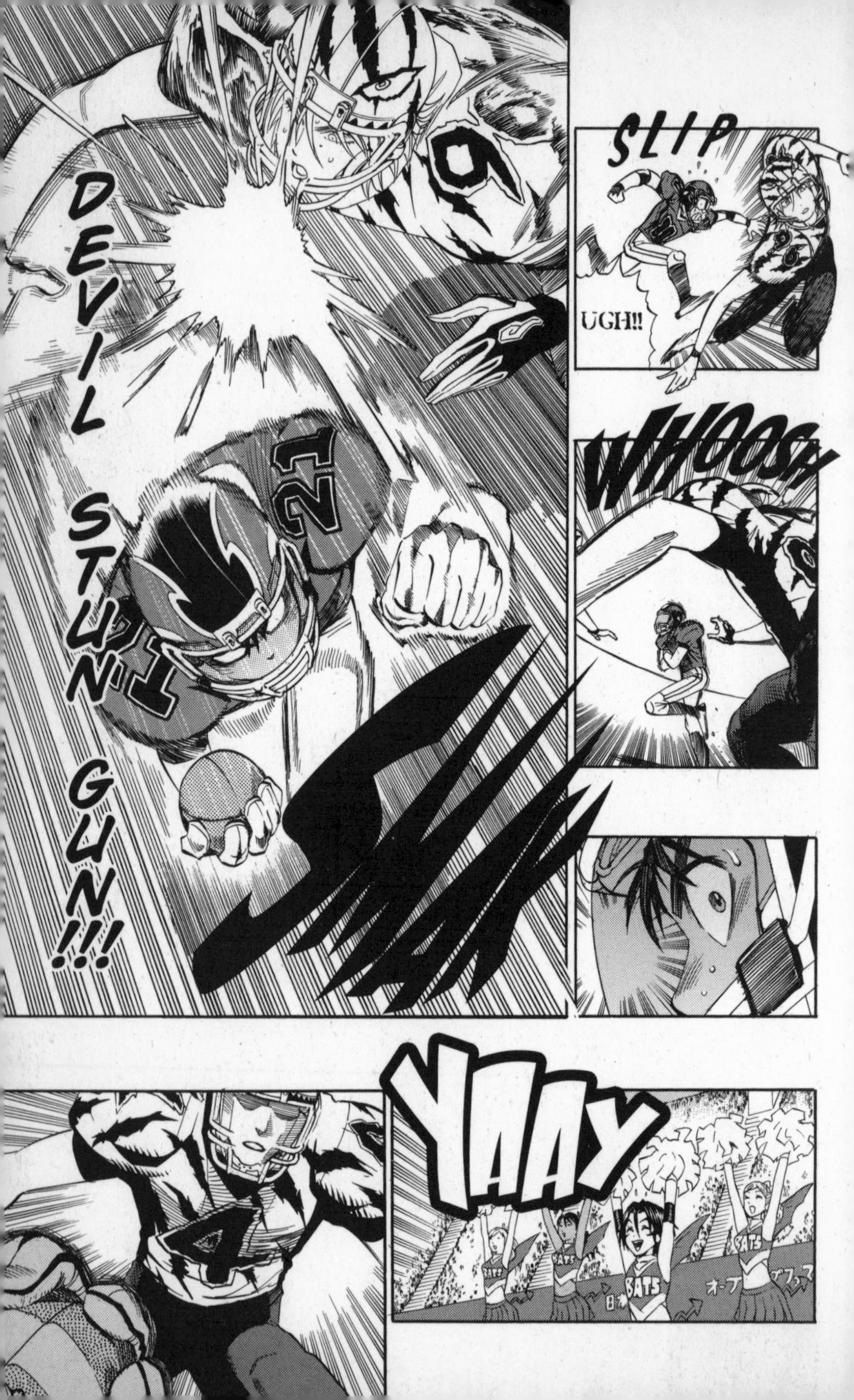
SLIP
UGH!!
WHOOSH
DEVIL STUN GUN!!!
YAAY

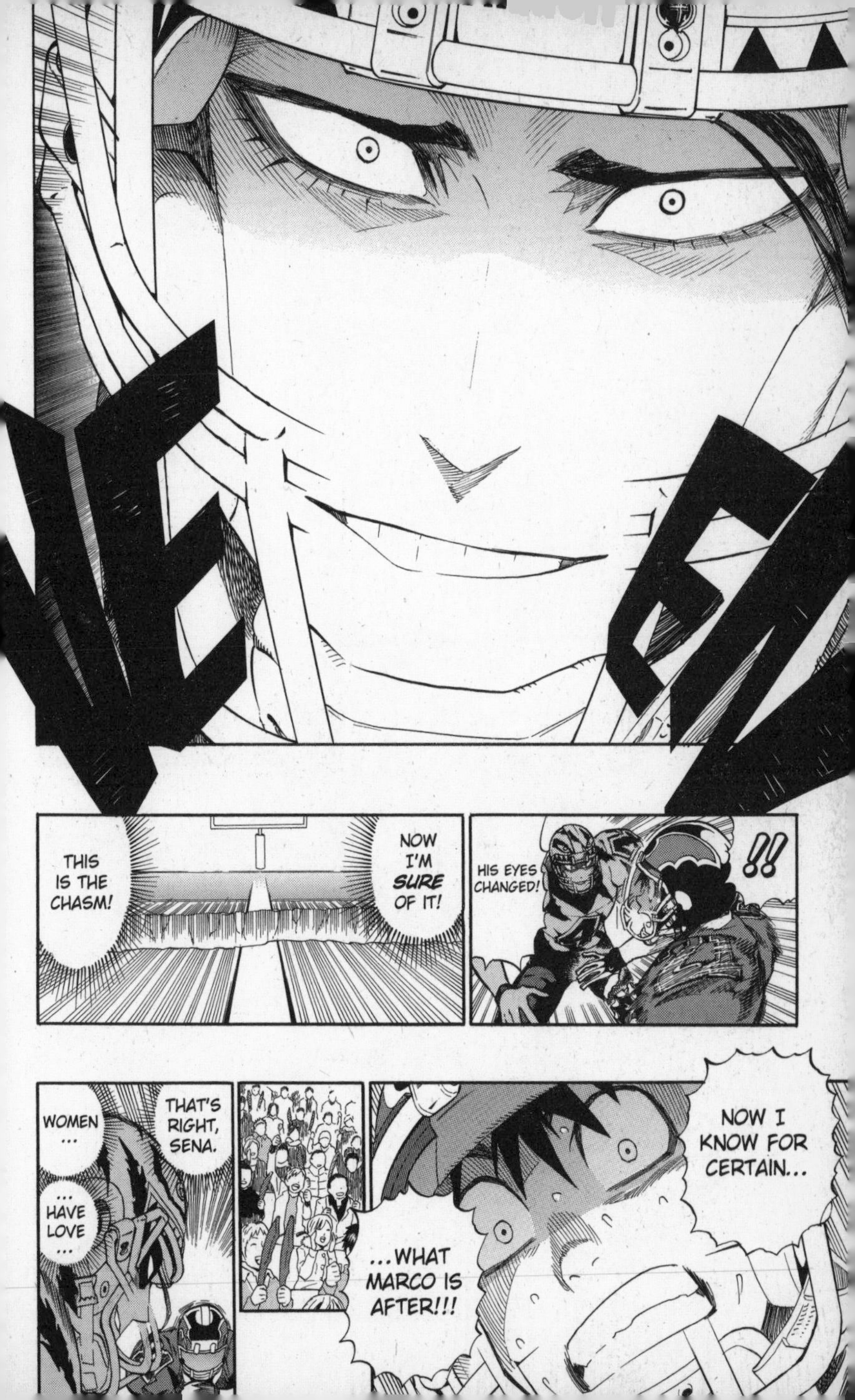
!!
HIS EYES CHANGED!
NOW I'M *SURE* OF IT!
THIS IS THE CHASM!
NOW I KNOW FOR CERTAIN...
...WHAT MARCO IS AFTER!!!
THAT'S RIGHT, SENA.
WOMEN ...
... HAVE LOVE ...

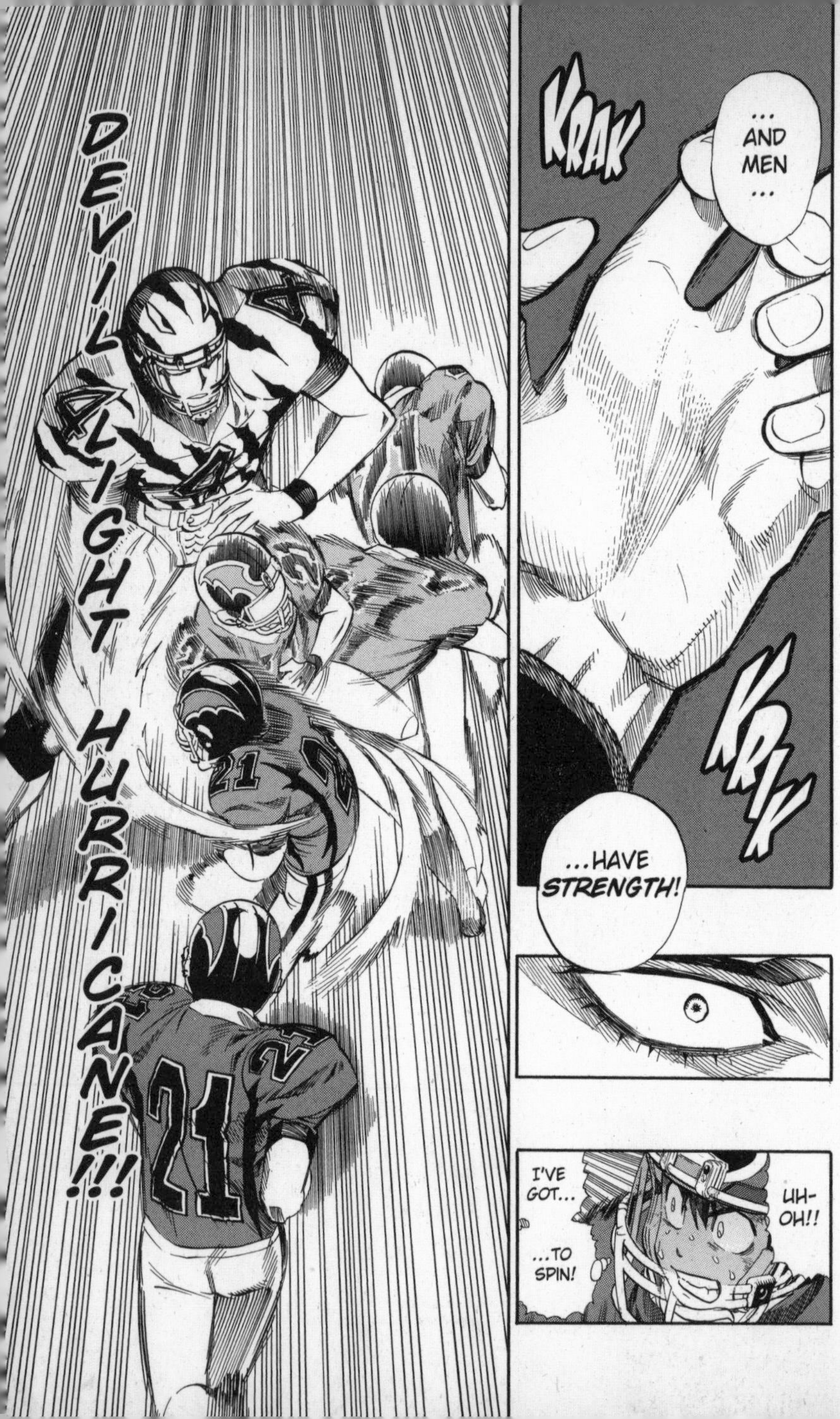
KRAK
... AND MEN ...
KRAK
...HAVE STRENGTH!
UH-OH!!
I'VE GOT...
...TO SPIN!
DEVIL LIGHT HURRICANE!!!

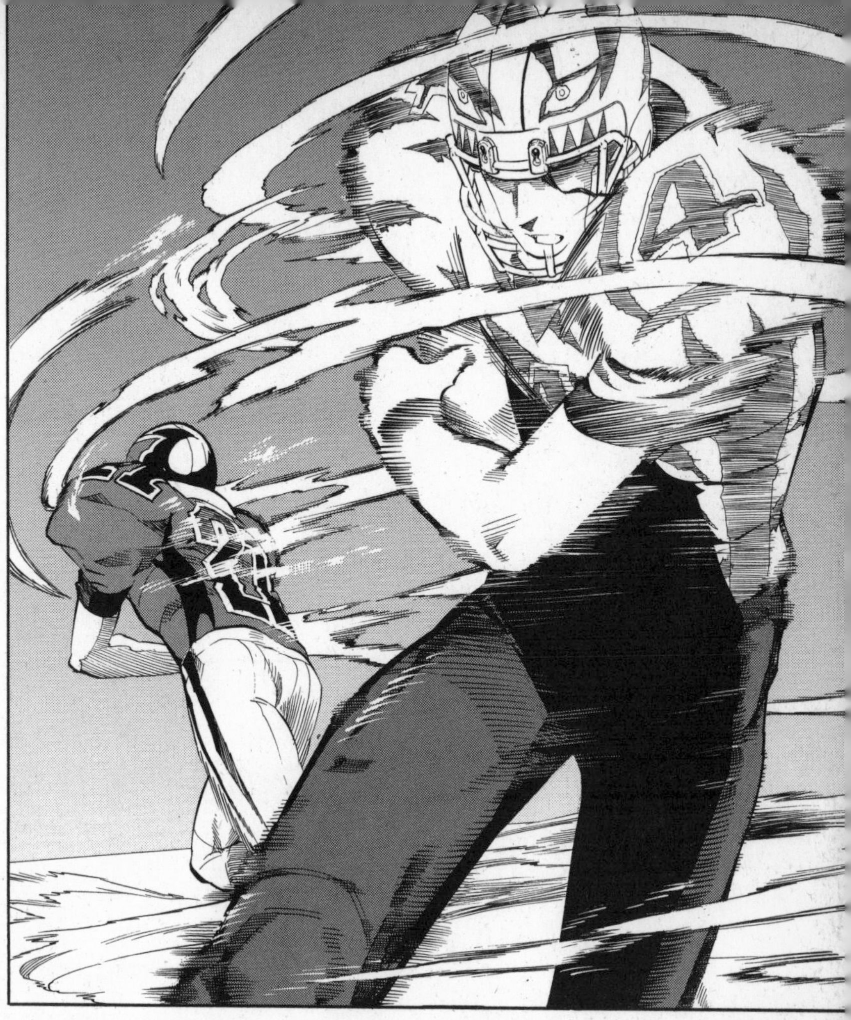
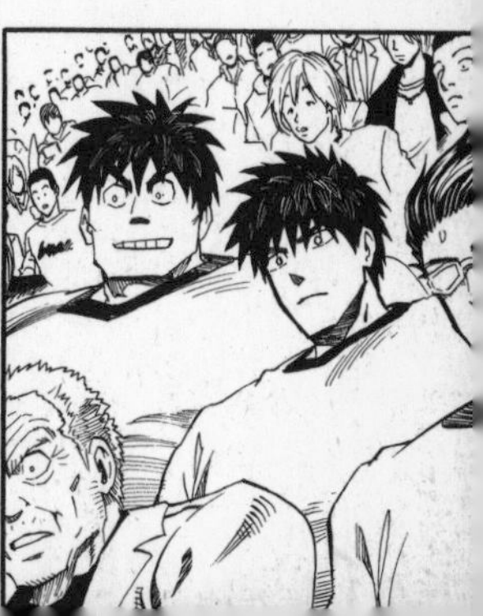
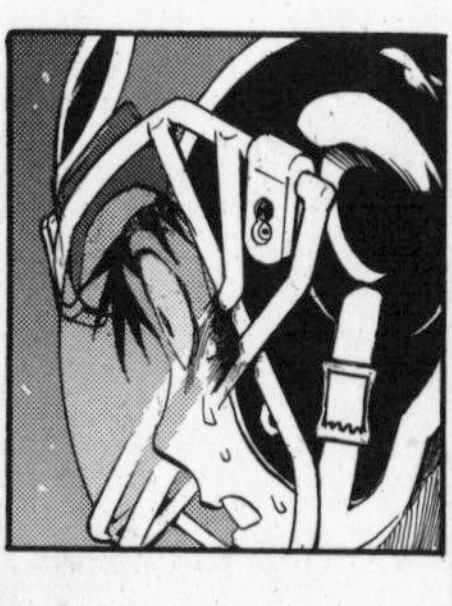
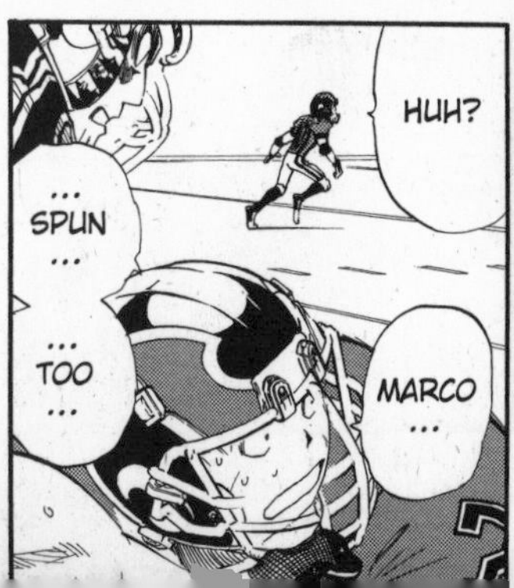
HUH?
... SPUN ...
... TOO ...
MARCO ...

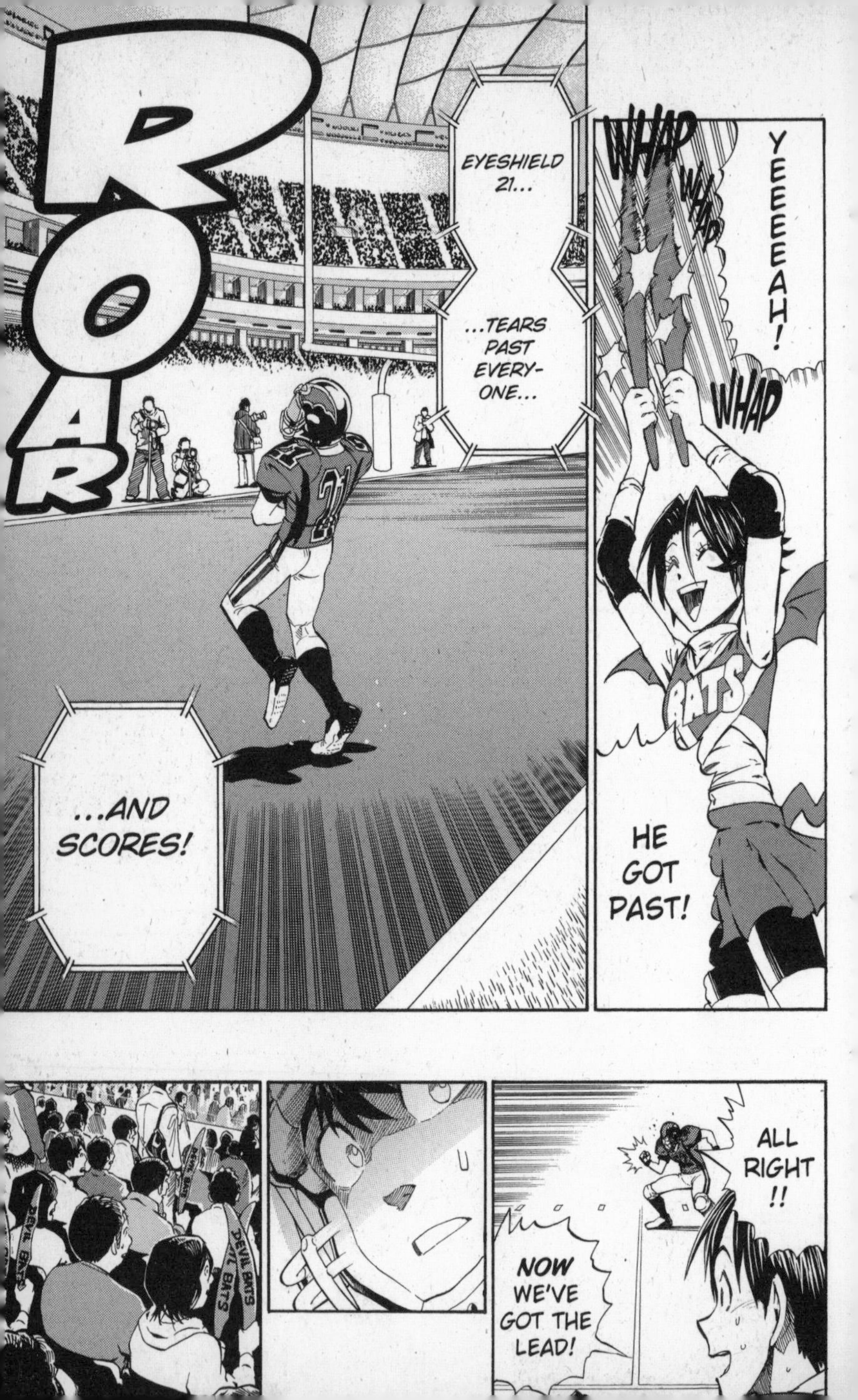
YEEEEAH!
WHAP WHAP WHAP
WHAP
HE GOT PAST!
EYESHIELD 21...
...TEARS PAST EVERY-ONE...
ROAR
...AND SCORES!
ALL RIGHT!!
NOW WE'VE GOT THE LEAD!
DEVIL BATS
DEVIL BATS

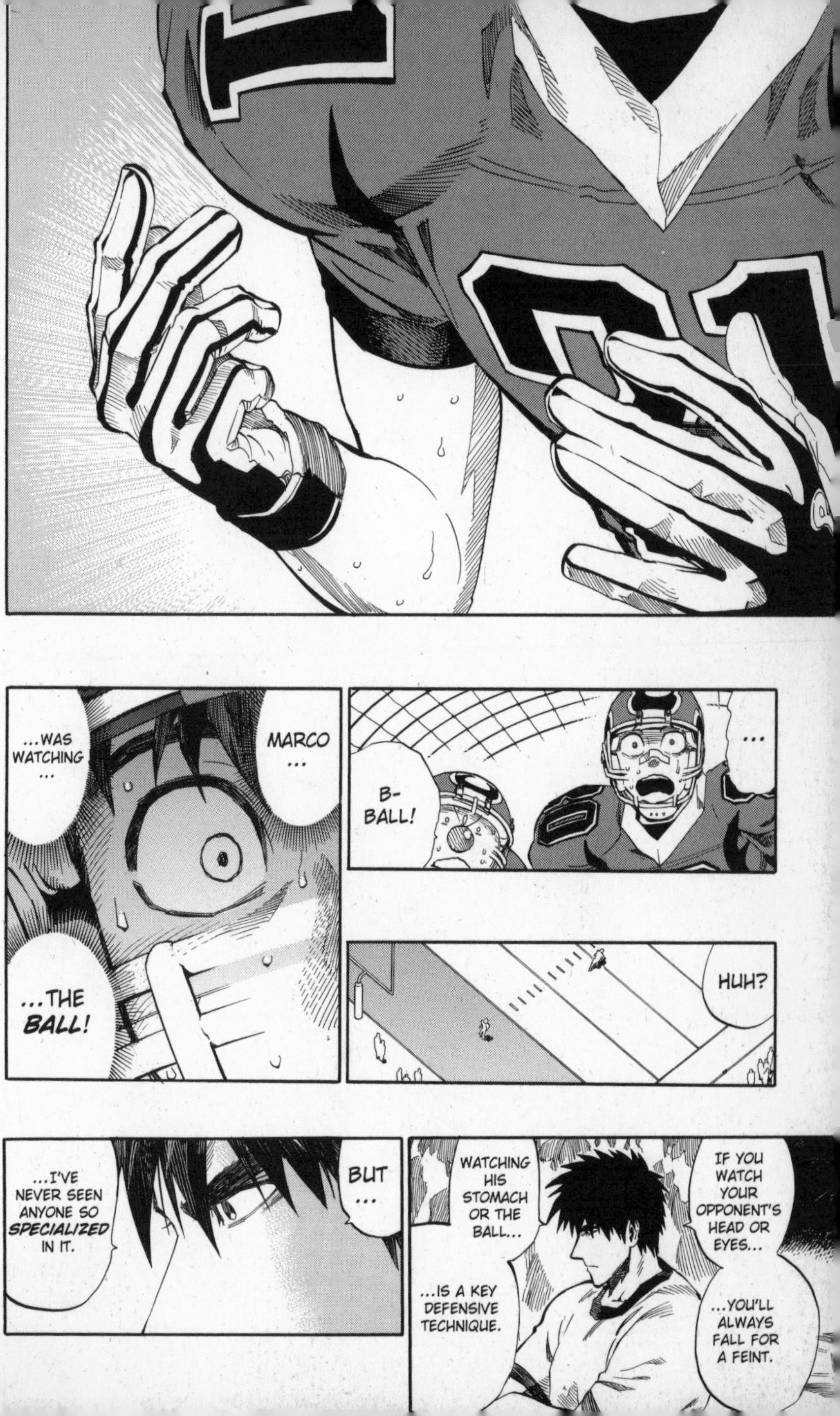
...
B-BALL!
HUH?
MARCO ...
...WAS WATCHING ...
...THE *BALL!*
IF YOU WATCH YOUR OPPONENT'S HEAD OR EYES...
WATCHING HIS STOMACH OR THE BALL...
...YOU'LL ALWAYS FALL FOR A FEINT.
...IS A KEY DEFENSIVE TECHNIQUE.
BUT ...
...I'VE NEVER SEEN ANYONE SO *SPECIALIZED* IN IT.

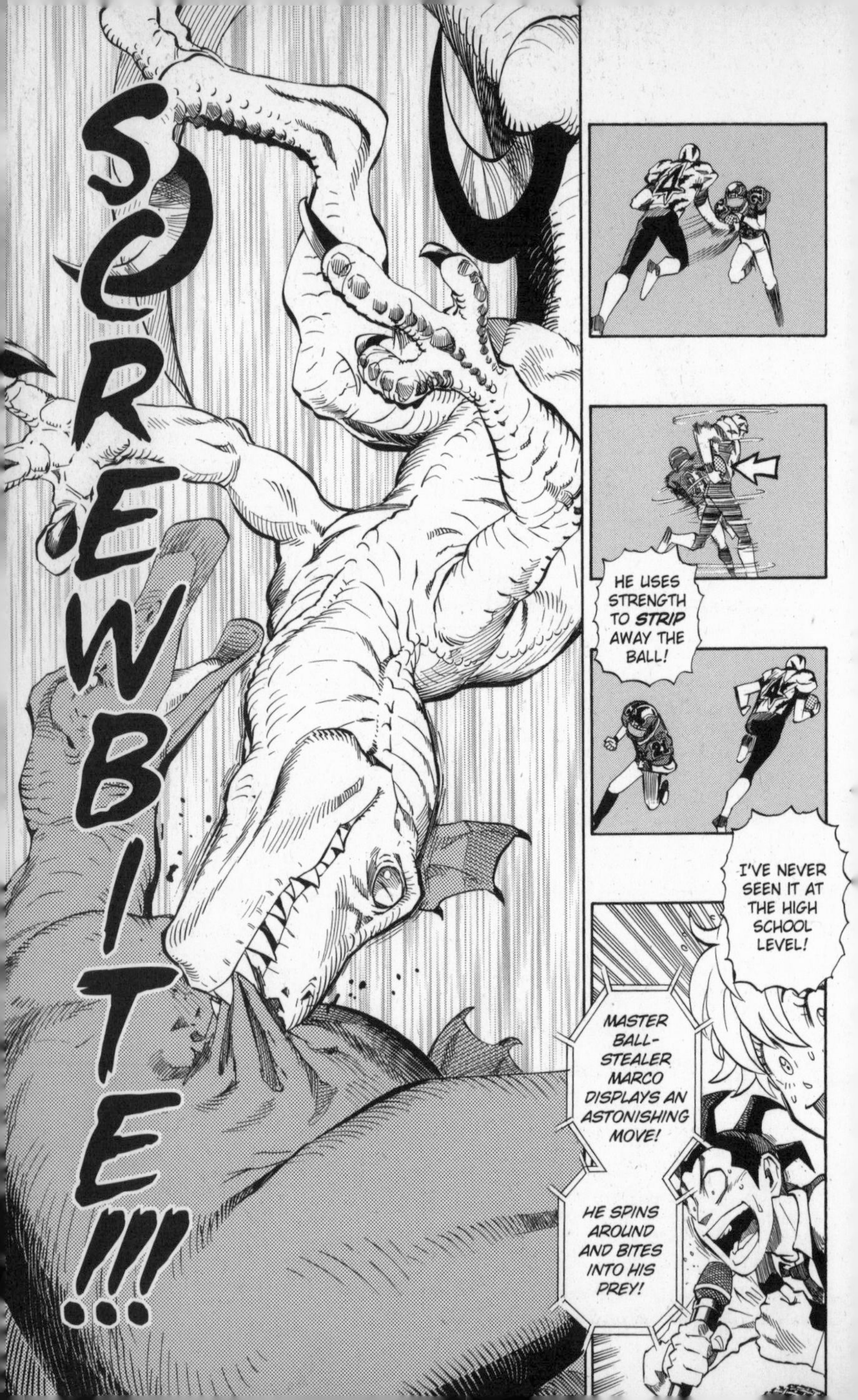
HE USES STRENGTH TO **STRIP** AWAY THE BALL!
I'VE NEVER SEEN IT AT THE HIGH SCHOOL LEVEL!
MASTER BALL-STEALER MARCO DISPLAYS AN ASTONISHING MOVE!
HE SPINS AROUND AND BITES INTO HIS PREY!
SCREWBITE!!!

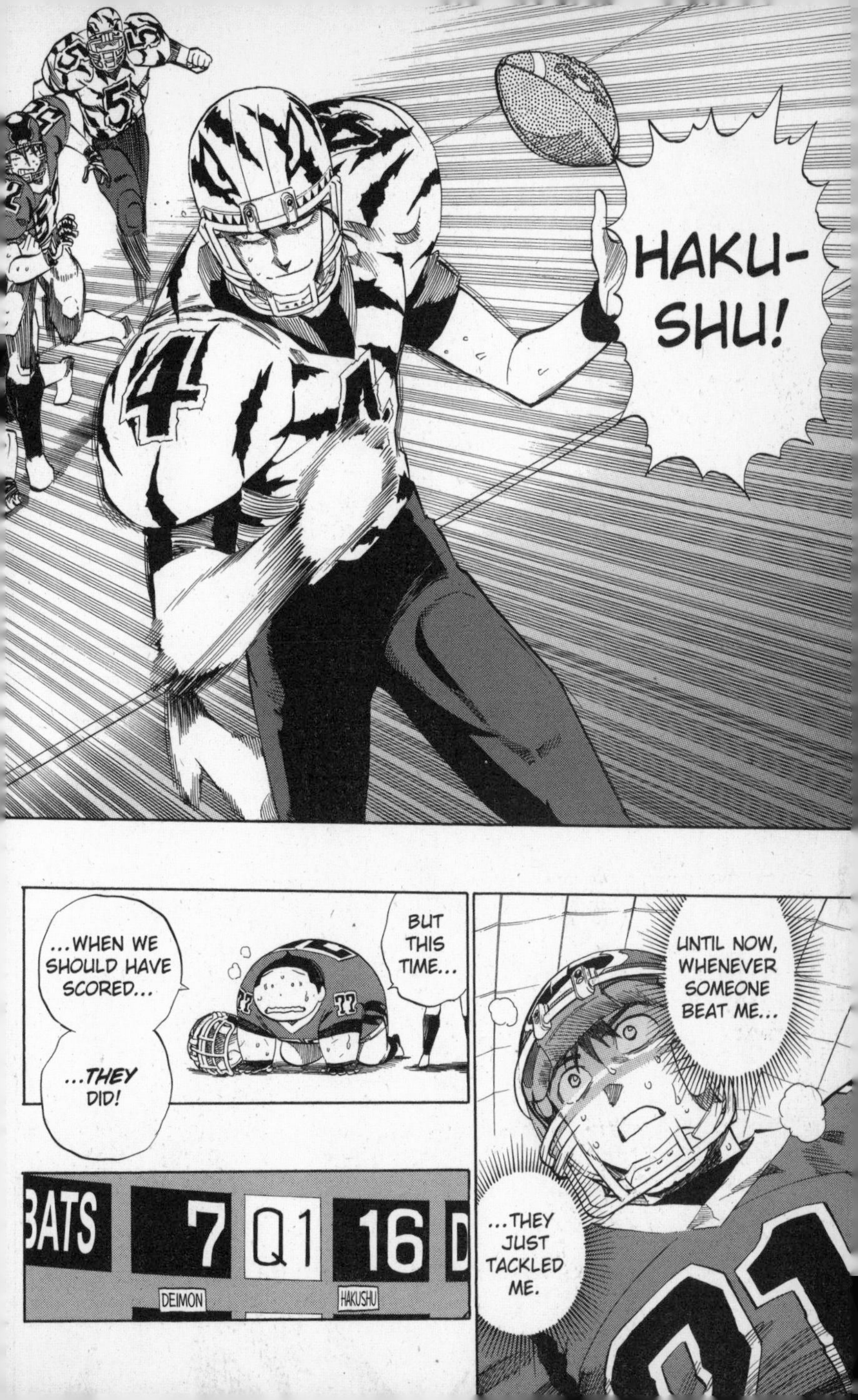
HAKU-SHU!
UNTIL NOW, WHENEVER SOMEONE BEAT ME...
...THEY JUST TACKLED ME.
BUT THIS TIME...
...WHEN WE SHOULD HAVE SCORED...
...THEY DID!
BATS 7 Q1 16 D
DEIMON
HAKUSHU

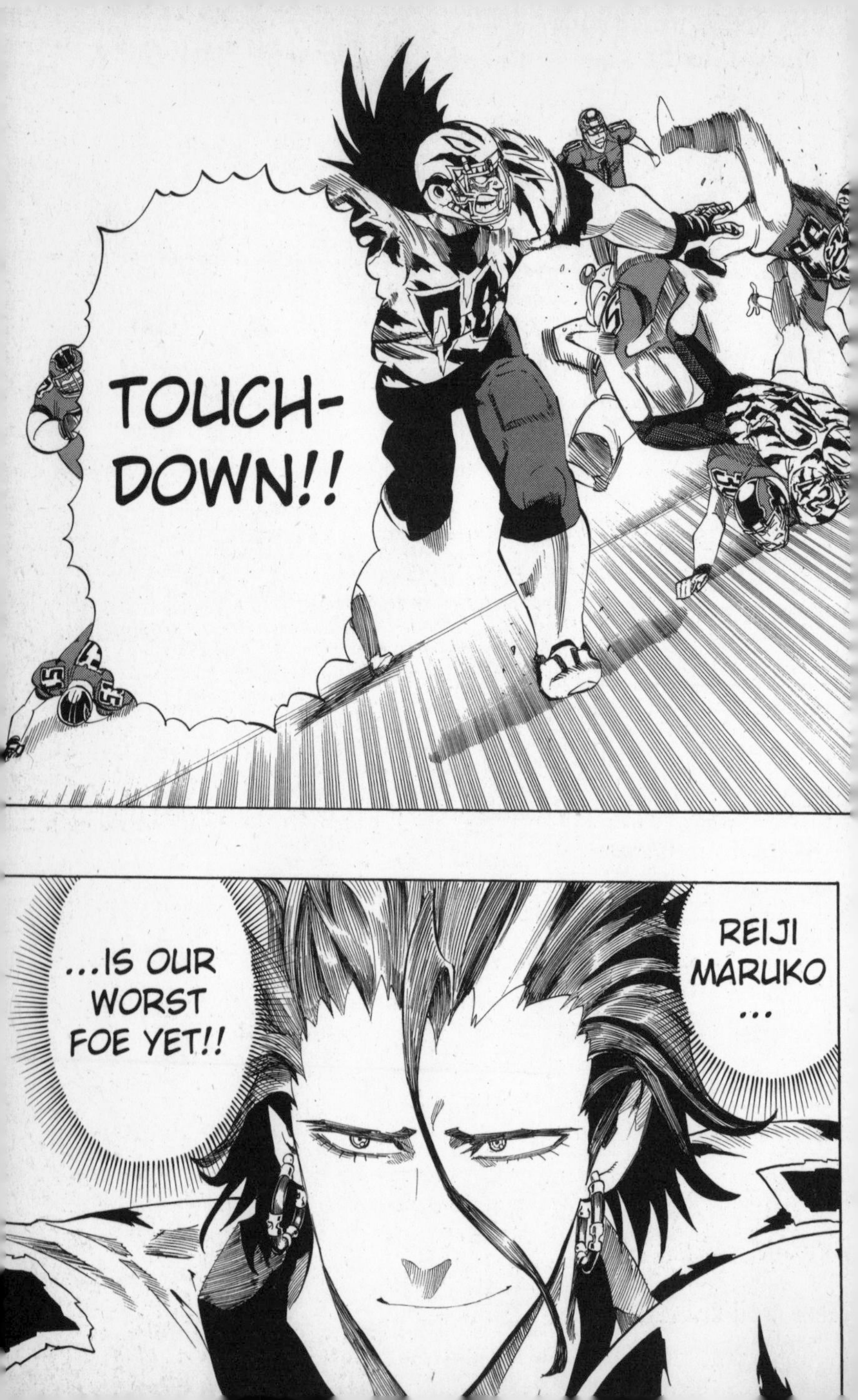
TOUCH-DOWN!!
REIJI MARUKO...
...IS OUR WORST FOE YET!!

Investigation File #101

Make an academic ranking of the schools!!

IS DEIMON'S ACADEMIC RANKING THE LOWEST OF ALL THE SCHOOLS TO APPEAR SO FAR? I WANT TO KNOW HOW THE SCHOOLS RANK ACADEMICALLY!!

Caller name: Namusan, Kanagawa Prefecture

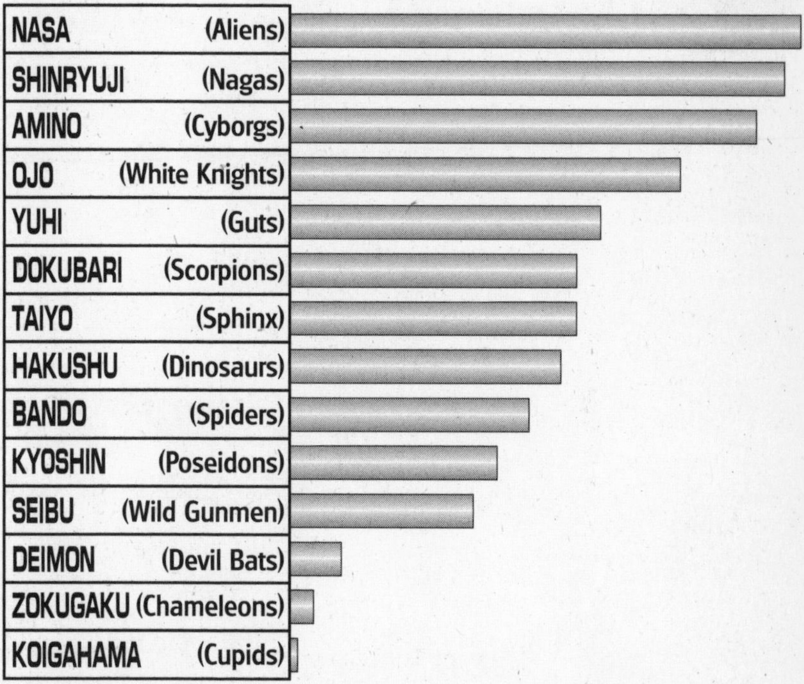

School		
NASA	(Aliens)	████████████████████
SHINRYUJI	(Nagas)	███████████████████
AMINO	(Cyborgs)	███████████████████
OJO	(White Knights)	██████████████████
YUHI	(Guts)	████████████████
DOKUBARI	(Scorpions)	███████████████
TAIYO	(Sphinx)	███████████████
HAKUSHU	(Dinosaurs)	██████████████
BANDO	(Spiders)	█████████████
KYOSHIN	(Poseidons)	████████████
SEIBU	(Wild Gunmen)	████████████
DEIMON	(Devil Bats)	██
ZOKUGAKU	(Chameleons)	█
KOIGAHAMA	(Cupids)	▌

AT MOST IT'S JUST A RANKING OF SCHOOL STUDIES AND TEST SCORES!

REMEMBER, GETTING HIGH TEST SCORES ISN'T THE SAME AS HAVING BRAINS!

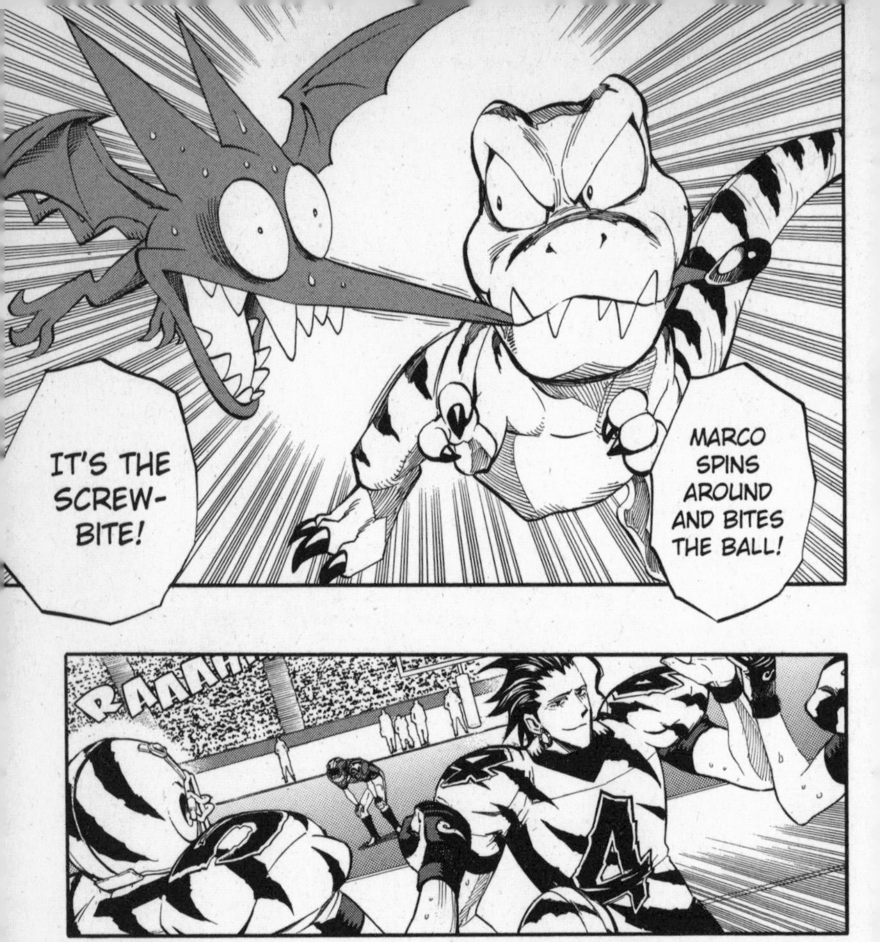
MARCO SPINS AROUND AND BITES THE BALL!
IT'S THE SCREW-BITE!
RAAAAH

Chapter 257 Hiruma vs. Marco

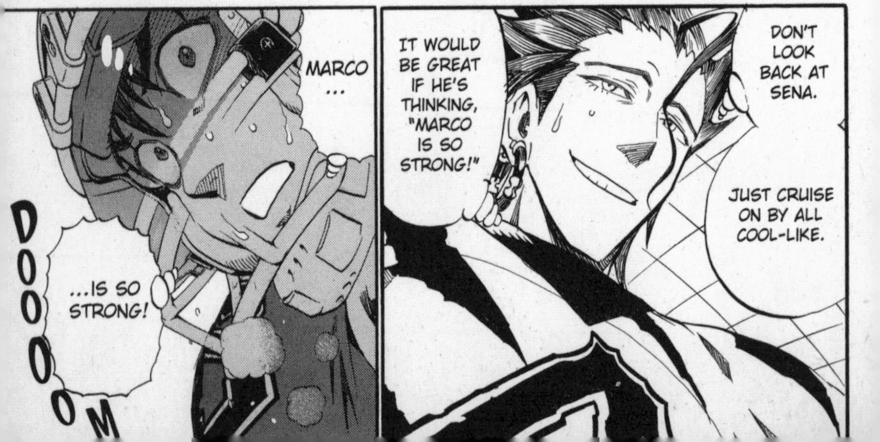
DON'T LOOK BACK AT SENA.
IT WOULD BE GREAT IF HE'S THINKING, "MARCO IS SO STRONG!"
JUST CRUISE ON BY ALL COOL-LIKE.
MARCO ...
...IS SO STRONG!
DOOOOOM

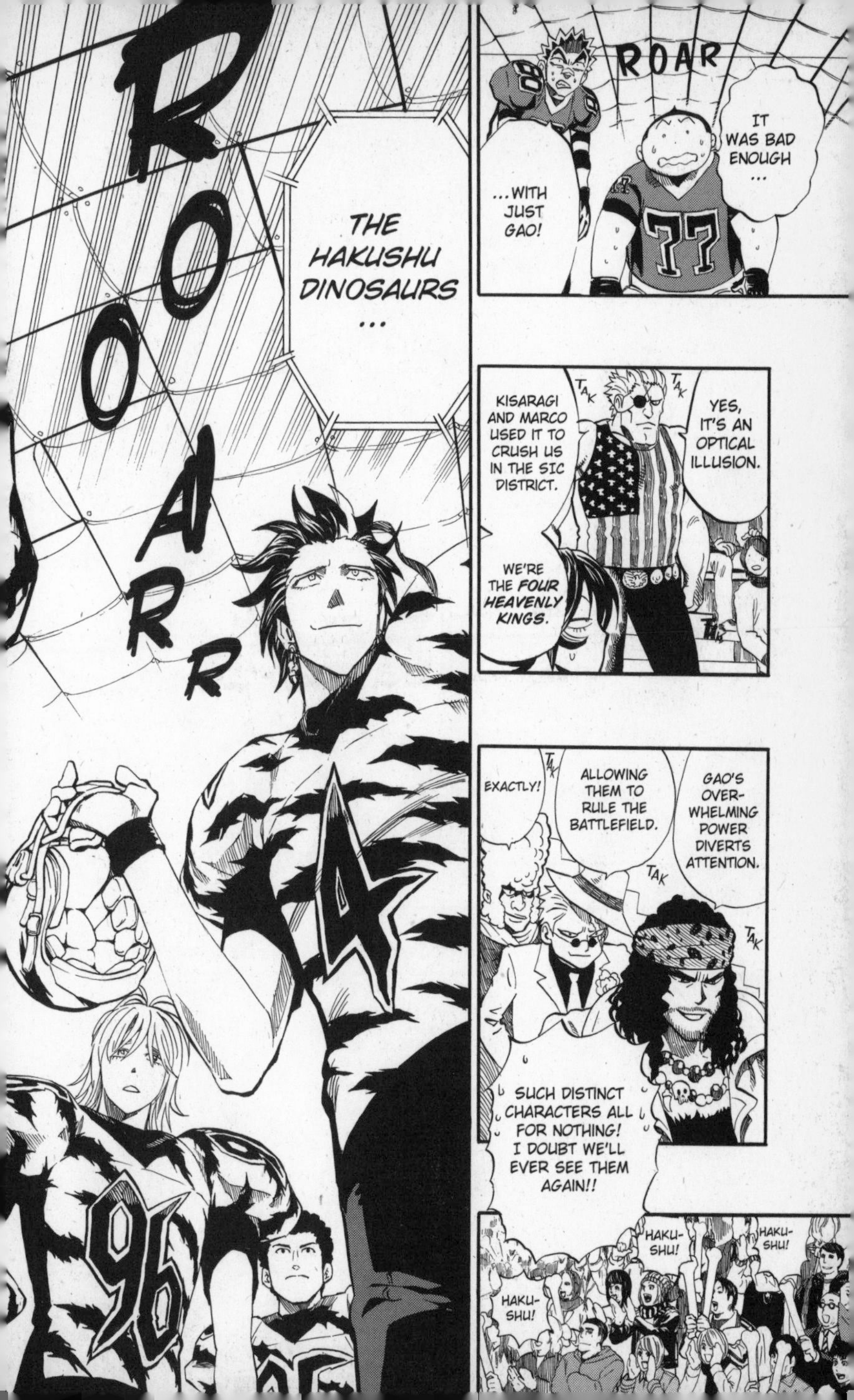
ROAR
IT WAS BAD ENOUGH...
...WITH JUST GAO!
TAK TAK
YES, IT'S AN OPTICAL ILLUSION.
KISARAGI AND MARCO USED IT TO CRUSH US IN THE SIC DISTRICT.
WE'RE THE *FOUR HEAVENLY KINGS.*
TAK
GAO'S OVER-WHELMING POWER DIVERTS ATTENTION.
TAK
ALLOWING THEM TO RULE THE BATTLEFIELD.
TAK
EXACTLY!
TAK
SUCH DISTINCT CHARACTERS ALL FOR NOTHING! I DOUBT WE'LL EVER SEE THEM AGAIN!!
HAKU-SHU!
HAKU-SHU!
HAKU-SHU!
ROOOARRR
THE HAKUSHU DINOSAURS...

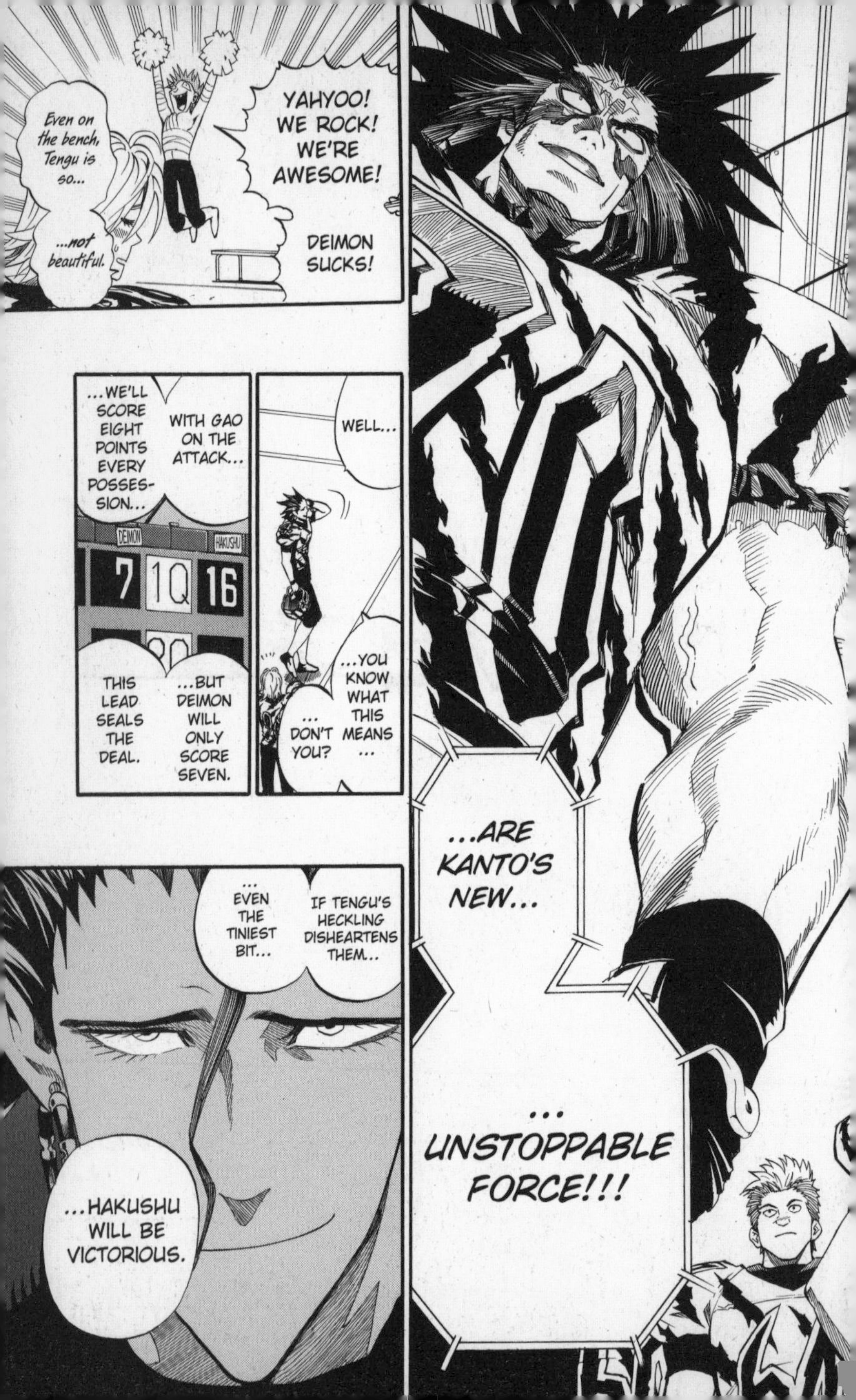
...ARE KANTO'S NEW...
...UNSTOPPABLE FORCE!!!
YAHYOO! WE ROCK! WE'RE AWESOME!
DEIMON SUCKS!
Even on the bench, Tengu is so...
...not beautiful.
WELL...
...YOU KNOW WHAT THIS MEANS...
...DON'T YOU?
WITH GAO ON THE ATTACK...
...WE'LL SCORE EIGHT POINTS EVERY POSSESSION...
DEIMON
HAKUSHU
7 1Q 16
...BUT DEIMON WILL ONLY SCORE SEVEN.
THIS LEAD SEALS THE DEAL.
IF TENGU'S HECKLING DISHEARTENS THEM...
...EVEN THE TINIEST BIT...
...HAKUSHU WILL BE VICTORIOUS.

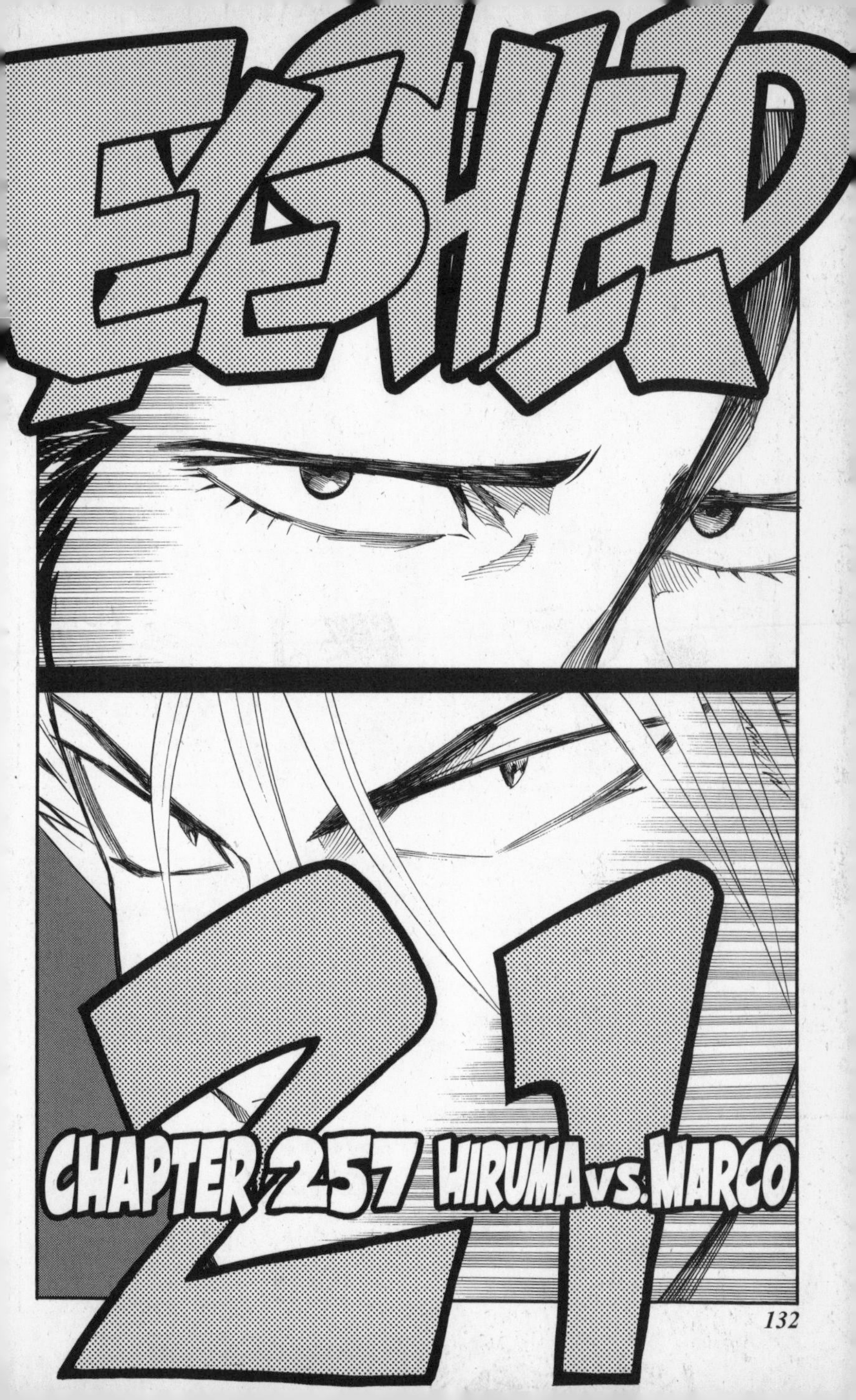
EYESHIELD 21
CHAPTER 257 HIRUMA vs. MARCO

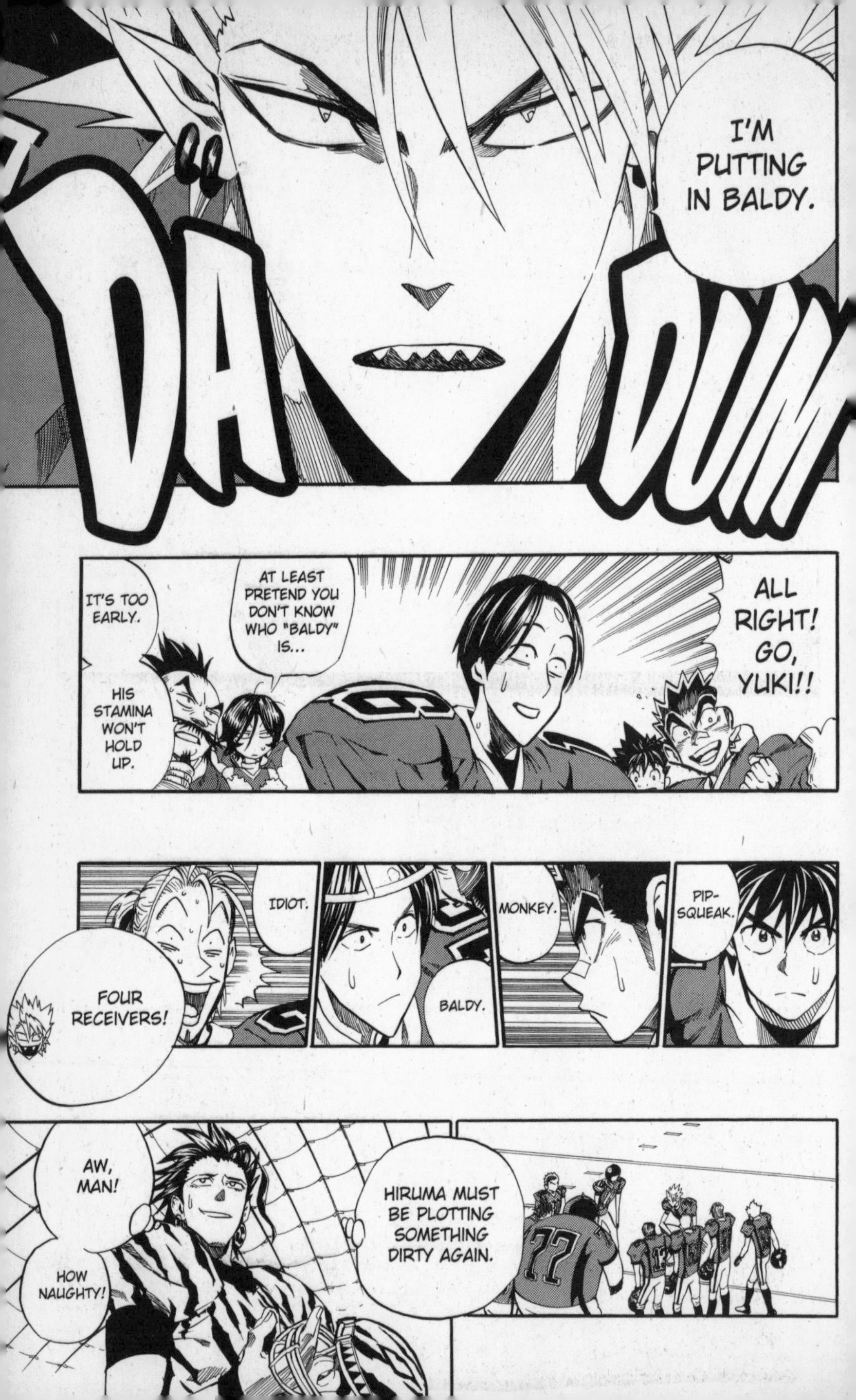
I'M PUTTING IN BALDY.
DA DUM
ALL RIGHT! GO, YUKI!!
AT LEAST PRETEND YOU DON'T KNOW WHO "BALDY" IS...
IT'S TOO EARLY.
HIS STAMINA WON'T HOLD UP.
PIP-SQUEAK.
MONKEY.
BALDY.
IDIOT.
FOUR RECEIVERS!
HIRUMA MUST BE PLOTTING SOMETHING DIRTY AGAIN.
AW, MAN!
HOW NAUGHTY!

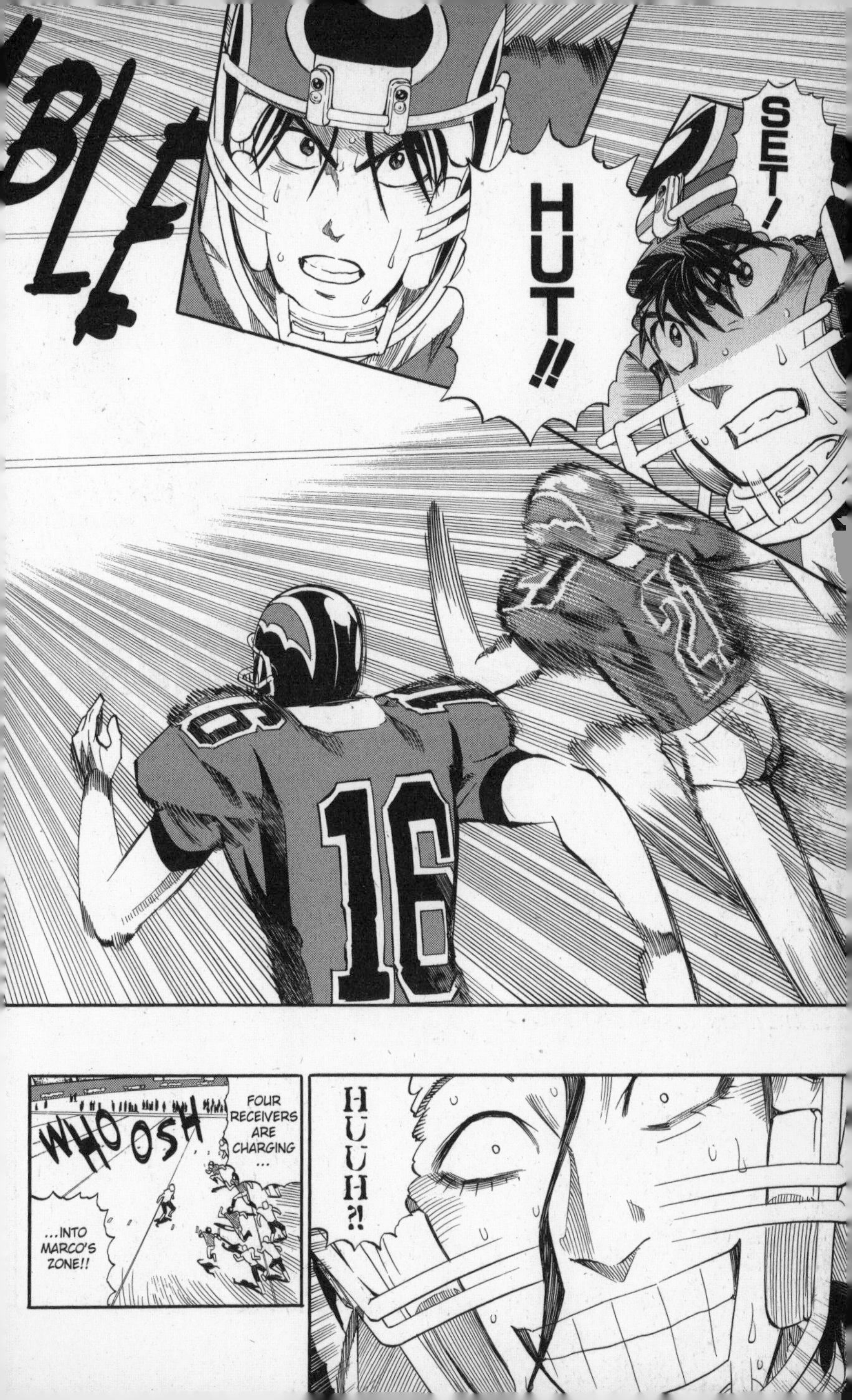
SET!
HUT!!
HUUH?!
FOUR RECEIVERS ARE CHARGING...
WHOOSH
...INTO MARCO'S ZONE!!

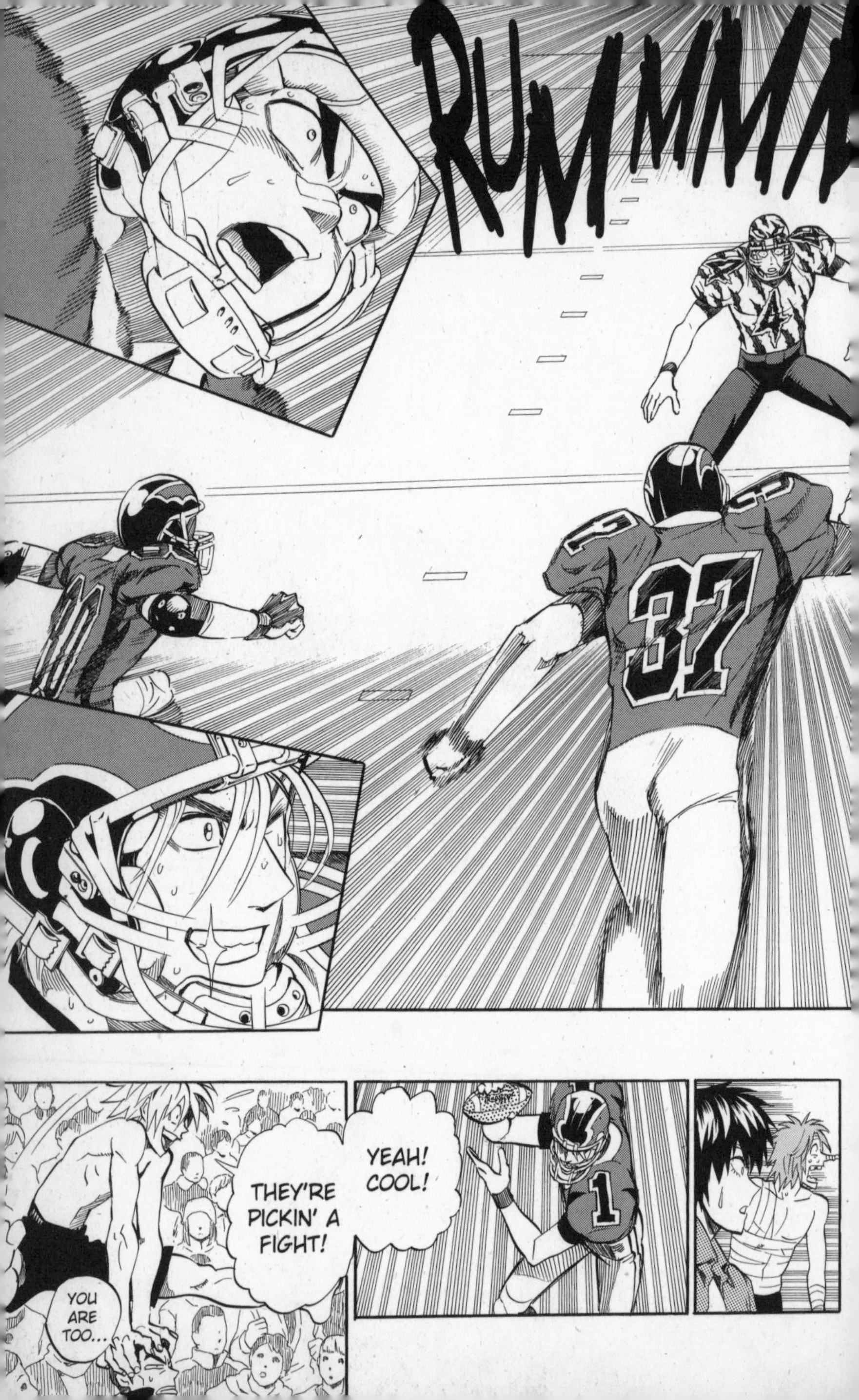
RUMMM
YEAH! COOL!
THEY'RE PICKIN' A FIGHT!
YOU ARE TOO...

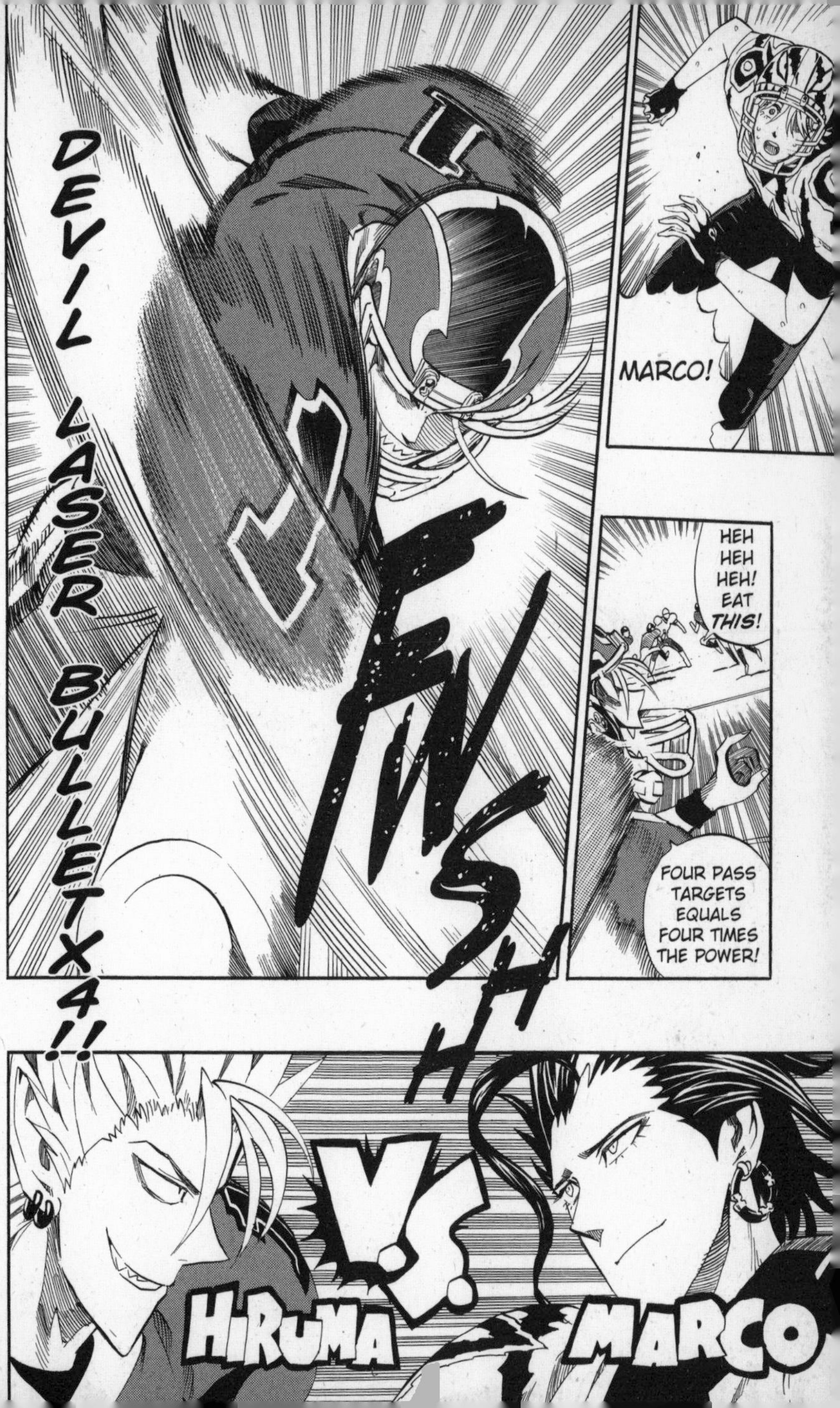

MARCO!
HEH HEH HEH! EAT THIS!
FOUR PASS TARGETS EQUALS FOUR TIMES THE POWER!
DEVIL LASER BULLET X4!!
FWSHHH
HIRUMA
V.
MARCO

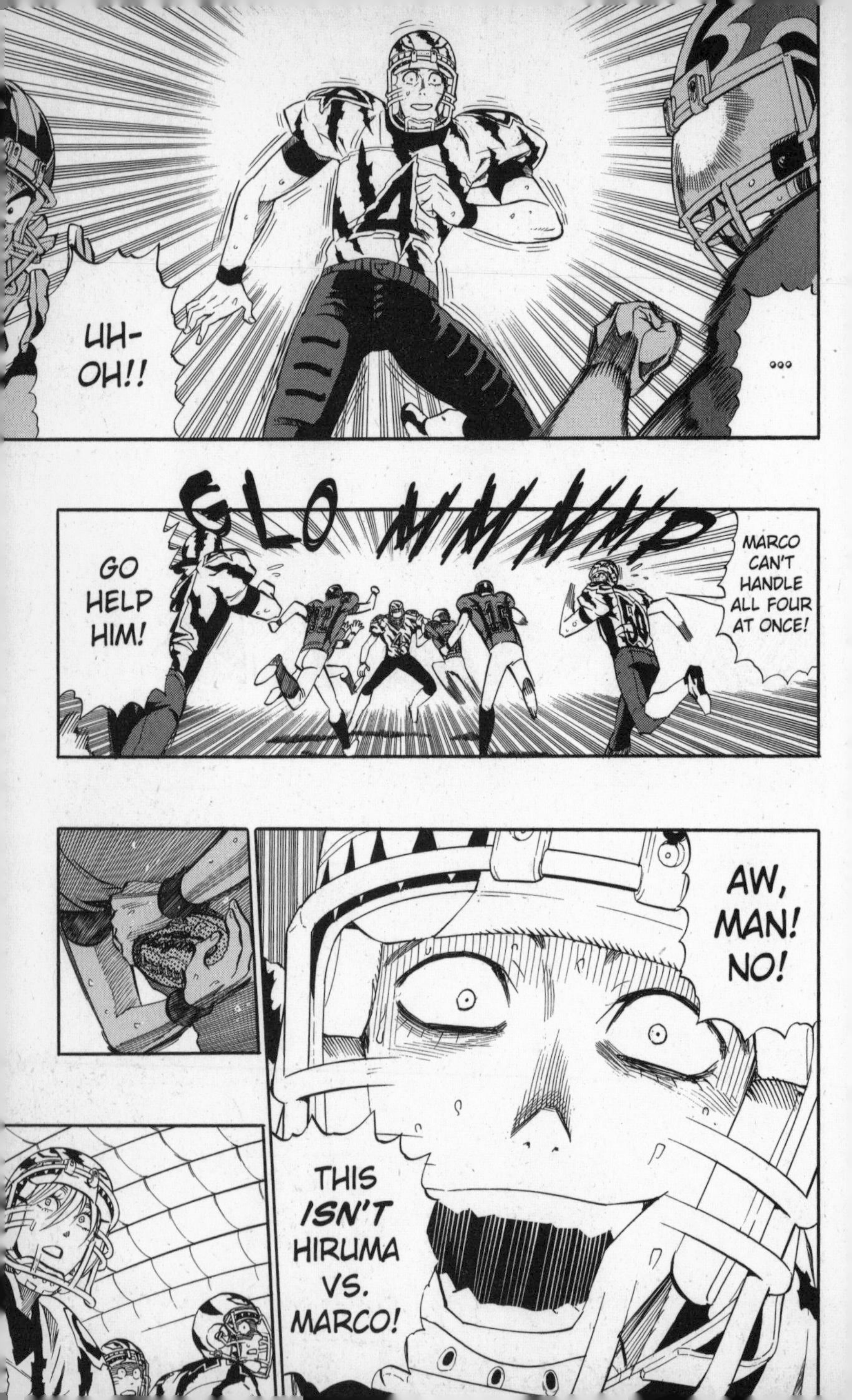
...
UH-OH!!
CLOMMMMP
MARCO CAN'T HANDLE ALL FOUR AT ONCE!
GO HELP HIM!
AW, MAN! NO!
THIS *ISN'T* HIRUMA VS. MARCO!

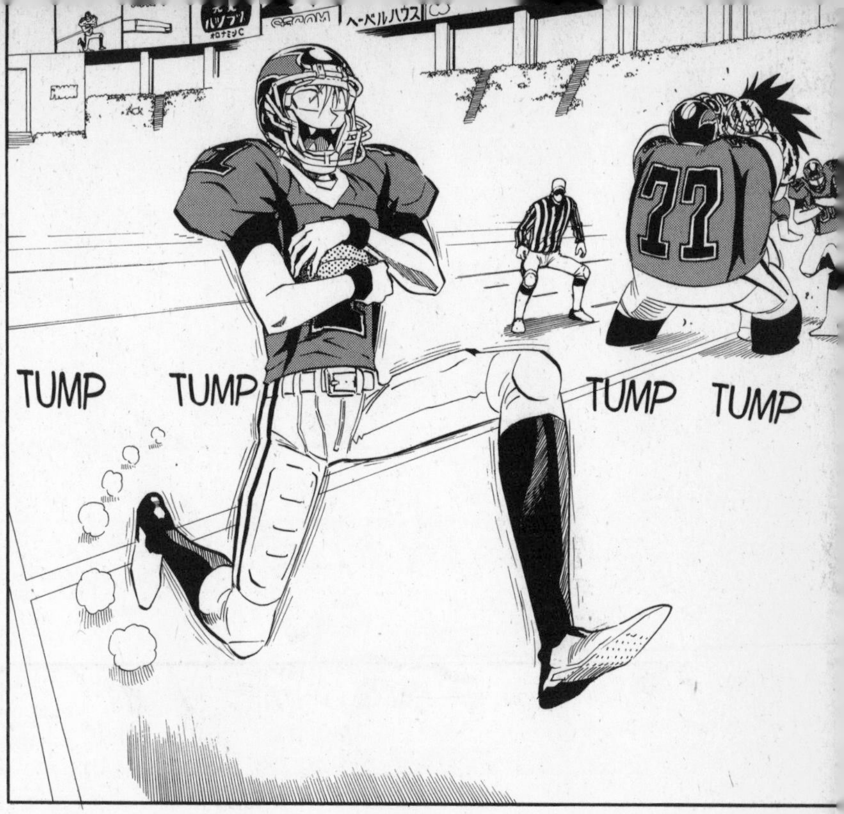
ヘーベルハウス
TUMP TUMP
TUMP TUMP

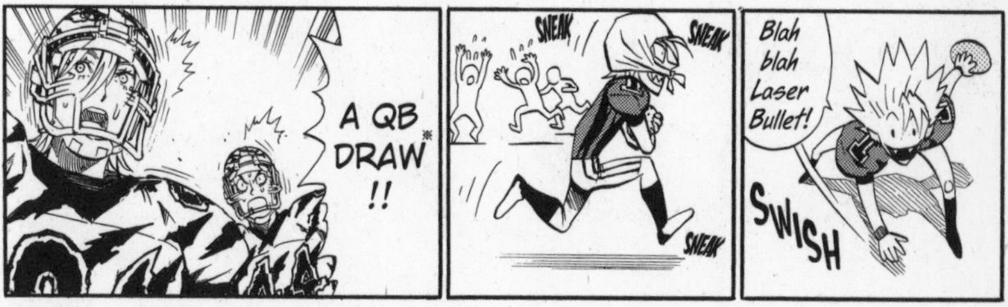
Blah blah Laser Bullet!
SWISH
SNEAK
SNEAK
SNEAK
A QB DRAW※ !!

※ THE QUARTERBACK PRETENDS TO THROW A PASS BUT THEN RUNS THE BALL HIMSELF.

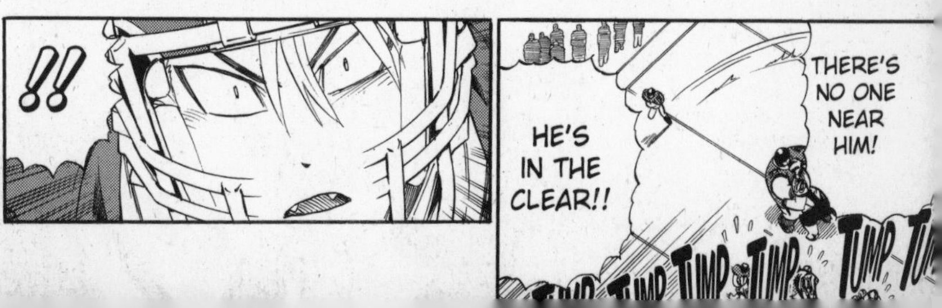
THERE'S NO ONE NEAR HIM!
HE'S IN THE CLEAR!!
TUMP TUMP
!!

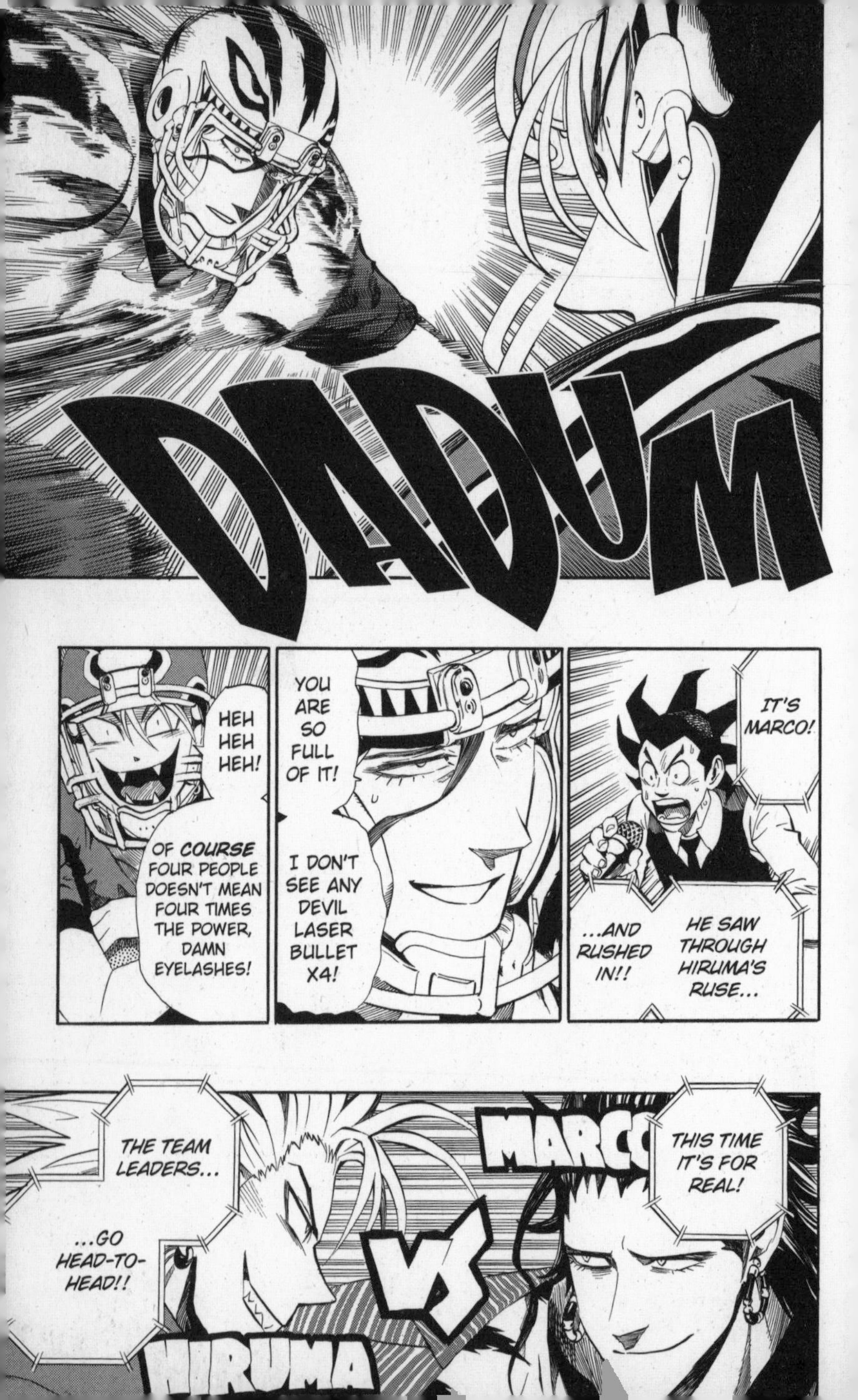
DADUM
IT'S MARCO!
HE SAW THROUGH HIRUMA'S RUSE...
...AND RUSHED IN!!
YOU ARE SO FULL OF IT!
I DON'T SEE ANY DEVIL LASER BULLET X4!
HEH HEH HEH!
OF *COURSE* FOUR PEOPLE DOESN'T MEAN FOUR TIMES THE POWER, DAMN EYELASHES!
MARCO
THIS TIME IT'S FOR REAL!
THE TEAM LEADERS...
...GO HEAD-TO-HEAD!!
VS
HIRUMA

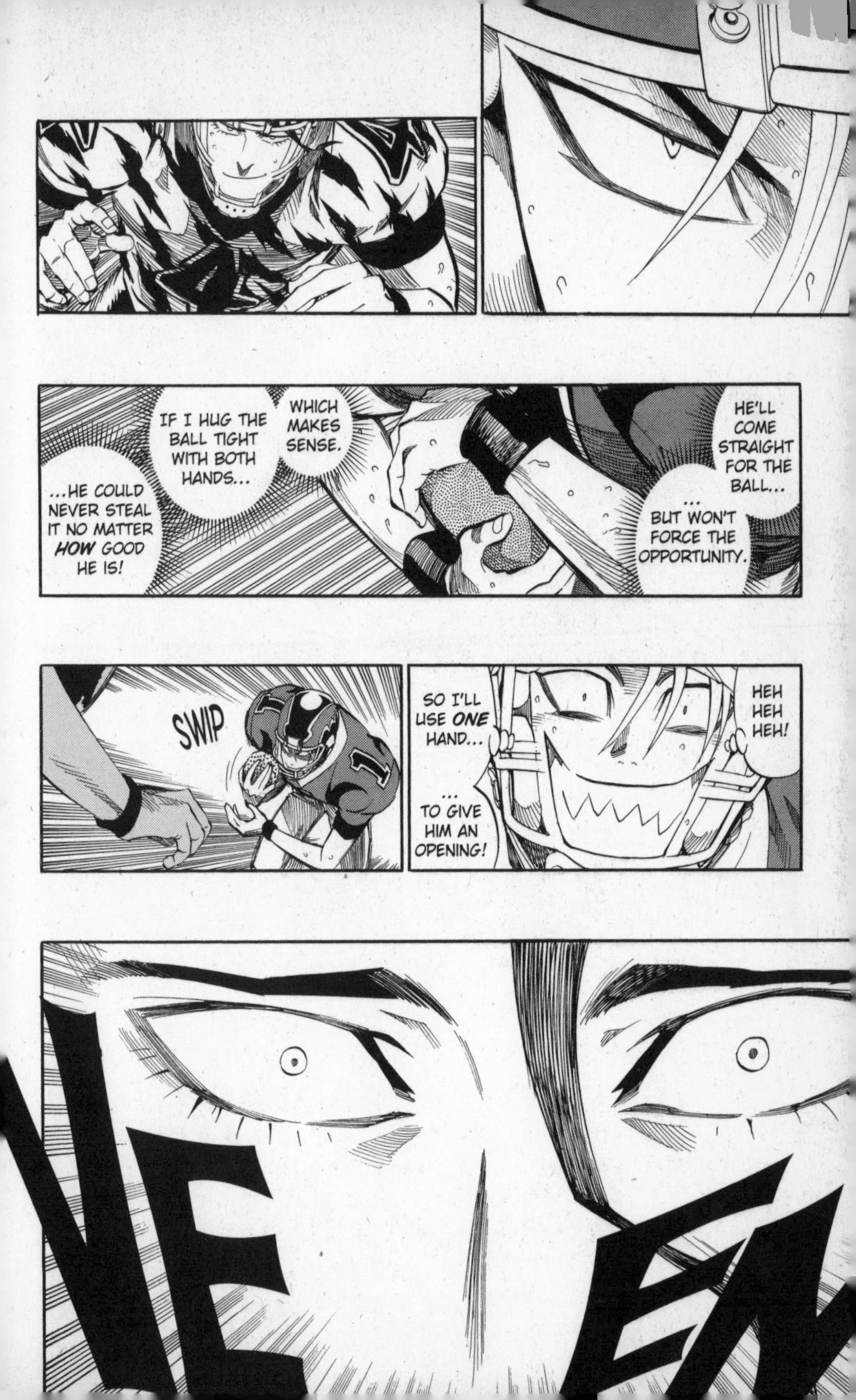
HE'LL COME STRAIGHT FOR THE BALL...
...BUT WON'T FORCE THE OPPORTUNITY.
WHICH MAKES SENSE.
IF I HUG THE BALL TIGHT WITH BOTH HANDS...
...HE COULD NEVER STEAL IT NO MATTER HOW GOOD HE IS!
HEH HEH HEH!
SO I'LL USE ONE HAND...
...TO GIVE HIM AN OPENING!
SWIP

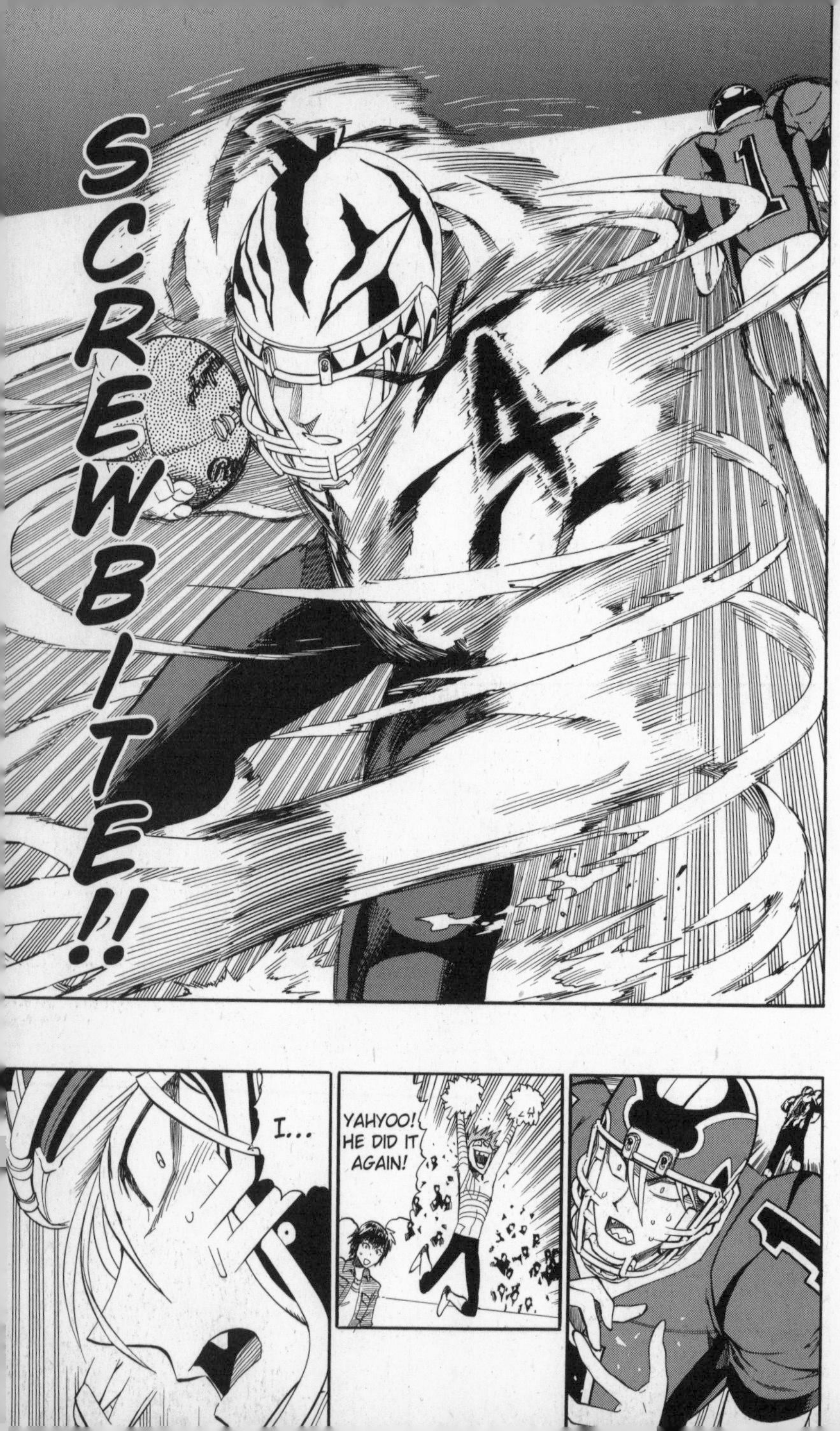
SCREWBITE!!
YAHYOO! HE DID IT AGAIN!
I...

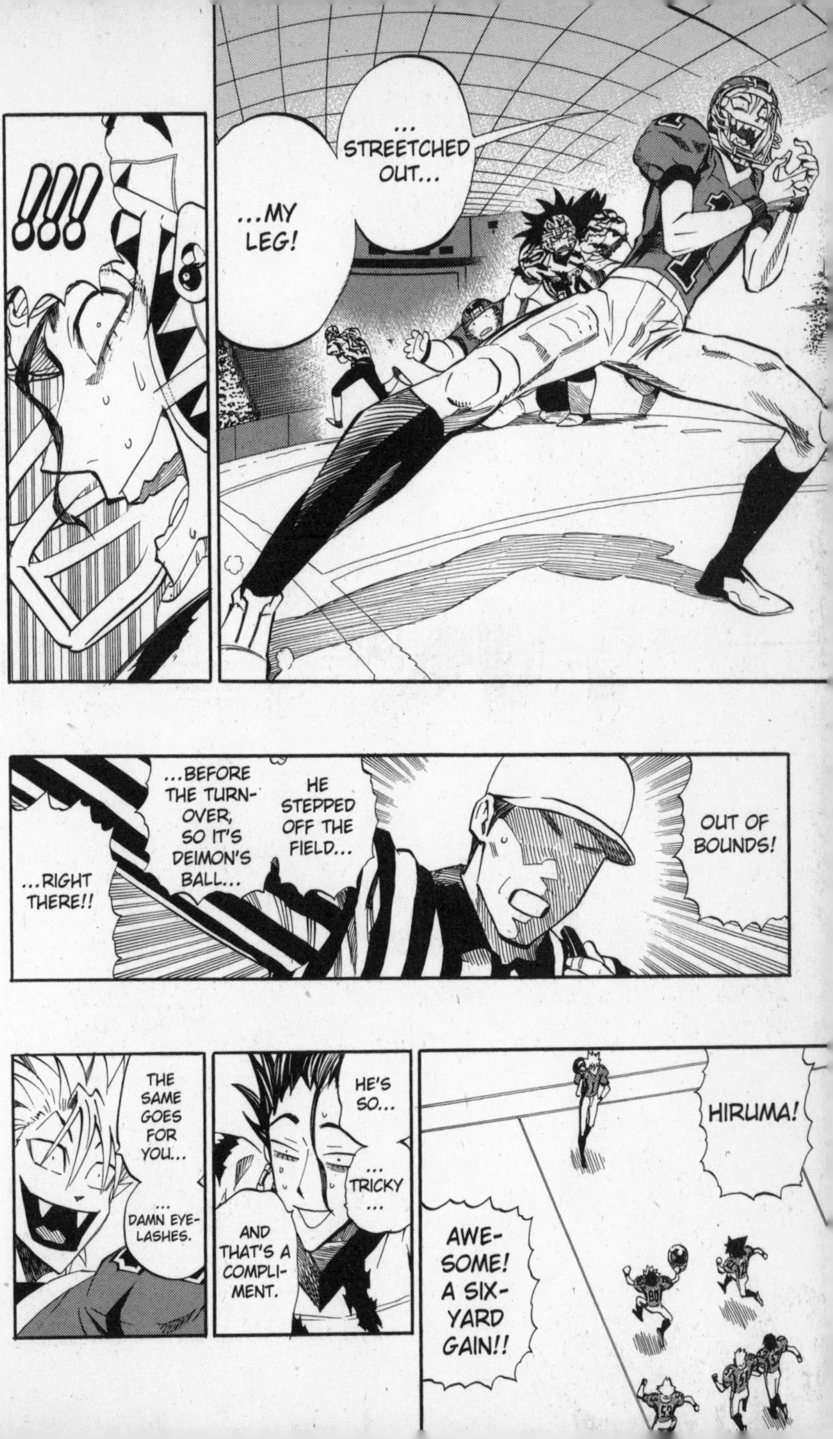
... STREETCHED OUT...
...MY LEG!
!!!
OUT OF BOUNDS!
HE STEPPED OFF THE FIELD...
...BEFORE THE TURN-OVER, SO IT'S DEIMON'S BALL...
...RIGHT THERE!!
HIRUMA!
AWE-SOME! A SIX-YARD GAIN!!
HE'S SO...
... TRICKY ...
AND THAT'S A COMPLI-MENT.
THE SAME GOES FOR YOU...
... DAMN EYE-LASHES.

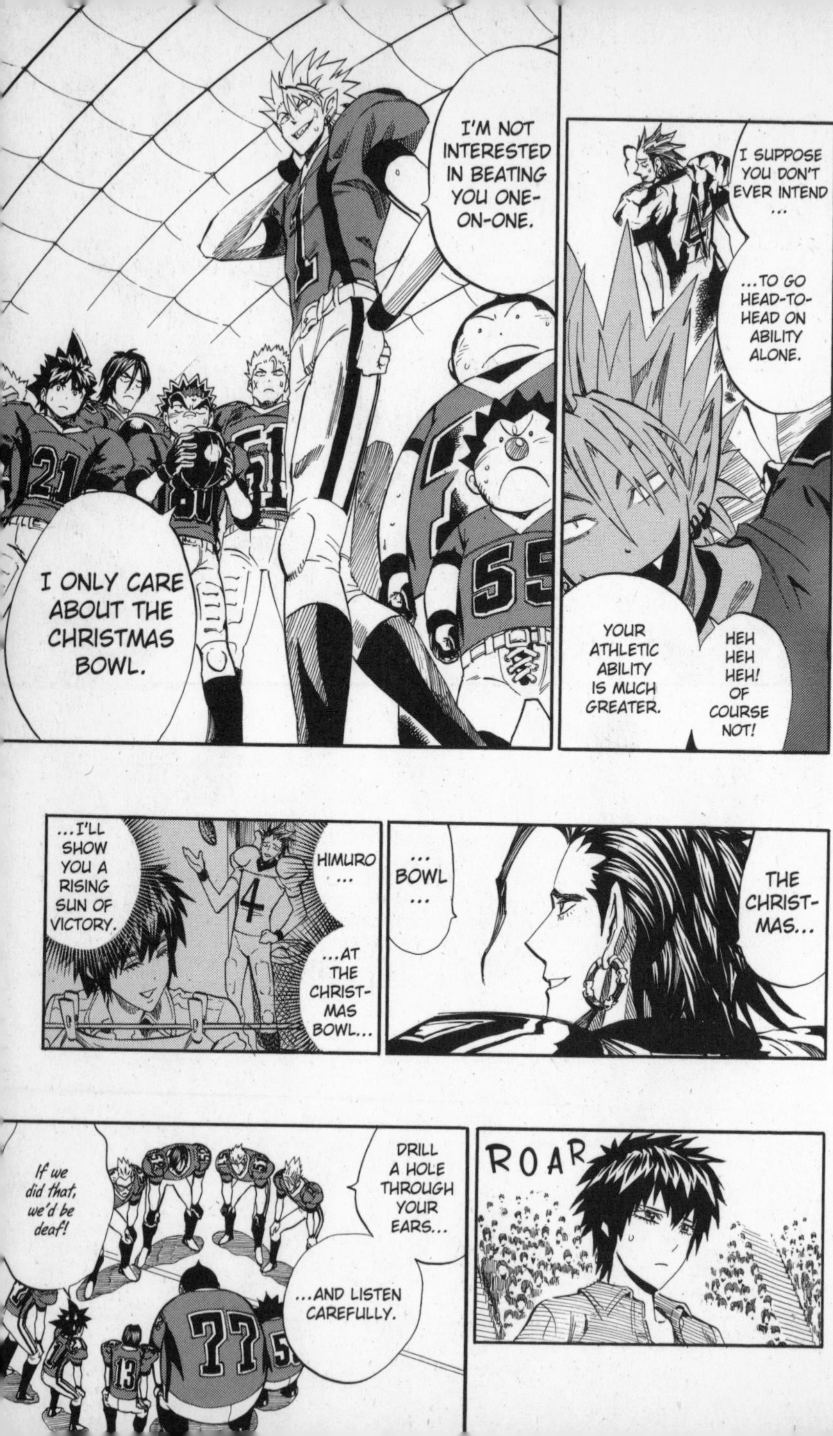
I SUPPOSE YOU DON'T EVER INTEND ...
...TO GO HEAD-TO-HEAD ON ABILITY ALONE.
YOUR ATHLETIC ABILITY IS MUCH GREATER.
HEH HEH HEH! OF COURSE NOT!
I'M NOT INTERESTED IN BEATING YOU ONE-ON-ONE.
I ONLY CARE ABOUT THE CHRISTMAS BOWL.
THE CHRIST-MAS...
... BOWL ...
HIMURO ...
...I'LL SHOW YOU A RISING SUN OF VICTORY.
...AT THE CHRIST-MAS BOWL...
ROAR
DRILL A HOLE THROUGH YOUR EARS...
...AND LISTEN CAREFULLY.
If we did that, we'd be deaf!

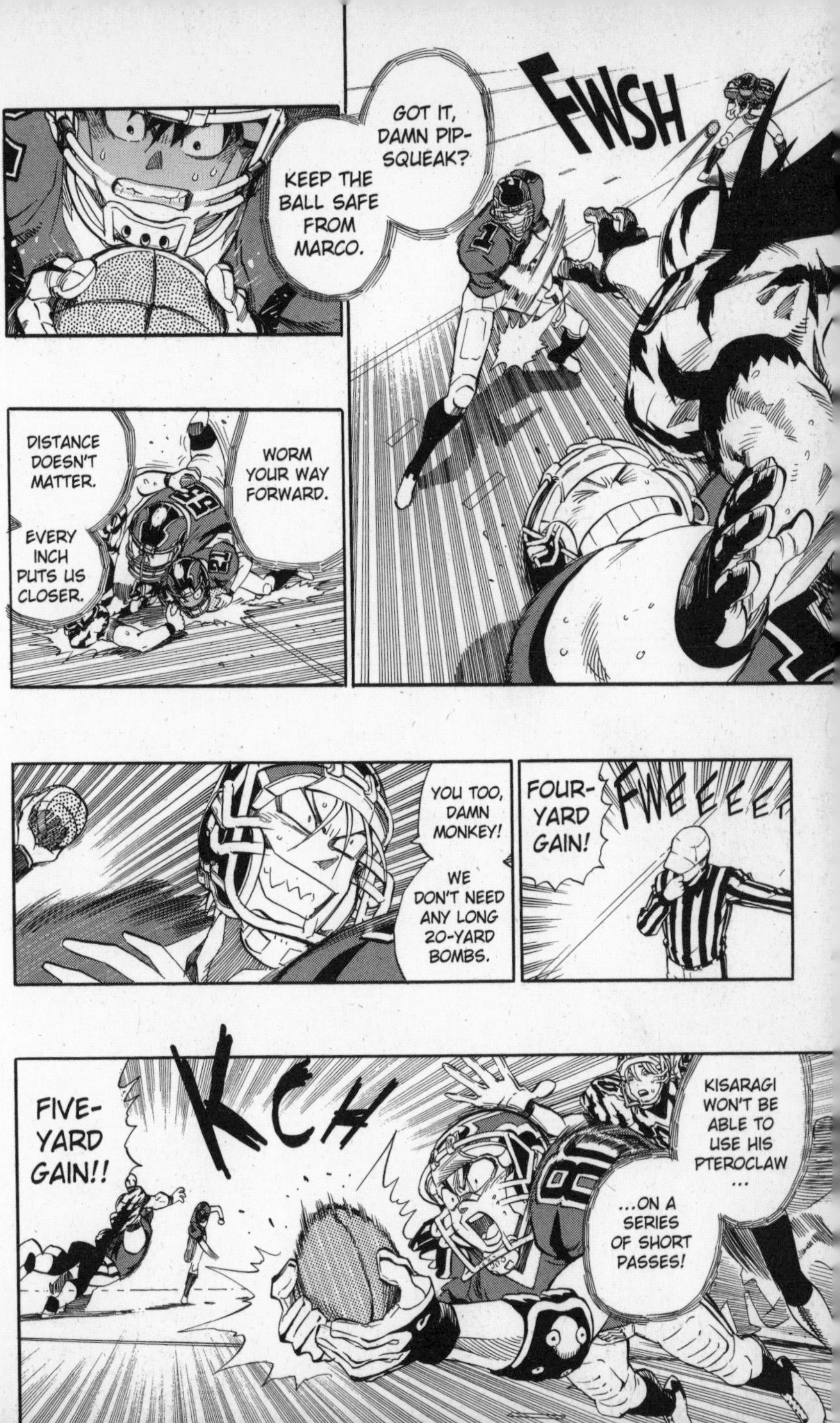
FWSH
GOT IT, DAMN PIP-SQUEAK?
KEEP THE BALL SAFE FROM MARCO.
WORM YOUR WAY FORWARD.
DISTANCE DOESN'T MATTER.
EVERY INCH PUTS US CLOSER.
FOUR-YARD GAIN!
FWEEEET
YOU TOO, DAMN MONKEY!
WE DON'T NEED ANY LONG 20-YARD BOMBS.
KISARAGI WON'T BE ABLE TO USE HIS PTEROCLAW...
...ON A SERIES OF SHORT PASSES!
KCH
FIVE-YARD GAIN!!

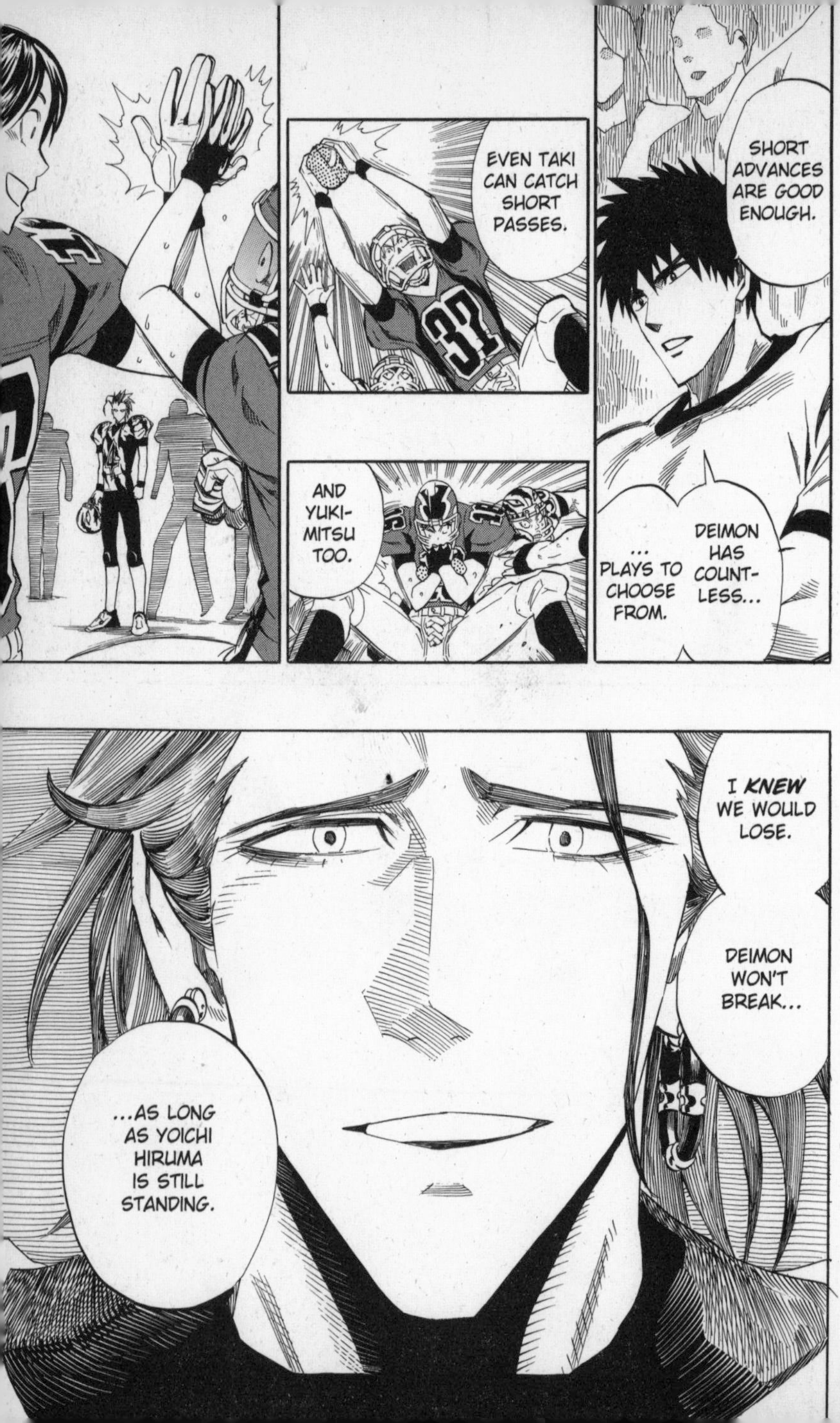

SHORT ADVANCES ARE GOOD ENOUGH.
DEIMON HAS COUNT-LESS...
...PLAYS TO CHOOSE FROM.
EVEN TAKI CAN CATCH SHORT PASSES.
AND YUKI-MITSU TOO.
I *KNEW* WE WOULD LOSE.
DEIMON WON'T BREAK...
...AS LONG AS YOICHI HIRUMA IS STILL STANDING.

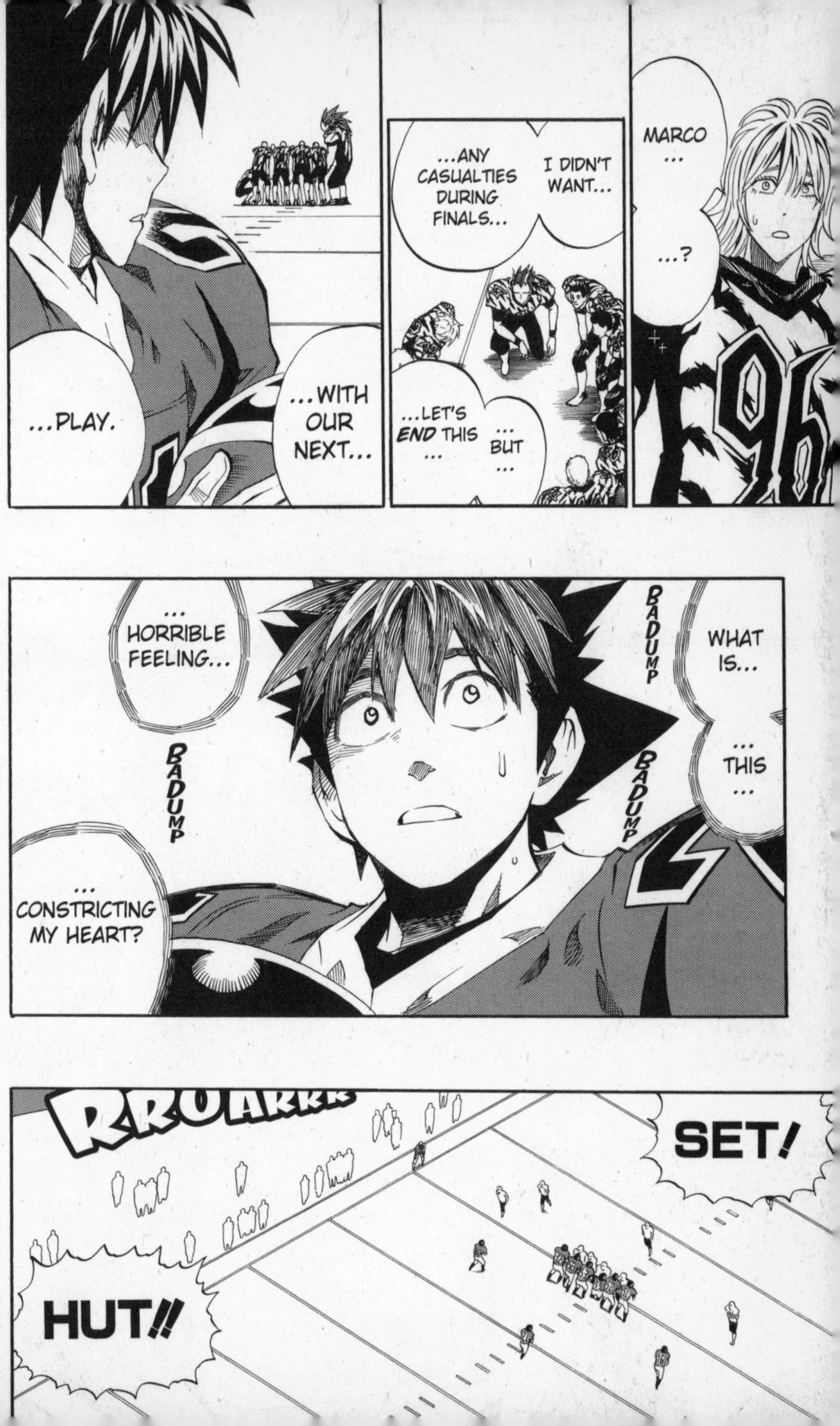
MARCO ...
...?
I DIDN'T WANT...
...ANY CASUALTIES DURING FINALS...
... BUT ...
...LET'S END THIS ...
...WITH OUR NEXT...
...PLAY.
WHAT IS...
BADUMP
... THIS ...
BADUMP
... HORRIBLE FEELING...
BADUMP
... CONSTRICTING MY HEART?
SET!
RROARRR
HUT!!

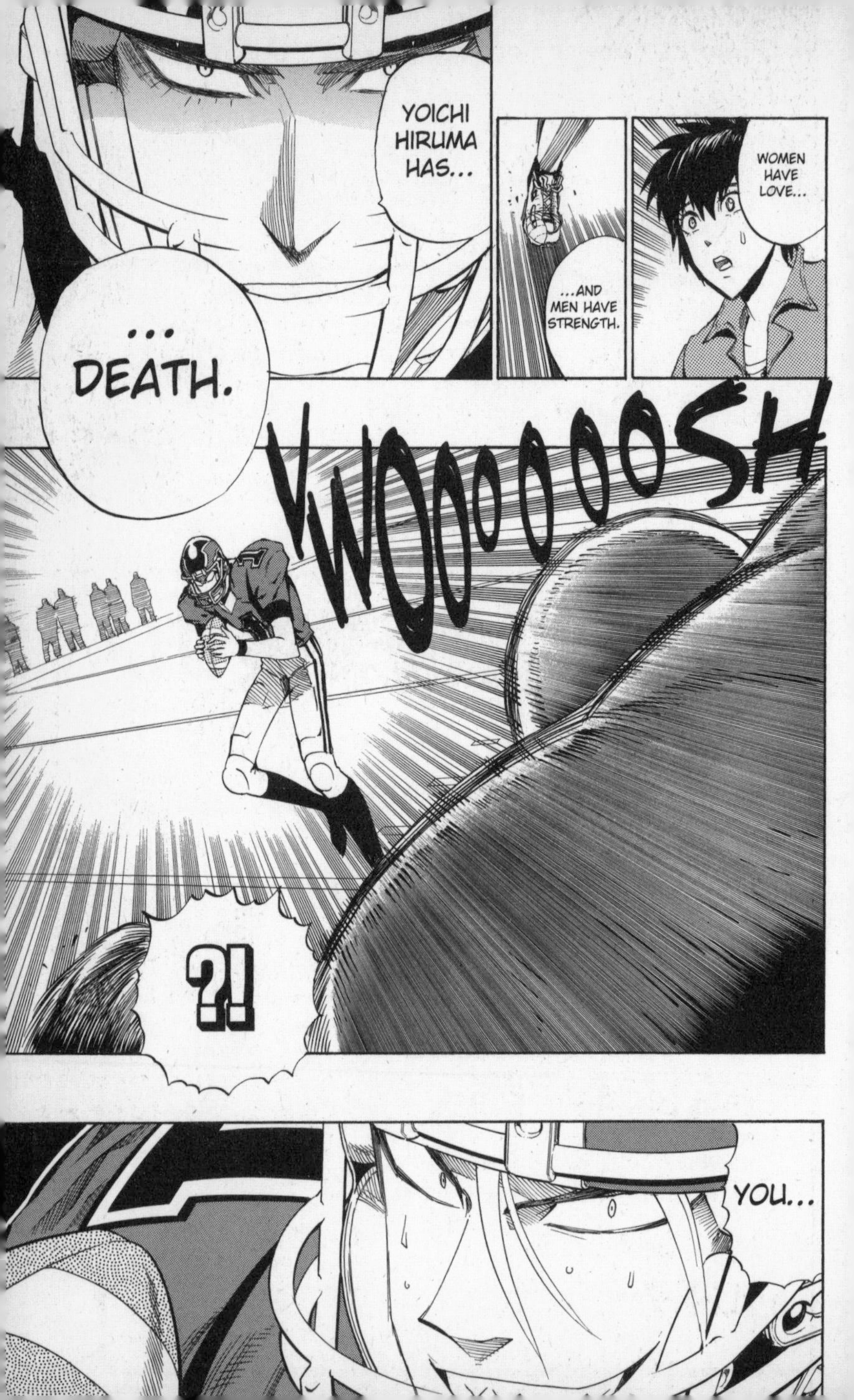
WOMEN HAVE LOVE...
...AND MEN HAVE STRENGTH.
YOICHI HIRUMA HAS...
...DEATH.
WOOOOOOSH
?!
YOU...

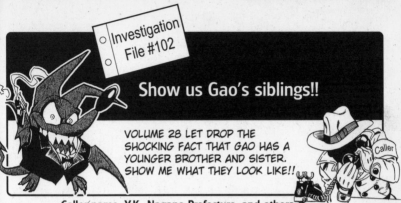

Investigation File #102

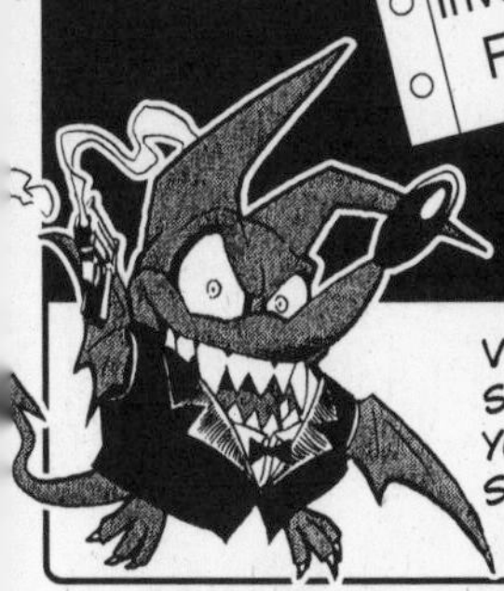

Show us Gao's siblings!!

VOLUME 28 LET DROP THE SHOCKING FACT THAT GAO HAS A YOUNGER BROTHER AND SISTER. SHOW ME WHAT THEY LOOK LIKE!!

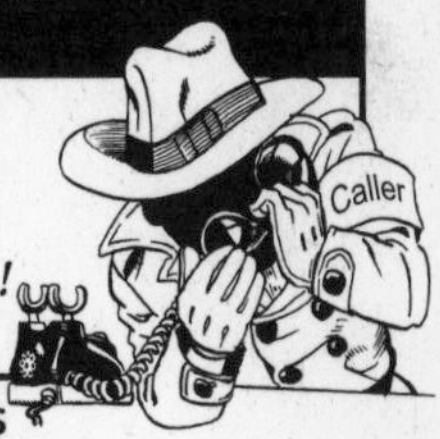
Caller

Caller name: Y.K., Nagano Prefecture, and others

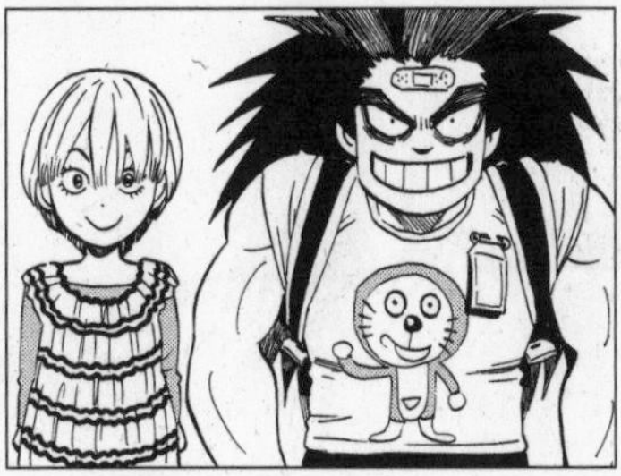

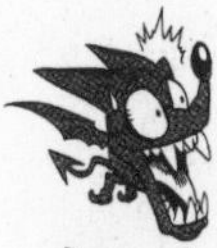

HIS LITTLE BROTHER IS SCAAAAAAARY!!

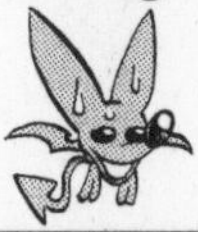

HOW COME HIS LITTLE SISTER IS SO NORMAL AND CUTE?

Send your queries for Devil Bat 021 here!!

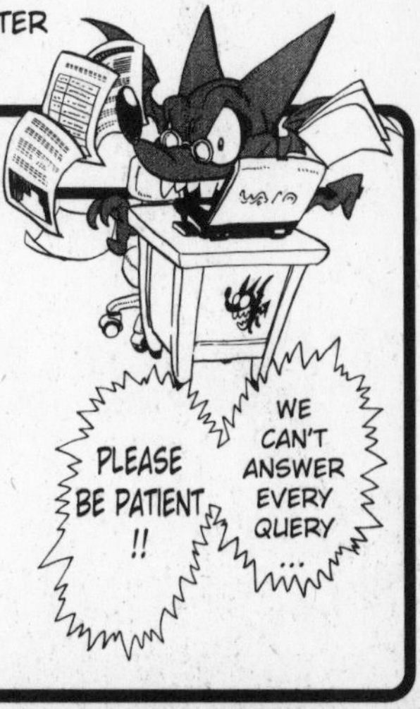
WE CAN'T ANSWER EVERY QUERY...
PLEASE BE PATIENT!!

Devil Bat 021
Shonen Jump Advanced/Eyeshield 21
c/o VIZ Media, LLC
P.O. Box 77010
San Francisco, CA 94107

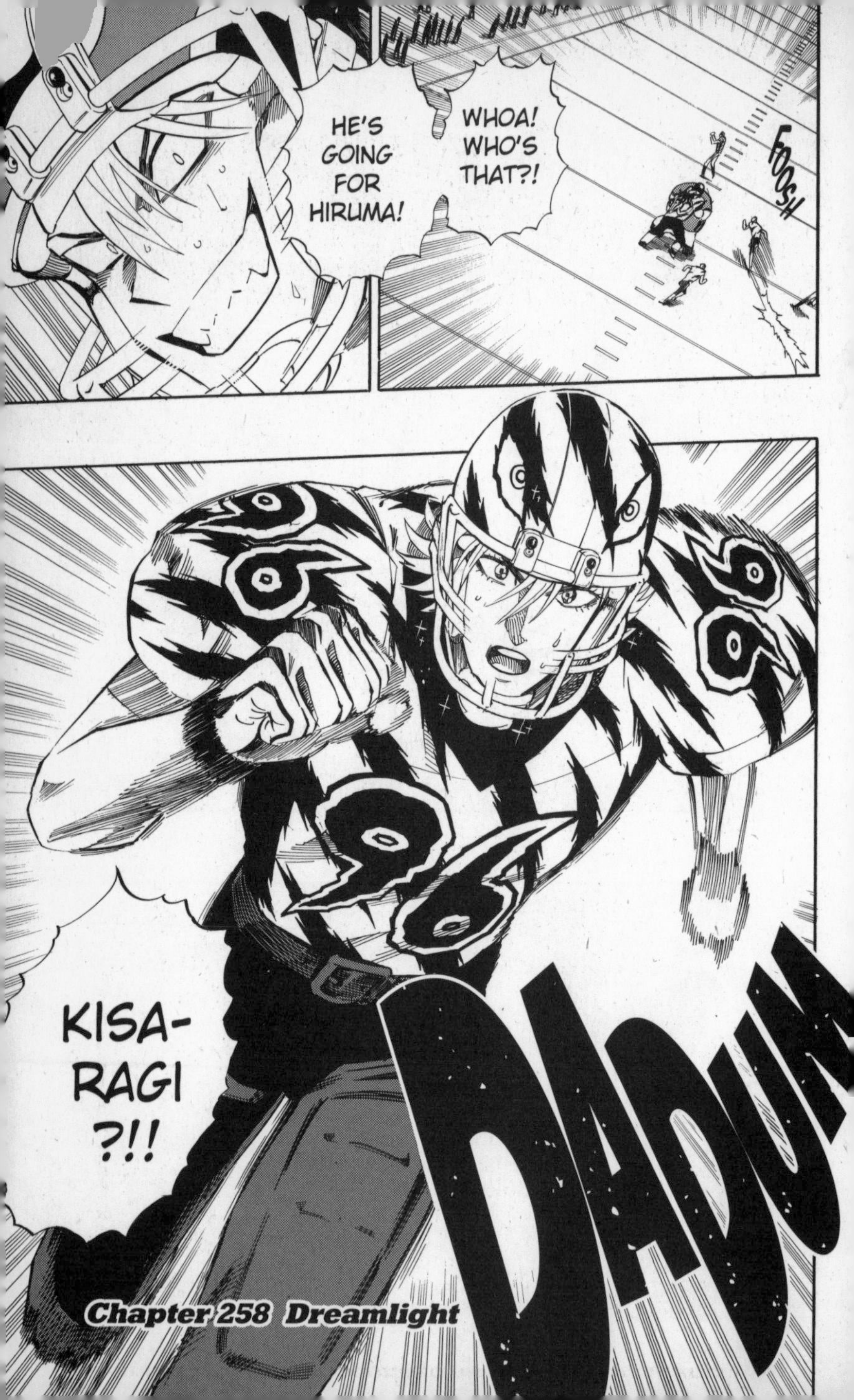
FOOSH
WHOA! WHO'S THAT?!
HE'S GOING FOR HIRUMA!
DADUM
KISA-RAGI ?!!

Chapter 258 Dreamlight

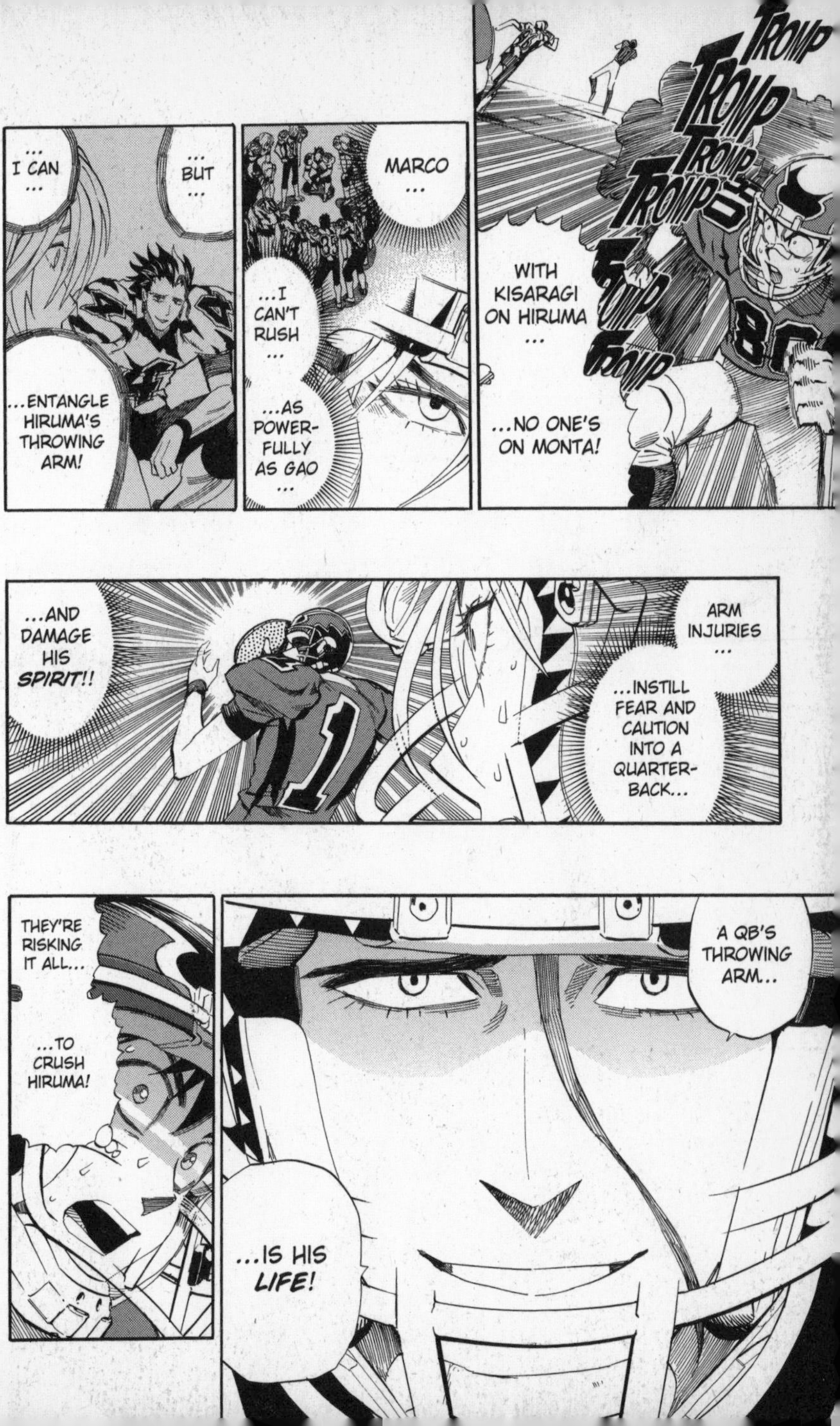
TROMP
TROMP
TROMP
TROMP
TROMP
TROMP
WITH KISARAGI ON HIRUMA ...
...NO ONE'S ON MONTA!
MARCO ...
...I CAN'T RUSH ...
...AS POWER-FULLY AS GAO ...
... BUT ...
... I CAN ...
...ENTANGLE HIRUMA'S THROWING ARM!
ARM INJURIES ...
...INSTILL FEAR AND CAUTION INTO A QUARTER-BACK...
...AND DAMAGE HIS *SPIRIT*!!
A QB'S THROWING ARM...
...IS HIS *LIFE*!
THEY'RE RISKING IT ALL...
...TO CRUSH HIRUMA!

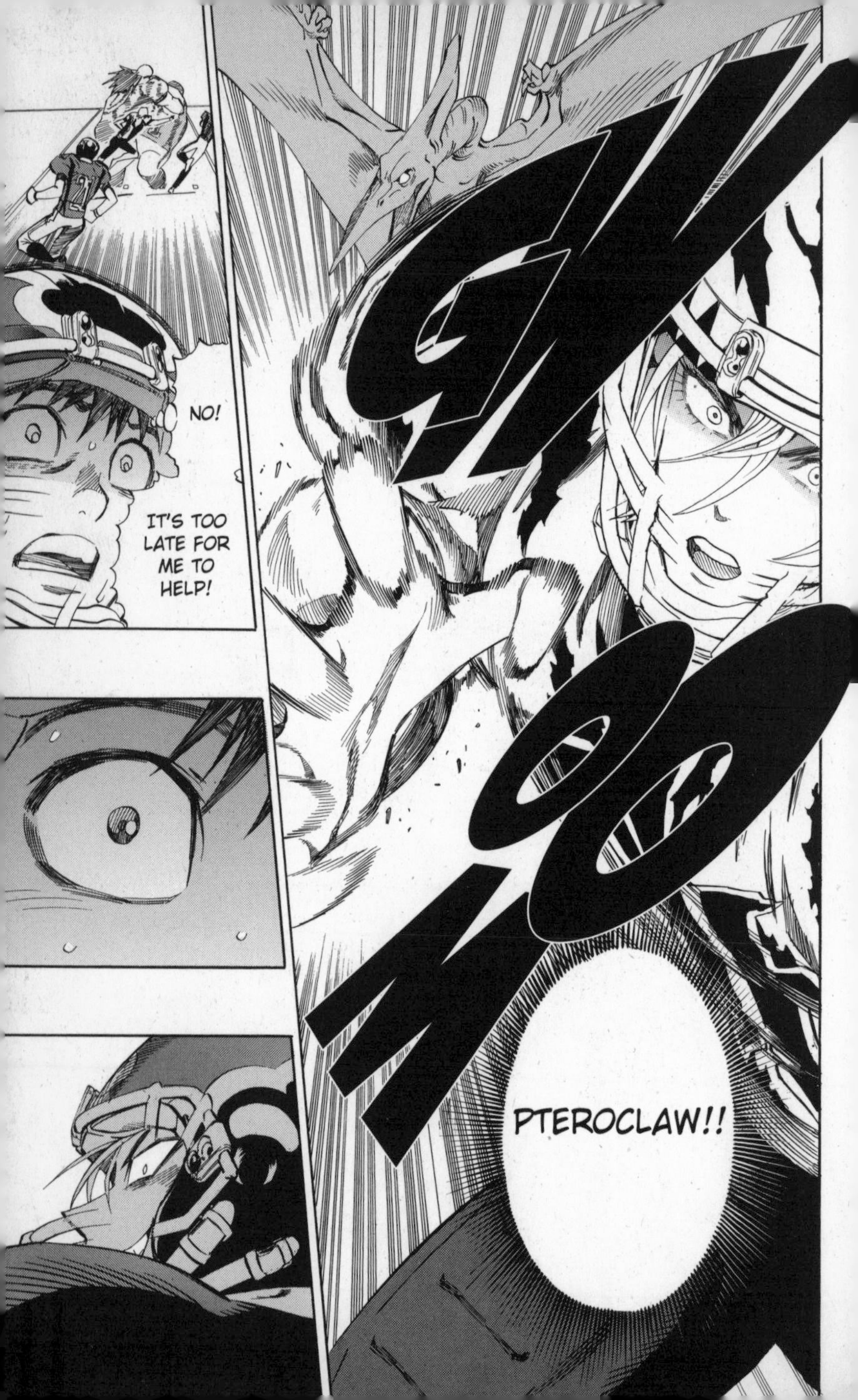
PTEROCLAW!!
NO!
IT'S TOO LATE FOR ME TO HELP!

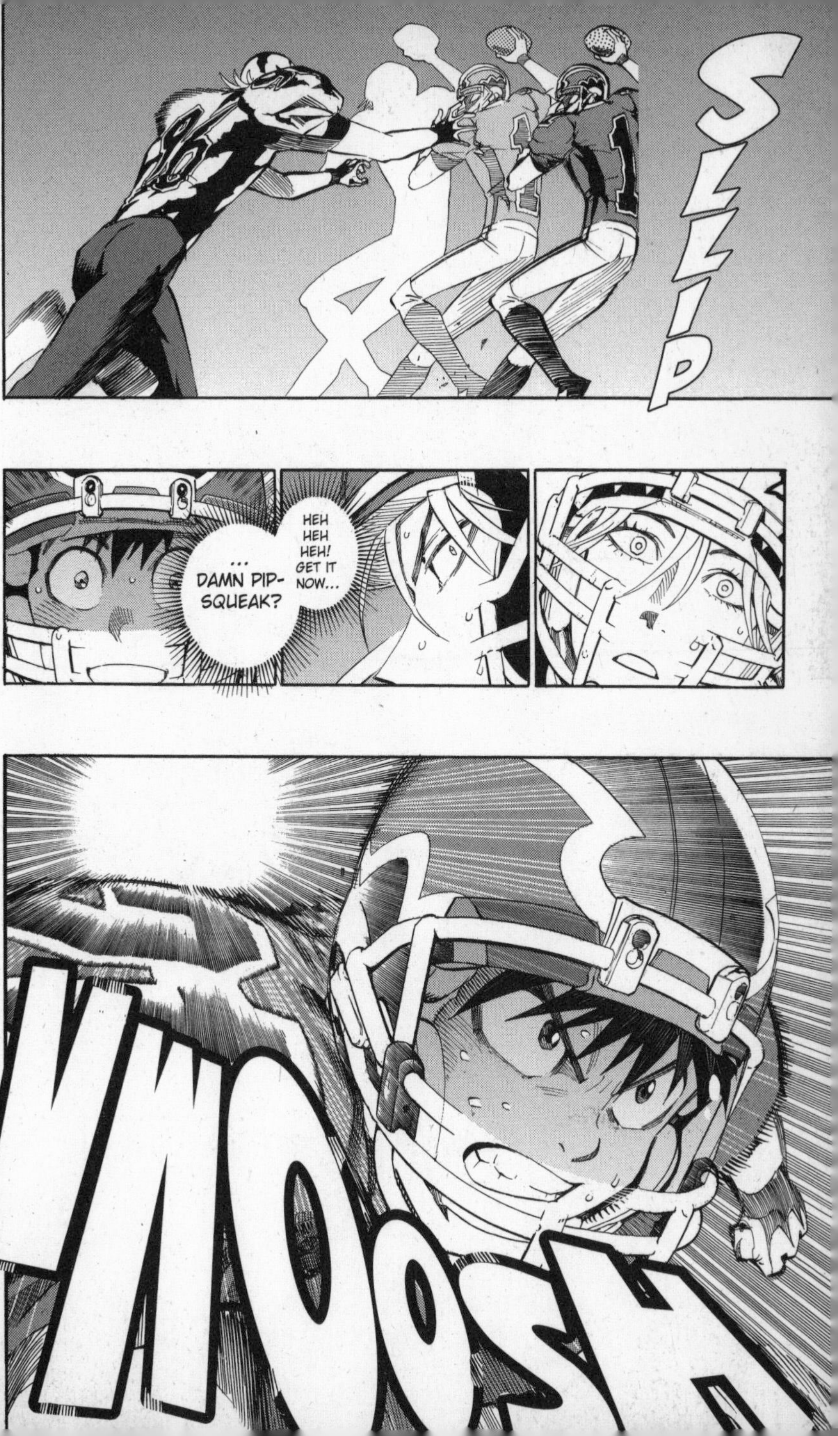
SLIP
HEH HEH HEH! GET IT NOW...
... DAMN PIP-SQUEAK?
WHOOSH

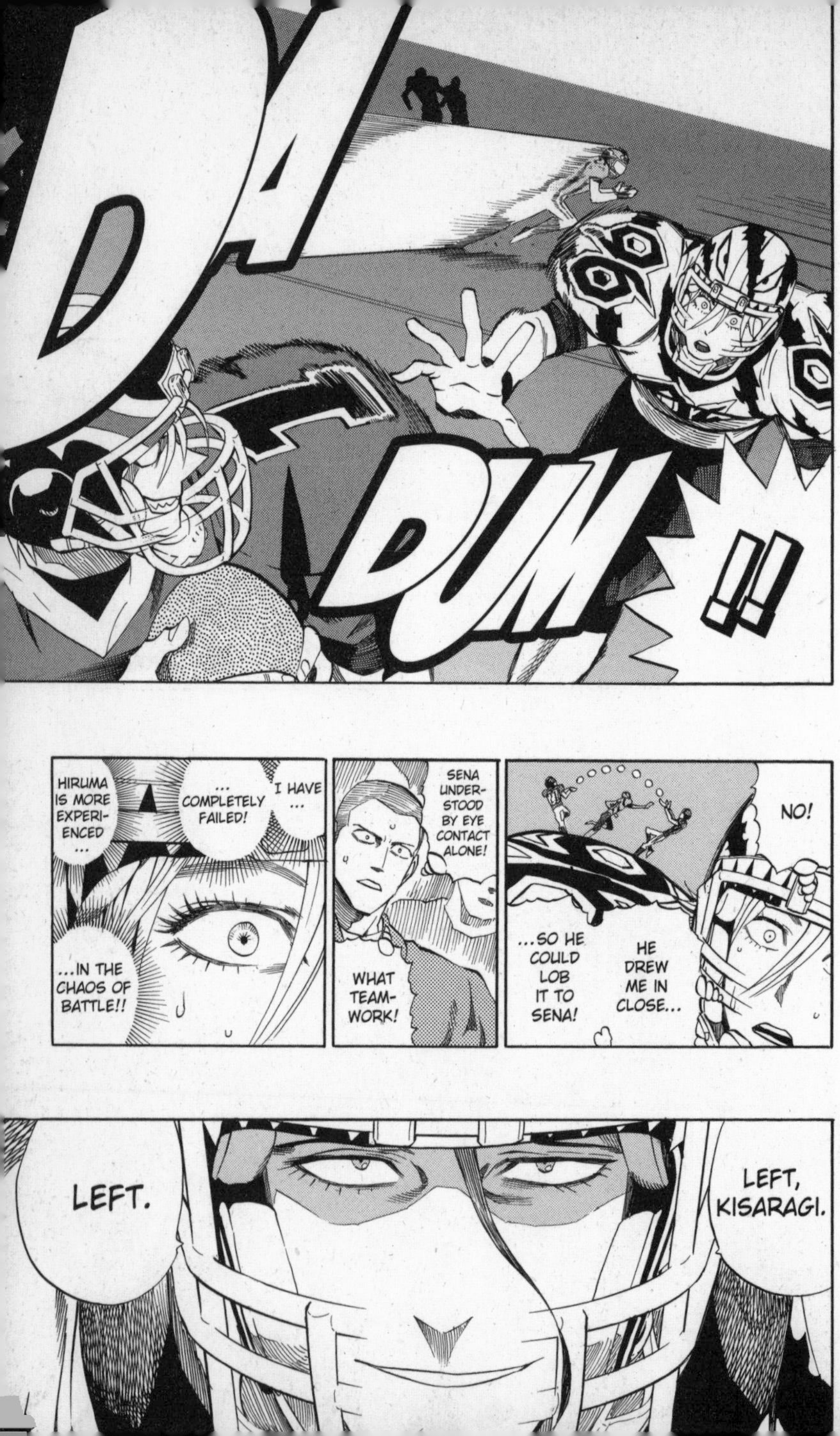
DA
DUM !!
NO!
HE DREW ME IN CLOSE...
...SO HE COULD LOB IT TO SENA!
SENA UNDERSTOOD BY EYE CONTACT ALONE!
WHAT TEAMWORK!
I HAVE ...
... COMPLETELY FAILED!
HIRUMA IS MORE EXPERIENCED ...
...IN THE CHAOS OF BATTLE!!
LEFT, KISARAGI.
LEFT.

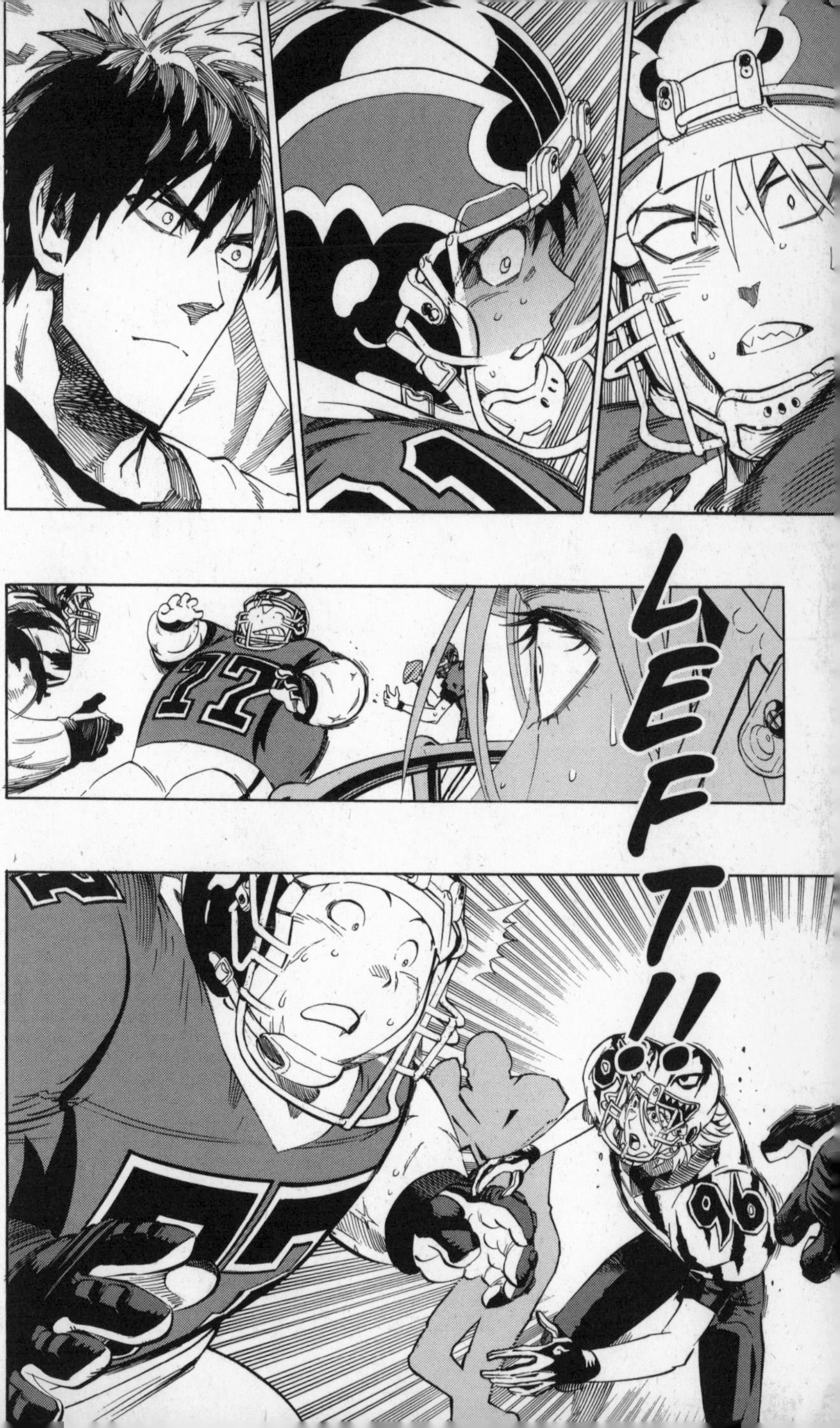
LEFT!!

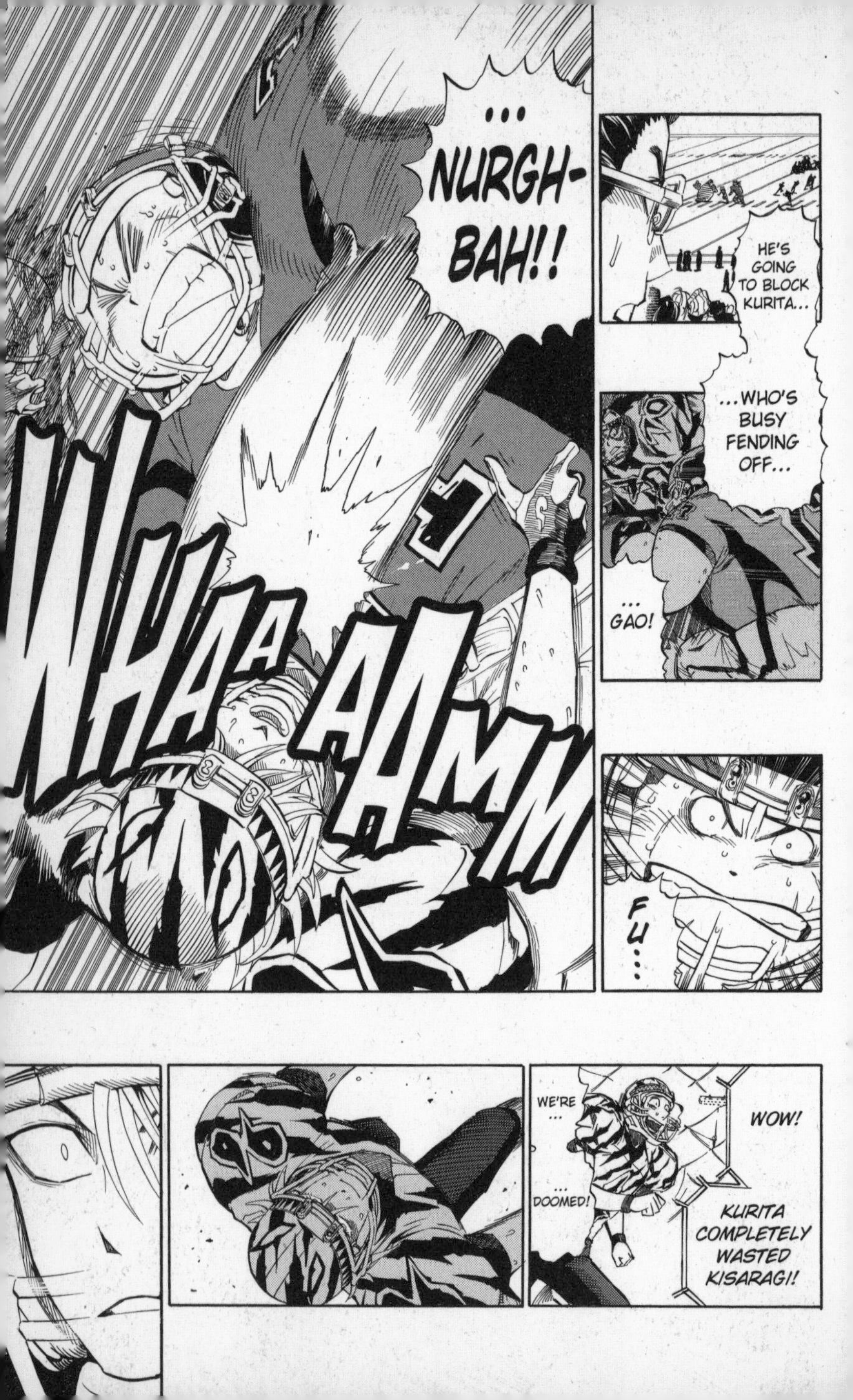
HE'S GOING TO BLOCK KURITA...
...WHO'S BUSY FENDING OFF...
...GAO!
FU...
...NURGH-BAH!!
WHAAAAMM
WOW!
KURITA COMPLETELY WASTED KISARAGI!
WE'RE...
...DOOMED!

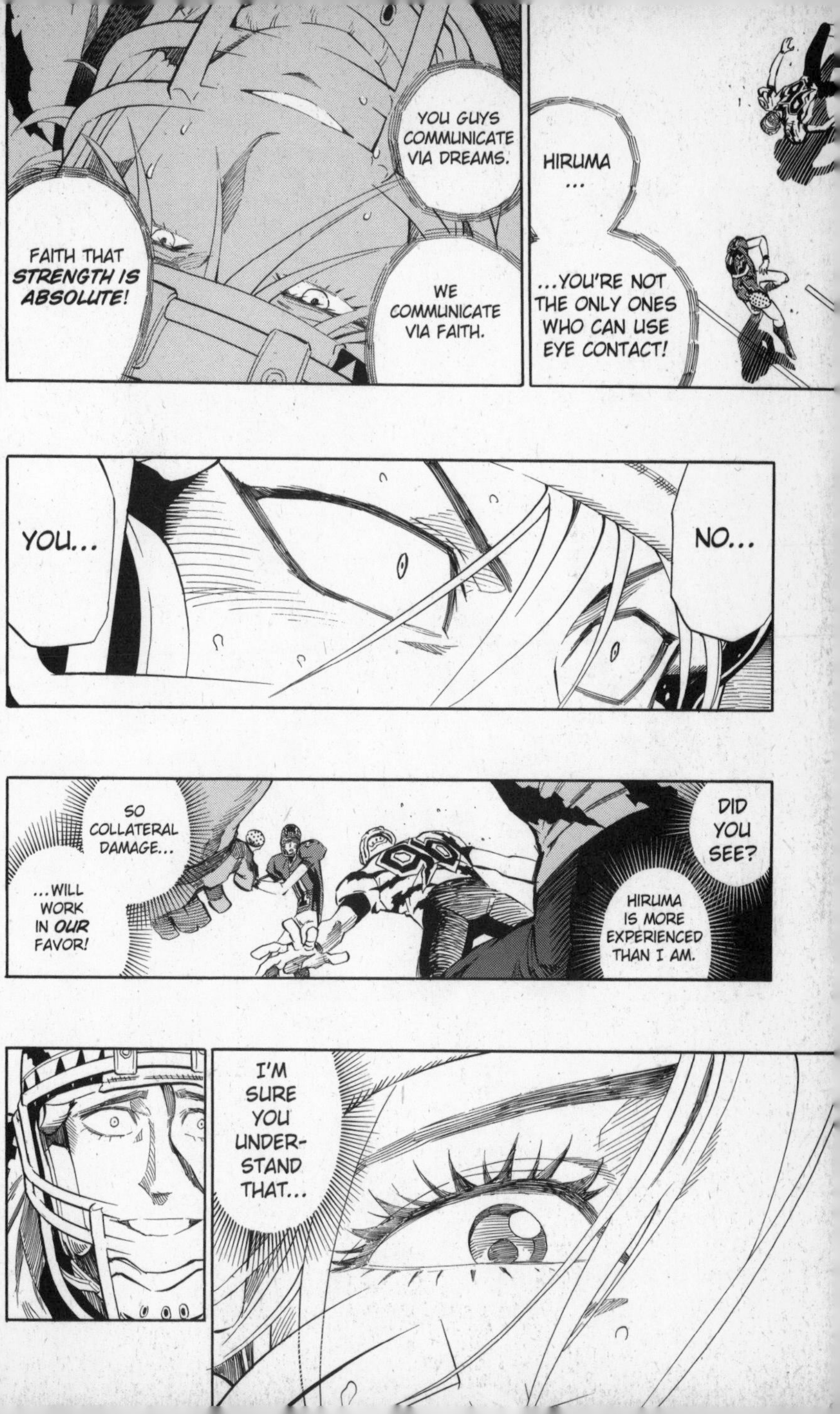
HIRUMA ...
...YOU'RE NOT THE ONLY ONES WHO CAN USE EYE CONTACT!
YOU GUYS COMMUNICATE VIA DREAMS.
WE COMMUNICATE VIA FAITH.
FAITH THAT STRENGTH IS ABSOLUTE!
NO...
YOU...
DID YOU SEE?
HIRUMA IS MORE EXPERIENCED THAN I AM.
SO COLLATERAL DAMAGE...
...WILL WORK IN OUR FAVOR!
I'M SURE YOU UNDERSTAND THAT...

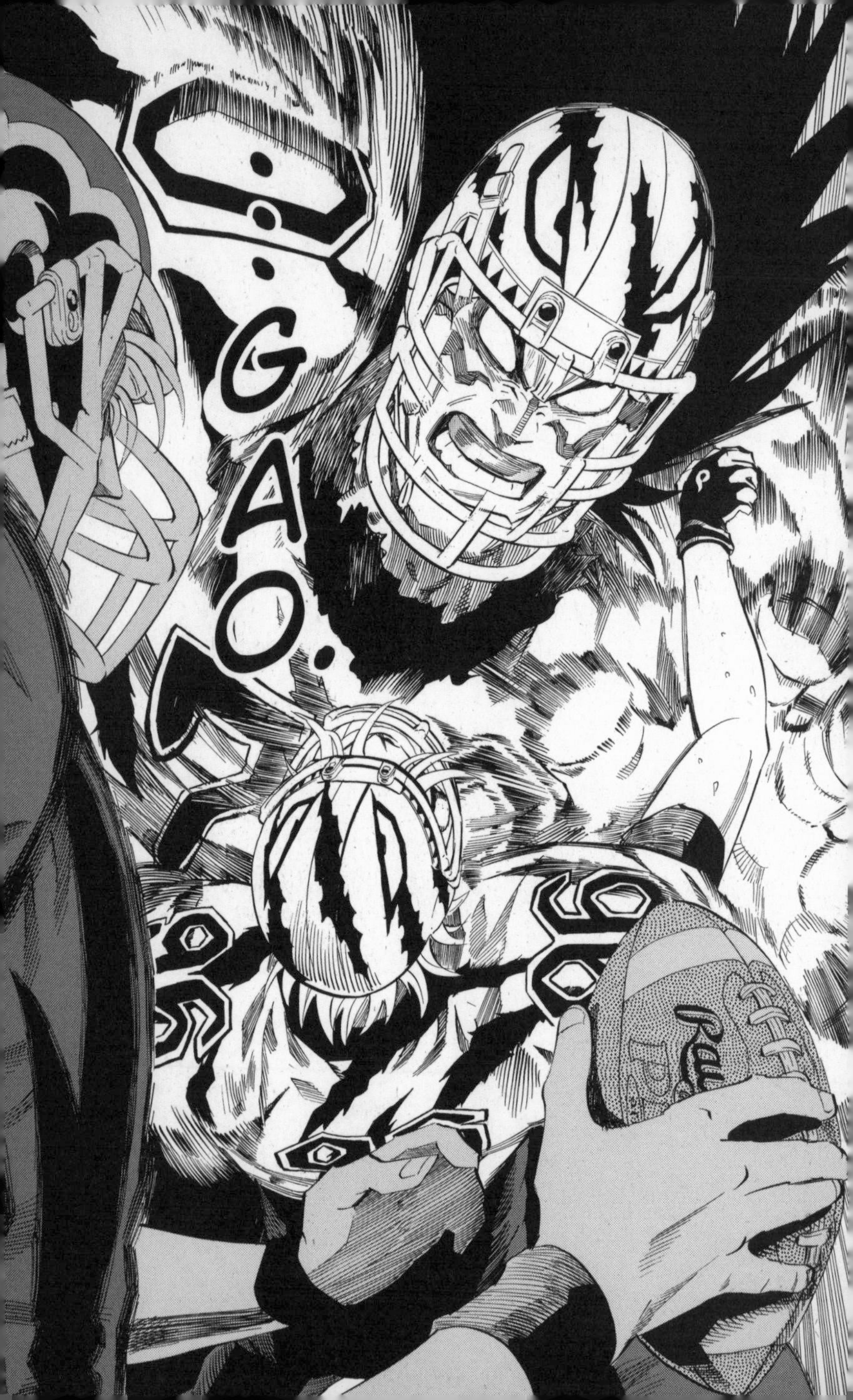
GAO

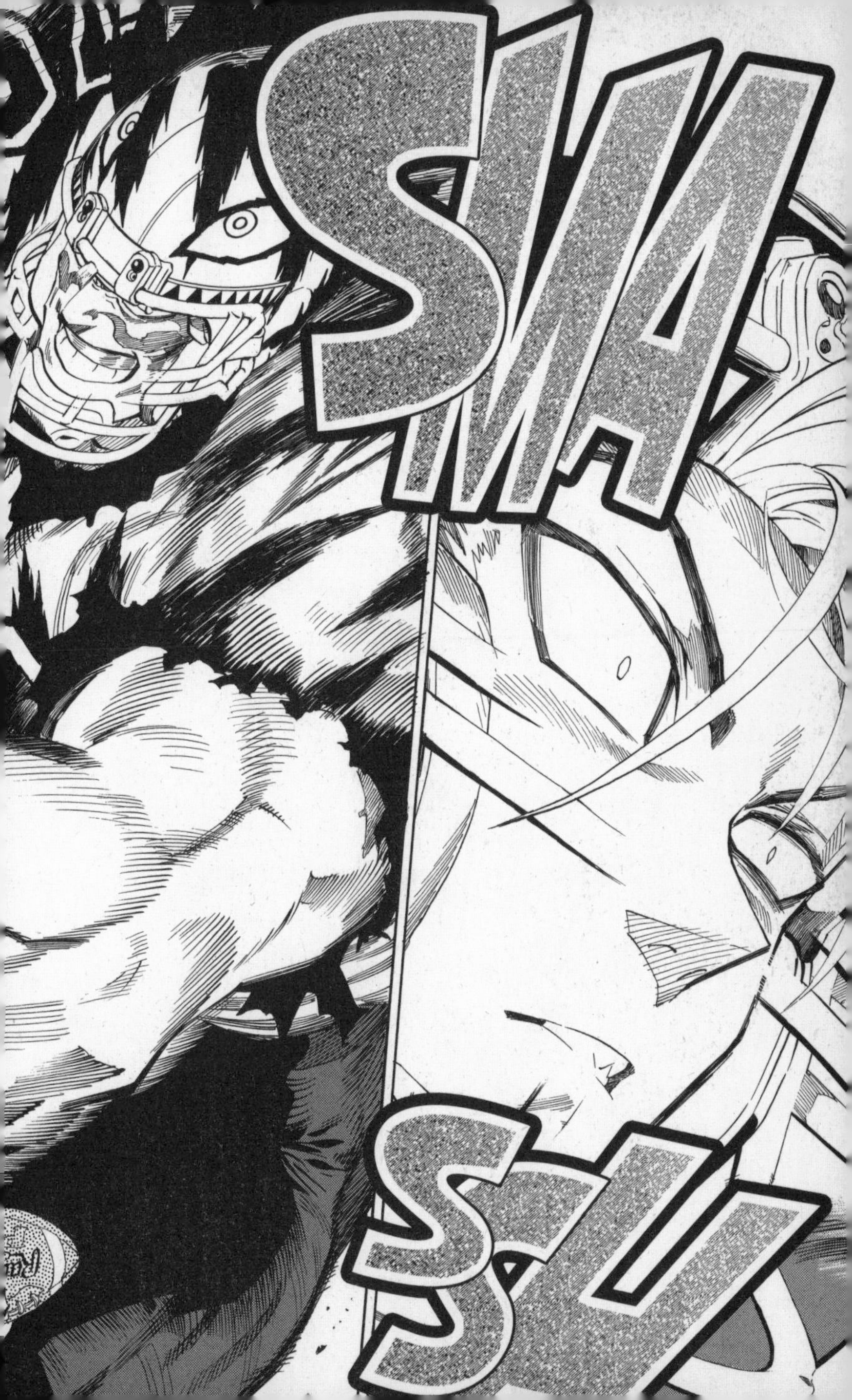
SWA
SSH

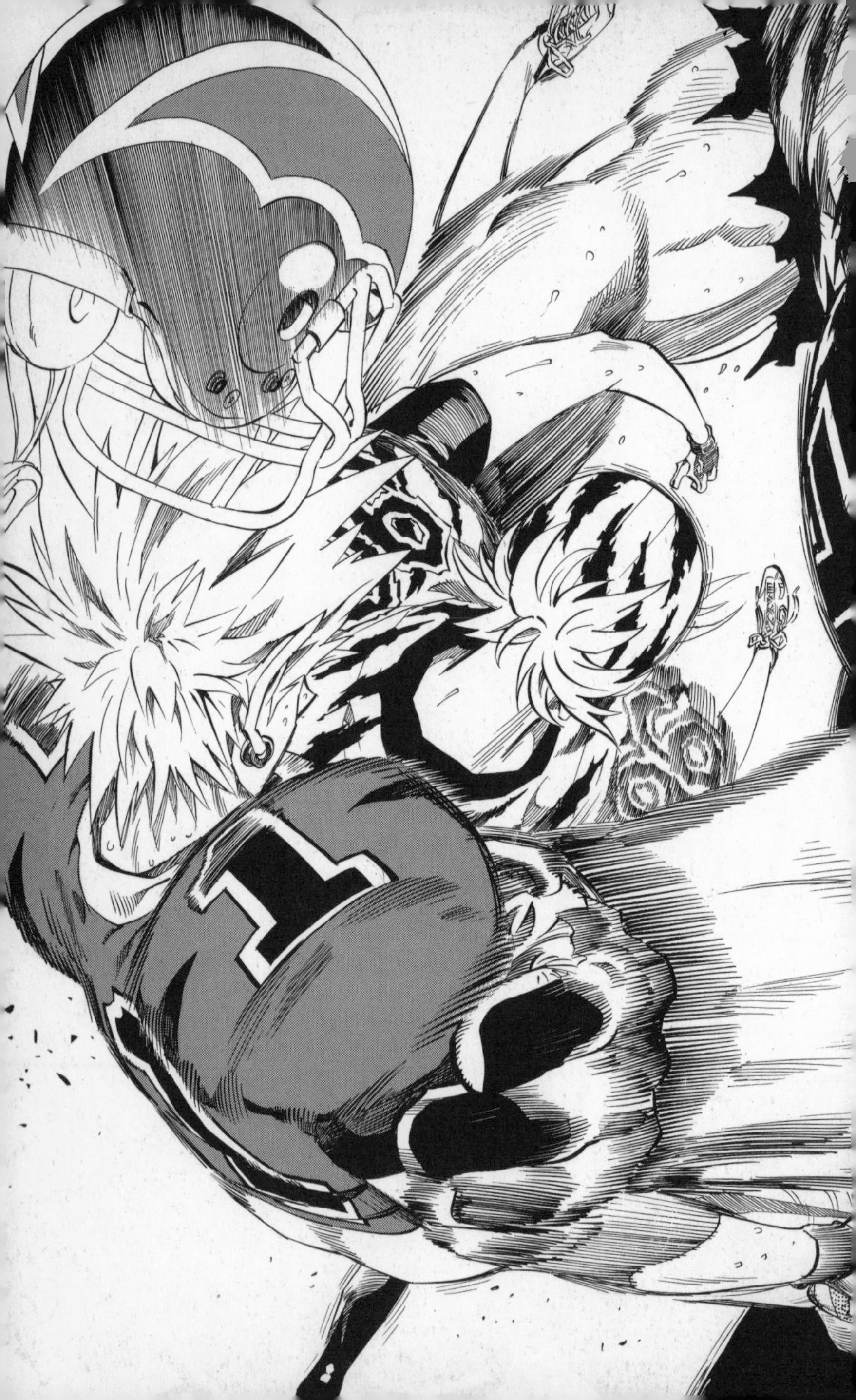

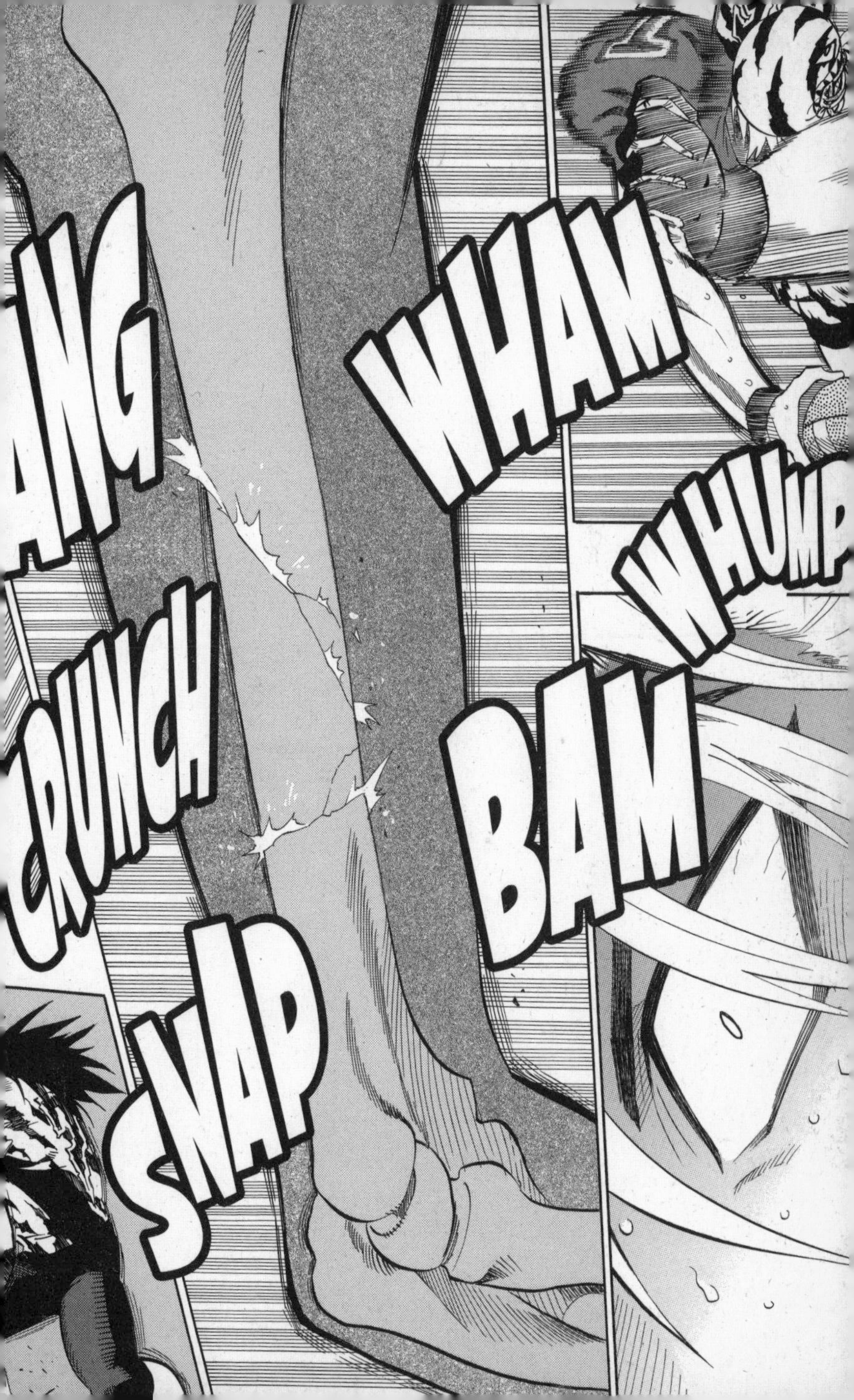
WHAM
WHUMP
BAM
ANG
CRUNCH
SNAP

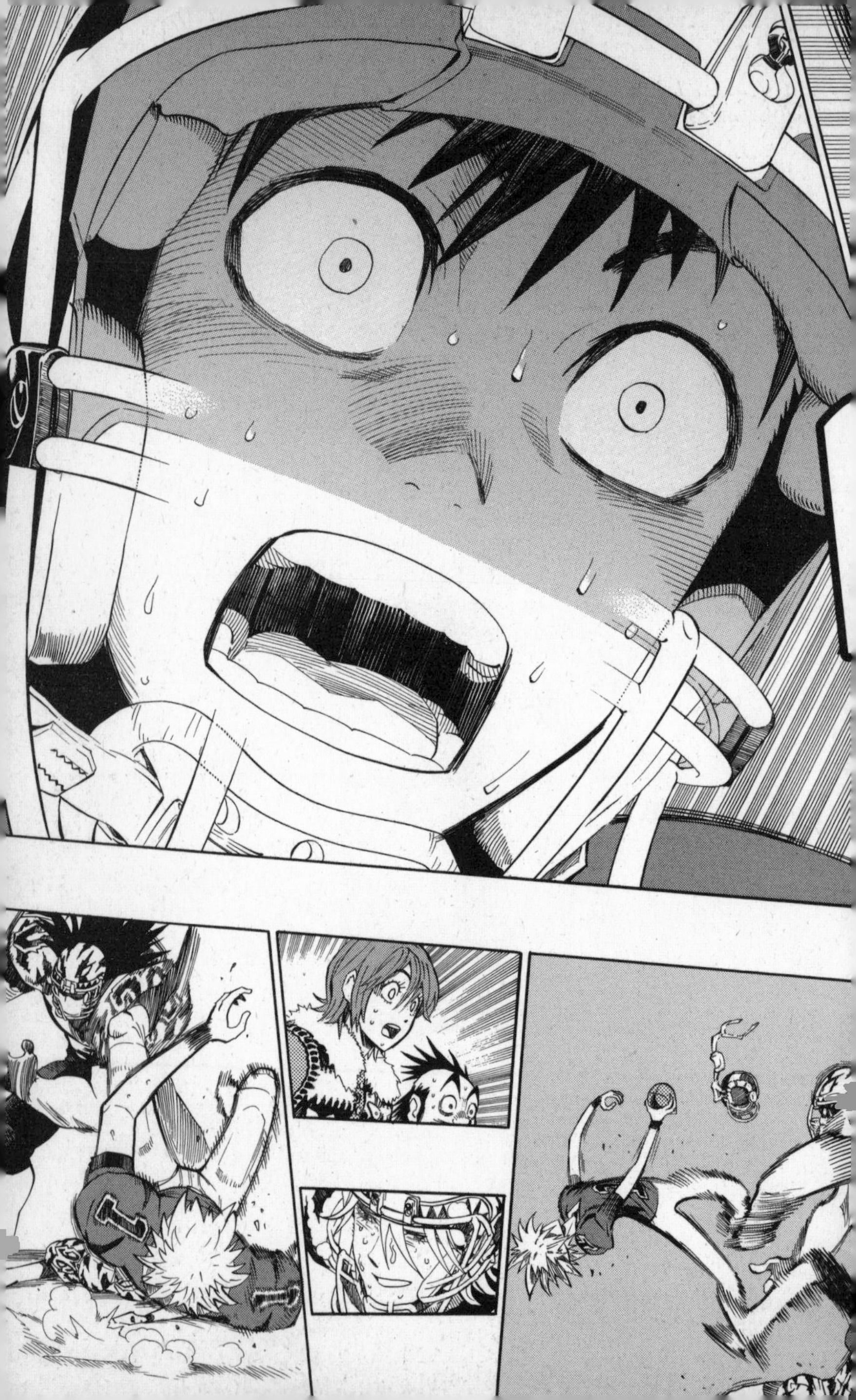

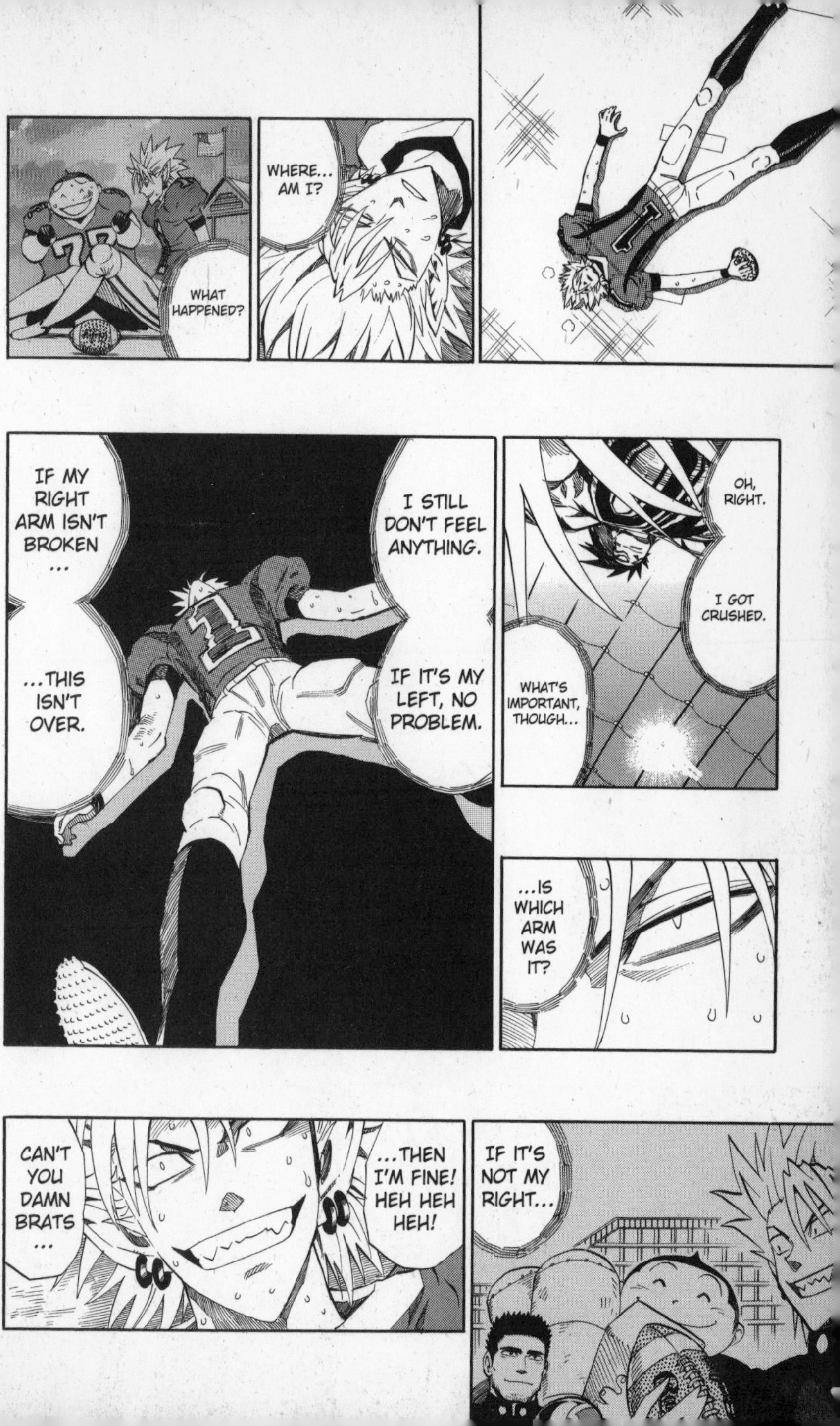
WHERE... AM I?
WHAT HAPPENED?
OH, RIGHT.
I GOT CRUSHED.
WHAT'S IMPORTANT, THOUGH...
...IS WHICH ARM WAS IT?
I STILL DON'T FEEL ANYTHING.
IF IT'S MY LEFT, NO PROBLEM.
IF MY RIGHT ARM ISN'T BROKEN...
...THIS ISN'T OVER.
IF IT'S NOT MY RIGHT...
...THEN I'M FINE! HEH HEH HEH!
CAN'T YOU DAMN BRATS...

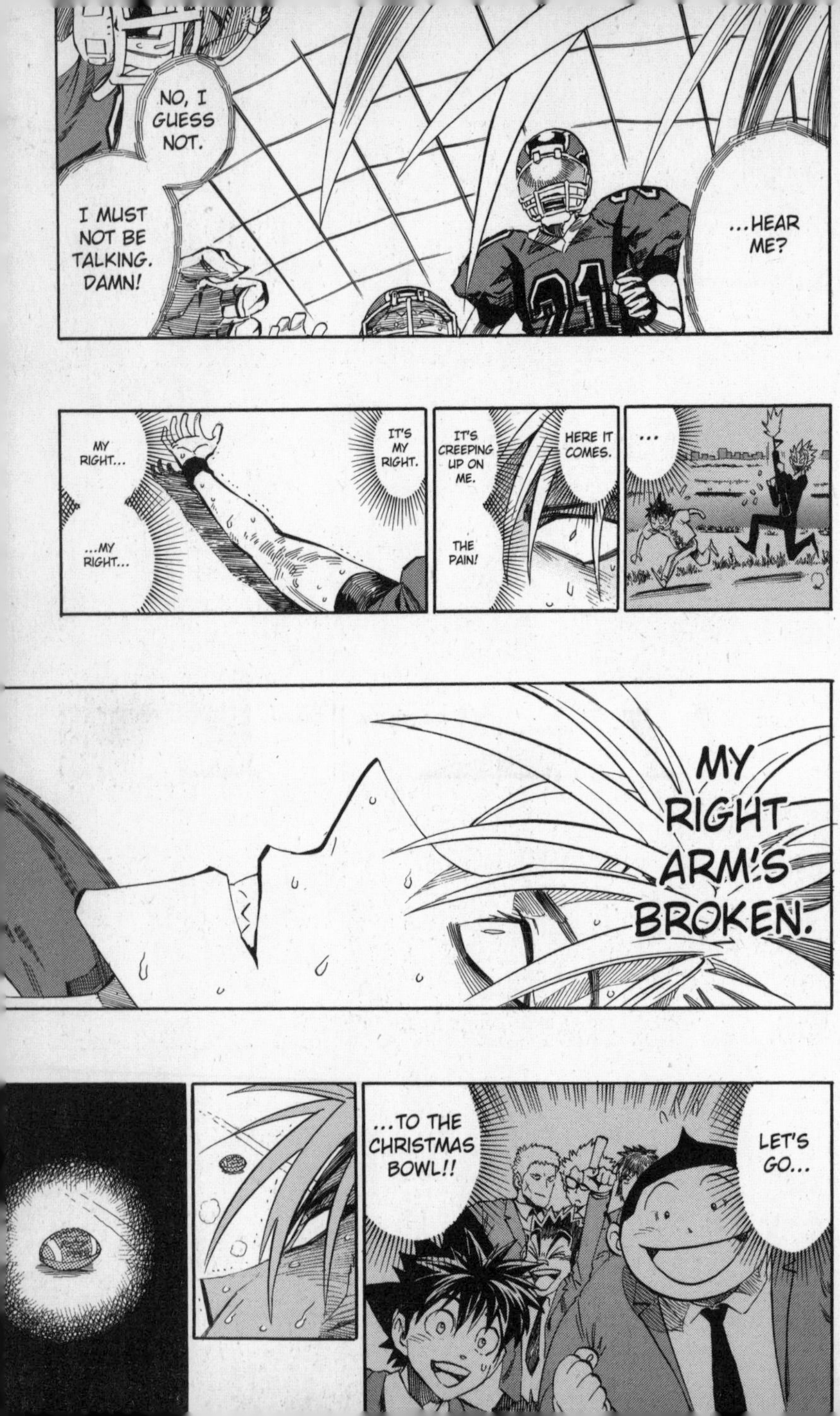
...HEAR ME?
NO, I GUESS NOT.
I MUST NOT BE TALKING. DAMN!
...
HERE IT COMES.
IT'S CREEPING UP ON ME.
THE PAIN!
IT'S MY RIGHT.
MY RIGHT...
...MY RIGHT...
MY RIGHT ARM'S BROKEN.
LET'S GO...
...TO THE CHRISTMAS BOWL!!

Chapter 258 Dreamlight

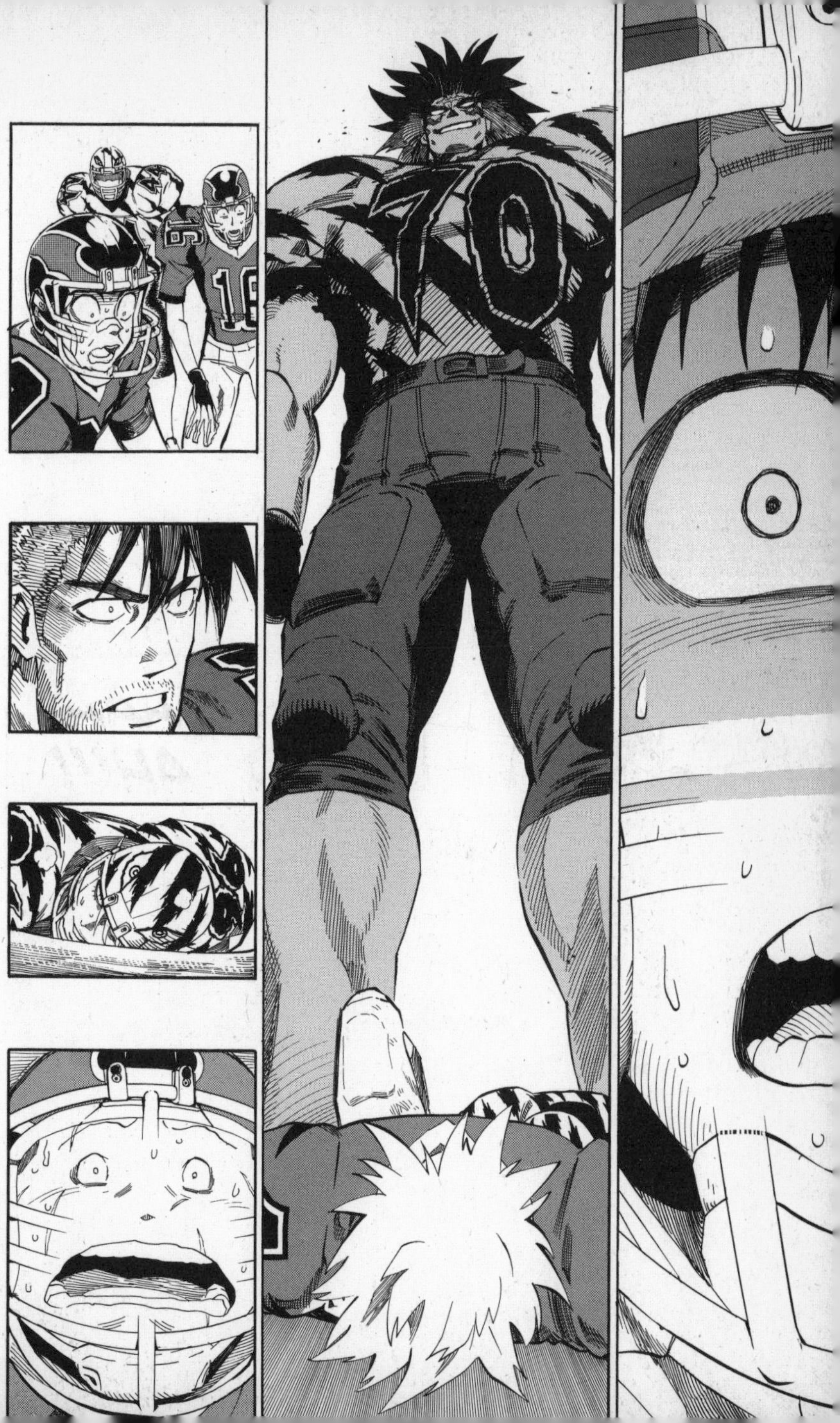

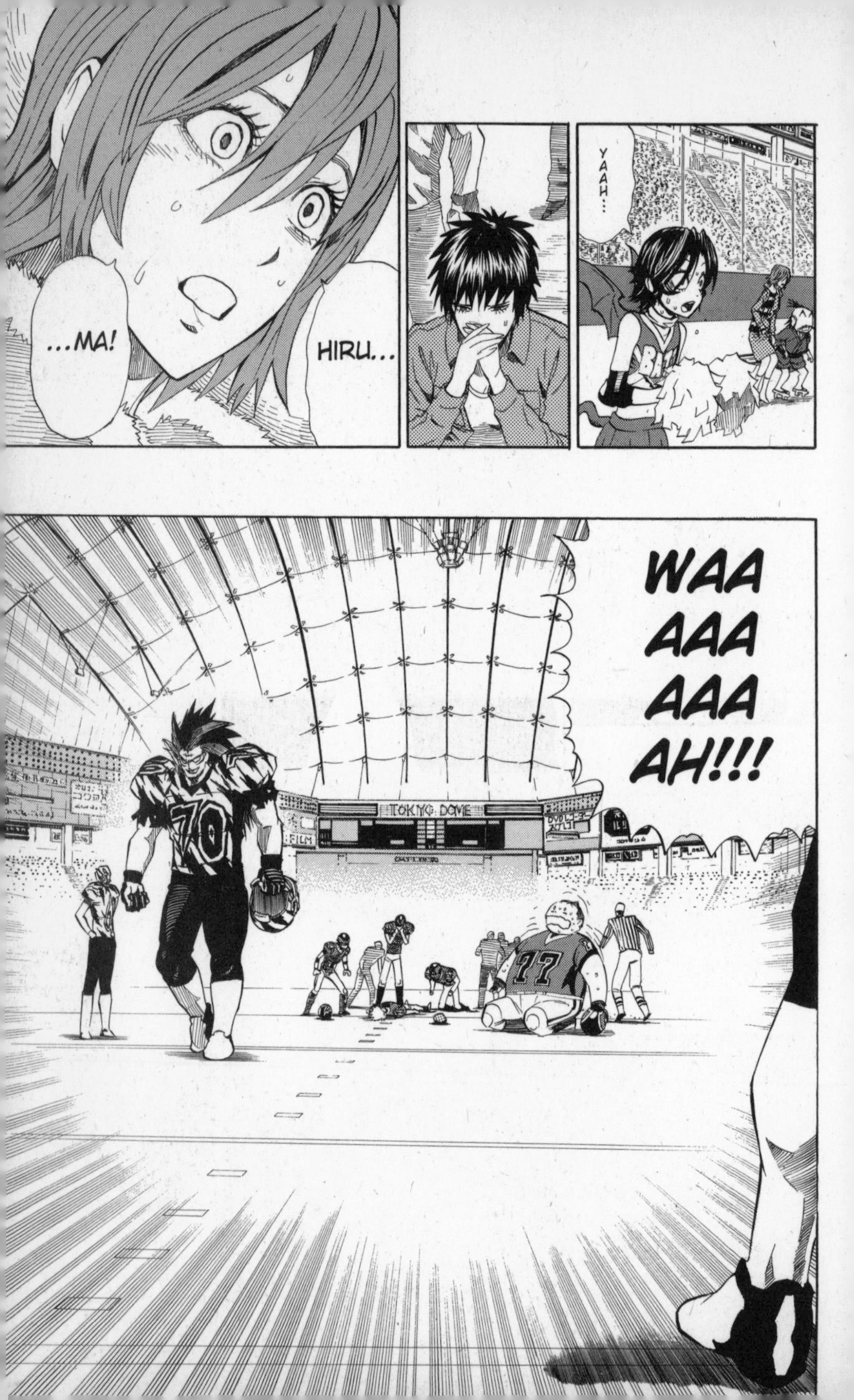
YAAH...
HIRU...
...MA!
WAAAAAAAAAAH!!!
TOKYO DOME
FILM

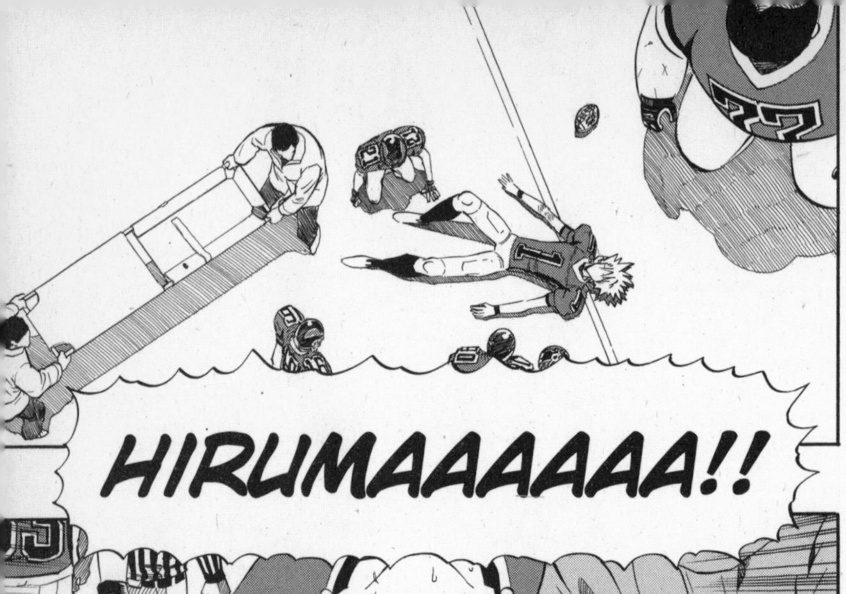
HIRUMAAAAAAA!!

Chapter 259 Second Quarterback

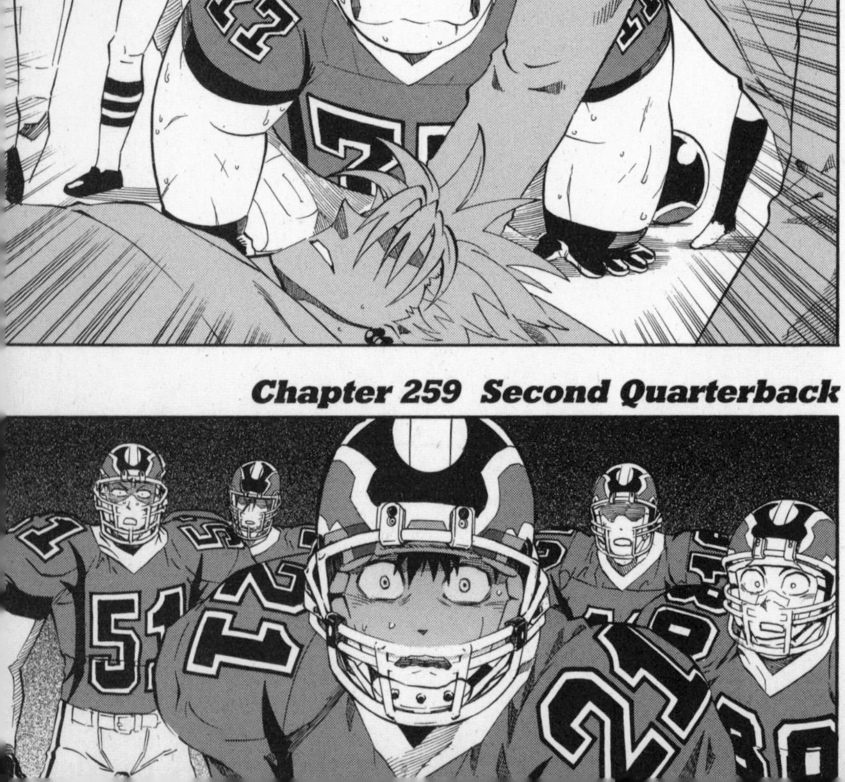

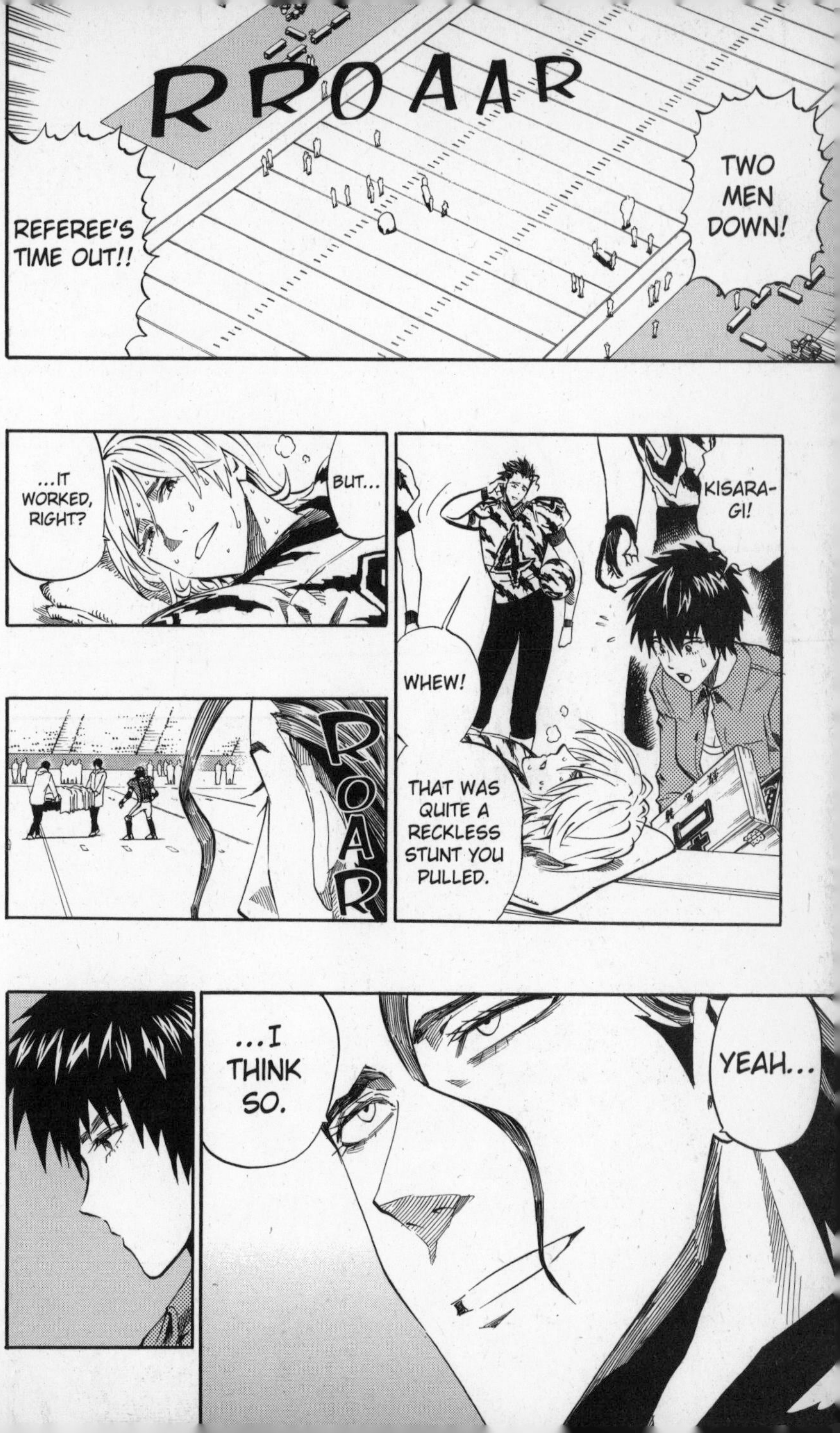
RRROAAR
TWO MEN DOWN!
REFEREE'S TIME OUT!!
KISARA-GI!
WHEW!
THAT WAS QUITE A RECKLESS STUNT YOU PULLED.
BUT...
...IT WORKED, RIGHT?
ROAR
YEAH...
...I THINK SO.

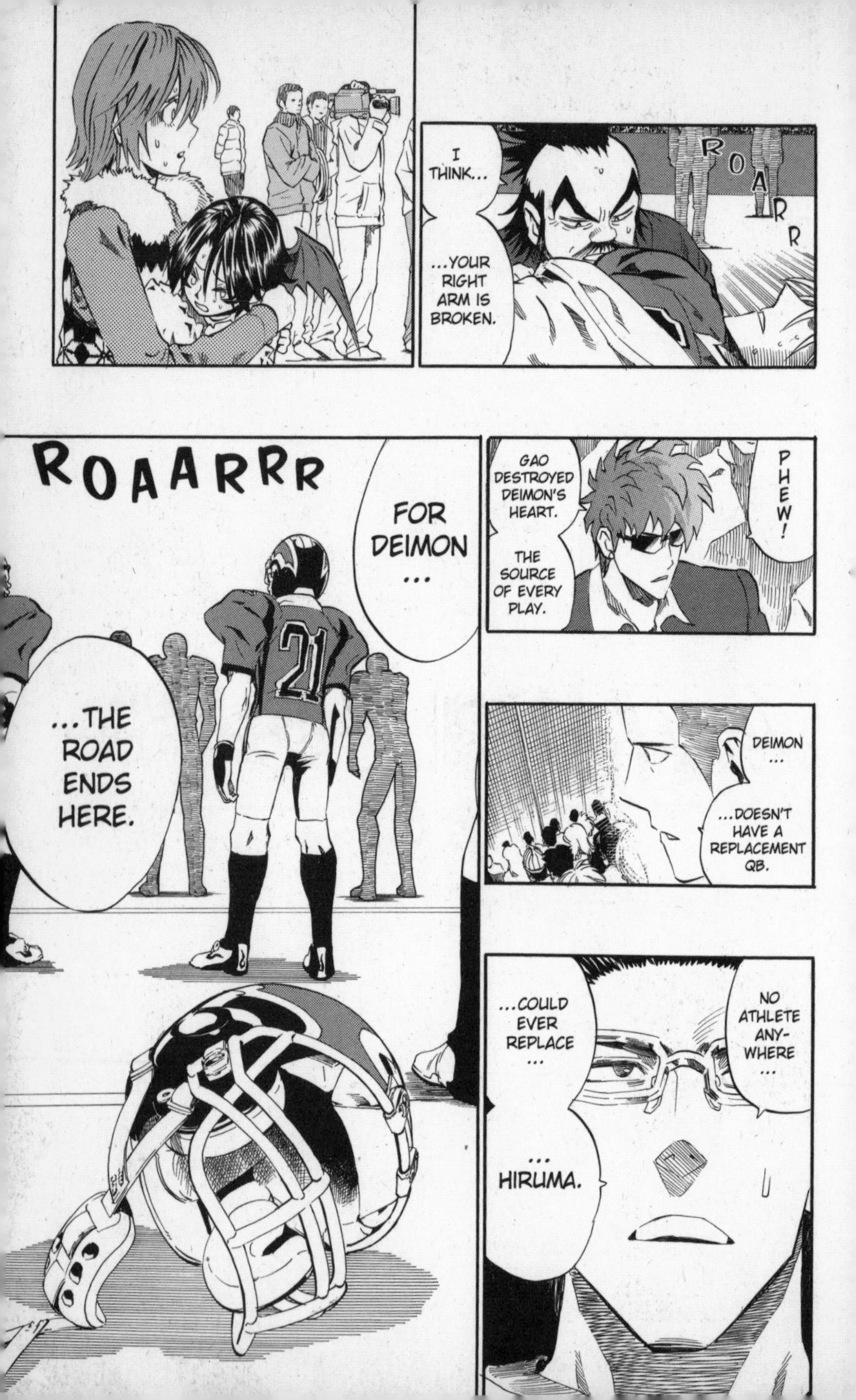
I THINK...
...YOUR RIGHT ARM IS BROKEN.
ROARR
PHEW!
GAO DESTROYED DEIMON'S HEART.
THE SOURCE OF EVERY PLAY.
DEIMON...
...DOESN'T HAVE A REPLACEMENT QB.
NO ATHLETE ANY-WHERE...
...COULD EVER REPLACE...
...HIRUMA.
ROAARRR
FOR DEIMON...
...THE ROAD ENDS HERE.

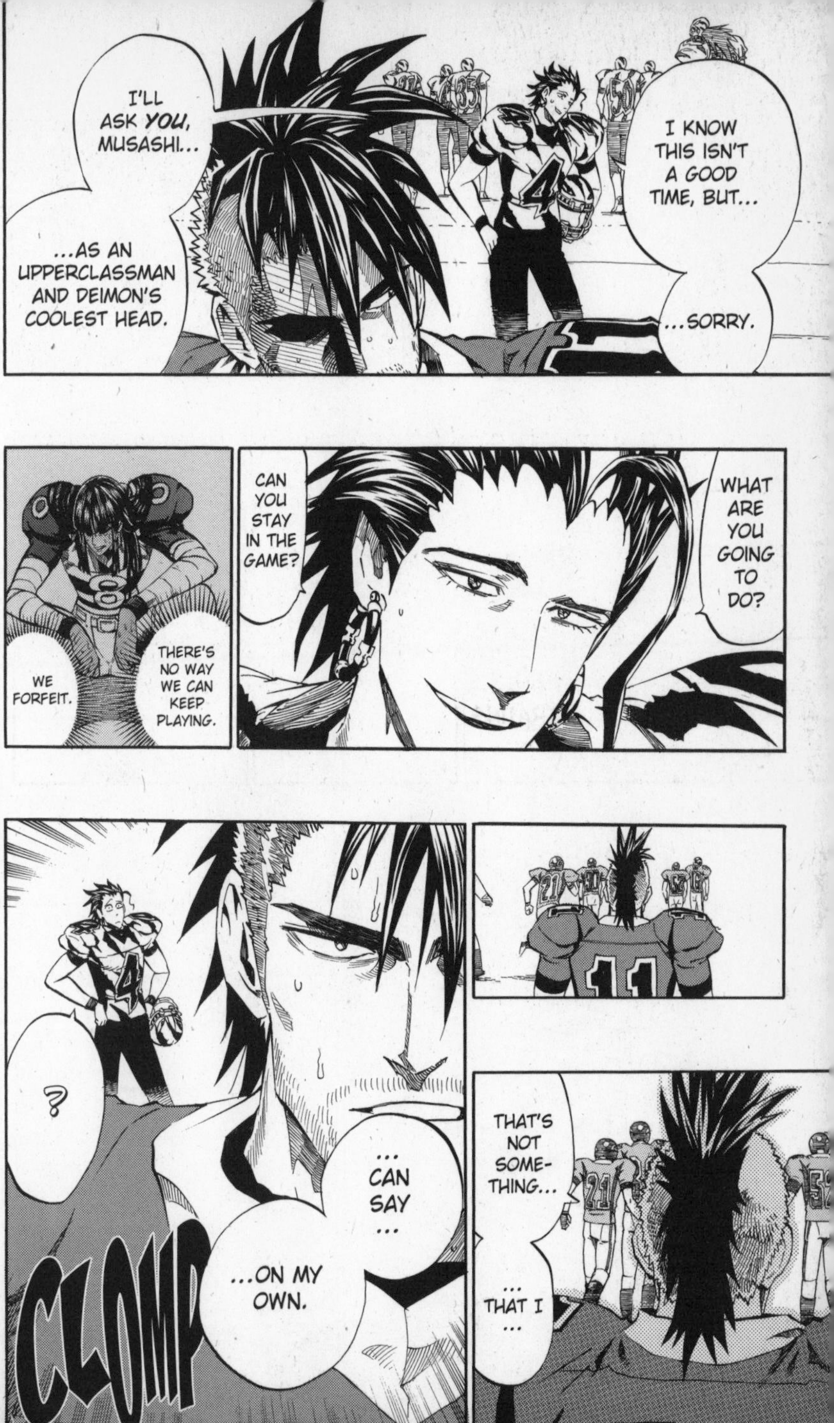
I KNOW THIS ISN'T A GOOD TIME, BUT...
...SORRY.
I'LL ASK *YOU*, MUSASHI...
...AS AN UPPERCLASSMAN AND DEIMON'S COOLEST HEAD.
WHAT ARE YOU GOING TO DO?
CAN YOU STAY IN THE GAME?
THERE'S NO WAY WE CAN KEEP PLAYING.
WE FORFEIT.
THAT'S NOT SOME-THING...
...THAT I...
...CAN SAY...
...ON MY OWN.
?
CLOMP

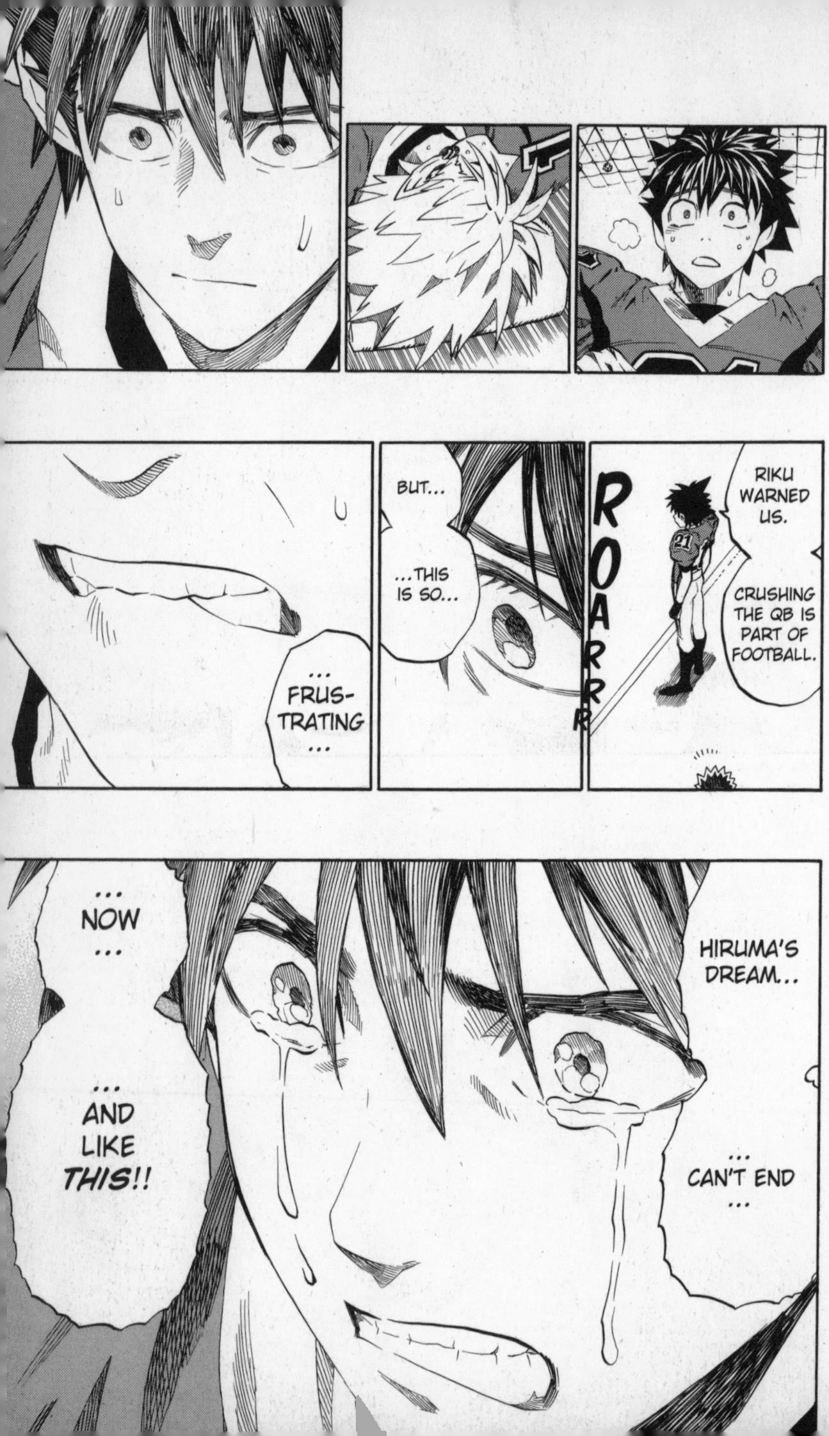
RIKU WARNED US.
CRUSHING THE QB IS PART OF FOOTBALL.
ROARRR
BUT...
...THIS IS SO...
...FRUS-TRATING...
HIRUMA'S DREAM...
...CAN'T END...
...NOW...
...AND LIKE *THIS*!!

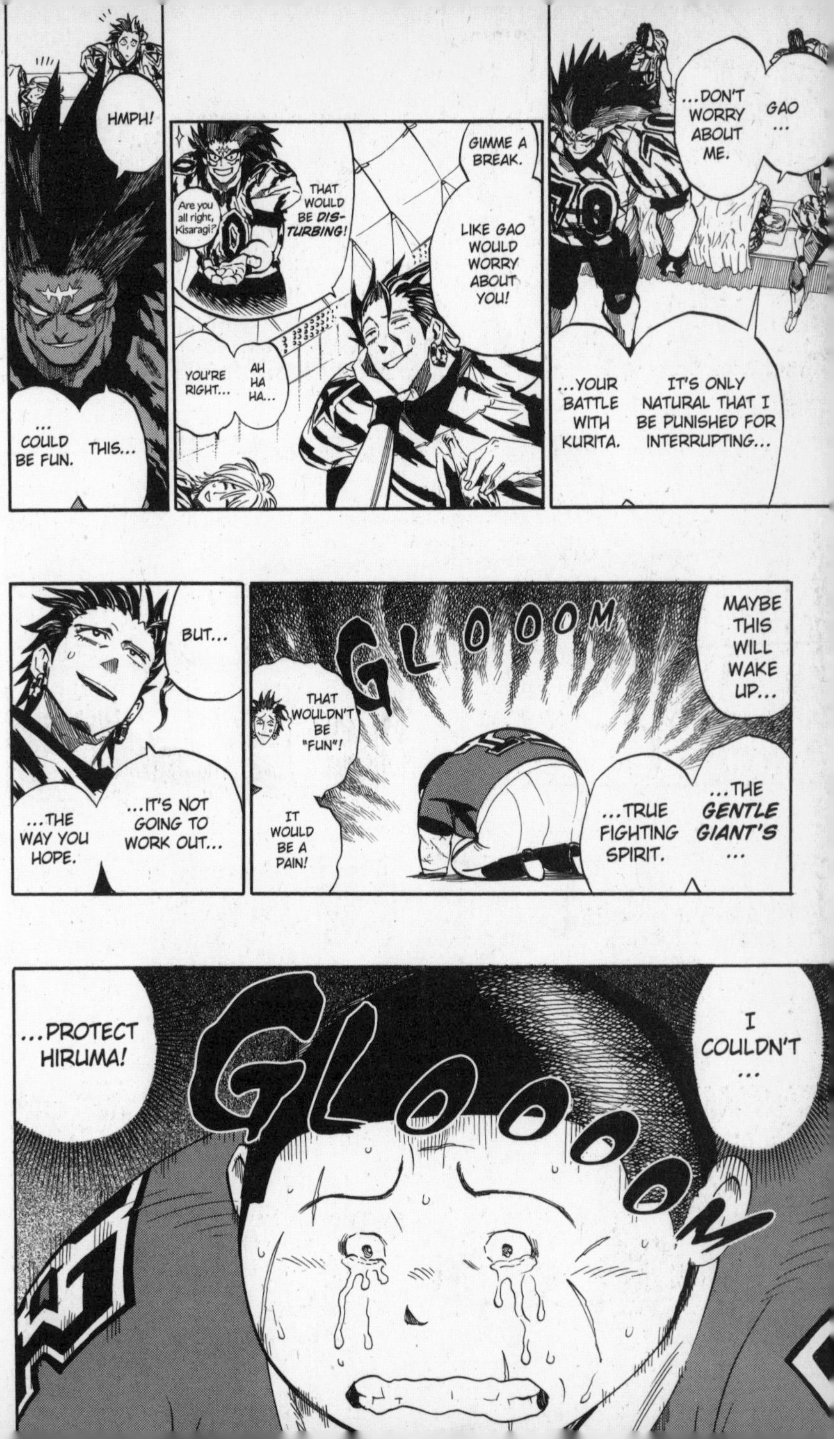
GAO...
...DON'T WORRY ABOUT ME.
IT'S ONLY NATURAL THAT I BE PUNISHED FOR INTERRUPTING...
...YOUR BATTLE WITH KURITA.
GIMME A BREAK.
LIKE GAO WOULD WORRY ABOUT YOU!
THAT WOULD BE *DISTURBING*!
Are you all right, Kisaragi?
AH HA HA...
YOU'RE RIGHT...
HMPH!
THIS...
...COULD BE FUN.
MAYBE THIS WILL WAKE UP...
...THE *GENTLE GIANT'S*...
...TRUE FIGHTING SPIRIT.
GLOOOM
THAT WOULDN'T BE "FUN"!
IT WOULD BE A PAIN!
BUT...
...IT'S NOT GOING TO WORK OUT...
...THE WAY YOU HOPE.
I COULDN'T...
GLOOOOOM
...PROTECT HIRUMA!

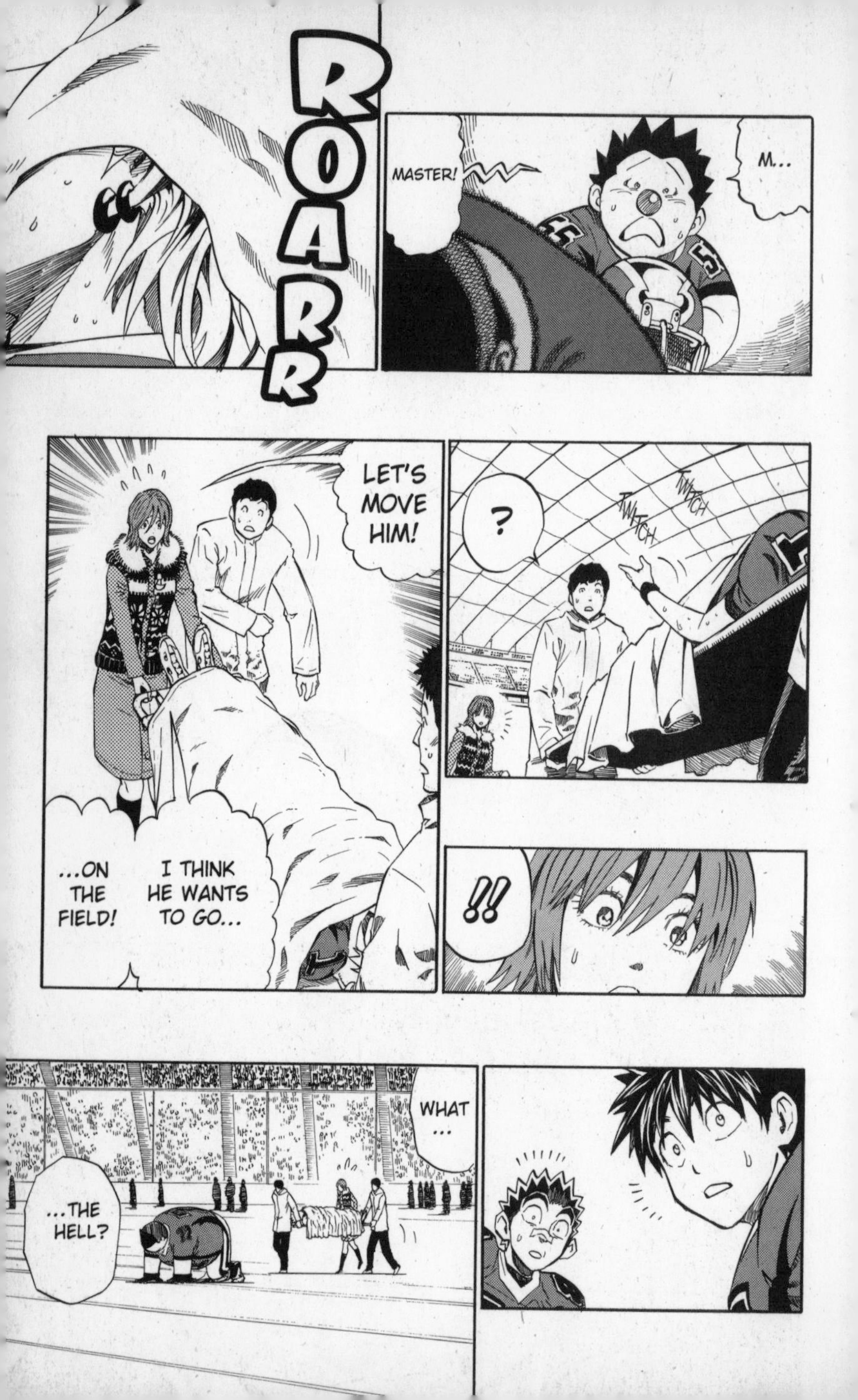
M...
MASTER!
ROARR
TWITCH
TWITCH
?
!!
LET'S MOVE HIM!
I THINK HE WANTS TO GO...
...ON THE FIELD!
WHAT ...
...THE HELL?

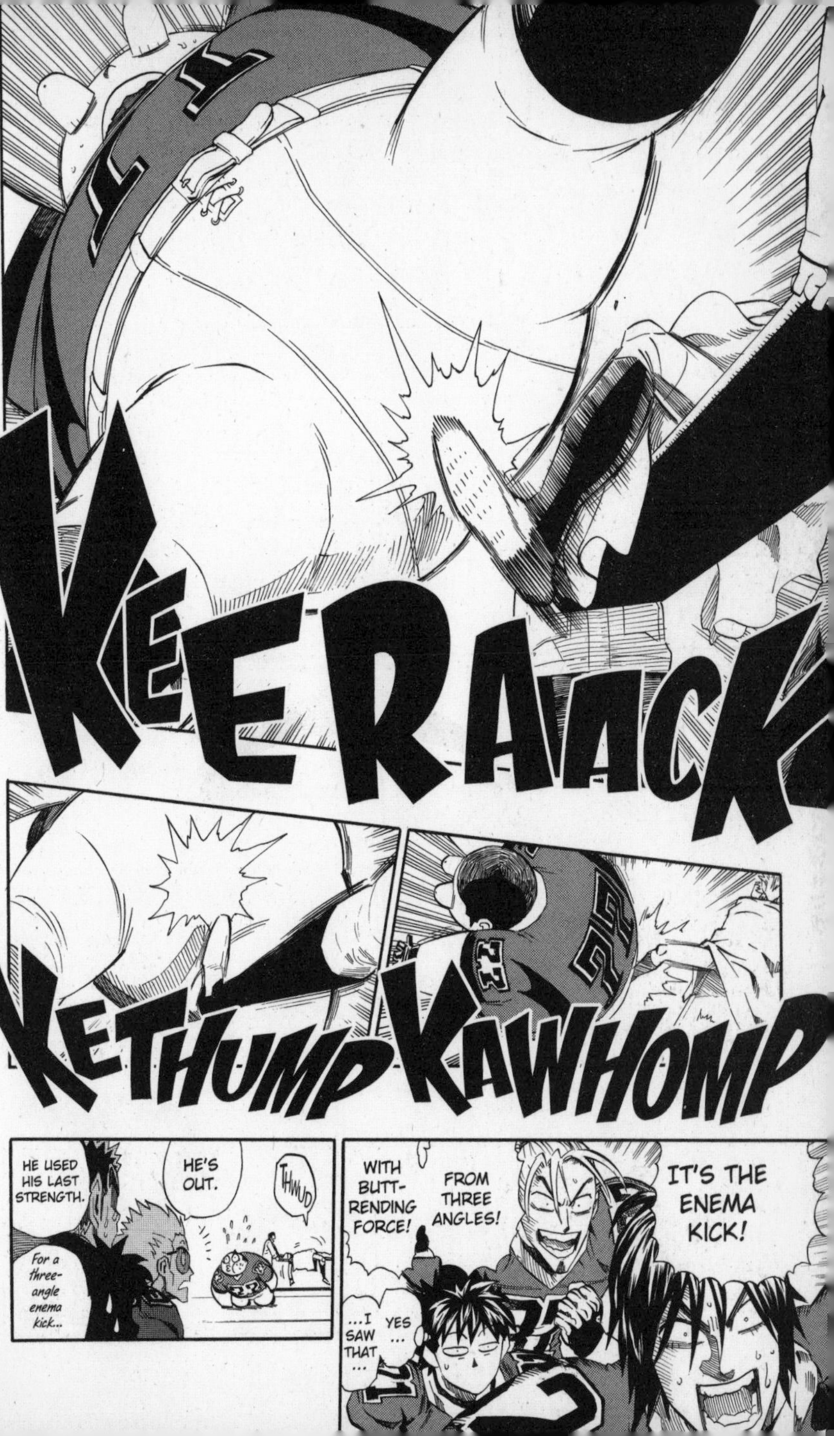
KEERAAACK
KAWHOMP
KETHUMP
IT'S THE ENEMA KICK!
FROM THREE ANGLES!
WITH BUTT-RENDING FORCE!
YES ...
...I SAW THAT ...
THWUD
HE'S OUT.
HE USED HIS LAST STRENGTH.
For a three-angle enema kick...

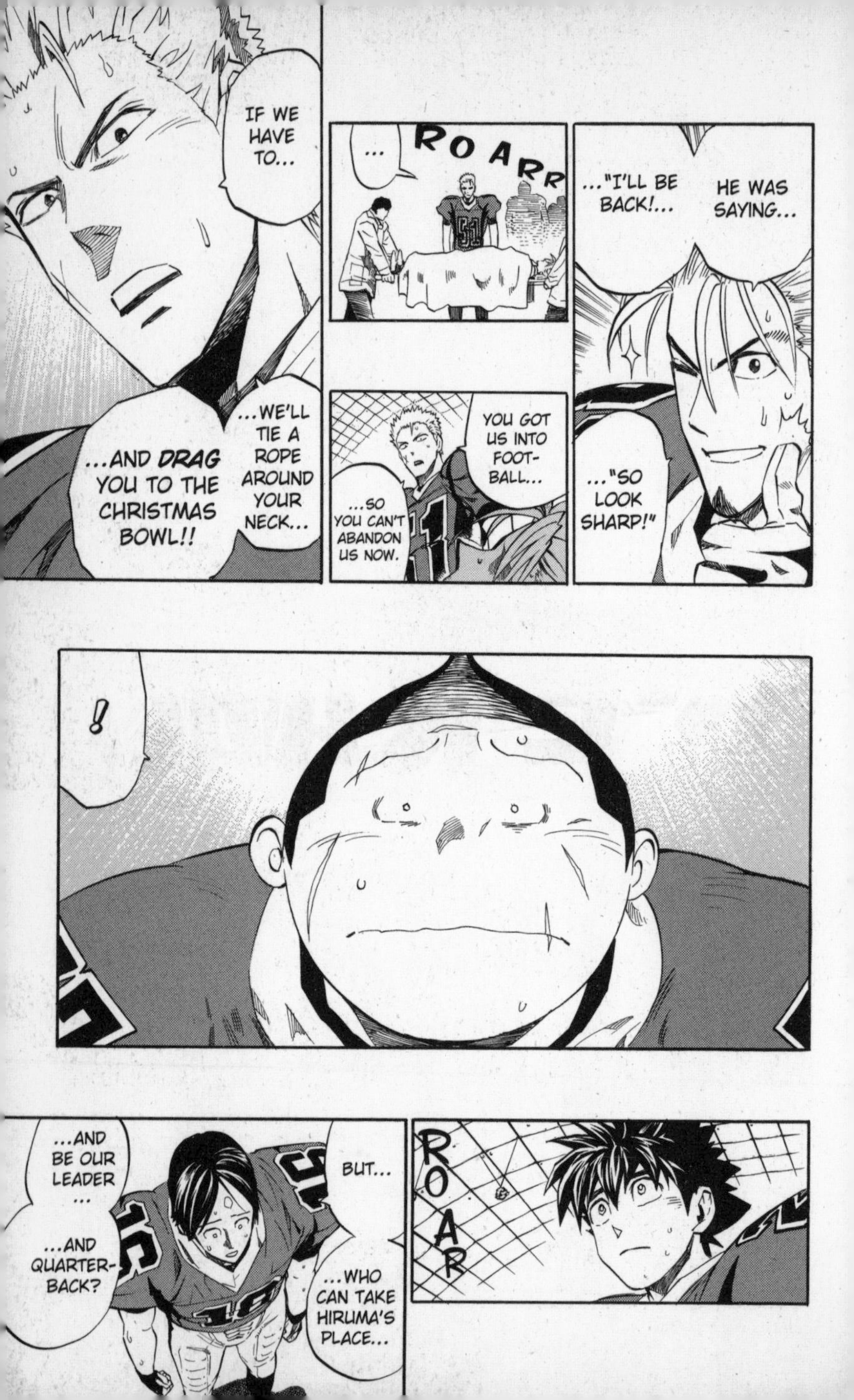
HE WAS SAYING...
..."I'LL BE BACK!...
..."SO LOOK SHARP!"
...
ROARR
YOU GOT US INTO FOOT-BALL...
...SO YOU CAN'T ABANDON US NOW.
IF WE HAVE TO...
...WE'LL TIE A ROPE AROUND YOUR NECK...
...AND DRAG YOU TO THE CHRISTMAS BOWL!!
!
ROAR
BUT...
...WHO CAN TAKE HIRUMA'S PLACE...
...AND BE OUR LEADER...
...AND QUARTER-BACK?

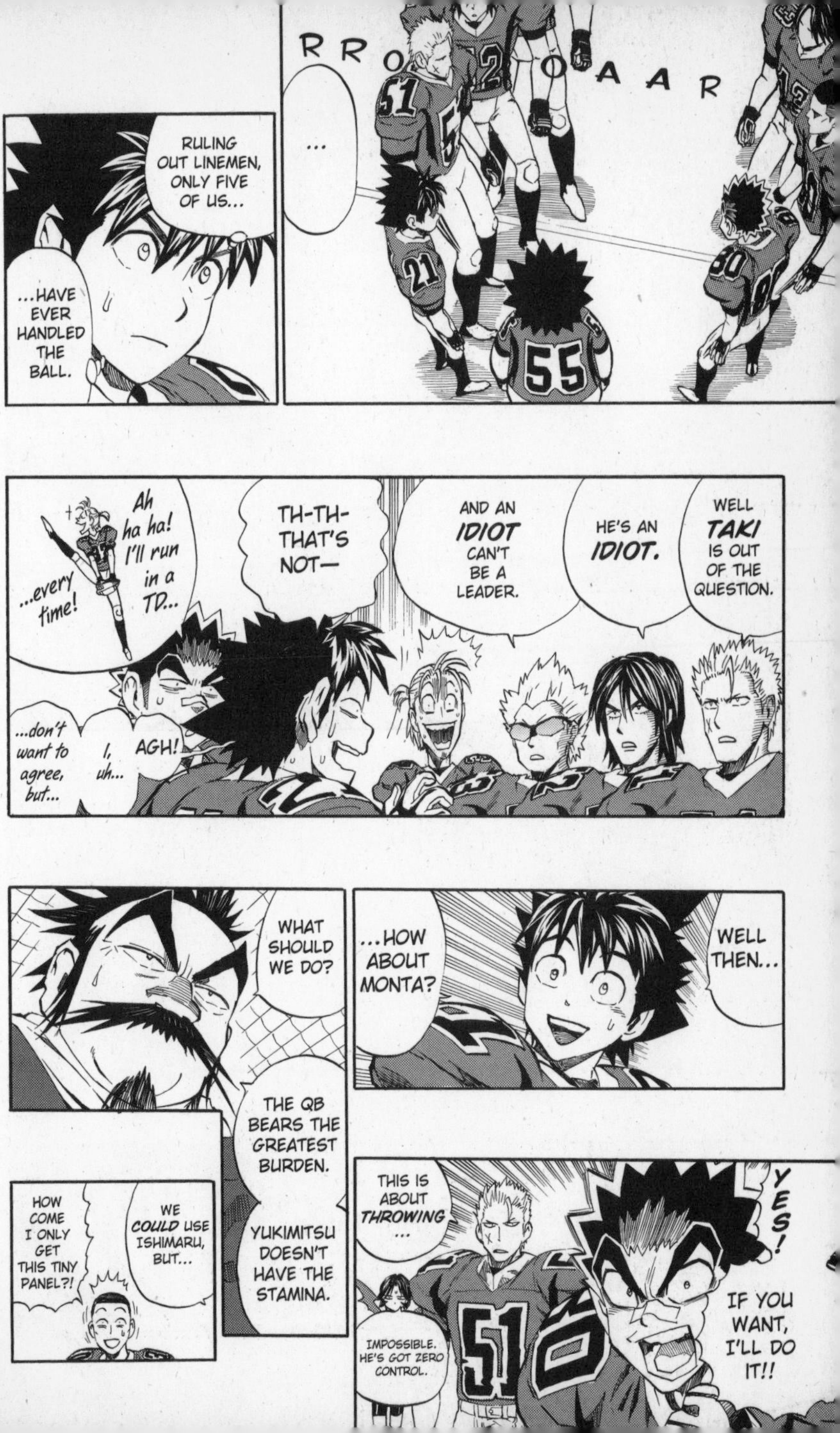
RROOAAR
...
RULING OUT LINEMEN, ONLY FIVE OF US...
...HAVE EVER HANDLED THE BALL.
WELL *TAKI* IS OUT OF THE QUESTION.
HE'S AN *IDIOT.*
AND AN *IDIOT* CAN'T BE A LEADER.
TH-TH-THAT'S NOT—
Ah ha ha! I'll run in a TD...
...every time!
AGH!
I, uh...
...don't want to agree, but...
WELL THEN...
...HOW ABOUT MONTA?
WHAT SHOULD WE DO?
THE QB BEARS THE GREATEST BURDEN.
YUKIMITSU DOESN'T HAVE THE STAMINA.
YES!
IF YOU WANT, I'LL DO IT!!
THIS IS ABOUT *THROWING*...
IMPOSSIBLE. HE'S GOT ZERO CONTROL.
WE *COULD* USE ISHIMARU, BUT...
HOW COME I ONLY GET THIS TINY PANEL?!

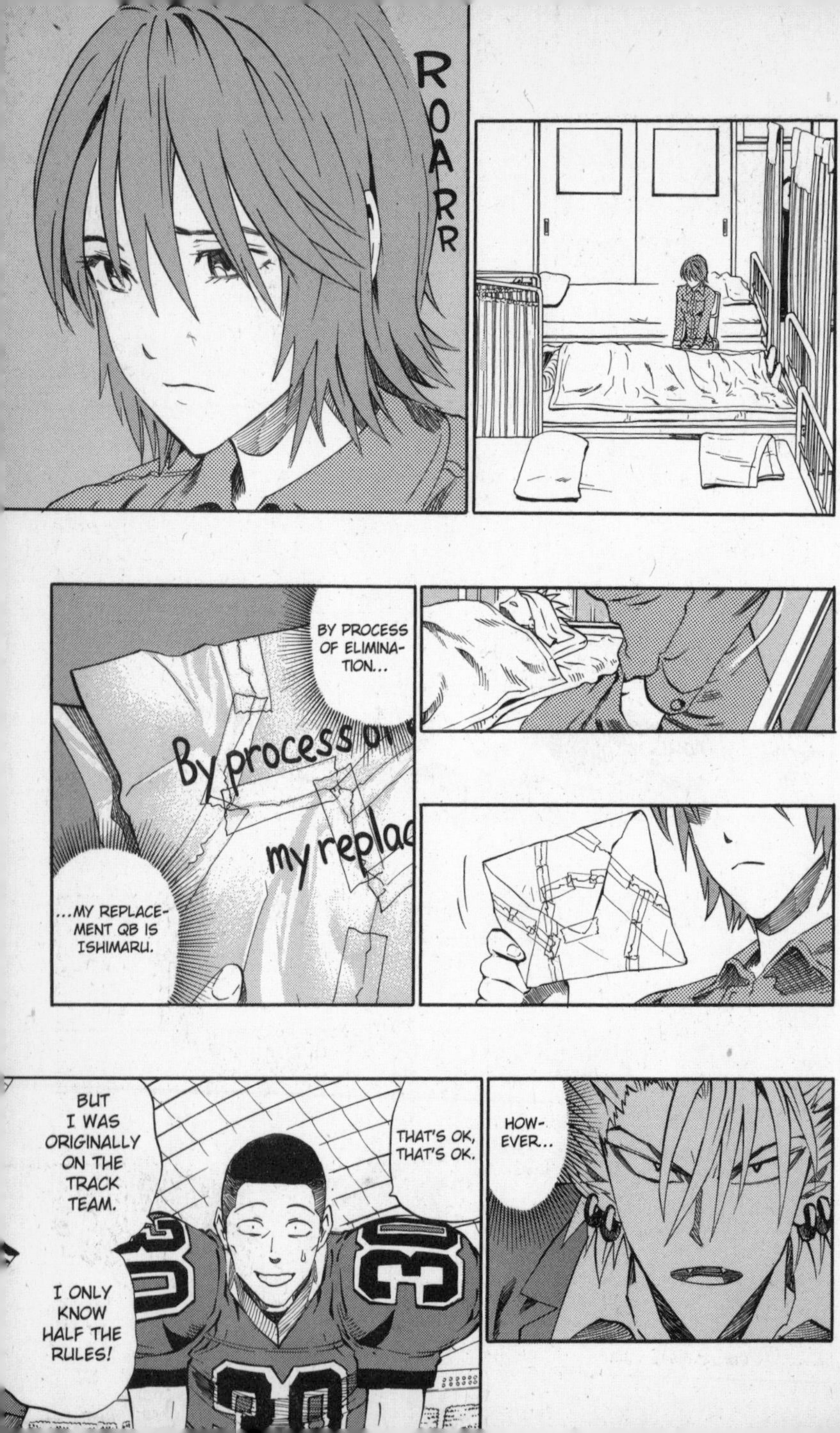
ROARR
BY PROCESS OF ELIMINATION...
By process
my replac
...MY REPLACEMENT QB IS ISHIMARU.
HOW-EVER...
THAT'S OK, THAT'S OK.
BUT I WAS ORIGINALLY ON THE TRACK TEAM.
I ONLY KNOW HALF THE RULES!

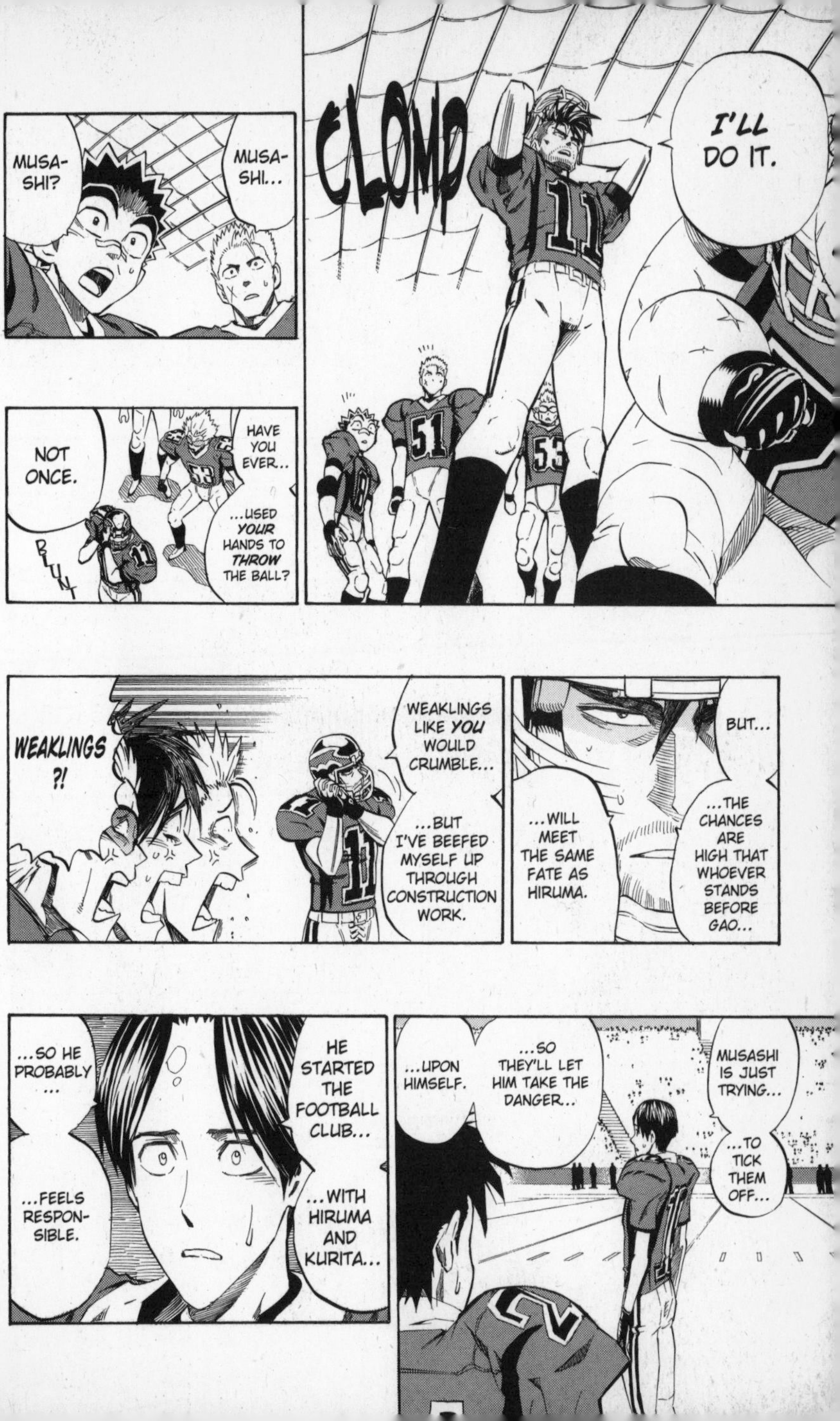
I'LL DO IT.
CLOMP
MUSA-SHI...
MUSA-SHI?
HAVE YOU EVER...
...USED YOUR HANDS TO THROW THE BALL?
NOT ONCE.
BLUNT
BUT...
...THE CHANCES ARE HIGH THAT WHOEVER STANDS BEFORE GAO...
...WILL MEET THE SAME FATE AS HIRUMA.
WEAKLINGS LIKE YOU WOULD CRUMBLE...
...BUT I'VE BEEFED MYSELF UP THROUGH CONSTRUCTION WORK.
WEAKLINGS ?!
MUSASHI IS JUST TRYING...
...TO TICK THEM OFF...
...SO THEY'LL LET HIM TAKE THE DANGER...
...UPON HIMSELF.
HE STARTED THE FOOTBALL CLUB...
...WITH HIRUMA AND KURITA...
...SO HE PROBABLY...
...FEELS RESPON-SIBLE.

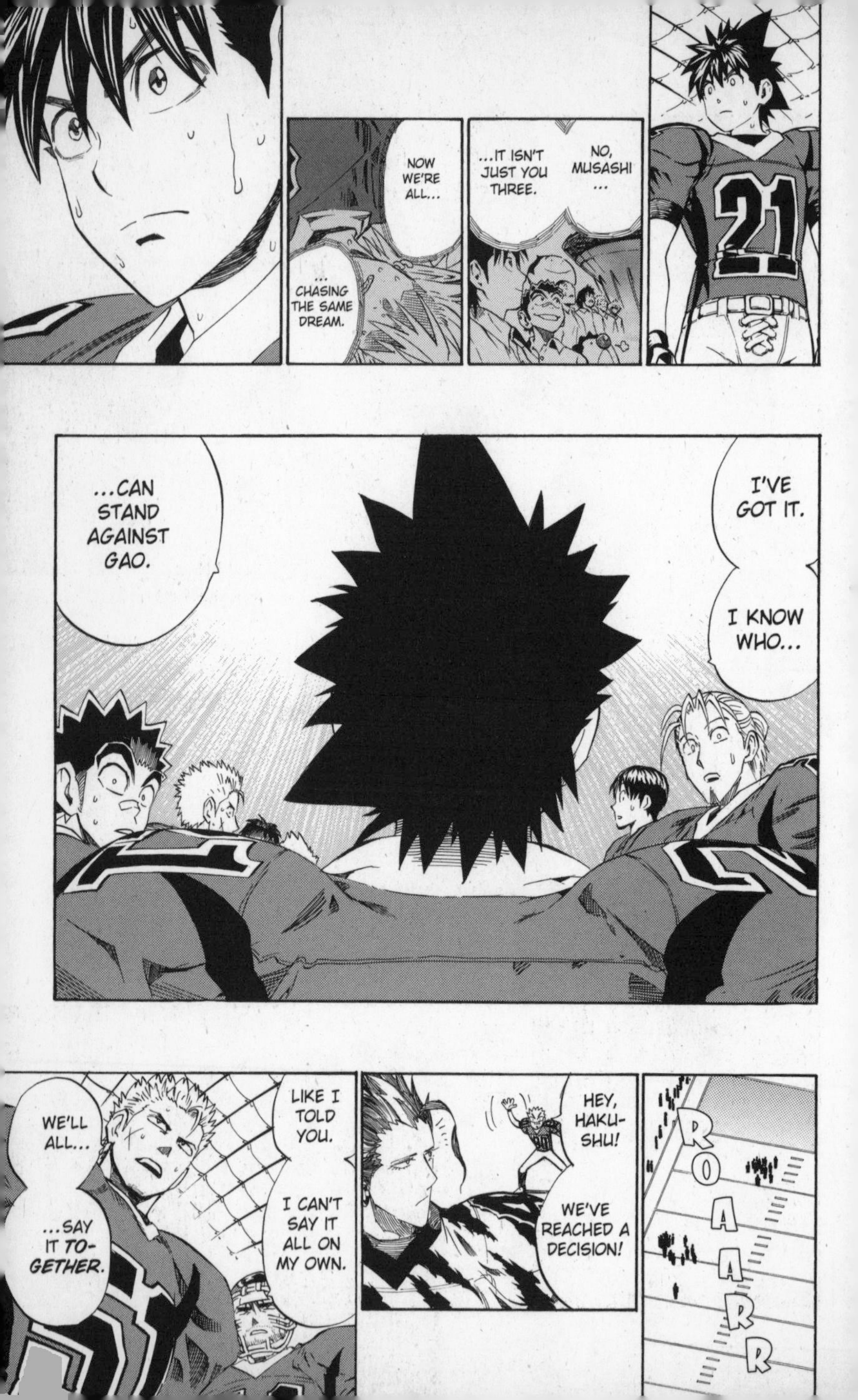
NO, MUSASHI ...
...IT ISN'T JUST YOU THREE.
NOW WE'RE ALL...
...CHASING THE SAME DREAM.
I'VE GOT IT.
I KNOW WHO...
...CAN STAND AGAINST GAO.
ROAARR
HEY, HAKU-SHU!
WE'VE REACHED A DECISION!
LIKE I TOLD YOU.
I CAN'T SAY IT ALL ON MY OWN.
WE'LL ALL...
...SAY IT TO-GETHER.

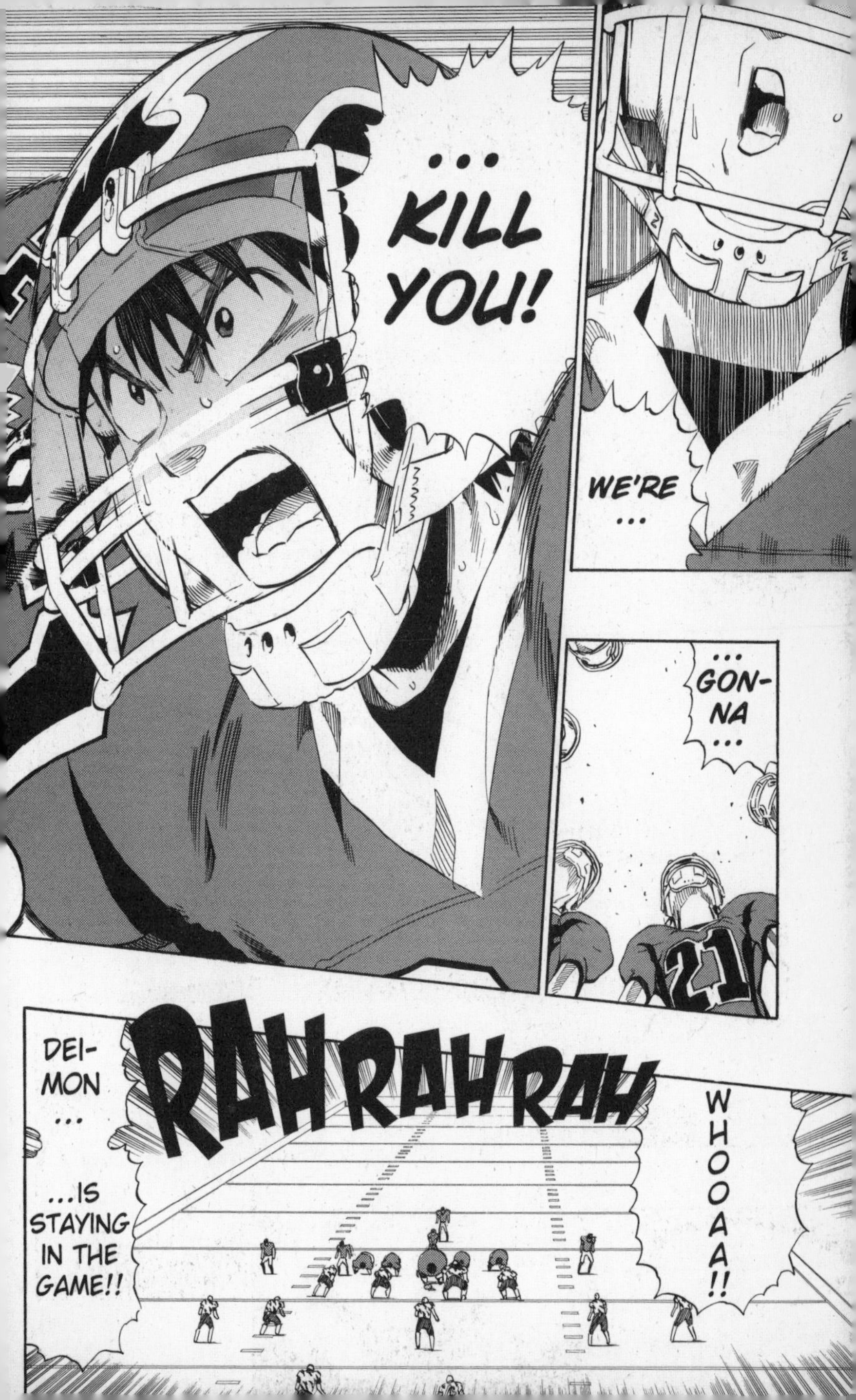
WE'RE ...
... GON-NA ...
... KILL YOU!
WHOOAAA!!
RAH RAH RAH
DEI-MON ...
...IS STAYING IN THE GAME!!

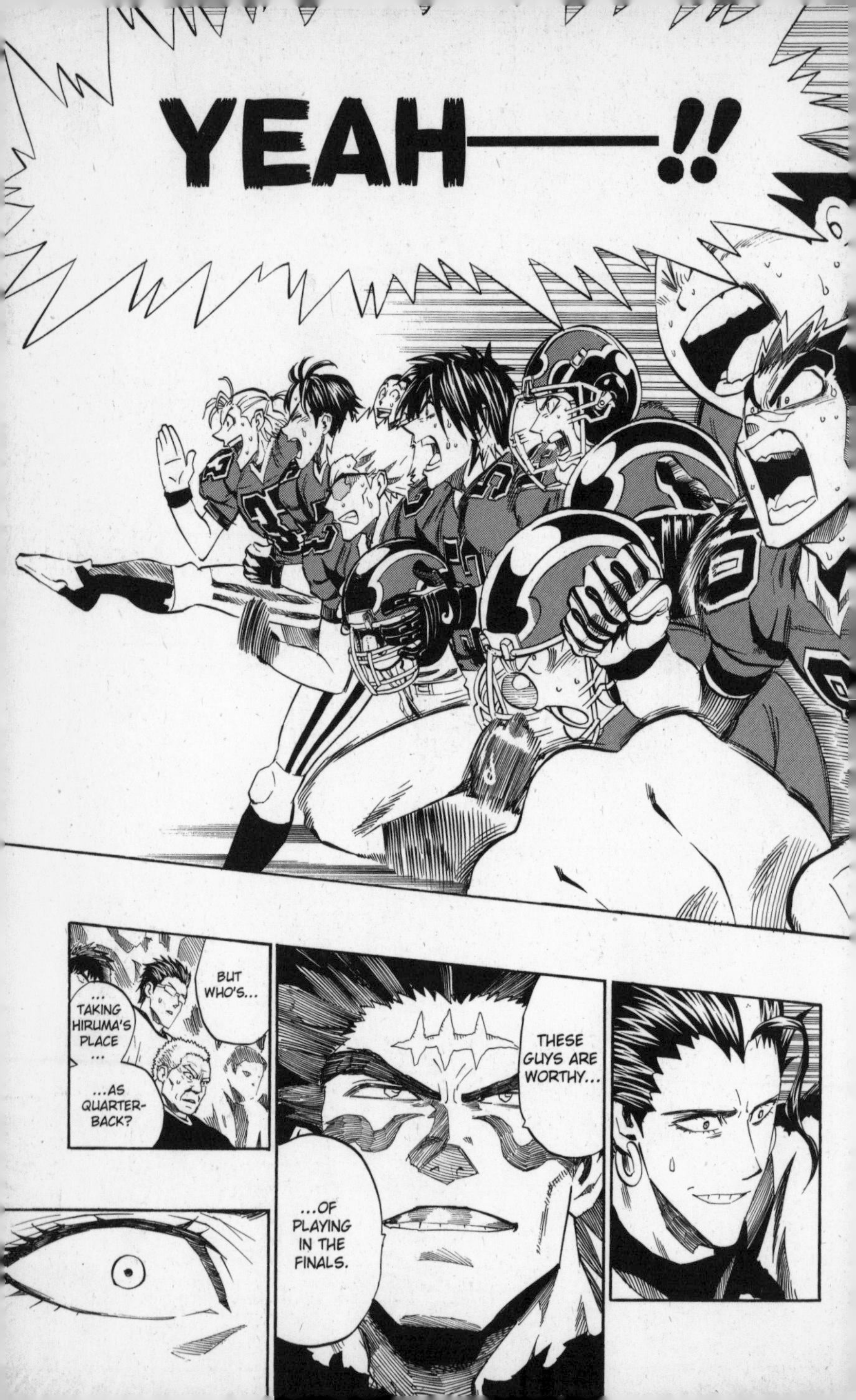
YEAH——!!
THESE GUYS ARE WORTHY...
...OF PLAYING IN THE FINALS.
BUT WHO'S...
...TAKING HIRUMA'S PLACE...
...AS QUARTER-BACK?

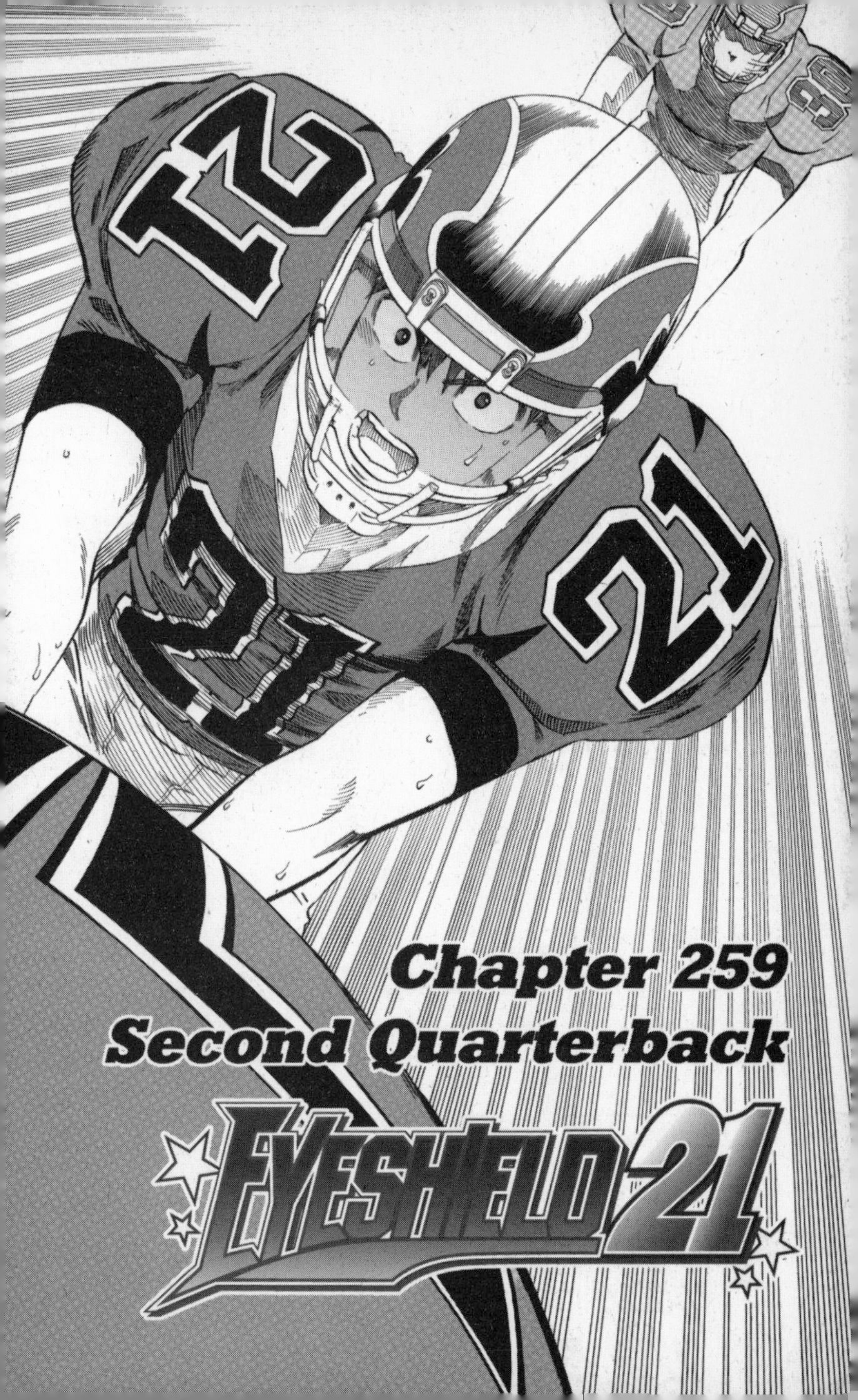
Chapter 259
Second Quarterback
EYESHIELD 21

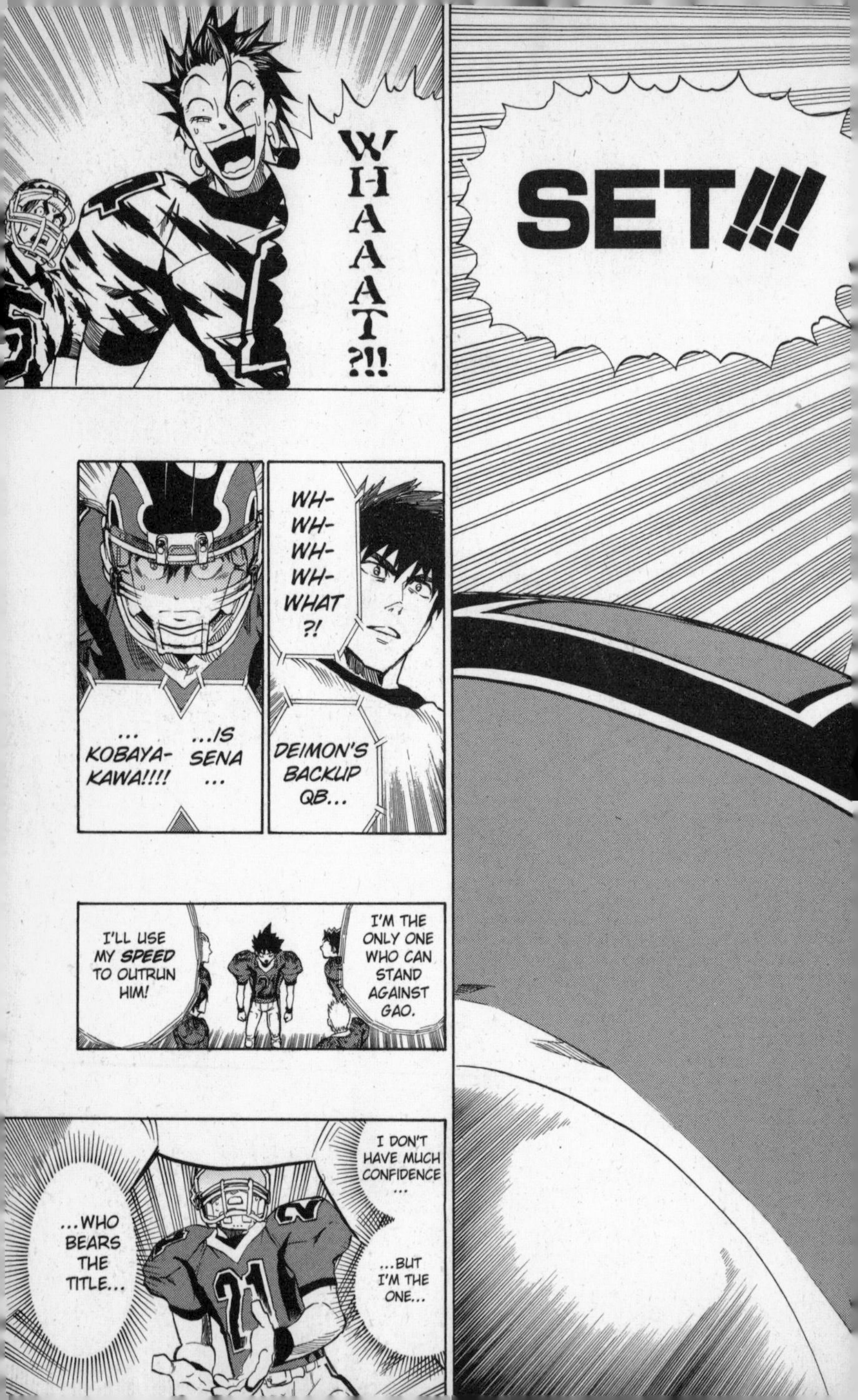
SET!!!
WHAAAT?!!
WH-WH-WH-WH-WHAT?!
DEIMON'S BACKUP QB...
...IS SENA ...
... KOBAYA-KAWA!!!!
I'M THE ONLY ONE WHO CAN STAND AGAINST GAO.
I'LL USE MY SPEED TO OUTRUN HIM!
I DON'T HAVE MUCH CONFIDENCE ...
...BUT I'M THE ONE...
...WHO BEARS THE TITLE...

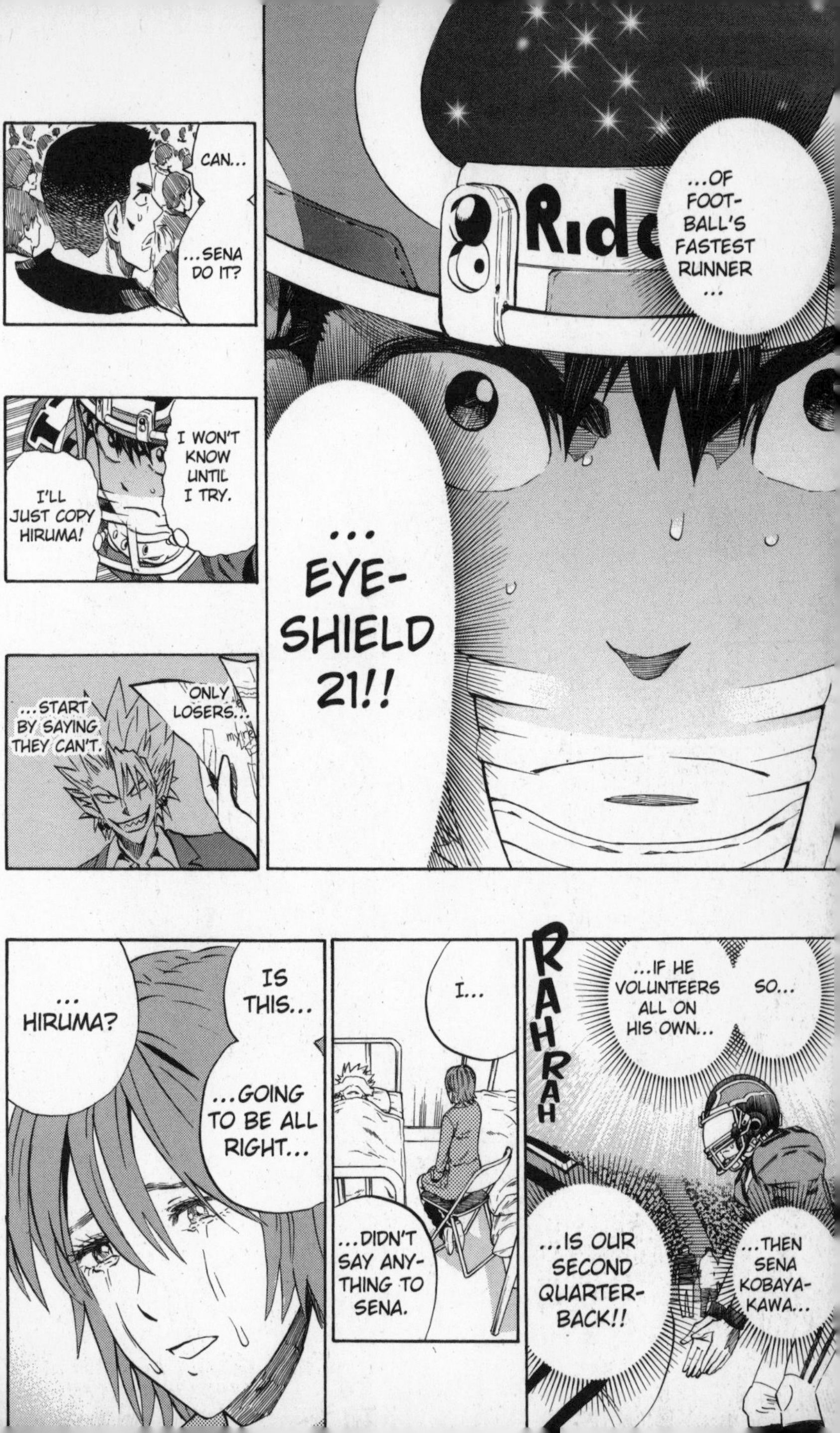
...OF FOOT-BALL'S FASTEST RUNNER...
...EYE-SHIELD 21!!
CAN...
...SENA DO IT?
I WON'T KNOW UNTIL I TRY.
I'LL JUST COPY HIRUMA!
ONLY LOSERS...
...START BY SAYING THEY CAN'T.
SO...
...IF HE VOLUNTEERS ALL ON HIS OWN...
...THEN SENA KOBAYA-KAWA...
...IS OUR SECOND QUARTER-BACK!!
RAHRAH
I...
...DIDN'T SAY ANY-THING TO SENA.
IS THIS...
...GOING TO BE ALL RIGHT...
...HIRUMA?

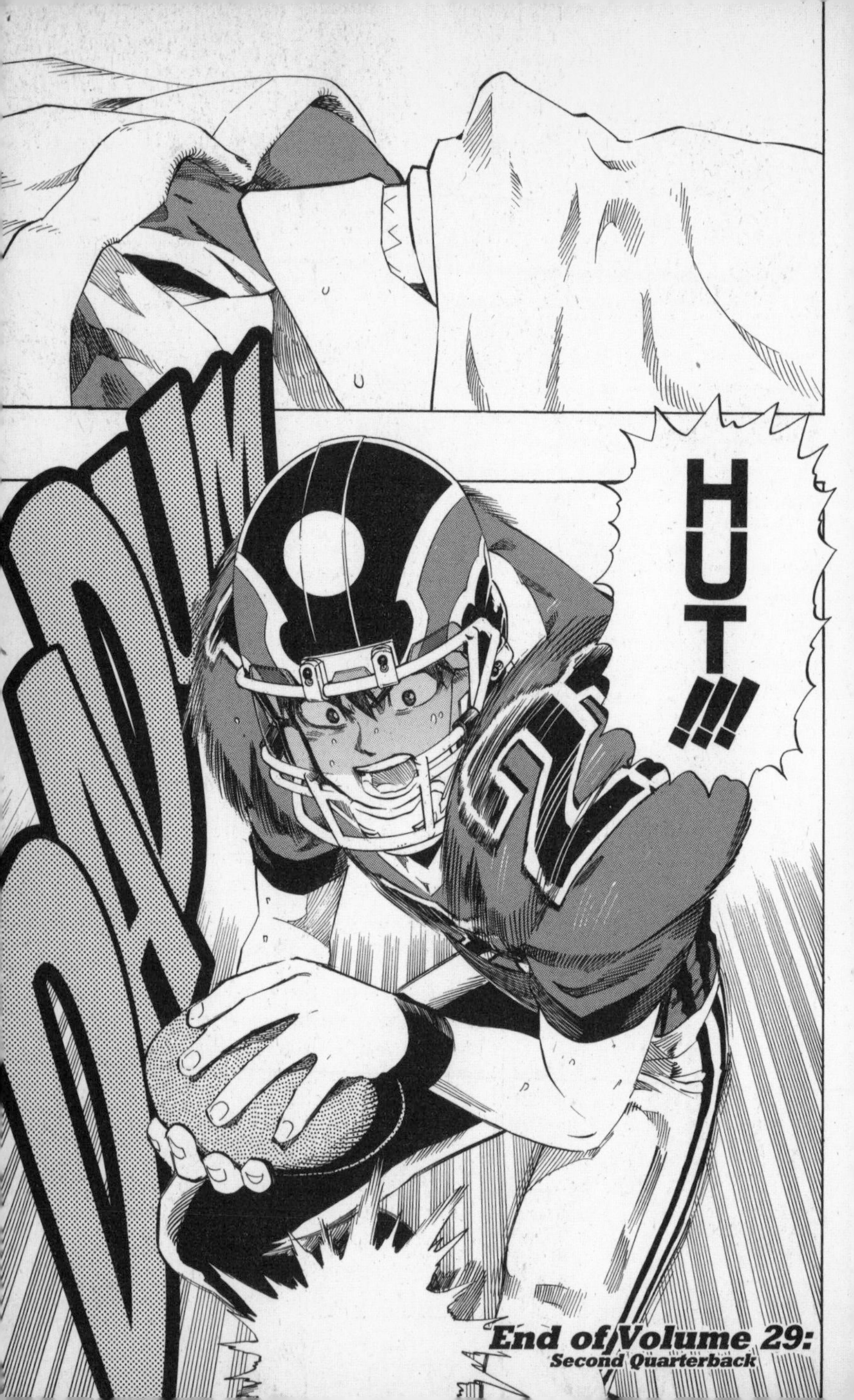
HUT!!!

End of Volume 29:
Second Quarterback

Deluxe Biographies of the Supporting Cast

Taiyo Boxing Gym

This is Taiyo High School's official gym. Trainer Tutan Khamen says this: "In 4,000 B.C. the army of ancient Egypt had already implemented boxing!" (It's true.)

The gym has developed pyramid-shaped gloves and golden headgear, but it's all ***against the rules so it can't be used***.

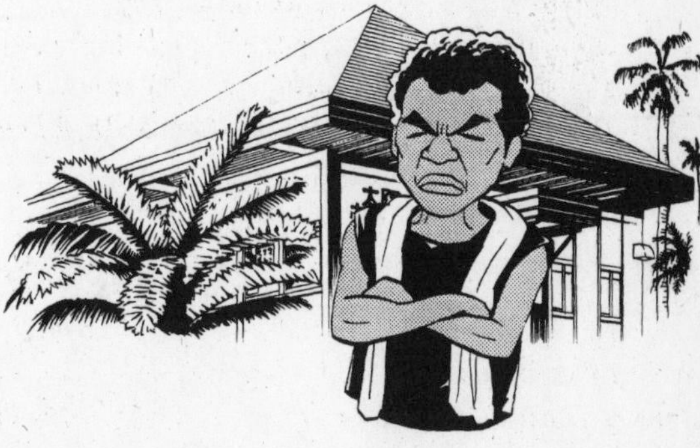

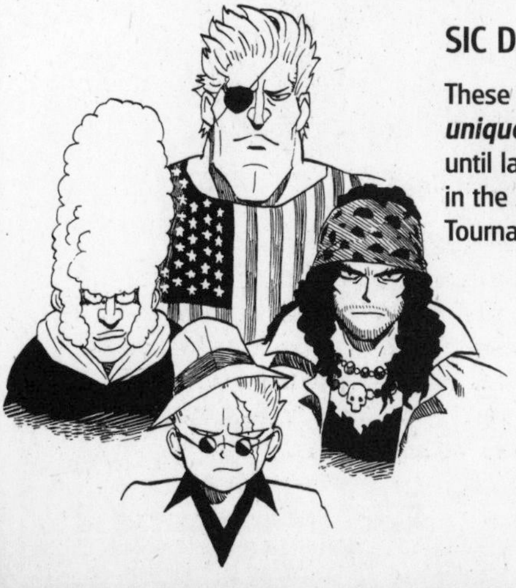

SIC District Four Heavenly Kings

These four aces, each with his own incredibly ***unique style***, are from the four teams that until last year boasted overwhelming strength in the ***SIC*** (Saitama-Ibaraki-Chiba) District Tournament.

● Teru Agoware

(Seijoki Stars: lineman)

The Stars-and-Stripes T-shirt he wears—
and never washes—is proof he has
committed his life to football. He doesn't
care if it's *unfashionable and smells*.
Therein lies his stoic spirit!

● Wataru Aranami

(Shiokaze Hippies: tight end)

Shiokaze is Karibu's sister school, whose
team the Pirates lost to Ojo. Whenever he
loses, he always says, "I'm a man of the sea,
so *it doesn't matter if I lose on land*."

● Hirao Chin

(Jimotono White Gang: safety)

His specialty is chewing out the refs. It's
called the Gangster Tantrum! As a result,
he always *gets thrown out of the game!*

● Hitsuji Shiroike

(Saimin Sleepers: quarterback)

Since he refuses to ruin his artistic hairstyle,
he has to special order his helmet just like
Kamaguruma of the Taiyo Sphinx. Don't know
what I'm talking about? Check out volume 6!
He exercises an overwhelming soporific
effect...on...his...opponents...

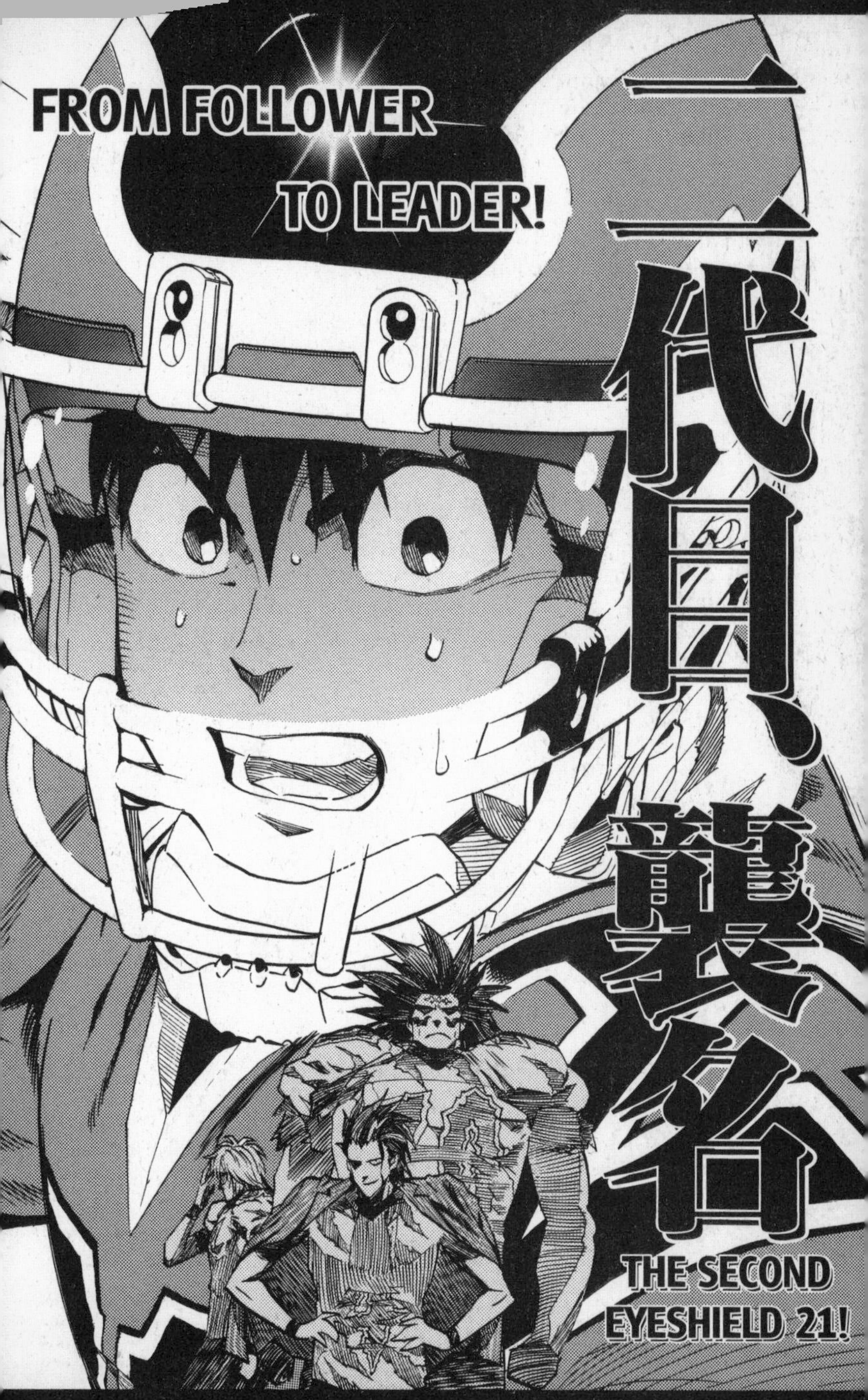
二代目襲名
THE SECOND EYESHIELD 21!
FROM FOLLOWER TO LEADER!

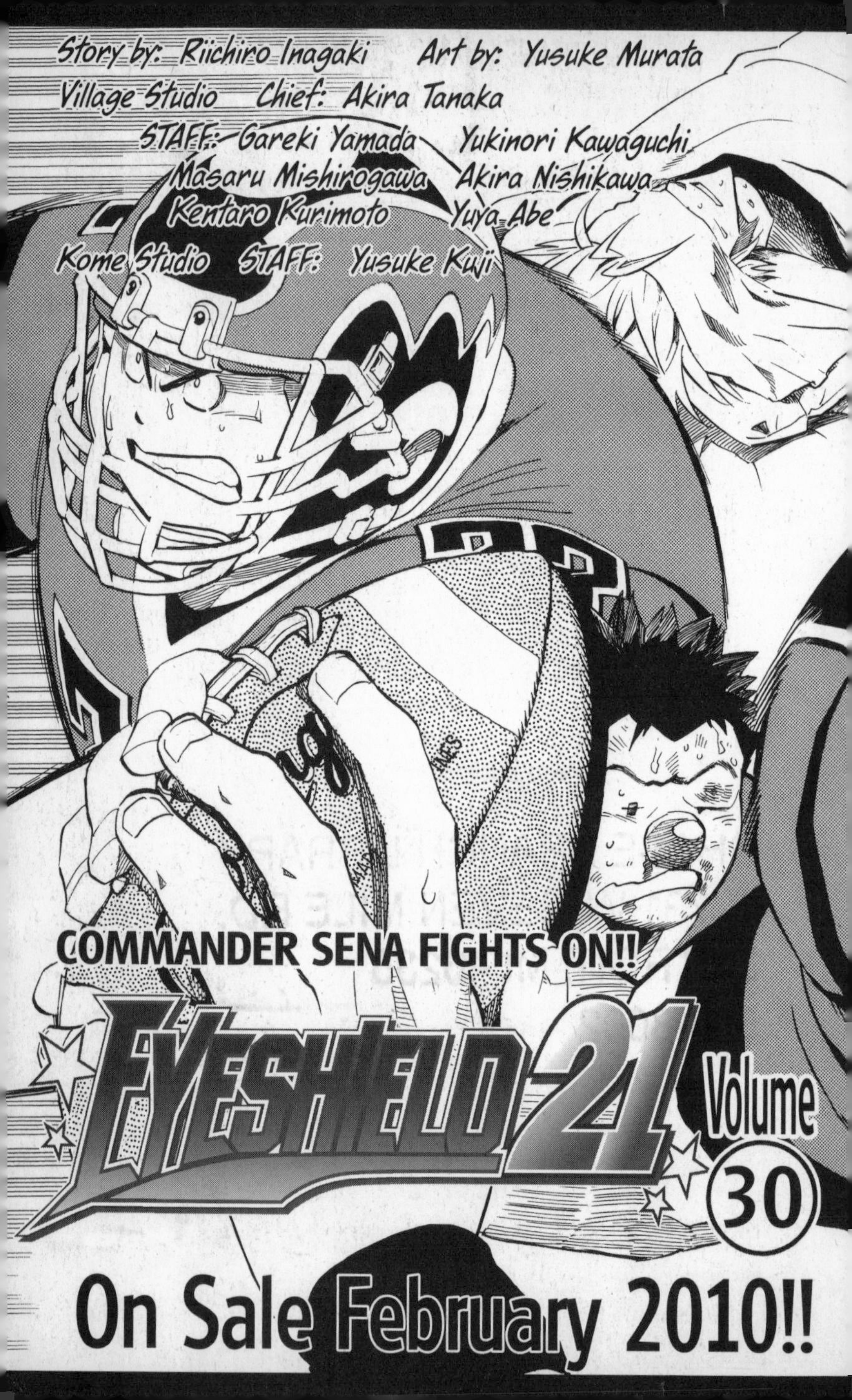
Story by: Riichiro Inagaki Art by: Yusuke Murata
Village Studio Chief: Akira Tanaka
STAFF: Gareki Yamada Yukinori Kawaguchi
Masaru Mishirogawa Akira Nishikawa
Kentaro Kurimoto Yuya Abe
Kome Studio STAFF: Yusuke Kuji
COMMANDER SENA FIGHTS ON!!
EYESHIELD 21
Volume 30
On Sale February 2010!!

Tell us what you SHONEN JUMP manga!

Our survey is now available online.
Go to: www.SHONENJUMP.com/mangasurvey

Help us make our product offering better!

THE REAL ACTION STARTS IN...

SHONEN JUMP

THE WORLD'S MOST POPULAR MANGA
www.shonenjump.com

ADVANCED

VIZ
media